The Art of Drag

The Art of Drag: A Practical Performers' Handbook is the ultimate guide for all drag kings, things, queens and queers who want to bring their best to the stage.

Filled with a wide range of exercises and advice from working performers, this book is a guide and support for every working drag act, and the drag-curious wanting to step a sequinned toe onto the stage for the first time. The book focuses on practical performance advice for creating new work, refining existing work and exploring new skills and perspectives from the world of drag. It also includes:

- Practical performance tips demystifying live performance skills such as singing, lip-sync, impersonation and comedy.
- Top tips on how to get bookings, get paid and make a profit.
- Advice on how to communicate with an audience and create an unforgettable live experience.
- Interviews with seven sensational acts who discuss how they use the art of drag: Adam All, Simply Barbra, Ada Campe, Hugo Grrrl, Le Fil, Me the Drag Queen and Son of a Tutu.

Written *by* a drag act, *for* drag acts, *The Art of Drag* is an invaluable resource for new and aspiring drag performers, along with academic performance courses covering Drag, Cabaret, or Queer Performance.

Michael Twaits is a drag act, actor and producer based in London. He is the creator and facilitator of *The Art of Drag* course at the Royal Vauxhall Tavern, which has run for over a decade and birthed over 200 drag acts. Michael is a prolific drag performer who has 20 years of performance experience; tiny clubs, huge Pride stages, films sets, theatres, embassies, trains and much more! He's worked across the UK and internationally and can usually be found at his West End residency *The Saturday Supershow* at the legendary Phoenix Arts Club.

The Art of Drag

A Practical Performers' Handbook

Michael Twaits

NEW YORK AND LONDON

Cover image: A selection of The Art Of Drag graduates (left to right, top to bottom): Pussy Kat Bangkok, The Black Flamingo, La Veronica, Kallum Kiraly, Dolly Trolley, Twerkish Delight, Bae Sharam, Michael Twaits Debbie Del Rey, Gem The Clown, Katastrofa Chernobyl, Vulgair, Seraphos, Chase Bush & Laura Nadia Hunt. Photography by Joel Ryder Media and Simon J Webb/Jack The Lad Mag. Cover design by Richard Dobbs-Grove at We Are Enriched.

First published 2026
by Routledge
605 Third Avenue, New York, NY 10158

and by Routledge
4 Park Square, Milton Park, Abingdon, Oxon, OX14 4RN

Routledge is an imprint of the Taylor & Francis Group, an informa business

© 2026 Michael Twaits

The right of Michael Twaits to be identified as author of this work has been asserted in accordance with sections 77 and 78 of the Copyright, Designs and Patents Act 1988.

All rights reserved. No part of this book may be reprinted or reproduced or utilised in any form or by any electronic, mechanical, or other means, now known or hereafter invented, including photocopying and recording, or in any information storage or retrieval system, without permission in writing from the publishers.

Trademark notice: Product or corporate names may be trademarks or registered trademarks, and are used only for identification and explanation without intent to infringe.

Library of Congress Cataloging-in-Publication Data
Names: Twaits, Michael author
Title: The art of drag: a practical performers' handbook / Michael Twaits.
Description: New York, NY: Routledge, 2025. | Includes bibliographical references and index.
Identifiers: LCCN 2025000039 (print) | LCCN 2025000040 (ebook) | ISBN 9781032812397 hardback | ISBN 9781032803104 paperback | ISBN 9781003498797 ebook
Subjects: LCSH: Drag performance–Handbooks, manuals, etc. | LCGFT: Handbooks and manuals
Classification: LCC PN1969.D73 T93 2025 (print) | LCC PN1969.D73 (ebook) |
DDC 792.02/8–dc23/eng/20250430
LC record available at https://lccn.loc.gov/2025000039
LC ebook record available at https://lccn.loc.gov/2025000040

ISBN: 978-1-032-81239-7 (hbk)
ISBN: 978-1-032-80310-4 (pbk)
ISBN: 978-1-003-49879-7 (ebk)

DOI: 10.4324/9781003498797

Typeset in Goudy
by Deanta Global Publishing Services, Chennai, India

This handbook is dedicated to my son and my husband.
And to those who fought before so I could have a son and a
husband to dedicate
a book to.

Contents

The Art of Drag: An Introduction ... ix
About the Course: The Art of Drag ... xvi
Who Wrote This? ... xviii
How to Use This Handbook ... xx

PART I
PREPARATION IS EVERYTHING ... 1

1 *Starting Here, Starting Now*: A New Beginning ... 3
2 *Being Good, Isn't Good Enough*: The Business of Drag ... 13
3 *Who Will Buy?*: The Economics of Drag ... 29
4 *The Best Thing You've Ever Done*: Measuring Success ... 43
5 *Memory*: Rehearsal and Development ... 53
6 *Why Did I Choose You?*: Building a Set, Range and Repertoire ... 63
7 *Sweet Inspiration*: Research and Further Reading ... 71

PART II
STAGE CRAFT FOR ALL DRAG ACTS ... 79

8 *Where Do You Start?*: Basic Drag ... 81
9 *It Had to Be You*: Alter-Ego ... 91
10 *Being Alive*: Making Choices and Finding A Voice ... 107
11 *People*: Audience Experience ... 117
12 *Anywhere I Hang My Hat Is Home*: Stages and Spaces ... 127

PART III
SPECIFIC DRAG PERFORMANCE SKILLS AND STYLES — 133

13 *Tell Him*: Talking On Stage — 135
14 *Make Your Own Kind of Music*: Vocal and Singing Techniques — 147
15 *Sing*: Sing a Song — 155
16 *Putting It Together*: Creating and Editing a Track — 169
17 *Gotta Move*: Rehearsing and Performing a Lip-Sync — 179
18 *Send in the Clowns*: Comedy, Reading and Roasting — 189
19 *Isn't This Better*: Parody — 203
20 *With a Little Help from My Friends*: Impersonation: Tribute and Parody — 217
21 *Where Is It Written?*: Text, Acting and Castings — 231
22 *Move On*: Hosting and Solo Shows — 239
23 *Don't Rain on My Parade*: Onwards — 251

PART IV
PRAXIS IN PRACTICE — 257

24 *My Man*: Interview with *Adam All* — 259
25 *My Name Is Barbra*: Interview with *Simply Barbra* — 265
26 *Keepin' Out of Mischief Now*: Interview with *Ada Campe* — 271
27 *The Way You Make Me Feel*: Interview with *Le Fil* — 277
28 *Simple Man*: Interview with *Hugo Grrrl* — 283
29 *Let's Hear It for Me*: Interview with *Me* — 289
30 *Mother*: Interview with *Son Of A Tutu* — 295
31 *As If We Never Said Goodbye*: Finale — 301

Glossary — 309

Acknowledgements — 313

Index — 316

The Art of Drag: An Introduction

An accountant, an estate agent, and a politician walk into a bar. The barman asks: *"What do you do for a living?"* They all respond: *"I wear a suit"*.

Sorry, that isn't a joke, it's an analogy I use when someone says they are a drag act. The barman asked *what* they do, not *how* they do it! Ok, you're a drag act – but *what* are you going to *do*?

Drag is a vast art form that spans many different modes. Each drag act may have a different approach, a different entry into the art form and often a different view on what is, or what isn't, drag. Some drag acts specialise in one performance mode, others are performance magpies who use a collection of skills from various areas of the arts. There is no single specific performance skill essential to being a drag act: a drag act may not talk, not sing, not lip-sync or in my case not dance. The only real rule is that somewhere within the work, whether visually or thematically, there is an exploration or play with gender.

We're in This Together

I have written this handbook for all drag acts; the professional, the aspiring and the drag-curious. Kings, things, queens and queers. It is a guide to the performance skills and techniques that can be used in drag. I have no intentions to police whether or not the work you produce as a result of using this book is drag. It doesn't matter to me. It's too easy to let language exclude, divide and separate communities. Please know, nothing written in this book should tell you that you can not do drag! I truly believe drag is an art form that everyone can learn from, partake in and enjoy. The only thing I ask from a reader is the desire to take their drag onto a stage of some description.

As I write I am trying to avoid bringing in too much academic theory: quotes, experiences and examples are mainly from experienced performers whose research and knowledge has grown out of practice and their lived experience. I'm a performer, not a scholar; I've pretended to be a good academic and thrown in a bibliography, nods to writing that has hugely influenced my journey. But personally, I've learnt more about performance from doing, seeing, failing and succeeding than I ever did from academia. And drag should be an open access art form, therefore the focus is on practice, performance and being academically accessible to everyone.

All Dressed Up with Nowhere to Go?

When discussing drag the emphasis is frequently on The Look: make-up, wigs, costuming and contouring. Of course, it is a visual medium, but what is the point in getting all dressed up if you don't know what you're going to do as a performer? The internet has given aspiring drag acts a rich world from which they can learn skills to create and finesse their aesthetic. The popularity of *RuPaul's Drag Race*[1] has given viewers a very specific format that some believe all drag should fit. But the world of drag is far wider than that, and is ever expanding.

Novice performers may mistakenly try to replicate what they *think* a drag performance is and forget the basics of engaging with an audience in a live space. *Drag Race* has brought lip-sync to the forefront of the drag skill set, but a drag act does not need to lip-sync. As an act I have never included a lip-sync in my set, it's simply not where my skill lies and does not help me fulfil my goals as a performer.

The popularity of *Drag Race*, and the visual emphasis on drag, means novice acts often come to the stage without an understanding, or discipline of basic stage craft. There is a belief that a strong aesthetic is enough to make a strong performance without any real rigour to rehearsal or development of the performance. Hours may have been spent on make-up and costuming: a big reveal has been planned, rhinestones painstakingly glued to every inch of fabric, but have they worked out what they are doing when on stage? My hope is, as you have picked up this handbook, you have a desire to avoid that pitfall. You have the aspiration to create your own unique performance style. A desire to plan, rehearse and execute a performance you can be proud of, and who knows, maybe even shape a strong career.

The focus throughout this handbook is always on performance: what you are actually going to do in drag. Performing on stage, but also the technical aspects of getting on-stage and finding opportunities to perform. The word stage has far reaching implications when it comes to drag; it could be the corner of a small bar or it may be the Hollywood Bowl. Let's try to prepare for all eventualities!

Having Something to Say...

Drag draws commentary on society, the patriarchy and heteronormativity. The belief that drag is simply trying to *trick* an audience both belittles and simplifies the art form and its importance to the queer[2] community. Many drag performers feel their performances actually present a more authentic version of themselves than they are able to express in everyday life. Drag gives the performer a voice and a space to express something which has often been denied in life. Until society is rid of homophobia, transphobia and misogyny there will always something political about a drag performer stepping out onto the stage, taking up space and performing. That doesn't mean all acts need a political theme, simply celebrating life (queer joy) as a minority, or a subcultural other is political. It's the age-old message of drag – *we are here!*

For some, the desire to be in drag is about escaping the constructs of society: the femme boy allowing himself to embrace, and own, his femininity; a woman adopting some of the male privilege denied to her on a daily basis. For others it is about escaping their everyday self; or perhaps finding the confidence to authentically be themselves.

Can I Be a Drag Act?

Drag has no governing body that says who is, or who is not, a drag performer. Unlike almost all other areas of live performance drag is an open access art form. No formal training, qualification or standard is required. No union is a gatekeeper. All that is required to build a career is an ability to fill a venue with an audience who will buy a ticket, or a drink at a bar. It seems everyone working across the drag scene has a different journey to the stage: a professional calling, a hobby, a freedom of expression, a form of escapism or even a journey of self-discovery. All approaches are valid and important; the variety of backgrounds and aspirations is what makes drag such a diverse scene. But those with longevity are also those who respect the craft, work their skills and are constantly challenging themselves to evolve.

As an aspiring drag act, where do you turn if you want to become a performer? Academic courses are starting to open up that include Drag, Cabaret or Queer performance. But academia and institutionalised learning isn't for everyone. A mentor is another possible option, but a seasoned drag performer will not always want to mentor someone, they may be too busy securing their own work. Without a guide are you just throwing yourself on-stage and hoping for the best? How do you rehearse a set? How do you come up with an interesting take on a song, an edit to a track or a fresh comic line? That is where this handbook comes in. It may be a book – but try to think of it as a mentor, a rehearsal buddy and sounding board!

Drag Is a Career?

What many don't realise is that being a drag performer can be quite a daunting and lonely experience. No director is sat in a rehearsal room giving notes or offering support. There are very few, if any, agents who will help shape and manage your career, especially in the early days. Initially you will be working as your own producer, promoter, marketing guru, director, seamstress and agent. It's rare to have invested collaborators, or someone to proof work prior to it being performed on stage. It makes drag nights full of the unknown, adrenaline and excitement.

There are few other careers where producers programme a performer and let them have such free reign on-stage. This creative freedom can mean performers don't always realise their full potential. Without support bad habits, lazy process and lack of professionalism can seep in. Work may be thrown together at the last minute, and if work isn't good enough you may not get feedback to help you improve, you simply won't get booked. I hope that's a gap this handbook can fill for you: a co-conspirator, someone to bounce ideas around with. The advice and exercises within these pages are ideas that will give any drag performer a boost of confidence and backbone with which to feel they are working to the best of their ability. And hopefully give your career a feeling of a trajectory.

Drag performances can be very simple and still be very successful, not everything needs to be overproduced or overanalysed. Walk out on stage, tell a joke, sing a song – these are seemingly the simplest of performance structures that most drag performers do. But there is an art to getting this right; choices should be made, a set structure and material must always be rehearsed! Knowing what you are doing, and often what you are *not* doing, is crucial to understanding the craft, and realising your full potential. Mastering the basic skills and understanding your unique point-of-view as a performer are key.

You Better Work

Through practice and experience you will slowly create a mode of working where you will be able quickly add new repertoire, and evolve your sets because as a performer you *know* your approach, your point of view and your skills. Both literally and figuratively, you will know where you stand.

This handbook will be equally useful to performers outside of the world of drag who may wish to step out of their comfort zone. I believe that all performers can learn from each other's toolbox; a cabaret singer trying to release a bit more freedom in performance, an actor trying to get into another character's shoes or a comedian trying to break old habits. The handbook will help performers look at their work and consider different styles of performance, ways of framing a performance and playing with audiences expectation and interpretation.

As you work through these chapters I hope you will start finding inspiration everywhere you go; over analysing people you see on the bus or hearing a song you had forgotten about in the supermarket. Like all art, drag draws inspiration from the world at large. Drag has a long history as a popular performance art from, a long history in the worlds of variety, vaudeville, music hall and cabaret. Part of that history is connected to being entertained and part of it is celebrating and subverting the world around us.

When talking to established performers, they often refer to drag as being a device that allows them to comment on society. To explore ideas they feel, within their off-stage life, they may not be able to. Drag is a form of armour which allows performers to take things further; to take up space, express unpopular opinions, give a voice to the underrepresented and explore ideas further. I love this visual of drag as armour for queer people, creating someone to protect us, help us and for us to rally behind when needed.

Drag Is Live

Drag is reactive; it is often at the vanguard of politics, fashion and the live experience. Where theatre, TV and novels may take months of writing and producing to respond to events happening in the real world, drag reflects on what is happening in the world almost instantly. Theatre and film are a document of what we have been through. Drag can be an outlet of how an audience is feeling in the moment, a way of processing what is going on in the world around them right now, be it responding to politics, pride, parties or plague.

Performance pieces are not created to be disposable. They should be performed time and time again, but always finding new life by adapting and bending to the present space they are being performed in. Keeping work live, relevant and in the moment is the most useful skill a drag act can learn. To perform *to* an audience, not at them.

Cynics may say that you cannot be taught to do drag and I completely agree to disagree! I do believe the essence of what you are performing on-stage comes from you, the performer. There are few scripts or blueprints of what your act should be within these pages – sorry! There are, however, countless ways of drawing those ideas out and finding inspiration, structure and momentum. Ways to rehearse, to create and ways to elevate your work. Drag is a personal journey, often a personal exploration, but that's not to say you can't have help bringing out ideas, shaping, refining and finding your unique take on the art form.

Dipping in a Toe or World Domination?

If you are reading this with aspirations of breaking the drag-glass-ceiling of where drag can currently go – brilliant! Equally if you want one fabulous night to dress up, make a scene and crack a few jokes that is equally valid. I come from a fairly traditional British end-of-the-pier drag format: song, patter, song, patter, repeat! Believe me I still have to work at this, rehearse and edit my set. Whatever you do on stage there is a structure, a craft and a rehearsal process that will help make sure you achieve your potential. My view is that if you are going to do something, give it your best. Drag is your hobby? *Great!* Planning a one off performance? *Amazing!* Let's make sure you do yourself justice.

I love seeing and working with those on the scene who are performing for a creative outlet or for their love of the community. It's one of the reasons I created *The Art Of Drag* course. Drag should be a place you can find your tribe, explore your identity and celebrate your idiosyncrasies. You don't have to have a desire to quit all other work, or be on a reality TV show! However, when I mentor students, and when I write ideas in this handbook, it always comes from the assumption that you want it to be successful, professional and a bookable act. Even if this is just a bit of fun for you, step up to the challenge of bringing your best self to the stage!

As you start performing and the opportunities arise, perhaps regular gigs begin to take shape, there is a point drag might become a career. There is no confetti or fanfare that marks when you become a professional, I tend to say it's when you start earning more for performing than you are spending on performing! And you get to that point quicker if you can learn two key skills: knowing your worth and spending less money! These aren't the sexy conversations people imagine having when discussing drag but organising the way you work off-stage can make all the difference to an on-stage career.

Don't Call Me Mother

There is a long history of passing skills down from one drag performer to another. Drag Mothers (and Others) represent the history and the continuation of traditions, as well as the building of a legacy and family. Personally, I have always steered away from the Drag Mother label, despite running a course which has birthed a couple of hundred performers on stage. My reasoning? I do not want to undermine the role a Drag Mother can have. I love passing on knowledge and ideas to young performers and a lot of my work reflects that. But Drag Mothers grew out of a point in time when 'traditional' family often turned their back on a queer child; a Drag Mother might provide literal shelter and sustenance, not just a couple of make-up tips and an old wig. Maybe this handbook can give a smattering of Motherly advice to a few fresh-faced children out there. Advice which may make you feel welcome into the extended family.

For me, this handbook is a way to pass on great advice I've received as a drag performer. My experience ranges from being a performer, host, singer, comedian, facilitator, producer, lecturer, mentor and occasional talent show judge. I've performed in West End Theatres, converted toilets, Hollywood film sets, cabaret clubs, queer bars, straight bars, the odd embassy and recently a train travelling across Europe. Audience sizes have ranged from Pride Stages with 15,000 people watching to cabarets with 12 people in the audience. It's a varied way of life where no two days are the same. But through my practical experience I have learnt how to prepare myself for any performance. How to *lean in* to the venue I'm working in whilst authentically performing in my own style. There will be personal anecdotes and examples throughout the book; my body of work has been my own form of research and praxis so it is inescapable. In drag, and queer performance, the personal is political – it has to be. So much drag performance originates from representing yourself because you do not see yourself represented elsewhere. My work, my politics and my opinions are baked into my performances, and this handbook.

Did I Want to Be a Drag Queen?

Art is a reflection of the world and many people see art reflecting back a world which doesn't include them and that is often a driving force for people to get on-stage. Time and again performers of my generation will reference when they first saw someone who was in any way *like them*. And for most of us that was far too late in life. That had a lot to do with why I was using drag, among other performance modes, to represent my own voice. Mine was not a unique story but I never felt it was one being told.

I arguably fell into drag as I was graduating from Drama School in 2006. The experience there was mixed; I was the only gay man on the course and was consistently pushed away from the roles I would probably be cast in within the real world i.e. the gay ones! To me there's a wealth of roles for a camp inclined gent; a restoration fop, Puck in *A Midsummer Nights Dream*, a Grieving Gay Son in *Casualty*, a victim of homophobic attack in *Casualty* (a multi episode arc?). But no, I was asked to play: a Sea Captain, a Duke, a Soldier, Macbeth. I spent most of the year being told to hold my camp tendencies back, square off my fluid movements and lower my vocal range. As a result I was walking on-stage physically restricting myself: I couldn't breath, I couldn't relax, there was no room to play and be present in the scene because I was holding so much back. I was a robot that was overheating and ready to implode.

As I graduated, I created my dissertation; a performance called *Confessions of a Dancewhore*, which celebrated the diversity of being a gay man. I played 13 different versions of myself, or what a gay man could be. I felt angry that Drama School had not let me 'play gay' and that they saw it as 'too easy'. They saw being gay as one thing, one choice, one style of acting. I created a piece that showcased my versatility and the diversity of queerness. I celebrated everything I'd been repressing for years and, as a performer, something clicked. Drag was the most obvious example of the release and the power it gave me was a revelation. I found that embracing the elements that were perceived as *feminine* whist also retaining the *masculine* was a very empowering and dynamic place to perform from.

I believe my queerness did not get along with being in an institutional environment. Queerness is about breaking conformity, not following societies rules or boxes, and it can make traditional, systematic institutes hard for many. Especially in performance where our body is inescapably a part of our work. As I said, there is no one way to do drag, or get into drag, this is just an insight into how my drag journey began. But this might give some context as to why some of these exercises have evolved from acting exercises.

When I took *Confessions* into the world outside of drama school I was rehearsing with Bette Bourne at OvalHouse Theatre. On watching a run through the main note I got was *"you've left college dear, no need to be clever"*. Bette brought a huge amount of fun to my work and helped me to see how I could combine fun, politics and academic ideas together but to focus on making a live, entertaining show. It keeps an audience engaged, and then they will be listening to everything you say.

Recently, looking over old rehearsal diaries I found a note: *"It's brilliant, intelligent work – now have some fucking fun with it!"* I'm unsure if that was a note from Bette but that ideal has really shaped my career. I can be politically engaged, intelligent and provoke a reaction from an audience whilst still being entertaining, engaging and charismatic. Politics don't have to be preached, personal histories aren't only told through an earnest monologue. In fact, the more likeable and accessible you can make yourself to an audience, the deeper I believe a message can hit. I like to use the term *Charm and Disarm*.

Prior to Drama School I studied Drama and Theatre at University and on a slightly simplistic level I think the theatre practitioner Brecht and his thoughts on theatre being like a boxing match is similar to my approach to drag. In theatre, it is easy for an audience to watch performances passively and not think about the meaning of what is being said on stage. Drag as a performance mode acts like a Brechtian alienation device reminding the spectator they are not watching reality, even though real issues are being explored. Thus allowing the audience to think independently about the arguments being presented. Taking Brecht further there is a sense of 'spass' in drag, an assumed tongue in cheek ('spass' literally translates to 'fun'). Brecht[3] wanted people to think rather than just observe, he felt when someone is laughing they are also thinking and comedy is a device through which to explore serious issues. To me this is how I approach presenting an argument within drag: it still needs to be fun, I still need to find a connection with the audience, rather than just talking at them and them remaining passive.

That is my background, it won't be yours. Whatever your background before drag is, don't view drag as a fresh start, rather the next chapter! Your history and experience can, and will, enrich the work you create. View drag as another step in an evolution, bring your history with you onto the stage and let that ring through in your performance to authentically show the world your unique point of view. I know that's easy to say – but I can almost hear you asking: *how?*

It's Time to Play

Now is the fun part; we need to play! Try things out, see what works for you. There won't be many definitive answers within these pages, it's not that type of book. Let's face it, drag isn't that type of art form; drag is punk, drag is fun, drag is political, drag is constantly evolving and putting two fingers up to anyone who tries to tell us what it is. Drag also moves fast. The idea of writing a 'how to' for drag is almost an oxymoron, it goes against the essence of what drag is. I am, therefore, hoping this handbook will serve as a *'this might help'*. And together we can get up, explore and discover.

I hope you will find courage in your convictions. Have the confidence to explore ideas that don't work at first, create something unusual and perhaps something you have never seen before! Be guided by your on your own unique journey rather than following someone else's, hoping you can just follow in their footsteps.

In case you've been skim reading, or are sat on the fence as to whether or not this is the book for you; I want to clarify three things before we move on. This will either make you cherish this handbook, or put it down and walk away.

1. **There are no definitive rules for drag.**

Anyone can do drag. I use the term Drag Act rather than queen, king or thing because to me it's an inclusive term for everyone in the field. And it's a field everyone is welcome in.

2. **This handbook is about performance.**

The world is over saturated with tips for drag aesthetics. This handbook is all about what you will do onstage, in rehearsal and of course how to keep those bookings coming in!

3. **This is *The Art of Drag* not *How to Be a Drag Act***

We are exploring the practical skills of drag performance. We are looking at the wide-ranging toolbox of practical stage skills. There isn't an exact algorithm, reading cover to cover won't instantly create a finished product.

The handbook goes through a lot of the skills a drag act can use on stage – but the words alone won't create anything. It is your commitment, what you do with the advice, exercises and ideas that will help you become a drag act!

Now that's out of the way. Let's get practical! Get creative! Get ready to be your creative best! It's time to give your performance process some of the rigour and rehearsal that it deserves. There will be exercises you love, others you won't, and some you will return to time and time again! And all the way through approach your work with an open mind and a sense of fun.

I can't wait to see what we'll create!

Notes

1. RuPaul's Drag Race has played a huge role in shaping modern drag. From here on when referenced I will just use Drag Race to refer to all branches of the franchise and cite specific episodes when relevant.
2. I choose to use the word Queer as an umbrella term for the LGBTQIA+ community. It's how I personally prefer to identify, it allows movement for an individual and a multiplicity of genders and sexualities to exist within one person should they so choose.
3. There is plenty of further reading and introductory writing on Brecht, Spass and Epic Theatre. My go-to is: Brecht, B., & Willett, J. (1964). *Brecht on Theatre: The Development of an Aesthetic*. [1st ed.] New York, Hill and Wang.

About the Course: The Art of Drag

This book grew out of the course, *The Art of Drag*, that I have run at the *Royal Vauxhall Tavern* (RVT) for the past decade. A ten-week evening course, split in two parts; five weeks on learning a variety of skills of drag and then five weeks working on an individual act. Guest lecturers join as we dive into lip-sync, singing, parody, hosting and more. Each week course members pitch one small idea in class, slowly building a range of potential performances before pitching one piece they will develop, rehearse and present at their showcase. From that point on we rehearse and refine their concepts until they debut them.

The course is open to all, with no pre-requisite of experience, background, gender, sexuality or aspirations. Some come to the course with dreams to break into the drag scene, others because they thought a book club looked a bit boring. Sharing and collaborating in a room as novice and experienced performers is a wonderful learning environment. The course structure gives a sense of accountability to developing work and seeing things to fruition as they have an audience waiting to watch at the course completion.

I have had around two hundred students on the course; all genders and sexual identities, even a few token heterosexuals, have taken to the stage in drag! The course harbours an ethos of bettering yourself and not needing to compare yourself against anyone else. No two performers are the same, no two sets are the same. Why bother comparing? Do your best, explore styles that interest you, try things out and see what happens. And then next time, do better.

I had no intentions of setting up a drag course but an opportunity arose so I said – yes! In the Summer of 2015 I had been hosting a variety night called *Finger in the Pie Cabaret* which we had run for a few years at *Madame Jojo's*. There was a spate of closures of LGBT+ bars and venues at this time. Amongst them was *Madame Jojo's*, and our show started roving between venues for the next few years. During this time we came to the *RVT*. It was a venue I already had a long history with as it was the first place to programme me when I was promoting my solo show *Confessions Of A Dancewhore* around 2008. The team at the *RVT* and *Finger in the Pie* were keen to run some introductory cabaret courses and I agreed to take on the drag course which eventually became *The Art of Drag*.

In the Spring of 2017 producers of *Finger in the Pie* dissipated but, with their blessing and the support of the *RVT*, I decided to take the course on and evolve it a little further. Since then I have run it twice a year at the *RVT*. Birthing many performers who have gone on to be successful acts across the London drag scene. Some now host, produce, a couple of have found their way onto franchises of *Drag Race* and others have enjoyed their showcase and returned to their *usual* life with just the remnants of eyeliner, glitter and fond memories.

I initially facilitated for two seasons of an eight week course along with guest lectures – Myra Dubois and Me The Drag Queen (at the time performing as Meth). As the course expanded so did the team of guests and a huge range of artists have stepped into our sessions and rehearsals: Adam All, Cosmic, Lolo Brow, Cookie Monstar, Rhys's Pieces, The Virgin X, Pi The Mime, Ada Campe, Joe Black, Stuart Saint and more.

I greatly enjoy running the course. Talking about drag and performance is a passion of mine. And something I believe consistently makes my own work and praxis better. Analysing performances and the choices of others helps me remember to keep working on my own craft. I'll often give notes in rehearsal that I need to be told myself. I hope too that I'll find use for this handbook as I continue to grow as an artist.

I often joke on the course that "*I take no credit, or responsibility, for what the performers create*". I simply open a door and start a conversation; the work comes from the performers. I feel the same for this handbook, it's up to you now to turn the pages and let your creativity run wild. The handbook is the impetus not the end result. The motivation and inspiration is here – but only you can act on it!

Find out more about the course at www.theartofdrag.co.uk/@theartofdraguk

Who Wrote This?

This handbook is for you, but is written by me and I have to acknowledge the personal experience that is shaping so much of my perspective…I feel you, the reader, knowing a little more about where I come from will help interpretation and understanding. I am a gay, white, cis-man who lives in the South of England. I have a Masters in Performance from Mountview Academy of Theatre Arts and before that a BA(Hons) Drama and Theatre Studies from University of Kent. During my undergraduate degree I studied for a year at UCLA; the year I spent in Los Angeles was formative with my perception of drag; by night the West Hollywood Scene and by day studying Queer Theatre with Professor Sue-Ellen Case at UCLA. In lectures my eyes were being opened to the performances of Split Britches, Holly Hughes, Tim Miller, Kate Bornstein, Alec Mapa and in the evenings life was being invigorated by drag acts at *Mickeys*, *Rage* and *The Abbey* West Hollywood. Some of whom later I would see on the world stage thanks to *Drag Race*.

When I came out, I wasn't legally able to get married. I wasn't able to adopt a child with a same-sex partner. I've stood on Pride stages and marched in parades campaigning for equality within the UK and for causes across the world. But I also do the grass roots work of taking my son to school and being the two dads at parents' evening. This is a good illustration of how there are different ways to take up space and put your politics into the world; sometimes arguing for a cause on-stage, but sometimes contextualising with a personal story. Hopefully one day two dads at a school meeting won't be an oddity.

Language changes and evolves. Fifteen years ago I wouldn't have written referring to someone being non-binary, the language was not commonplace (There may have been precursors; gender non-conforming, gender-fluid, queer, etc.). As soon as something is in writing it makes it permanent and LGBTQ+ politics are anything but permanent. We keep evolving, we keep trying to create space for more people, for more letters in our alphabet and for more people outside of the patriarchal binary that Western Society thrives on. I opt to use the, not always popular, word queer as an umbrella term for anyone who feels they are somewhere within the ever-growing acronym of letters.

If at any point the language feels to have excluded you or anyone else, just know you are welcome here. Your drag is valid. Your label, or name, for your drag is correct. It is *your* drag and you are naming it, how could it not be correct? Within a few years of publication I'm sure there'll be new terms and new language I would wish to include, and some of language from this first edition will feel clunky.

Throughout the book I have tried to open exercises and ideas up to all types of drag performer who may use elements of drag. Occasionally, I may mention something that implies drag queens (such as tucking) I may not always open it up and give a drag king (for example binding) just to balance the conversation but know this is implied. Everything within the book can be explored by everyone. My experience coming from working as a drag queen will feed into the writing and references but I am part of a scene which is becoming more diverse and more colourful all the time. I hope this book can continue to make the world of drag a more varied place.

When talking of performers I will use the pronoun they perform under at the time of going to print. But again, for many, gender is fluid, people will carry on evolving, transitioning and transcending. I also have to acknowledge this handbook does not look at all forms and uses of drag in a live space. There is a rich history of drag from shamanism, activism and much, much, more. I have written this handbook placing the performance in the frame of a Western, queer performance space be that a bar, club, brunch, theatre, Pride stage, or other. There are of course areas of the world those safe spaces don't yet exist. There are performers who don't wish to ever step onto a stage. Not including those journeys in the handbook is not to try to declassify them as drag or devalue their importance. I'm writing from my experiences, and I hope you will take the advice useful to you and create the next steps in yours.

Find out more about the author at www.michaeltwaits.com/@michaeltwaits

How to Use This Handbook

I hope one day to meet a drag act who has a dog-eared copy of this book covered in scribbles, highlights, doodles and make-up! A practical performance handbook is meant to be well used and loved – not just an attractive book on a shelf!

This is not a book to sit and passively read, rather something to actively engage with. A conversation starter. A rehearsal assistant. My advice is to treat this handbook like a buffet; have a look at it all, assess the situation. Try a little of everything. Then come back for more of the bits you loved and walk by the rest. But try everything, and dig in!

Accompanying this book you will want a blank notebook, highlighters, pens, hopefully you have a phone (or similar device to record, film, voice note during the process) and access to a computer where you can play music, do research and create a folder to keep things organised. There are a few extras (like a pack of cards) but essentially everything is hopefully accessible – and if you can move some furniture in your bedroom you have a rehearsal space! The handbook is designed for you to produce work with: there will be times to write, to think and to get up on your feet.

A physical notebook is essential. As we go through there are plenty of opportunities to write and work through ideas, scraps of paper get lost, the above is to help you stay organised. Digital notes are too easy to erase, a notebook will serve as a great creative document that you can revisit over and over again and ideas can be transferred to a computer when appropriate.

The handbook is accessible for an act starting from scratch, but there will be times you might get a booking and need to adapt some existing work or another time you might only have a ten minute set but have been asked to do 15! All moments to return to the handbook, and your notebook, and dig deep!

As a facilitator of the course *The Art of Drag* I have seen first hand how not every exercise works for every performer. We all have different ways *in* to rehearsing and developing our work. As a result, most chapters have a variety of exercises; many compliment each other but others may just not work for you at this time. That's ok, try the next one. This journey won't be linear, you will come back round and perhaps on the second time around different things click.

The main thing I ask of a reader is not to be too obstinate; I truly believe it's the worst quality a performer can have. We always need to be open to conversations, new ideas and new arguments: try seeing things from a fresh perspective, try performing something in a different way. Don't assume you know the answers to a question before it's even asked. In fact, don't assume.

If I may break may own rule and make a quick assumption about you; you have a desire to learn, a curiosity about drag performance – why else would you have picked up this book. Nurture that curiosity. Keep asking why and how. The search for these answers will be the driving force on your journey.

For simplicity of writing, I have always written as if the performer is intending to perform in a traditional drag bar environment. There is a stage (or at least an area called that), an audience, usually a bar and a space you are sharing with the audience. The stage area isn't necessarily where the entire performance takes place, but it is the expected focal point of performance – but drag acts love a surprise entrance from the rear!

There is a chronology to the handbook that will make sense as you work through but creativity isn't linear. Here's an indication of what's to come, and why it's there:

Part I: Preparation Is Everything

Setting the ground work and broadening your horizons. What can you do in drag? The chapters here cover how to be professional, make drag economically viable, and how to achieve your best with realistic goals. Before heading into stage craft you will become familiar with rehearsal and development techniques, repertoire and take a look at some of the variety of what is out there in the world of drag!

Part II: Stage Craft for All Drag Acts

There is a stage craft that every drag acts needs to master on-stage. Here you will learn to explore basic drag and have pointers that can help bring the best from every performance. You'll explore your alter-ego, and the way in which you find your voice and bring your unique point of view to the stage. Focus will then shift to the audience connection and how you can utilise the live space you are in to create a unique experience and achieve your best.

Part III: Specific Drag Performance Skills and Styles

This is where you get into the specifics: talking, singing, creating a track, lip-syncing, comedy, parody, impersonation and more. Each subject has a range of approaches, ideas and exercises to help any act master these specific skills and how you apply them to your set. And when one set is no longer enough you can explore more: creating a piece which defies categorisation, hosting or perhaps a full length show.

Part IV: Praxis in Practice

It's all well and good reading the what's, why's and how's but it can feel quite daunting in the hypothetical. To help add more colour and context you have seven very different acts, who use *The Art of Drag*, discussing their process, their motivation and why drag is the art form for them. Interviews with *Adam All, Simply Barbra, Ada Campe, Le Fil, Hugo Grrrl, Me The Drag Queen* and *Son Of A Tutu*.

Part I

Preparation Is Everything

Ozzy Mandeus photographed backstage at the Royal Vauxhall Tavern by Fox Al Rajim

1
Starting Here, Starting Now:
A New Beginning

This is the start of an amazing adventure, a new chapter in drag! Picking up this handbook you have decided to invest in yourself: as a performer, as a drag artist and as the person off-stage who needs to handle the realities of being a fabulous creature in the spotlight! Before we get practical, let's look at the wider world of drag performance.

Anyone can wear a suit, that doesn't make them a CEO. When you put on your drag – what type of performer do you want to be? This chapter is going to give a breakdown of the three key areas of drag: what you might do on stage, what you might look like and how to turn that into a business!

This chapter will help you explore the breadth of styles and forms drag can take, curating a dream list of things you think you should do, can do, and might want to do! It is worth taking stock of your own preconceived ideas of what drag is; firstly, so you know where you might fit within the world of drag; secondly, to make sure you don't cut yourself off from any potential areas that might lead to exciting opportunities.

Drag acts are creative magpies; borrowing from all areas of the arts, fusing forms together to create new and unique performance experiences; calling on cultural references from everywhere. Drag acts are superheroes who can do anything on-stage; don't limit yourself or think small, challenge yourself and indulge in the excess to drag. Be the full Barbra Streisand: actor, singer, comedian, writer, producer, director…why can't you do it all?

What Are You Doing? And Why?

These are *essential* questions to consistently ask yourself throughout your career. For each set you perform and each gig you get; what and why? What is your role within the bigger picture of that show? What are you giving to the audience? Why you? Moment to moment within your performance, ask: why did you take a step forward? Why have a reveal at that moment? Why are you making eye contact on that specific line?

Performance is about the relationship between the performer and an audience: never create a performance because someone told you that's how you *do* drag. Create it because you want to communicate something to an audience. With the success of *Drag Race* certain styles of performance have come to the forefront as the *expected* performance modes for a drag act. I always recommend; focus, at least initially, on your existing strengths and the skills that you can use to communicate with an audience. Rather than attempting to create what you may feel is expected. If you are a naturally funny person – get into drag and tell us a joke or a story! Build your craft from the places you feel confident and slowly reach out into new areas.

EXERCISE 1: THREE BRAINSTORMS – THINK BIG

You will need: Your notebook, pens and a timer.

You have barely started *Chapter 1* and – BANG – you have an exercise! This is an e*ssential* exercise that every performer can benefit from: whatever experience you might have, whatever preconceived ideas you have about drag, take a moment to look at the art of drag with fresh eyes. You are going to create three separate brainstorms; free flowing notes around a subject. I have given a starter brainstorm for each of the three subjects: Figures 1.1, 1.2 and 1.3. You are welcome to carry on from there, although I imagine you'll need more space as the creativity pours out (and if this is a library book then best use a notebook – let's not ruin the book for the next reader!).

For each brainstorm set a timer for five minutes; the challenge is to keep writing the whole time, don't edit or limit yourself – *keep writing*. If you run out ideas, see if anything written down has the potential to be broken down into more specific areas. There will be storms within storms as your brain works its magic.

Don't worry about yourself as a performer yet: be as open as possible, broaden those horizons. You might include ideas specific to being a King/Queen that, currently, you don't think apply to you – that's great!

Tackle each brainstorm subject separately, but do all three before moving onto the analysis below. There are no wrong answers and unless you choose to share, no one else will see it. Don't hold yourself back – use every second that you have! Five minutes per brainstorm – start the clock!

Brainstorm 1 – Performance

What types of performance can a drag act do?

Write down as many ideas as you can as to what type of performance someone could do in drag.

The Obvious: *comedy, singing, lip-sync…*

The Less Obvious: *acrobatics, modelling, fire-eating…*

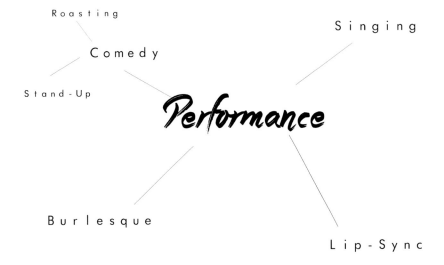

Figure 1.1 A Starter 'Performance' Brainstorm

Brainstorm 2 – Aesthetics

What can a drag act use to create their look? Think; heels, beards, padding, make-up, facial hair, wigs – then wig size, wig colour, wig style…

Figure 1.2 A starter 'Aesthetics' Brainstrom

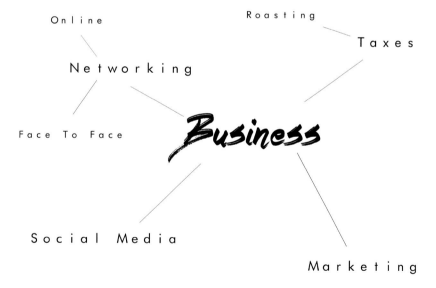

Figure 1.3 A Starter 'Business' Brainstorm

Brainstorm 3 – Business

What does a drag act need to do offstage to get work, make money and promote themselves?

Many find this the hardest one, dreaded words: *accounting, networking, research, self promotion, self care, taxes…*.

Well done!

I hope you ran out of space and are still thinking of more! If you found that hard, do not worry: this is not a definitive document, you can keep adding and editing! Now that you have started to think about the basics of a drag career it's time to dig into each area in detail.

Performance

How is your *Performance Brainstorm* looking? I said in the *Introduction* that there won't be many definitive answers within this handbook. However, I have one for you here: **there is no type of performance that cannot be done in drag!**

Some of the things that you might have included: *opera, circus, mime, acrobatics, host/compere, juggling, magic, burlesque, lip-sync, comedy, performance poetry, acting, dancing, fire breathing, impersonation, playing instruments, improvisation, character comedy, bingo calling, plate spinning, chat show host…*

The list is almost almost endless! Did you miss any? It might be quite revealing what you missed out. I think through omissions you will have revealed to yourself a few of your preconceived ideas on drag. Which is brilliant, you are learning about yourself and what you think drag is!

As an art form, drag is not one specific performance mode. As I mentioned at the start of the book, saying you do drag does not tell someone much about what you are actually going to do on-stage. It tells them more about the aesthetics, and assumptions may be made on styles or themes explored. For this reason many established drag acts will refer to themselves as something specific; a comedian, a host, a lip-sync act, etc. Rather than *just* a drag act. Drag is not what they do, but the way in which they achieve it.

As drag artists, you are chameleons of the arts: adapting your skill set to any given situation, to express what you wish to depending on a list of variables of any given performance. It's why you can do *Drag Queen Story Time* on a Sunday morning and a risqué club night that evening. You use different skills, styles and approaches of drag for different audiences and shows. Drag is fluid; both adaptive and reactive, creating unique, bespoke live experiences.

EXERCISE 2: WHAT ABOUT YOU?

You will need: Your *Performance Brainstorm* and at least two highlighters.

It's time to take drag performance out of the hypothetical and into the specific: let's look at you! Your skill set and aspirations. What are you going to do? Revisit the *Performance Brainstorm* with two coloured highlighters; one of them is your *I Can Do That* colour and the other *I Want to Do That*. Take a few moments going through your brainstorm and highlight which you *can* do and which you *want* to do.

The *I Can Do That* are things that as a performer you feel confident doing: speaking, dancing, singing, comedy? Perhaps you are segueing into drag after a career in a different performance art. Brilliant! These are all skills to incorporate and adapt into your drag work.

The *I Want to Do That* are things which are possibly going to require some work and a leap of faith. A step into a new world, which at the moment, isn't in your skill set. When you have drag on it is your armour, and will help you find new ways to perform on stage. As you become more experienced on stage, I encourage you to find new skills and performance modes. No matter how experienced you are, artists are always evolving, improving and playing with new ideas and forms.

Off you go! Get highlighting! There's no time limit just come back to this when you are ready.

Now you've highlighted your brainstorm, draw up a simple table with *I Can Do That* and *I Want to Do That*. Table 1.1 is an example of what your list *could* look like.

Your list may be longer or perhaps one side is very small and the other is huge: no wrong answers! As you move forward through the book hopefully some from your *I Want to Do That* list might be able to move into the *I Can Do That* list and new *Wants* will appear. When you are creating new work, building your repertoire (see *Chapter 6: Building A Set, Range and Repertoire*) you can return here and decide if it's time to expand your rep with existing skills, or jump in and do something completely different!

I Can Do That	I Want to Do That
Tell A Joke	A Trapeze Act
Sing	Magic
Talk To An Audience	Character Comedy
Acting	Dance

Table 1.1 An example of a table assigning what skills are an "I Can Do That" and "I Want to Do That".

This is an exercise I often come back to for inspiration and to give me ideas on what I might want to create next. I included *"Do a trapeze act"* on the example because I always have wanted to do that. I am still not a circus performer but I do currently open the second half of my weekly show in an aerial hoop whilst in full drag. Why? Because it's camp! It's unexpected and it's visually exciting for an audience. I've previously spent an hour singing and chatting standing up, so to have a different dynamic brings the audience back with anticipation that they haven't yet seen everything I have to offer. I still have aspirations to learn a trick or two, but for now, the visual of a trapeze, or aerial hoop, adds an unexpected dynamic twist to the show. And is a lot of fun!

No Excuses

With your *I Can Do That* list you can create a new act, or add material to an existing set, because you are aware of your existing skill set. You have identified a variety of performance skills you know you have. They will need rehearsal, work, polish, but they are achievable ways for you to perform. You may need help structuring the material, working out how to perfect it – but that is what this handbook is for!

If you need to create some new work: look at your list and choose a skill, or skills, and then jump into those chapter(s) of the handbook! Dive in and expand your repertoire. When creating new work you do not have to feel you are always re-inventing the wheel. You can return to *Chapter 15: Sing A Song* for example numerous times, every time you add a new song to your repertoire! As you work through the handbook new ideas will be cropping up everywhere. Some will be things you can quickly drop into your repertoire, others will be ideas that need to be developed, others you'll keep to one side until the moment is right. In *Chapter 6: Building A Set, Range and Repertoire* there is a structure for how to manage all of this so ideas don't get lost. But identifying your existing skills is a great place to start as a performer.

Aesthetics

It's time to return to you *Aesthetic Brainstorm*. The visual, the appearance, the look, the make-up and more! This is often the first thing that comes to mind when thinking about drag but this is a *Practical Performers'*

Handbook, so it is coming second. You cannot ignore the ways in which creating our aesthetic in drag will affect the work that you perform, and the way in which an audience will interpret your performance because of it. What are the tools drag artists *can* use to play with appearance and gender? And how do these affect what the audience see and perceive?

Nothing makes me more furious than a drag act being told what they *should* be doing with their aesthetic, or even worse hearing the phrase *"that's not how you do drag"*. Queens don't have to wear nails. Kings don't need to bind their chest. Queers don't need to portray any form of gender norms, in, or out, of drag. There is no rule book for drag or drag aesthetics, just a smorgasbord of delicious *options* to be played with.

What was on your brainstorm? It could have featured: wigs, lashes, eye shadow, glitter, binding, tucking, facial hair, reveals, corsets, heels, tights, toupees, breastplates, jewellery, hats, jackets, gowns, sequins, contouring, contact lenses, exaggerating lips, reducing foreheads….

The list, again, is almost endless and each item could bring a different effect to your performance on stage. As a drag act these are areas you will keep playing with throughout your career, aesthetics are always evolving (look at some of your favourites on social media and compare a picture from today and three years ago).

I have another definitive answer for you: **no single item on your *Aesthetic Brainstorm* is essential to creating a drag aesthetic.** Some of these options will be things you wish to play with, others things you wish to avoid. But knowing and considering, all the options is invaluable.

It is careful curation of various elements of aesthetics that creates a drag *look*. What every drag act does need to know is the affect their aesthetic has to an audience. Your drag look may wow, unsettle, charm, bemuse or confuse an audience before you have taken a second step on to the stage. Know what your aesthetic is doing!

There are queens who don't wear wigs, kings who don't stuff their pants, queers who don't wear eyelashes! It is how, as artists, you choose to opt in or out of each option that will shape your drag aesthetic. How they are used in conjunction with each other, and with your performance, that will create your brand, your drag identity.

EXERCISE 3: WHY OR WHY NOT?

You will need: Your *Aesthetics Brainstorm* from *Exercise 1*, a pen and highlighters.

When discussing drag, and performance, I always want to know *why* you are doing something, or why you are *not* doing something. It is one of the biggest strengths you can have as a performer: to question everything will give clarity. These choices are what make you unique, give you a point of view. Having a unique stance will help you shape your alter-ego, build your brand and show you how you want to engage with the world. (That's a lot of pressure to put on whether or not you wish to contour your cheeks!)

Spend a few minutes going over your *Aesthetic Brainstorm*: highlight with one colour the *Will Use* and another the *Won't Use*. This is not locking you into anything permanently, it's an exercise to see what you are thinking, at the moment, you might explore! Don't feel you need to put every element into either category. Again there's no time limit here – just come back when you are ready! Get highlighting!

Well done! Now the tricky part: pick the five you feel strongly towards for *Will Use* and for *Won't Use*. Draw up the table (like the example shown in Table 1.2) in your notebook and also write *Why* after each one. A justification! The only rule is the answer can't be *'because that's how you do drag'*.

Will Use	Why	Won't use	Why Not?

Table 1.2 A Blank Table to Be Filled with 5 Aesthetic Choices a Performer Will Do and 5 They Will Not.

It may be too early for you but I would highly recommend returning to this once you know more what your drag act is going to do! It may also help to talk this through with someone. Or even role play that you are trying to justify your choices to someone. Below is an example of my thought process, you do not need to agree with any of it, I don't want everyone having the same approach as me, but it will be useful to see how opinions help me make choices. And it's also a nice way for you to get to know me better:

> As an artist I often refer to myself as a 'gateway' drag act! For many people, straight theatre going audiences, I am the first drag act they have seen in the flesh. The way I present myself is one reason this works so well to them. As a performer I have a layer of honesty and being present in the room, they feel charmed by me, I'm approachable and despite looking how you might expect a drag queen to look, they don't feel I have tried to 'trick' them.
>
> Aesthetically, when I walk out on stage there is something familiar about how I present. I look how they would expect 'a drag queen' to look. Sequins, pretty, on the glamorous side, big hair. Compared to many other drag acts there's something almost understated about my aesthetic. It isn't too challenging or aggressive. In many ways, I walk out and I meet their expectations and they relax because they were correct in preconceived assumptions. So, before I even begin my set I have established a dynamic, or a relationship with the audience, which is all to do with the choices I have made towards my aesthetics.
>
> This is my perspective, my choices, my drag style; I am a white, cis, British man who is 6'3 who opens most sets saying *"I'm Michael Twaits, a man in a dress"*. This won't be your story or point of view, so don't let me influence you! But do see how I carefully select what I *Will Use*, and *Won't Use* to reinforce my point of view.
>
> **Will Use**
>
> Heels: I am tall, and rather than apologising for that and trying to look demure I want to visually celebrate it! My height helps me command a room or stage. I wear six inch heels, stilettos. Exaggerating my height also helps me look narrower, the proportions of how I look on stage seem more traditionally elegant (i.e. tall and thin) because I am making myself taller.
>
> Wigs: I have quite a feminine facial structure and I want to look beautiful/pretty/femme as part of my look. I balance this out by choosing hair slightly larger than life and often choosing an un-natural colour so straight away it's visibly obvious I'm a drag act. The size and volume of the wig also balances out my proportions. (In the early days of my career some questioned if I was trans which wasn't a problem for me personally but does alter the way an audience take my politics and humour so I used wigs to be a large drag signifier to the audience.)
>
> Body Make-Up: I like a little bit of sparkle or tinted moisturiser on exposed flesh. Spending time on my face and it mismatching my neck/arms seems to break the glam illusion. I do some simple shimmer foundation or moisturiser.

> **Won't Use**
>
> Breast/Hip Padding: I've already established I'm a 'man in a dress' I am not trying to look like a woman or create a gender illusion that will 'trick' an audience. I aim to visually celebrate being a camp man – *"why can't a man look glam and wear a dress?"*
>
> This approach has a knock on effect to lots of costuming my choices too. Certain styles of outfit *need* padding to look 'right'. Generally I don't wear leotards or anything too figure hugging. I wear lots of tulle, pom-pom, ruffles and layers to create movement and build shape where it's needed and to still give me a waistline.
>
> Body Make-Up Contouring: No to contouring or anything which gives a cleavage illusion. Again, my aesthetic is retaining my male body whilst looking glam.
>
> Eyebrow Blocking: My face is naturally quite femme and I have large eye sockets with enough space to paint a good eye shape. I like my face looking more natural than the majority of modern drag acts. I also find drawn eyebrows can slightly limit facial expression, or set one style of face. And I have an animated, funny face that I utilise in performance.
>
> These are just a few examples of how I use different areas of drag aesthetic to build my brand, reinforce my politics and to visually establish how I relate to an audience. I want to look a certain way because of the effect it has on the audience and the story it tells them. There is also an undercurrent of reclaiming things I wasn't allowed to like or play with growing up. Reclaiming something, taking up space or ownership is a great justification for aesthetic drag choices. As is a personal gender exploration. It might be you have a selection of aesthetic choices which fall under that category: embrace them, just always try to acknowledge why you are making those choices and the effect it will have on your audience.

Aesthetics Ongoing: Always Ask Why?

As an ongoing part of my practice – I am nosey. And I encourage you to be the same! As artists you are always learning, and you can learn a lot from others.

In a dressing room, if I see someone using a new make-up item, undergarment or accessory I am not familiar with (or something I am familiar with being used in an unusual way) I always ask about it! What does it achieve? Is it better than what they used to use? Is it cheaper? Longer lasting? Obviously be polite and friendly but be inquisitive! Always be open and alert to new ideas of how your practice might evolve.

If you aren't yet working with other acts and getting onstage, take a look at a few of your favourites online. (It seems everyone has a makeup tutorial on YouTube!) Think about a few of the big aesthetic choices and ask yourself: why? See if they tell you in the video. Why have they done that? What's the reason? What does that give an audience? And the follow up question is always: have I learnt anything I could apply to my own aesthetic?

Often with make-up a lot of it is an evolution of classic stage craft; white around the inner eye can draw an audience in, over drawn lips will help emphasise the accuracy of the lip-sync to the back of the room. Often the answer *"it looks good"* may come up, but try to be specific: *why* does it look good? Or even why do you want to look good? Does having a harsher jaw contour make this drag king look stronger? Does an oversized wig make it more obvious the way gender is being parodied?.

Performance and Aesthetics

From exploring these two brainstorms I hope you are beginning to see an endless world of possibilities. Styles, forms and ideas to play with. This variety is what makes drag shows so exciting. Even if watching a show with every performer doing, for example, a lip-sync – the evening will be varied and dynamic because no two performers are bringing the same ideas or options to the stage. They all have their own unique approach to what they are doing and what they want to do.

This is not a chapter to finish and feel ready to get on stage with but I hope these two explorations have broadened your horizons and got your ready to challenge yourself moving forward to explore all the things a drag act can be. These are ideas to help create your own unique approach rather than replicating what you have seen someone else already do.

Business

There's no business like drag business! Drag is a tricky business to navigate with no singular clear path to success. But a professional approach to drag, and a good grasp on the business basics can help make any drag journey more successful.

The *Business Brainstorm* exercise nearly got put to the back of the handbook, to leave you thinking about the longevity of your career. But as the handbook developed and I spoke to more students, young acts and novice performers it became clear: the business side of drag needs addressing from the very beginning! As soon as you step off the stage from your first gig, you are looking for your second gig and you have already started to build a reputation, a brand and hopefully momentum!

Take another look at your business brainstorm. Perhaps you've started to worry that this is a lot to take on. But actually it's all about having a positive approach to your work ethic and developing a level of professionalism to help sustain the career that you want. Or at least not have your hobby become a financial and emotional drain!

Your brainstorm could have included: social media presence, networking, researching who books what, taxes, budgets, rehearsals, promotion, professionalism, reputation, websites, branding, logo, getting booked…

If you are wanting to shape a career, earn money and get those bookings: it all needs addressing! And in detail, because being good isn't good enough, you also need to be likeable, professional and find your audience.

That's a lot to be getting into.
More than a few paragraphs.
In fact it's become the next two chapters.
Let's get down to business!

Professor Q Cumber photographed backstage at the Royal Vauxhall Tavern by Fox Al Rajim

2
Being Good, Isn't Good Enough: The Business of Drag

You could be a talented comic, a natural stage performer or a world class make-up artist: that does not guarantee a successful career. To achieve the best, a drag act needs to be organised, professional and personable, things that don't always come naturally to the drag inclined! This chapter is going to give the best practical advice to help you do your business best and set you up with the tools that can shape a sustainable career.

The business of drag is a minefield: performers have to self-produce, promote, market and manage themselves. It's a lot of hats to wear and if you aren't getting the balance right, you simply won't get the bookings. The business advice in this Chapter is not just for new drag acts; established acts will find ways to save time, improve their brand and they may even realise why some venues aren't inviting them back.

It doesn't matter how accomplished you are, people want to work with those who make it easy and fun. If you are hard work, badly organised or underdeliver there will always be an equally talented drag act waiting to take your spot. Professionalism is key to longevity.

Most of this book focuses on what to do in rehearsal and on-stage to be your best, here we are focusing on how to get onto that stage! This chapter will give you a strong business backbone: you will build your online brand, create a professional online resource for bookers, look at how to approach people (venues, producers and performers) and how best to get networking to help you find more bookings. We will then focus on being professionally prepared for the gig, knowing what questions to ask and finally some top tips to help you get the most out of every opportunity. I haven't framed any of this chapter as a dedicated exercise because it's all on-going work and professionalism. Some elements you will want to do straight away, others just keep in mind as things move forward. But get your note-pad, computer and phone ready because there is a lot to do!

Before You Get the Gigs

Prior to looking for performance opportunities every act needs to get set up for business. There are two parts to this; firstly preparing yourself as a professional performer and secondly actively doing your homework!

Preparing Yourself Professionally

A first impression can last a lifetime. Prior to approaching *anyone* asking for work, think about what you are presenting. What will they find if they search for you online? What can you do to present yourself as an organised and professional artist? How can you make sure they see you at your very best?

A good place to start is to know *what* you are, be brand aware. In TV and Film, they refer to an elevator pitch: selling an idea to someone succinctly and clearly between floors. That's what your online presence needs to do. It should grab people's attention and let them quickly *get* who you are.

The Online Basics

You're going to build your online presence. Try and set it up as you go; if it's too early for you then make a note and comeback to it. If you already have a presence, brilliant, it's time for an online health check. How could things be improved?

Email: Have a designated drag email address. A free one is fine but something that keeps all your drag admin in one location and lets recipients know exactly who they are communicating with. It should be your drag name @ address, so everyone instantly knows who is getting in touch. Not your government name, your old witty nickname or chat room handle!

Social Media: All acts need to have a presence. Initially it could be basic with a holding picture or two. People will usually do research on an act before booking them, so make sure you are *findable*. Social media names should be as close to your stage name as possible. Again, it should be a dedicated social media account for your drag act, not an extension of your personal one. Try and find one @handle to use across all networks that you are using (ideally that matches your email address too), this helps create a strong brand identity. Consistency always helps branding.

You do not need to be on every platform, choose the ones that suit your style. Find the networks that fit in with your personality and use them to your benefit. If you are witty, and like trying out one liners – tweet. A visual artist might prefer to use Instagram. Chatters might focus on Instagram Stories. Dancers may TikTok. Find what fits your style and what can serve you best. Perhaps look at a performer you would like to be compared to and see how they manage their socials – how frequently do they post? What's their following like? What's their content like?

It's better to do a few platforms well rather than spread yourself too thin. When I investigate an act I check the date of the last post, did they work recently? If someone's booking them then they must be doing ok! If you have a social media account that you are no longer using then shut it down or make it private. The online world is forever shifting so join new networks and see if they work well for you. But if they don't close or hide them.

Consider the first impression. Most let you pin a post to the top of your profile; choose one that represents the best of your work and showcases who you are.

Social media algorithms are always adapting. Newer acts often want to build numbers and beat the algorithm doing the latest trend. The best advice is to keep being authentic and representing yourself as best you can. Try and look at your accounts with an objective eye; if you were booking an act and the last post was them drunk or talking about how they were late to a gig – would you book them?

Website: Many acts do have websites but for most it's more of a holding page or portfolio with links to their social media and/or upcoming gigs. If you have merchandise or want to sell things then investing more in a website may be worthwhile. But it is definitely not a drag essential. Much like different social media platforms it's better not to do it than to not do it well.

Ongoing Promotion and Marketing

With all social media content remember less can be more. A few strong images are more powerful than 12 shots of the same look in a bedroom mirror. Cameras on phones are amazing, so even if you've never been on a stage, you can get a few good shots of yourself in drag that will represent you well as you're setting up your presence.

The other key is to **not put your whole set online**. Audiences come to see a live performer; if they've already seen the full set prior to coming along – what are they paying for? If you have a show-stopping costume try to not do the big reveal online, save it for the stage! Let the live experience have the 'wow' moment. Use social media to tease people, to make them want to see more, make them feel they missed out not being at your last gig! Share a video with a good joke and an audience reacting so people want to see more! But do not post the full set!

The Online Promotional Drive

All of the above is what I call front of house: anyone can find it. It is also essential to have private, shareable content collated and curated for producers and bookers. To increase the chances of getting a booking you want to make a producers' life as easy as possible. Present them with your best from the outset. Create a Google Drive/Dropbox (other services are available) filled with the following documents and share a link to it in your initial email. This will answer many of the questions a producer may have. This presents you as professional and organised, which makes them want to work with you!

The drive will constantly evolve as you get better content, higher quality footage, photos, etc. Initially you may not have everything listed, but you are aiming for:

- A Biography:

Within this have a one-line catchphrase, a one paragraph biography and a couple of quotes. A performance CV is an option if you have enough credits and experience but make it clear, relevant and succinct.

- Reviews/Highlights:

These could be slipped in the bottom of the biography or a separate document. A few quotes can really help promoters sell you as part of their show. It also means you don't need to tell the producer you're great, the reviews have done that for you.

- Press Shots:

A selection of press or professional quality photos. Essentially a small selection of shots you are happy to be used for publicity. Often promoters will need something they can 'cut out' and add to an existing design so one should be a head and shoulders with a simple background to allow this. All photos should to be saved as your name and then the photographers. (e.g. *Michael Twaits by Joel Ryder 2024*).

Make sure the shots are representative of how you look – not overly photoshopped, or even worse a decade old. It's why I like to add a date on the end of the photographs' name.

- Live Shots:

Professional quality shots that represent you in performance. It's great to have one which is on a grand scale and shows off if you have worked on big stages but limit these as what's more useful is the close-up details of you in performance.

- Videos:

Where previously we said you don't want to share your full set with a potential audience, this is the opposite! If you have recorded versions of a set, include it in the folder so producers can see exactly what they are booking. Montage videos of a variety of work are good to show range but limit to one and let the other videos be a full set/performance. For multi-skilled performers I recommend labelling the videos – 'hosting', 'comedy set', 'parody song' etc. If you are pitching to a specific show, wanting to perform a particular set, then put that set in the folder as a video and let the producer know which you wish them to watch.

The link to this drive can be set to private and then attached to the bottom of any correspondence with potential producers, bookers or collaborators. They may not look at everything but even a cursory glance will show you are professional and showcase your strengths as a performer.

Chicken or Egg?

It may seem a little early to be discussing these things but every time you get into drag it is an opportunity to create content: get new footage, new photos, new posts for social media. Initially, use a few selfies or photos taken by a friend. When you do the first open mic night, or heat of a drag contest – make sure someone is there to support you and take photos and, if possible, film it. Each time you get a new, or better, photo, update your online drive and your pinned post on social media.

Photoshoots

If you are confident in your aesthetic and have some finances, you could book a photo session at a studio. A simple way to find a good photographer is to research the professional shots of any drag acts who are local to you, find shots you like and see who took the shots. The costs vary but it is an investment in your career, and also (as we'll discuss in *Chapter 3: The Economics of Drag*) a tax deductible cost.

Venues and producers always prefer professional photographs and again it sets you out as someone taking their career seriously. When you are discussing packages and prices with photographers make sure you know how many photos are included, if any retouching will be done and if you have permission to use the photographs as you wish. Some photographers hold copyright and won't let you use them on posters or in publications. Be sure to have a clear conversation and get it in writing prior to moving forward.

Research

Before reaching out to a venue, producer or programmer always do some research!

I often make acts repeat that sentence out loud like a mantra! Go on. Read it aloud! It's incredible how many performers don't do research when the internet makes it so easy. Through social media, and websites, you should be able to find essential information on any venue, producer, performer or potential gig. Before making contact with anyone ask yourself – how would my set, or act, fit into these line-ups?

With drag having a wide spectrum of styles you need to make sure you are being specific about where you think you will fit in. Venues and producers are always wanting to find new talent but you need to be clear about what you are offering and make sure it's suitable. Try not to waste people's time. (e.g. If you aren't a lip-sync act, don't reach out asking questions about a lip-sync competition!)

Canvassing

The mistake a lot of eager acts make at the beginning is not doing enough research and not knowing where they might fit. They blanket message all venues and producers but clearly show that they haven't looked into how they could fit in.

> As a young performer I had a huge amount of confidence: the 'arrogance of youth'. If I had a show, I would write to everyone who, possibly, might be able to book me, hire me or use me in some way.
>
> I was indiscriminate in my approach. *"You have a venue – you are on the list"*. Everyone got told what I was doing, what my show was about, a few press clippings, a nice promotional photo. I was selling the product. What I wasn't doing was any form of homework on each contact, so often the work was falling in the lap of someone who wasn't actually in a position to help me.
>
> Fifteen plus years later, when people contact me I read the email and ask: *"Why are you contacting? How can I help you? What can you offer? Why are we a good match to work together?"* I want people to be specific and show their research! If the answers to these questions are clear, I'm much more likely to reply to their email.

Researching Venues and Events

Most venues have websites that list their nights. Check them; look at the programming pattern. What's the routine? Who are their audience? Are the nights themed? What styles of performance do they programme, and on which nights? Which night might be suitable for you?

Once you think you have found a regular night you might be a fit for **buy a ticket and go along**! Check you were right. Try to say *"hello"* to the host or an act, maybe a producer, and introduce yourself briefly. Maybe take a business card with you? Ask what's the best way for you to make contact with them? Then you follow up a day or two later with an email or message reminding them you were at their show the other night, it's a great opener to an email.

Many think business cards are outdated but they are brilliant for performers who often meet other performers/producers when they are in costume and don't have a phone to hand. A card can just be slipped away and then they have all your details and a little reminder of you.

Social Media Groups

Social media is a great place to keep an eye out for casting calls and upcoming shows. There are specific performer groups for different genres of performance, for local areas, some nationwide. They are great ways to keep in touch with what's going on, see who's performing where and when. It's a resource for learning a lot about your local scene. There are also specific groups for Kings, Trans-Drag Performers, Performers of Colour, Non-binary Performers, etc. These are well worth getting involved with, if that's how you identify, as it may provide more specific casting calls and opportunities.

Approaching Venues and Producers

When corresponding venues, producers or bookers can often tell if they want to work with you simply from how you come across in emails. Don't bombard them with numerous emails or information; be clear, professional and to the point, let them know why you are getting in touch and where to go if they want to see more.

Here's an example of a simple email that says: *"I know your venue, I'm looking for work, you can find out more about me here, who do you think I should speak to?"*

Filling in the **bold** with specific detail also shows you have done your research and set yourself up as a professional performer. Adapt it to your needs or personal style but from a producer's point of view this will tick a lot of boxes.

> Dear **[Name]**
>
> I visited the ***[venue name and a specific performance]*** and loved the atmosphere and performances. I am a ***[basic skills overview – up to three points]*** who would love to be involved in some future shows. I think I could fit ***[specific shows they produce/host from your research]***. I don't know if you are the person to speak to, if not, perhaps you could point me in the right direction?
>
> I have recently ***[contextualise who you are, or give some recent experience]***. I am keen ***[why are you emailing now]*** and want to work with new venues. I have a drive <u>here</u> with a biography, images and some video.
>
> I am sure I'll be back at ***[venue name]*** again soon and hope to get the chance to say "hello"! If you need anything further don't hesitate to get in touch.
>
> Best wishes,
>
> **[Drag Name]**
>
> **[Contact number]**
>
> **[@socialhandles]**
>
> **[Press quote if you have one]**

As a producer I am ticking off a list of positive things:

- They saw a show. They've done research!
- They are professional, proactive and keen.
- They have a range of skills and know where they would fit.
- They are checking if they're speaking to the right person before bombarding with information.
- They are linking to the piece of work they want me to see.
- They have good communication so moving forward it should be an easy working relationship.
- I want to click on a link to see who this person is and find out more.

Top Tips

You will find your own voice and way of approaching people. But do check these quick pointers before sending any opening correspondence looking for work:

- Be polite and honest.
- Let them know why you are contacting them now.
- Email during *usual* working hours. Avoid messaging via social media.
- If you have an upcoming gig include the details.
- Use spellcheck.
- Name drop, if you have been recommended by someone, don't be afraid to mention them. (e.g. "*Dave passed on your email as he thought we'd be a good match*".)
- Show your research.
- Let the work you provide sell itself. Too much ego can put people off.
- The drag world is small. Assume everyone knows each other; avoid talking down venues, performers or producers.

Approaching Performers

Often you may not know who programmes a night but know a performer connected so you could approach them. This can work when done correctly, but often going directly to an act shows lack of research so keep it as a last resort.

I have had a few variations on this message:

> Hi Michael, I would love to come and host *The Saturday Supershow* at the Phoenix Arts Club.
>
> *Sent on Instagram at 3am*

Firstly, I am the host of *The Saturday Supershow*, they are literally asking for my job?

Secondly, they have messaged me on social media at, what I would consider, an out of hours time. Try and always use an email and send during usual working hours to give a sense of professionalism. If someone makes an approach in the wee small hours of the morning, I assume they are; international, drunk or having a late-night existential crisis. If you're a night owl, wait until you are acquainted before messaging late or simply schedule the message to go at a suitable time.

Finally, it's an Instagram message. Like most people my email is in my Instagram bio, so this shows little thought has been given. That's not to say you can't initially communicate through social networks but if a professional message starts on social media try and move it over to email ASAP.

What might have got me to respond or start a conversation?

> Hi Michael, I saw you at the *Phoenix Arts Club* last weekend and loved the space and the show. Who would I need to speak to about guesting on one of the shows? Here's a link to some of my work. Thanks so much.
>
> *Email sent at 3pm*

Despite being only three sentences this message has a lot of positives and I would probably get back to them.

Networking

Being proactive is a rule to live by: energy breeds energy. The more work you are out there doing the more work it will lead to. When you are working, share it on your socials, let people know about upcoming gigs. Also, when you are out watching (and researching) the scene take a good photo, tag the venue, tag the performer. Be seen to be out and about.

Keep going and seeing shows, firstly because this will provide artistic inspiration and keep the creativity flowing into your own work. Secondly, the networking is equally important. If there's a show you enjoy, or think you would be a good fit for, find out who programmes it. If you met someone connected to the show, or any other potential contact, follow them on your socials. When I meet someone new and add them on socials I often send a swift message that has no questions and no follow up required: *"Great to meet you last night, what a fun show. See you soon I'm sure"*. It puts the ball in their court but shows builds a little connection, they now know where to reach me and often after a busy show one can forget a few of the faces they've said *"hello"* to. It's a nice little reminder without instantly chasing or asking for work.

Often in programming meetings people will mention someone I haven't worked with but I have bumped into, even if it's on social networks, and it helps when people in the meeting say – *"I know her, she came my last show, she looks great"*. Being on people's radar is really useful!

Correspondence – Before a Show

Very few producers on the drag scene will send out any form of contract or formal agreement. It is essential when working with someone new to have an email trail that clarifies everything and confirms expectations on both sides. *One clear email trail*, not hundreds of small notes and questions across multiple platforms or messages.

Make sure you have timings (technical rehearsal, show time, expected arrival and finish), the fee and any other essential details confirmed in writing for your own piece of mind. Resend the link to your online drive and clarify that there's a biography and pictures they can choose from for promotional purposes. It's much easier to do this upfront, rather than wait to be asked, or worse have someone in the team find an image of you online, because they will always choose one that you dislike!

The last part of the booking/confirmation email should say: *"Thanks, see you there! If you need anything else let me know"*. It clarifies that you have all the info you need and, hopefully, so do they.

A Rider

I am a drag performer, not J-Lo! I will not be asking for white roses or a midcentury chez-lounges. However, when accepting bookings there is nothing wrong with letting the booker know what you need as a performer. Most drag or cabaret venues do multiple shows a week, so it's usually straightforward and they are prepared technically to support most performers' needs. With venues you are new to, double check any possible issues that are relevant to you and your set.

- Will there be space in the dressing room for me to get ready?
- What type of microphone do you have?
- What are your stage dimensions?
- Is there parking?
- What's the ceiling height? (Am I ok to wear platforms and a beehive? Many drag venues are in basements.)
- What time is the technical rehearsal? Where am I sending my tracks?
- What time can I access the dressing room/stage for a technical rehearsal.

Not all these questions need to be asked in every instance, but in the confirmation email it is always useful to get essentials clear from the outset. If you saw another show using a wind machine for example don't assume you can use it. It may have been bought in for a specific night; ask in advance so you are fully prepared.

Technical Correspondence

Usually, at this point you will be introduced to the tech team via email, this is often one person who works part time at the venue. Technical time is often limited so being prepared will help everyone to do the best with the time allowed. You need to present your tracks and any specific requirements in advance, clearly and concisely. (In *Chapter 12: Stages & Spaces* we'll dive into more details of what to do and expect at a technical rehearsal.) In your correspondence, keep it simple; cabaret and drag bars lighting is usually basic, blackouts aren't often black and there are minimal *special* effects – create your set with that in mind! The tech team is often one person operating lighting, sound and more, so simple is best! Give suggestions for lighting and the tech team can offer you their best. If working to a track, put the timings down that you want things to happen, or dialogue. Large physical actions can be a cue but make sure the tech can see you – which isn't the case on all stages!

Let the tech team know of any surprises in advance; for example, if there is a cut in the track, or it intentionally gets very loud or quiet, otherwise they may think there's a technical fault with the track and try to fix it during the show.

Tell the technical team if any of the following applies:

- Any mess/clean-up to your act?
- Any health and safety/dangerous audience interaction?

- Any special/dangerous effects – fire, aerial, bubble machine, confetti cannons, scissors, etc.
- A false start or finish, does anything 'go wrong'.
- Anything needing to be pre-set or tidied up after.

Performers Technical Drive

Similar to your *Online Promotional Drive*, create a *Performers Technical Drive*. A place to keep all your backing tracks, lighting plans and cue sheets. When booked for a gig create a folder with the title of the show and the date, and then drop specific tracks and notes into it. Send a link over to the tech team (I would CC in the producer too as an FYI) and then they will have everything they need laid out clearly for them.

Within the folder name each file with your *drag name* and then the track title or document. If you are submitting multiple tracks number them (e.g. *1. Michael Twaits – One Night Only, 2. Michael Twaits – Like A Prayer*). Often, bigger shows will confirm with a more formal contract and you will need to provide a *health and safety/risk assessment* form. If there is a dangerous element to your piece have these ready in the folder (e.g. *Michael Twaits – risk assessment.doc, Michael Twaits – Public Liability Insurance.doc*).

Working with a Host

A good host will always try to talk to you prior to introducing you. Let them know if there is anything specific you would like said or not said.

- Name, pronunciation and preferred pronouns – in drag there are layers of gender play so it's easy for the wrong assumption to be made. If it matters to you always reiterate your pronouns.
- How do you wish to be introduced? Not a full biography or paragraph of awards but simple facts – Comedy? Lip-sync? High energy? etc.
- Is there a key selling point?
- Are there any surprises – does anything 'go wrong'. If you are a fire performer – is the fire a surprise? Or should the host mention it?

What the host does prior to you going on-stage is get an audience ready to watch you; the better they know what is coming, the better they can do their job. They don't need a long detailed introduction written down, just a clear overview of who you are and what you are about to do. A host often won't have seen your whole performance – so clearly let them know what you need.

Union, Union, Union!

As a solo artist it's easy to feel you don't have a support network and producers can take advantage of that. In the UK, Equity now has a department that deals with drag and cabaret acts. All performers should join a union if possible. Most offer career support, basic legal advice and will help if you ever have a dispute over pay or work conditions.

Insurance

Drag acts perform in close proximity to an audience, doing potentially dangerous things; climbing through an audience, throwing off items of clothing or walking down a staircase in six inch heels! If it were to go wrong you want to know you are covered. Venues and producers should have liability insurance but as a performer having cover is invaluable and a union membership often includes this. Many union memberships will include liability insurance within their package.

Corporate or Private Functions

Drag performers often get requests to take drag out of the bar and into an unusual environment! Work at weddings, office parties, event openings, galas; all loosely fall under the category of *Corporate or Private Functions*. These tend to be for more established acts, when people have seen you at a show or two, but some performers make a living purely in this area and there are agents who specialise in this work. The following pages may scare you off of this type of booking, but there is good money here! Being professional, asking the right questions and telling the booker your expectations is key to making things run smoothly. These events are often in venues not designed for performance and frequently organised by people who do not work in live events. There is generally an assumption it will all be alright on the night, and it will, as long as you ask the right questions, and insist on the right answers.

A producer who works outside of live events in a venue, that may not be their own, can be a recipe for disaster. Venues may not have a built in sound system, microphones or stage. Producers may actually be office managers who were tasked with managing a Christmas party. They may not realise you need a dressing room or someone to play your tracks. With all corporate and private gigs, state the obvious, always ask specific questions and insist on a contract. If you have concerns, or any additional outlay, ask for a deposit/part payment in advance. Keep all emails as one trial of what has been agreed upon.

I always ask the following questions upfront:

- What type of PA system do you have?
- Who will be operating the tech on the day?
- What time can I have a technical rehearsal?
- Can you confirm there will be a private dressing area for performers? With mirrors and lighting?
- Where do I fit in the running order/timings of the event?
- Who will be introducing me?
- Is the dressing area secure whilst I'm onstage?
- It takes me over an hour to get ready, I will need a sink, and ideally a bathroom, nearby.

These questions are written assuming the answer is positive. Not" *do you have a PA system?*" – but "*what type*". Not "*can I have a tech rehearsal?*" – but ". *with?*" This sets the expectation that these things are all essential.

No answer needs to be a deal breaker, but you need to be prepared to offer solutions and make it clear there could be extra costs as a result. If no dressing room is provided – fine: they will need to pay for a taxi, to and from the venue. If no tech team is available, perhaps suggest someone you've worked with previously.

As for the performance, do not expect an easy ride. Frequently the person booking thought having a drag act would be a great moment but the other 150 people in the room simply aren't interested. Or a drag act is booked as a bit of token diversity, a 'wow' factor or even a shock factor. There is a big difference between an audience at a show where they have bought a ticket and an event where a performance is thrown at them. So be prepared!

> I have been booked knowing the producers don't really care what I do on-stage, they just want to be seen to be booking a drag act. And I took that money!
>
> I call this *Mickey Mouse Drag*, because I feel like the people inside the costumes at Disneyland. I have a smile for everyone and four fixed poses for the photos. I can fake laugh my way through it. But, honestly, inside I am dying. I am a performer and want to be performing on a stage.
>
> I have also been to corporate bookings where I've done my set and then, when finished, have been asked to "*work the room*". If agreed in advance and included in my timings/fee – fine. But an assumption that once I've done my actual job I will be happy to hang around is not right. Clarifying expectations in advance is essential.

> If they ask for longer than agreed I simply say *"I'm sorry but I'm going to my next job"* and then show the receipts of their email, or contract, with confirmed timings. If they want to pay more to cover the extra time or travel arrangements, we can talk. But it is fine to say *"No"*.

Some Warning Signs

Performers learn on the job, especially from every bad, or odd, experience. When you are getting ready in a dimly lit Accessible Toilet – remember to go over the emails and see how this happened! How can you stop this from happening again?

I have some key phrases I look out for when approached.

- **"We really want to have a drag act at our wedding"**.

The novelty of drag is more important than what the act does. They haven't asked for a comedian, or a singer, they just want the drag. If you take this job, you will be awkwardly milling around, posing for photos, possibly not even performing. It also implies the happy couple will love it, but it could be awkward with extended friends and family.

- **"It's going to be an immersive experience"**.

This is a euphemism for there being no stage or lighting. You probably won't have good tech support or sound quality. Half the room won't be able to see or hear you.

- **"We'll find somewhere private with a mirror for you to get ready"**.

Unless you clarify in advance this will end up being an Accessible Toilet.

- **"A small fee but exposure"**.

They already know they are underpaying you. Why? What sort of exposure?

- **"You can stay and have dinner"**.

They want you to mingle but if they offer you dinner they think that is the payment.

- **"We are a new company"**.

They are trying to make money as a business but expect people to be underpaid in order to make their business a success? I'm afraid drag is my business and this is how much I charge.

- **"Would it be cheaper if you do 10 minutes rather than 20"**.

Once I'm onstage I can do 5 minutes or 40 minutes and still charge a similar amount. The travel, the prep, the hour plus getting ready and the fact that this booking has taken away the opportunity for work elsewhere is really what I am charging for. As an established act I have plenty of options for my set so how long I'm on stage for makes very little difference to the amount of work I do for a gig.

Facing the Music

The truth with corporate and private work is that you never know how it will go until you are there. Look out for the warning signs, ask the right questions and be as prepared as you can be; then smile and get on with the job.

If something at an event does not feel right though, you do not *have* to do it. Politely explain why this won't work, what is missing or what was agreed in advance. Then see what solutions might be offered, and refer to earlier correspondence. You have fulfilled your part and are ready, if they don't have a microphone/technician/dressing room that is not your fault.

Final Business Tips

There are numerous ways to keep work coming in, but the best one is to be a good act who people enjoy working with! If everyone enjoys working with you, they will want to work with you again; they know you, they like you, it works! These tips can help to leave a good lasting impression that will get you booked again and again.

Time Keeping

Always be on time. My advice is that 'on time' is 15 minutes early, not walking in the door at the time the tech starts. **15 minutes early**. Get to the venue, find a space in the dressing room and then be at the side of the stage ready to start your tech rehearsal.

Once in the building you also need to get ready on time, allow enough time to get into drag and do whatever level of warm up you may need to do!

"Thank You"

After a gig, send a quick message thanking the producer/promoter. Sign-off saying *"can't wait to do it again"*. This leaves the ball in their court as they know you are keen to return. When putting video/photos on socials: tag producers, promoters and thank everyone. It goes a long way and also helps give that illusion of the busy, well connected, drag act!

Backstage Professionalism

Before you put on your wig and shoes and head to the stage: tidy your shit up! Put all day clothes in one area or bag. Put the majority of your make-up kit back in your suitcase/bag. Once your kit and clothes are tidy, take a make-up wipe and clean the surface where you got ready. Leave it how you would want to find it! Before leaving at the end of the evening do the same.

Names

Always learn the names of the people you are interacting with at a gig: the host, other acts, the tech, the producers, etc. If in a venue more than twice: the bar staff, security, the person on the door. People like working with people who make them feel appreciated and validated. Be a team player.

Be Human

A lot of this chapter sounds quite formal but actually being human and interacting well with people is the art of the business. Having a friendly chat and not always being *on* or looking for work. As you build relationships with producers and colleagues get to know them, make friends. Be professional but also part of the community.

Photographers

Good photographers are a drag acts best friend. If a photographer is working an event and there is a moment when nothing else is being photographed (pre or post show, an interval) ask them for a couple of quick shots elsewhere! Be cheeky and get exploring; go outside the venue, find a stairwell to sit in, jump behind the bar, get creative! Don't monopolise their time but you are looking fabulous and someone is with you wanting to create content, so why not ask? Some of my favourite publicity shots have come from the unexpected photos at events. Photography is a collaboration so, if there's time, put some ideas forward to get some varied and interesting shots.

Crediting Collaborators

Always credit collaborators. Photographers especially will get annoyed when their images are used without a credit. It goes back to the thanking point, it helps build the relationship, so people will want to work with you again. If you share an image on socials, tag the photographer and in your *Online Promotional Drive* label all photos with the name of the photographer to be credited!

Don't Be a Dick

A cover all rule for drag! It's the most likely reason you won't be rebooked. A poor performer can improve, a bad attitude usually doesn't. When in a new venue, take the temperature of how the night works, be courteous and follow the lead of those more experienced or regulars. Don't start asking for free drinks, talk over someone else's tech rehearsal or make the night all about you. You want to make a lasting impression, and build an ongoing relationship to get more work.

It's a rule for life – *don't be a dick*.

Overview: Business

You may not be ready to do all of this straight away but get the framework set up and keep adding and improving it as you get more content, more photos, more video and a wider range of experience.

- Build an *Online Promotional Drive*: Simply show the best of yourself. A few images, videos, a short biography and any quotes that can show bookers who you are and why they should want to work with you.
- Keep social media simple: For every post ask – is this looking professional, fun? Ask yourself, would I book me? Would I want to see this act?
- Network and build relationships: Be seen at shows, keep in touch with people, thank people, credit people.
- Do your research: Know you are a good fit for a venue or night before approaching. If you are unsure, go and watch the show before reaching out.
- Clear communication: Don't just bombard people. Clearly tell them why you are getting in touch, share a link where they can see more and try to respond to messages in a timely fashion.
- One point of communication: Where possible funnel all of your communication for bookings to one email and keep hitting reply to build an email trail with all information in it.
- Don't be a dick: People want to work with people that make work seem simple and fun!

Having looked at getting bookings and being professional there is one huge area of being a drag act we have so far avoided. Making that money! This chapter has armed you with the knowledge of how to get the bookings, now it's time to look at which bookings to take, how much money to spend and how to keep a track of it all.

Alegria photographed backstage at the Royal Vauxhall Tavern by Fox Al Rajim

3
Who Will Buy?: The Economics of Drag

Every performer has their own financial situation, budget and skill set. Drag is not a fair playing field, but what industry is? Every performer should aspire to earn more than they spend. Drag is expensive: how much should you spend, and how much should you charge?

Many acts give up on drag because it costs them more than they earn; this chapter is going to help you watch your pennies so you can have a long career trajectory. It might be the chapter you *enjoy* the least but it will be the one your accountant, and savings, will thank you for reading!

> When I was starting as drag performer, I had many jobs: weekdays in a call centre, teaching drama to children at weekends and picking up occasional waitering shifts after both. I could have dropped some of those jobs much sooner if I had been wiser with my drag finances.

Drag careers take many forms; many readers will be hobbyists who may think this doesn't apply to them. But even as a hobbyist you still want to make sure you aren't always paying to perform. Money coming in should exceed money going out!

Money, Money, Money

The reason there are so many *moneys* in the ABBA classic is to remind you of all the different ways a drag act needs to keep on top of their finances! There are many obvious ways money is important in drag, but also a few that are frequently overlooked! Firstly tax: you will need to pay it. Top tips: research tax rates properly for where you live, register as self employed and keep all receipts. Currently[1] as a guide: if you receive more than $400 (US) or £1000 (UK) a year this needs to be declared. Even a hobbyist drag act will need to know their *income*.

The second overlooked area of finance is the outgoings. Drag acts can lose track of what is being spent, get carried away with the sequins! From the outset keep track of what money is being spent: keep every receipt. Log everything, a note book, a spread sheet, screenshots when you buy something. This is your *outgoings*.

Income: Getting Paid

Before worrying about how much, it's worth taking a look at the various ways a performer can be paid:

DOI: 10.4324/9781003498797-4

An Agreed Fee

A fixed amount is agreed in advance of the performance and paid within 30 days after the performance (hopefully quicker). Performers send over an invoice after the performance.

Box Office Split or Door Split

This happens with young producers or collectives, producing their own night. This is a way to heavily encourage acts to promote the night themselves to ensure enough people buy tickets so they get paid more. Producers *may* offer a minimum fee and then a split of the box office/door depending on how successful the night is. For example, £50 and then once the show has broken-even the remaining profit will be split.

If working for a Box Office Split there is nothing wrong with asking a producer what the expected level of audience numbers is to break even. Anyone producing a show paying this way *should* be transparent about numbers; if they aren't then be prepared that performers probably won't be receiving much.

Working for Tips

An act is given the stage time and makes their money from the tips. Often this can be in conjunction with a small, agreed fee by the producer. In the UK this doesn't happen, you may occasionally get tipped, but a producer would never expect an act earn enough through their tips as the UK doesn't have a tipping culture. In the USA a drag act can make an awful lot from tips.

Expenses or Voluntary

This happens a lot, especially at the beginning of your career: entering drag contests, open mic slots, charity nights, etc. If you are in a country with a tipping culture you may be able to earn a little extra, with a successful act, from tips.

If working for expenses, ask in advance: what is included as expenses and what receipts they may need. Some producers may do a blanket 'expenses' fee for example £20 to each performer, others will ask for itemised receipts of every expense! Always ask what is required.

Disparity

This is not a way of being paid but something to be aware of; not everyone on the bill will be paid the same amount. Some might be seen as *headliners* who are pulling a crowd in due to experience, or perhaps a TV credit. Too often kings are being underpaid compared to queens. Later in this chapter we'll look at knowing your worth. As a performer, it's good practice not to publicly discuss fees backstage, but obviously discuss with colleagues and friends to help make sure you are getting the right amount. But in the dressing room, or during the show, is not the time to do it.

Make sure all the questions regarding payment have been asked, answered and confirmed in advance of accepting the gig.

Invoicing

As previously discussed in *Chapter 2: The Business of Drag,* with every booking; the best practice is to have an email trail between yourself and the producer. Once the performance is done reply to that email; thanking them for a great night and attaching the invoice for the agreed amount. Once a fee or payment has been agreed it would be bad form on either part to try and renegotiate. Replying to the email highlights that this invoice is for the amount agreed in advance. If requesting reimbursement for expenses, you will also need to attach receipts.

Always fill out a full invoice; it is easy to find a template online. Make sure it includes:

An Invoice Number: I use MT (my initials) then the year 24/25 and then and then add 1 each time I create a new invoice. i.e. MT2425001, MT2425002, etc.

Personal Details: Legal/Government name, trading as name/drag name, address. Also your National Insurance, Social Security, Unique Tax Payers Number or your country's equivalent.

Gig Details: The date, the title, where it happened and what your role was.

Their Details: Name and business/venue address.

Bank Details: This is how they'll pay you. Bank name, sort code, account number, swift/BACS

Keep track of which invoices you have sent and which have been paid. I would recommend having a spreadsheet so you can see what you need to invoice for, what you have been paid for and which invoices you have sent but haven't been paid. An invoice should be paid within a month and there is nothing wrong with a follow up email if you are waiting for payment simply asking when you can expect payment and reattaching the invoice.

> As a freelancer, in the UK, all my invoices clarify at the bottom that I am responsible for my own tax and include my UTR (Unique Taxpayer Reference). If anyone I work for ever gets audited they can track where the money went, and see that I filed my taxes that year, without contacting me. I also add one line clarifying all invoices and expenses to be paid within 30 days.

EXERCISE 1: INCOME VS OUTGOINGS

You will need: A computer. (Paper can work, but digital is simpler.)

Depending on where you are in your drag journey this could be a quick exercise setting up the spreadsheets for future use or a longer process that will help you organise your annual tax return.

On your desktop create a folder called *Drag Budget*. Position it on your desktop so it's easy to find and hard to escape. Within it create two further folders – *Income* and *Outgoings*. Finally create a spreadsheet with two tabs named *Income* and *Outgoings*. Your task is to keep these up-to-date. Every time you are paid document: add the invoice to the *Income* folder and the numbers to the *Income* spreadsheet.

Every time you spend money, itemise it in the *Outgoings* tab on the spreadsheet and add the receipt (or a photo of it) to the *Outgoing* folder. In the spreadsheet add a little detail; what was the item, what is it for, where it was bought from, the price and the date. You think you'll remember – but you can't remember everything. It might work to set a routine that this is a job you do on the first of each month.

Did you buy this book? A wig? Anything that is wholly or exclusively because of being a performer should be documented in your outgoings. An accountant, or finance professional, can clarify allowances in your country or territory and it's always best to show too much and let them say what is or isn't allowed. Most of the expenses are deducted from income before calculating your tax, so doing this is essentially saving you money! This does not mean it's free to buy drag items. The money has been spent, but expenses will come off of your income prior to you paying tax.

Tax vs. Expenses Overview for Dummies!

If your *outgoings* are higher than your *income* – you have earned nothing. Or worse, you technically *paid* to work. Or even worse, if you don't save the receipts from the *outgoings* you will pay the tax on your full *income*.

The folder you created – *Drag Budget* – is what you will eventually use to file your own tax return or send to your accountant. If you don't have the receipts, you can't claim it. I can't stress enough: keeping track of everything will *save* you money. A brief example:

> I was paid £200 last night for a show but spent £150 on expenses: I only earned £50. The £150 has been spent either way. But when it comes to tax, I only wish to pay tax on the £50 I earned not the £200 I invoiced for. So, I need to receipt to *prove* the £150 was spent on costume/travel/expenses used wholly and exclusively for my performance work. Tax at 20% on £200 would be £40. Without the receipts, I would have to pay £40 tax, and therefore would have only have £10 to take home! Tax at 20% on £50 (because I have my receipts for the £150 in expenses) is £10, meaning I take home £40.

This is a broad, slightly crude, example but it's essential to have the mind set that **what you are being paid is not what you are taking home**. What you are paid (Gross Earning) has to have expenses and tax deducted to make your take home (or Net Earning). This is the important figure, it's the money in your pocket at the end of the day. Below is a look at how drastically your tax bill can vary if you haven't saved your receipts.

How Much Does Drag Cost Me?

As a performer it's important to understand how much each drag gig is costing you. It will guide which offers to take, what sort of fee to charge and show whether it is financially viable.

> ### EXERCISE 2: WHAT ARE YOUR COSTS?
>
> **You will need: A computer with a fresh spreadsheet.**
>
> The amount performers spend on their drag isn't universal. However, using Table 3.1, as a framework you can calculate your average, essentially calculating how much it costs every time you get into drag. You may need to add a few rows that are specific to your drag, and others may not be relevant. But the table will provide a simple breakdown of your costs.
>
> Create a spreadsheet in your *Drag Budget* folder using the example below as a template. This is something to come back to and review during your drag journey. If you are already an experienced drag act you could use previous years *Income/Outgoings* to show you how much you've spent in each area.

Drag	Costs	Example
Travel:		£14
Wigs:		£10
Make Up:		£15
Costuming:		£20
Accommodation:		£0
Food/Sundries:		£0
Gig Specific Costs:		£0
Lost Work Elsewhere:		£0
Ongoing Costs:		£5
Total Costs:		£64
Gross Income Total:		£250
Tax: (20%)		£50
Net Total:		**£136**

Table 3.1 A Table to Work Out How Much Is Spent on Performing in Drag.

For each row above, insert the specific cost for that gig OR an approximate average cost per gig for all reusable items.

> I have included an example within this exercise and have put my numbers into Table 3.1. How much I spend on a wig is not what matters, it's an illustration. The balancing out of *income/outgoings* and how that reveals what I am actually earning is what matters.
>
> For this example, I am offered an evening show in a West End, London location for £250. I don't need to invest in accommodation and can perform an existing set so don't need: a new look, backing tracks, or any single use props. However, I am still wearing make-up and costuming so need to factor that into a budget – it isn't free just because I already own it!

Travel: How do you get there? Trains, petrol if driving, taxis, etc. If you travel in a regular pattern, a weekly gig at the same venue then that usually isn't a deductible expense but as a gigging act to different venues, it is.

> It costs me £14 for a day-travel card, I'll assume I finish before the last train home so won't need an additional taxi fee.

Wigs: A variable cost. How much does the original wig cost? How much does a restyle cost? How frequently is that done? Or is it cheap enough you can buy a new one each time? Maybe you use your own hair – £0.

> My wigs cost around £200 and I can wear them 8–10 times before needing a wash and re-style. I have a professional who does that for me which costs around £60. One wig lasts 4 restyles before being too tatty. Therefore the total cost is *around* £400 for 40 wears.
>
> I average this out to be £10 per gig that goes to my *Wig Budget*.

Make-up: How many products do you use to get into drag? How cheap/high end are your brands? How long do they last? You need to replace and replenish them. A small amount from every gig should go into your *Make-Up Budget* so you can constantly replace products when needed.

> This isn't an exact science. I use around 18 products ranging from £5–£40 each. They all have different usage and need restocking at irregular intervals. After a little back and forth I have approximated £15 per gig towards my *Make-Up Budget*.

Costuming: It is easy to over spend. One costume can be used over and over again, but could cost a lot more than you are paid for one gig. Again, a small amount from every gig should go into a *Costuming Budget*. Include all worn items in this budget: shoes, undergarments, jewellery and accessories.

Set a budget, try to only spend that and as gigs and payments increase, so will your budget.

> I have lots of mid-priced dresses rather than a few very expensive looks. I work a lot and like visual variety. I have gowns that are more expensive and make more impact, but are less practical for day-to-day gigging. I budget £20 from each gig to go into my *Costume Budget*.
>
> The more I work, the more I can spend on costumes. £20 may not sound a lot but I am working four nights a week: £80 a week. Every month I can invest around £400 on costuming. Sometimes that could be one costume, or save up a few months' budget on a bespoke outfit. Other times a few cheap bits of jewellery and a new pair of shoes. It's actually quite a large budget for me.

Accommodation: Overnight accommodation, etc. Can you get back and sleep in your own bed? Occasionally work comes up that seems well paid, then you factor in a hotel and suddenly – was it worth it?

> For this example I can get home – £0.

Food/Sundries: It's best to try and factor gigs into your eating schedule rather than spending money as it can be a tax grey area. But every gig is different and sometimes you do have to buy a meal or two.

> For this example I am being fed at the venue – £0

Gig Specific Costs: Is there a theme where you need a particular look? A prop or accessory that you have to buy? Or does your set use a single-use item; sparklers, confetti cannons, runner beans, etc?

> I have no one off costs for this example – £0

Lost Work Elsewhere: This is really important as you move forward, if you are starting out you may be taking holiday days from a day job to do your drag. As you become established you might be cancelling a residency night to do a one off job elsewhere.

> No lost work elsewhere – £0

Ongoing Costs: Union membership, website, email, business cards, etc. Small costs which all add up over a year are still worth factoring into your ongoing running costs.

> I have a website, Equity Membership (which gives me liability insurance), a personalised email address and business cards. All of these are fairly insignificant amounts when worked up per gig. However, it adds up to around £1,000 a year. Four gigs a week, that's 200 gigs a year. I need to budget £5 for my ongoing costs.

Tax: <u>You are going to need to pay this.</u> Put a percentage of income into a separate bank account so you have it ready. Set the percentage depending on expected income and earnings elsewhere. If you are unsure I'd recommend assuming a minimum of 10% the invoiced amount or 20% of your earnings after other expenses to start with.

> I used a tax estimate at 20% of the invoiced amount, this isn't the exact amount that will be due. When my tax bill comes in I have usually over saved. It is always better that way round. It also means I can then re-invest the extra into my drag, or my life. It's a bonus!

Earnings Overview

As an act to say "*I earn £250 for a gig*" sounds alright? But how does it sound when to say "*I take home £136*"? You can also now see that for every gig, it costs me £50 plus travel to get into drag! How much is it costing you? Use the above exercise to get to know your numbers: how much does it cost you to get into drag? And how much do you have left to live off?

> Save Money!...You need to be able to pay your rent so you can make art. You need to be able to eat food so that you can make art.
>
> Le Fil[2]

Why Do Receipts Matter?

If you aren't keeping evidence you will pay *more* tax than you need to. For one gig it may not seem much, over a year it is a lot! It is getting a little maths heavy now, but everyone needs to learn this lesson: **more receipts = less tax!**

> This is a hypothetical, simplified example for illustration only. Imagine I will earn and spend exactly the same amount four times a week, for one year (leaving two weeks off for a holiday). I have saved all receipts and my accountant approves them all as fully deductable. Using the average costs from *Exercise 2*, I can save around £3,500 from good budgeting.
>
> Income: £250 x 4 (gigs a week) x 50 (weeks a year) = £50,000
>
> Outgoings: £64 x 4 x 50 = £12,800

Table 3.2 shows the tax due *With Receipts* vs *Without Receipts*. (Remember the £12,800 I spent on my expenses has been spent whether I have receipts or not.) The difference in the Net Total with receipts in the UK is £3,584 and at current US rates it's slightly less: £2,337.25.)

	With Reciepts	Without Reciepts
Income	£50,000	£50,000
Deductible outgoings	£12,800	£0
Total Taxed Income	£37,200	£50,000
Tax Due According UK HMRC	£6,896	£10,480
Net Total (UK)	**£30,304**	**£26,720**
(Income minus Outgoing and Tax Due)		
Tax Due According to Current US rates	£6,791	£9,128.25
Net Total (US)	**£30,409**	**£28,071.75**
(Income minus Outgoing and Tax Due)		

Table 3.2 Tax Calculations for a Year's Income Showing the Difference With and Without Receipts. (Tax Calculated at 2024 rate on HMRC and IRS.)

From *Exercise 2* I have put aside £10,000 for tax: £50 per gig, 4 times a week, for 50 weeks a year. This is more than enough for both UK and US taxes. Without receipts I would have to pay an additional £3,000–£3,500 with current taxes rates. How many months' rent could that cover?

A tax return will never be as simple as this example, but it will always be this beneficial to save your receipts!

So, How Much Should I Charge?

To have a clear, set fee for every gig is not feasible. However, knowing how much it costs you each time you get into drag, and what additional costs each show can add to that amount, is a brilliant starting place for working out what a fee should be. Maybe the goal at first is to cover all costs, then it becomes to take home £20, then £50, £100, etc. These are goals, and hopefully once they become the average you can shift that goal. (You'll dig deeper into this in *Chapter 4: Measuring Success*.)

Fees for performance are very often about negotiating. As you become more established you may be negotiating at a higher level, but the negotiating never really goes away. However, the financial reward is not the only reason to be taking a gig.

Should I Take This Gig?

Drag is a passion project for most; these passions could be artistic goals, personal explorations, community connections or a fun creative outlet. Acts need to find the balance between finance, fun and furtherance. Every performer needs to answer a few questions to decide if they want to accept a gig:

- Will I earn enough?
- Do I want to do it?
- Will it further my career?

It's rare that one answer is enough to inform your decision. The challenge is then to work out if the combination of all three answers is enough. These three questions can form a Venn diagram (Figure 3.1). It would be great if every gig hit the central sweet spot, but realistically that is rare. As a rule you want to try to only take work in the crossover of two rings. If offers don't meet any of the rings criteria, have the courage to turn them down straight away!

The Economics of Drag

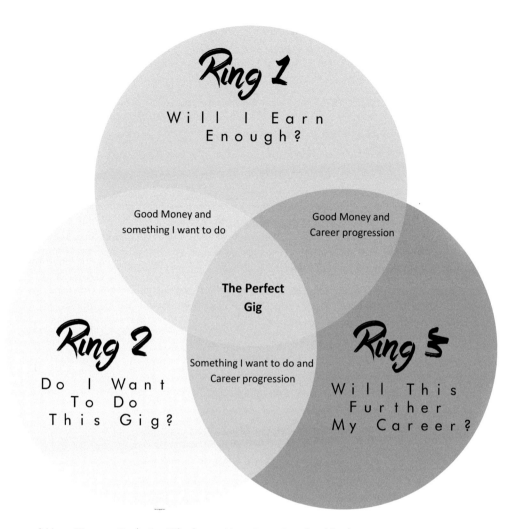

Figure 3.1 A Venn Diagram Exploring Whether or Not a Drag Act Should Take a Gig.

Ring One: Will I Earn Enough?

This seems self-explanatory, but notice the word *earn*. It's not about what they are paying but what you take home. **How much are they paying vs. How much it will cost?** You have filled out the spreadsheet from the previous exercises, now it's time to use it. Have a quick look at how much they are paying compared to your drag costs and any additional gig specific costs: travel, accommodation, specific costumers, props, etc. Could you save costs by using existing costuming, material and repertoire? Are there any additional non-financial perks? (That is, high quality videography, photography, transport, meals?) In the early days paying enough to cover your costs might be enough for you.

Occasionally a gig will have a fee that makes you just take it (we all have bills to pay). Do the job and think of the money! But ideally, you want finance to balance with one of the next two rings.

Ring Two: Do I Want to Do This Gig?

Drag should be fun and fulfilling! Will this gig satisfy the reasons you got into drag? Will it be fun, social or artistically rewarding? Will you be working with people you like working with? Perhaps you are able to perform something you want to perform but don't often get the chance to.

At the beginning of a career Ring Two is often a "yes" because acts just want to be working. As a career evolves it's easy to get slightly stuck in a routine of similar, fun, gigs that are not truly paying enough or helping you move forward. Always keep an eye on Ring Three.

Ring Three: Will This Further My Career?

Furtherance. It's hard to guess where a career will go and what doors may open up to you. But a career needs trajectory, a sense of progression. Will this gig lead to more work? Will this build your following? Is it a venue or event you want to be associated with? Does it introduce you to a new audience, or take you outside of the usual circuit? Will it introduce you to new venues, producers, promoters? Is it an opportunity to move forward, perhaps to headline or host, when you don't usually?

At the beginning of your career Ring Three is often a *Yes* answer because simply working feels like a move forward in your career. The money does not matter as much as getting established but at every gig it's worth spending a moment looking at how it's moving you forward.

> I worked for ten years at *Pride In London*; producing, programming and hosting their show at Trafalgar Square. I also hosted and produced their annual talent show *Pride's Got Talent*. I was working as a volunteer and claiming expenses, Ring 1 was never enough. So why was I there for a decade?
>
> The reason for staying is the amount I got from Rings 2 and 3. Each year I evolved the role to help further my career; my goal was to be the host at Trafalgar Square, and I wanted to increase my skills as a programmer/producer. The programming and stage time I received increased each year.
>
> I was performing in a West End Theatre for *Pride's Got Talent*, receiving high quality videography and photography. At Trafalgar Square getting wonderful pictures, and footage, of me on the huge stage and working with amazing international artists like Renee Zellweger, Ian McKellan and Billy Porter. Politically I was also supporting many causes that were near and dear to my heart and able to do my part in progressing queer causes.
>
> On paper this was *costing* me money. However, as a cabaret act used to performing in small venues, I knew I wanted to be associated with the large stage of Trafalgar Square, the high-end performers and to make myself stand out to other acts on the scene. I knew hosting was my core skill as an act and what was a bigger stage to host on? The work I received off the back of these opportunities has shaped the longevity of my career.
>
> I was the go-to host within the scene for all sorts of work and a knowledgeable, experienced producer of large-scale events. My 'little black book' of producers, promoters, performers and sponsors filled up with contacts that have proven to be useful to me time and again. I was a professional and organised person when we worked together through *Pride In London*, so they are happy to work with me outside of it too.
>
> I was hugely privileged that I had enough income from work elsewhere to allow me to invest in my career. The pay off in the long run was worth it. But I had to take other work on that paid well to support myself.

Working for Free

At the beginning of your career you most likely will be doing nights *without* a fee: competitions, charity fundraisers, etc. and you will be grateful for the stage time! Hopefully, your costs will be lower as you'll be spending less on costuming and make-up. Keep an eye on how much you are giving away because if you are getting into drag and working for *free*, you are actually *paying* to work. (In my case £64.) How much is working for free costing you?

The networking that comes with working on a range of different gigs is priceless: meeting different producers, seeing different venues and working with other acts will help you shape your career. However, knowing your worth is essential as many will take advantage of those eager to work for free. As an industry the economics don't add up if acts *always* offer their skills and services for free! (Undercutting other acts is not on; constantly working for free does the industry no favours). There will always be a young drag act who will undercut you on a fee, but don't let that stop you from moving towards commanding a professional fee.

Knowing Your Worth

Performers need to know what they are bringing to a gig, and the fee that commands. If it's something quantifiable: experience, high following, quality in aesthetic, notoriety of performance skill, find ways to politely make that clear when negotiating a fee. Sometimes working less enables you to charge more. Will producers feel comfortable charging audiences £10 a ticket to see you if the night before you are working at a venue that doesn't charge? It's tempting to take every offer that comes in but your brand, and your value can be lessened if you do too much work seemingly for free.

Payment In-Kind

Occasionally companies may offer payment in-kind. This means no fee is handed over but a return of their goods or services. Payment in-kind can be beneficial for both performers and bookers. However, make sure it's a gift in kind that you want. A photographer may want to use you to build their portfolio and you can get some great promotional shots in return – great!

> I have an annual job I do with a world-class hotel. It is two short rehearsals and then an easy evening show. Rather than payment, I receive a night, dinner and drinks in the hotel at a date of my choice. It would cost far more than I would charge for a gig and probably costs them a lot less than they would pay me. So, my husband and I usually go there to celebrate our anniversary! Everybody's happy.

Save Your Pennies

Starting out, it may feel you need to buy everything all at once to create your drag aesthetic: you do not. Get crafty! Be a bargain hunter! Beg and borrow! Visit charity shops and flea markets.

Drag acts re-use looks! *Drag Race* makes it seem a costume is worn once and then discarded; that is not the case. For initial looks try and find costumes you can use time and again, freshen it up by changing accessories. A consistent look initially will help with establishing your brand.

Spend less at first and slowly upgrade your aesthetic over time. Always create the performance first, costuming should complement and enhance your performance, not dictate the performance. Test run a costume, or get a trial wig from the cheaper end of the spectrum first. Make sure both the performance and the costuming work before investing too much.

> I once spent three years making a costume with as much free time as I could spare. It's been booked twice.
>
> Adam All[3]

Once you know a look suits your set, by all means spend some time and money on it: but gradually. Perhaps update the wig, then the shoes, then add a few sequins. Do not bankrupt yourself by spending too much on something which isn't earning enough.

A recurring theme on *The Art of Drag* course, is a student, on Week One, ordering an expensive gown and trying to create a performance that suits it! The money has been spent because they thought the dress was pretty. For a singer standing still, this *could* work. But what if they want to add some choreography and they can't move in the dress? Suddenly they have a dress that does not work for the act. Or worse, they end up creating a piece that isn't what they wanted to do, because of the dress.

There are many networks (groups on Facebook for example) where drag acts are buying and selling costumes, wig styling services, jewellery, etc. This is a great place to pick up some second-hand costumes you could work with for a while.

Time Is Money

Remember, your time is a commodity too; if you are making a new costume or doing additional rehearsals this should be factored into how much you are being paid. There are many ways to be crafty yourself and save money on costuming, wigs, and more. But be realistic about your skill set and put your efforts into what you do best.

> I have tried a few times to improve my wig grooming and styling skills; I have also ruined numerous expensive wigs! Even if I spent money on the right tools I feel I would only do an *ok* job. I am much happier to spend the £10 off the top of every gig for wig maintenance.
>
> I have a sewing machine and can fix or alter costumes. I have made a few costumes but again it isn't where my skill set is. The time I save hiring a professional to do these things I can invest into finding more work, writing more material and using my strengths to make myself a better performer. Drag acts don't need to do absolutely everything themselves.

Overview: The Economics of Drag

Prepare yourself, highly paid gigs don't start coming in from day one. The cost of drag, however, is there from the outset; you need make-up and costuming at the very least. Focus on trying to keep costs down and making sensible choices.

- Know how you are getting paid. Invoice swiftly and use it as an excuse to contact the producer saying you would like to work with them again.
- Keep a log of everything. Money coming in and money going out. All in your *Drag Budget*.
- Work out how much getting into drag costs you. Know the figure so as soon as a gig is offered you can work out, roughly, what you will take home from it.

- Try not to spend more money than you are earning.
- Save money by getting creative and crafty, find ways to reuse, repurpose and up-cycle drag.
- Only take gigs that are worth your while. Use our Venn diagram (Figure 3.1) to find the balance between the three rings; finance, fun and furtherance.

The first year or two of your career will be a lot of trial and error. You may spend more than you planned, earn a little less or realise it's taking longer to get established than you hoped. But having the details of how much your *income* and *outgoings* is can help you set goals for the following year and beyond. You should be able to track down where you overspent, or which gigs perhaps weren't the best idea to take. It's important to find time to take stock and review how things have gone on then to look forward and plan what's next.

Setting goals is a simple way of keeping an eye on a careers trajectory. Whether it be short-term, long-term or life-long goals – they can all help you find ways of keeping you moving forward and *measuring success*.

Notes

1. This was written in 2024. All acts should check each tax year what changes have been made to declaring income. Never assume it's the same as the previous year.
2. *Le Fil* in interview with *Michael Twaits*, July 2024. See Part IV for full interview.
3. *Adam All* in interview with *Michael Twaits*, July 2024. See Part IV for full interview.

Scarlett Love photographed backstage at the Royal Vauxhall Tavern by Fox Al Rajim

4
The Best Thing You've Ever Done: Measuring Success

What makes a successful drag career? The last two chapters focused on the business and the money; these are two of the least likely reasons that anyone got into drag in the first place. What do you want to achieve? And how are you going to do it?

Goals are simple ways to quantify success and view career progression, and ways to hold yourself accountable. This isn't an industry where you will be called in for an annual review and given targets for the year. There will be no written warning that you aren't doing a good job: you simply won't get the bookings. So: hold your own annual review, do your own evaluation after a performance, set targets and keep moving towards them. We are going to set up a structure to help you measure your own success and find a momentum in your drag journey.

Why Are You Doing Drag?

Why aren't you wanting to be a traditional stand up? An actor? A dancer? Drag isn't an obvious choice for a hobby or a career. There is no set path, no guaranteed income and it's not a stress-free life. Usually, it's a calling; a passion to express oneself. It may be a love of drag, a community calling or the need to explore something through performance. Why have you picked up this handbook?

EXERCISE 1: FREE WRITING

You will need: Your notebook and pen.

Set a timer for three minutes and write out some answers to the question: *Why Drag?* There are no wrong answers, simply keep writing for the full three minutes and see what comes out. Why did you decide you wanted to explore drag? What do you want to achieve? What drew you in? Start the timer and get writing!

Excellent! Some will have found that really tricky, others will have filled pages. There's no need to over analyse your results (yet). As you carry on more ideas may come – add them to the list! Which of the following categories were answers in? Or is it a combination of them:

Community – meet like-minded people, give a voice to lesser represented people, etc.

Exploration – to take up space as your authentic self, find who you are on-stage, etc.

Ego – stardom, fierceness, a natural performer, be on TV, etc.

Politics – breakdown the patriarchy, reclaim your queerness, change the world, etc

DOI: 10.4324/9781003498797-5

Career – you have skills pointing towards drag performance, earn money using existing skills, etc.

Fun – have a laugh, meet people, celebrate queerness, etc.

These are just a few suggestions. It is interesting to see roughly which area was the impetus for you getting into drag, and possibly picking up this handbook. Drag doesn't need to be your only source of income, or the main driving force in your life: if it's a fun outlet for your 9–5 then great! Keep this free writing exercise to hand; as you move forward you will want to refer back to it.

> I think success is a calm nervous system. And I don't think anyone is being paid enough in drag to live a life of high stress.
>
> Hugo Grrrrl[1]

Career: How Can You Measure Success

Now that you have a few thoughts around why you do drag, think about what you want to get out of drag. What do you want to *achieve*? The following exercises are going to set up some long-term goals, as well as some immediate goals which will get you moving in that direction.

A novice drag act's goals might simply be to have fun, or get regular bookings. A more experienced act's might be to get more headline slots, or work in a specific venue. An established performer might wish to up their fee, or step away from working in certain venues.

> I like putting smiles on people's faces, but also leaving a thought in their heads.
>
> Son Of A Tutu[2]

As a career evolves it is easy to forget why you got into drag in the first place. Initial hopes get forgotten because, as soon as you have achieve them, your ego sends messages to start looking for the next thing. Having a document, something written down that reminds you of where you were and how far you have come, is priceless. Allow yourself to celebrate victories as they come in *before* moving on.

The Grass Is Always Greener

Whatever you have, whatever you achieve, whatever you do, it is human nature that the shine will wear off once you achieve it and you will want something more. There will be times you care more about what your peers have achieved, and how that makes you feel in comparison to yourself. Try to focus on yourself. Remember, for most performers you only see how they are doing through their front of house lens: their social media, which is very easy to *rose tint*. There will be times you doom-scroll through the social media of a colleague whose career you wish you have. I can obviously tell you to stop it, but will you listen? Will you listen to yourself? Remember your success is relative to what you want to achieve. And theirs is, essentially, none of your concern.

Artists are usually their own harshest critics: a glowing review with stars aplenty can be twisted in your mind due to just one word. It's human nature to focus on the tiny negatives and not the overall positives, especially with artists. Find ways to be kind to yourself, let go of envy and celebrate *your* achievements. To do this, you need a set some goals and commit pen to paper so you can refer back to them time and again!

EXERCISE 2: SO MANY GOALS YOU CAN'T MISS THEM ALL!

You will need: Your notebook and pen.

Find a clean page in your notebook and write some goals. What do you want to achieve as a drag performer? Some could be very simple, achievable, some long-term, some short-term. Dream big! Maybe some goals are what you hope to get out of this handbook others may directly refer back to your *Why Drag* free writing.

Put Yourself First: Often I refer to *removing* the ego, but here *indulge* the ego; use the phrase "*I want...*" as the start of each goal.

Be Specific: How much money? How many gigs? How many social media followers? Which specific venues? Put down numbers and names!

Make Professionalism a Goal: If you can frame the *business* and *economics* of drag as goals, it makes it much more likely to happen. Think about *Chapters 2: The Business Of Drag* and *Chapter 3: The Economics Of Drag*: getting better at tax, approaching venues more proactively, spending less on costuming, etc.

Give Yourself the Power: You cannot make the Oscars have a new category for *Drag Performance Of The Year*. But you could make a short-film worthy of that award. The film is the goal, the work is the goal, your performance is the goal. Not the accolade.

I often see *I want to be on Drag Race* come up in this exercise. Getting cast is a lottery, it's reality TV. If that really is what you want, find a way to give yourself the power – "*I want to be Drag Race ready.*" Maybe set smaller, specific goals that would make you feel ready.

Be a Realist: *I want to be as big as Lady Gaga* is a great aspiration but not a goal. Pick specific factors that she's achieved and make them goals for yourself: release an album of your own music, be forward thinking with fashion, etc.

I am not stipulating a time limit on this exercise as I'm sure it's something that will evolve and you will come back to and add a list. Think seriously about what you wish to achieve through your performing. Refer to your notes from *Exercise 1* and put pen to paper! Set those goals!

Below are a few goals I have heard over the years from students. You don't need to agree with them all, I don't agree with them all, but they might make you think of a few additional ideas for your own. Hopefully they'll give you some more inspiration!

I want to be regularly working. Two gigs a month minimum.

I want to be able to pay my mortgage.

I want drag to be my only income source.

I want to see more drag shows and broaden my range of inspiration.

I want to only accept work paying £200 or more per gig.

I want to have fun and make new, like-minded, friends.

I want to have an enjoyable work/life balance.

I want over 2,000 Instagram followers.

I want to be programmed as a headline act.

I want to start hosting my own shows.

I want to produce my own hour-long solo show.

I want to stop working at brunch venues.

I want to improve my make up skills.

I want to confidently sing a song on-stage.

I want to become a better performer.

Hopefully you have a list brimming full of great goals for yourself. If, like me, your free writing gets a little chaotic, it's worth spending a minute copying them out into a clear list.

Give Yourself the Power

With all your goals the next question to ask is: "*What's stopping me?*"

The answer should be: *no one*.

If there is someone in the way: how can you shift the goal, or reframe the expectation, to give yourself the power?

For example: kings notoriously get booked less and paid less. It's a huge problem across the scene. They also don't have the same level of exposure in the mainstream. Could you aim to be the most visible, or booked, drag king in your city rather than to *make* every bar in your city book you? Be a pioneer, lead the way and smash through ceilings: but try not to allow those people who won't shift, change or evolve to have the power in you measuring your own success.

Simply put, the world is not an even playing field: and drag is no exception. Many acts have complex barriers due to marginalisation, gender inequality, racial inequality, and more. Re-addressing, or rebalancing, the patriarchy is too much pressure for one person. The work you create can be brimming with these themes, but for your own goals focus on where you are going rather than how you are going to change the world. Some people have to work harder, have their elbows out more, to create their own space. Other people seem to have an easier journey. If you are someone who does have it easier: could some of your goals be community focused? To help support diverse programming, create more opportunities for under-represented voices or those from lower socio-economic backgrounds?

Before moving on, have one last look through your goals: be specific, be realistic and give yourself the power. If you need to reframe a goal – do it!

EXERCISE 3: THE GOALS TABLE

You have your goals: how can you achieve them? Hopefully, you have a wide range of goals so that soon you can start ticking some off and feel you are achieving! Create a table and categorise your goals into the following three columns:

Immediate: What can you start working towards right away? Learn a new song, rehearse a stand-up set, email a venue, etc.

One Year: Not everything is instant, what are you working towards for this time next year? Perhaps to phase out the day job, get a headline gig, stop accepting work that pays poorly, etc. This is a list to be working *towards* and frequently looking at to keep you motivated and feeling you are working towards something.

Five Year: I say five years because you always want something on the horizon. However, putting a goal here doesn't mean you *can't* achieve it for five years! To go from making £0 from drag to it being your only source of income in one year may be a little ambitious, but over five years that could be achievable. These could be artistic goals (write a one-person show) or practical (pay my mortgage with drag). I am not here to tell you what is, or is not, achievable; each reader will have different priorities, different skill sets and be at different points of their drag journey. Try to be realistic – Ru wasn't built in a day.

Date the List: This table will be in constant flux and evolution. Every time you add or edit it put the date next to it. If you're a spreadsheet fan you might like to add a *date set* and *date achieved* column

Table 4.1 is an example of how a *Goals Table* might look:

1 January 2025

Immediate Goals	One Year Goals	Five Year Goals
• To become a better performer.	• To be regularly working (two or more gigs a month).	• For drag to be the primary income source.
• To improve make up skills.	• To have an enjoyable life style.	• To have a 'red carpet moment'.
• To confidently sing a song on-stage.	• To not accept work for less than £200.	• To produce an hour long solo show.

Table 4.1 Example of a *Goals Table* Divided into Immediate, One Year or Five Year timelines.

Always Aiming to be a Better Performer

Being a better performer should **always** be in that first column! It's something every artist should consistently be working on: almost all of the *One Year* and *Five Year* goals will be more likely to be achieved by becoming a better performer. Spoiler alert, that goal is also why you have picked up this handbook!

If you haven't already, add that to your immediate goals column and then give it a tick because you are doing it! You are on your way! But this is a goal that shifts as you shift. The better you become as a performer, the better you need to become to keep achieving that goal. This doesn't mean you can't acknowledge achievements, or improvement, but always aiming to be better is what will give you a trajectory, a momentum to move forward.

Evaluation

This table is a constant work in progress: Updating it at the beginning of each month will give you motivation and trajectory, as will an annual investigation. Set a reminder in your calendar to regularly revisit and have a review. When a goal is achieved, can the parameters be re-set to keep you moving forward? E.g. if you were after £100 a gig and got there, is £150 realistic for the next step?

Small steps make a big change: adding £10 to every invoice adds up! Likewise finding one extra gig a month could make a big difference to your yearly income. Don't feel these, seemingly, small achievements aren't worth celebrating. Have a moment to be proud of your achievements. And possibly question why some escaped you? Do you need to edit the parameters? Be more realistic? Or work harder? You may find at a review stage some of your *Five Year* goals no longer apply, or have evolved. That's fine, but what's changed? Return to this chapter and redo the exercises: things can change but you need to be aware of the direction you are travelling in!

> Talk to me about this five years ago and there would have been a bit of me that was absolutely distraught that I hadn't been on *Drag Race UK* yet, but not anymore. I don't see "mainstream success" as success for Me anymore.
>
> Me The Drag Queen[3]

Flow

How will an *Immediate* goal help you achieve something in the next year? Or the next five years? Sometimes you need stepping stone goals: something that can provide a path. If you have a *Five Year* goal that none of your *Immediate* or *One Year* goals are guiding you to achieving, how are you going to get there? Visa versa, you may have some *One Year* goals that once achieved will leave you wondering why you wanted that.

Moving Forward

The *Goals Table* will act as a rudder for your drag career; steering you in the right direction, and sometimes steering you back on course. The *Immediate* goals can be your day-to-day motivation: a drag to do list.

Reviewing the list on a regular basis and acknowledging achievements is how to track long term success. You may not have reached international acclaim, but if your goals were to have fun and make new friends – then that is success! You may now return to the exercises and ask: "*What's next?*"

> A piece of advice from drama school was to do one task everyday, to make me feel like a performer: rehearse a monologue, take a class, read a play, email a casting director. Even on a day working in a call centre, I was a productive, *resting* actor trying to improve my craft.
>
> I have adapted and developed this into my drag. I do *something* as a drag performer every single day: to get ready for my next gig, improve my skills, rehearse a song, adjust a costume, rehearse new material, see a show or network! All of these things are about investing in a career and in yourself as an artist. Find a little creative moment to remind yourself everyday – you are a performer!
>
> If you only work on your drag when you are working towards a booked gig, things will move very slowly. If you aren't 'booked and blessed' find a few more daily tasks to make you a better drag act. Little and often is a far more productive approach than rushing to create an entire set in a single day.

Hold Yourself Accountable

As an artist, often working solo, it is easy to not see things through to completion. Find ways to hold yourself accountable and not run away just because things get tricky. Throughout upcoming chapters are opportunities to write, rehearse and create new sets. You will have brilliant ideas that you *start* developing and at some point come to a block: something that stops the creative flow, a reason it isn't quite working. In a supported rehearsal room this would be addressed, talked through and collectively worked on to get to the end goal. When working solo instinct will be to abandon ship: run away! ("*This isn't working, what was*

I thinking!") Please don't – screw your courage to the sticking place and work through that block. Or around it. Or over it!

The easy option is to say *"that's not working"* and move to a new idea: the cowards way out! If everything comes easily then it probably isn't the most interesting piece of work. Performances are exciting because they are challenging, thought through and worked on. So keep jumping over the hurdles.

A few techniques that may help you:

- Tell a friend. Send a quick message to a trusted colleague or friend: *"I'm working on a new Parody Song. I need a week on it. Can you check in on me next week?"*
- Give yourself a deadline. Set reminders on your phone/calendar.
- Announce on social media that you are doing it – *"debuting a new song next week!"* Now your audience are expecting this new piece. You have to follow through.
- Find creative minds to bounce ideas around with. Often talking through an idea, or a block, provides the solution without the need of much response from the colleague. Hearing your thought process explained out loud can show you where the issues may lie. Talk to people.

Each Gig: How Can You Measure Success

Drag is subjective; performances won't always be to everyone's taste. *You* are the best person to judge whether or not a performance has been successful. Other barometers of success can be audience reaction, venue reaction, producer reaction…but going onstage with a specific few goals you can personally measure success by is very useful.

For every gig, when wheeling your suitcase up to the venue, remind yourself of two things. Firstly, how this gig is moving towards any goals, and tick it off. Then the show is a success in your career trajectory before you have even stepped on-stage:

- *"Being paid more than I normally am tonight"* – tick!
- *"Fourth show this week"* – tick!
- *"Headlining tonight"* – tick!

Secondly, some simple goals that will make this gig a success *for you*:

- *"Working with XXX tonight – get a photo for socials"*.
- *"Performing a new song tonight: going to get the lyrics right"*.
- *"Find out who programmes this venue midweek for future work! Schmooze the staff"*.

The list of what you wish to achieve can be as simple or sophisticated as you need; depending on where you are in a career, if this gig is a new venue, or new content being performed, etc. Always ask yourself: *"what will make this gig a success for me?"* And remember: being present, having fun and not becoming complacent are all great goals!

In many ways this is a mindfulness exercise, to keep you engaged with *your* journey: to connect with why you are doing the gig. It also gives energy and trajectory to each gig so you don't fall into autopilot or go through the motions. It will also help you focus on the job in hand, rather than multi-tasking with all the other things going on in life.

If you feel you have achieved these small goals then it was a success! You are progressing. Each progression is a step forward in your career, and each step adds up no matter how small.

My success is if I do a show and I leave with mission accomplished: people smiling and the roof has come off that for me is success!

Son Of A Tutu[4]

Review

Many acts find it useful to record their set (video or audio) when there is the opportunity to. Find a colleague who can point a camera phone at the stage, or even simply set your phone up nearby so you can capture some of the gig. The recording is not for social media or promotion but a record, for you, of how the set went. Adrenaline kicks in on-stage and often acts don't quite remember moment for moment how things went, what got said, what got the laughs. The recording won't capture the magic of the live experience but it will document your pacing, when the audience reacted and what lyrics you got right. This can then be taken back into rehearsal to show you what you need to work on and help this set become the best it can be.

I try and record new stuff, mostly on audio for myself, on my phone. If I can get people to do it on video for me, when setting new things, great!

Ada Campe[5]

Lack of Success Does Not Mean Failure

Not every gig is a success; not every pay cheque was worth it, not every joke will land. There will be times you come off stage and think you bombed. These gigs are also stepping stones in the journey to success, you can learn from what happened and improve. Get cross about it if you need to: let it out and then let I go, move on! How can you stop that happening again? Usually the answer is more practice, more professionalism and more preparation.

Overview: *Measuring Success*

A drag journey is full of unexpected opportunities and a limitless variety of directions they can go in. Having your own, ever evolving, list of goals, a roadmap to where you wish to go, can help everyone. Remembering why you wanted to do drag in the first place and finding ways to keep control of your own career are essential for sustaining trajectory and momentum.

- Ask yourself why you got into drag? What do you love about it? What do you want to get out of it?
- Create a list of goals. Desires your wish to achieve.
- Structure the goals into *Immediate*, *One Year* and *Five Year* goals to give a structure and realistic timeline.
- Remember not everything needs to be a financial or professional gain: have fun, give back to the community, celebrate under-represented voices.
- Each gig is a small step in a bigger journey. Always look at how this gig is helping the bigger picture. And how this gig can be a success for you?

The best way every performer can improve their journey, and create a long-term career, is by improving their craft as a performer. This handbook is full of ideas of how you can do that; if you feel the momentum dropping: re-read this chapter and ask yourself why? Pin point areas for improvement and revisit those chapters. If you are not getting the bookings you want, revisit *Chapter 2: The Business of Drag*. If you are struggling with finance revisit *Chapter 3: The Economics of Drag*. Find some active goals from there that you can work on. Once a month, have a cup of tea and look over your goals, make amendments, tick some off and let that set your motivation for the coming month.

Now, as a performer, having addressed the business, economics and the trajectory of your drag journey we need to address something few drag acts seriously do, and even fewer talk about: rehearsal!

Notes

1. *Hugo Grrrl* in interview with *Michael Twaits*, July 2024. See Part IV for full interview.
2. *Son Of A Tutu* in interview with *Michael Twaits*, July 2024. See Part IV for full interview.
3. *Me The Drag Queen* in interview with *Michael Twaits*, July 2024. See Part IV for full interview.
4. *Son Of A Tutu* in interview with *Michael Twaits*, July 2024. See Part IV for full interview.
5. *Ada Campe* in interview with *Michael Twaits*, July 2024. See Part IV for full interview.

Gem The Clown photographed backstage at the Royal Vauxhall Tavern by Fox Al Rajim

5
Memory: Rehearsal and Development

Occasionally drag acts are lucky: a large scale show may provide a rehearsal schedule, a space, even a director or choreographer. For the other 99.9% of drag performances the onus is on the drag act to rehearse, shape and prepare their set, to be ready and present the best work possible. Preparation is everything.

This chapter is a selection of tips and tricks guiding you to a productive time rehearsing and developing your work. Whether it is a full out rehearsal or simply running lines a few times on your way somewhere else. Seize every moment you can to hone your craft and improve your technique. Knowing your content so well that in performance your focus is on the live moment: the words, movement and the emotions.

> Don't be underprepared. Fail to prepare and prepare to fail.
>
> Adam All[1]

More Than a Memory

Live performance is not the act of proving that you know your lines, moves or lyrics; the audience have paid to see you *perform* the material to the best of your ability. Once learnt, that's when the craft of rehearsal can really take shape: bringing the piece to life, making choices and creating a dynamic experience for an audience.

Rehearsal Definitions

When I refer to rehearsing in this handbook I am visualising you pushing furniture to the edge of the room and making the most of it. Rehearsal is about getting your material ready *and* about bettering your performance skills – so running well structured pieces, focusing on vocal range, articulation, sharpness of movement, for dancers even flexibility is part of your rehearsal process.

Very few drag acts have a rehearsal space; you need to become adept at rehearsing in your bedroom, or lounge, or if you need more space – a local park. Make it part of your life to be having mini-rehearsals on-the-go between other things you are doing. Drag acts aren't usually earning enough to hire rehearsal spaces – remember *Chapter 3: The Economics of Drag* – don't spend money that you don't need to, work with what you have! As a career develops you may build relationships with venues who will open up their space for rehearsals occasionally.

DOI: 10.4324/9781003498797-6

You Need to Rehearse

When developing work on paper the ideas often flow, put smiles on faces and feel good. When you first get on your feet however there are often blocks, things that aren't working and the temptation is to change the idea you were developing. Instinct is the writing, or content, is the problem – not the delivery. It takes time and effort to bring something to life on your feet. It takes time trying to get the rhythm of your delivery right, finding the beats and connecting to the audience in the desired way. Rehearsal is the way through! The same is true when reviewing work after its first few performances: If it didn't all land the way you wanted, it needs more work and more rehearsal. Not a full rewrite or edit. Train yourself not to run away from the work: remember you need to rehearse.

Always Rehearsing

There will be times where acts have a formal rehearsal for a new piece, you can set aside some time to get up and work! This chapter is full of tips to help structure and get the most out of those times. However, building mini-rehearsals into your everyday routine is the best way to constantly be working on your craft. In the modern world everyone is multitasking, embrace that with your drag! Look out for simple ways to incorporate running material and improving your skills into your everyday life.

- Headphones are a drag acts best friend: listen to songs, edits or useful audible material on the go. If you are working up some comedy, record a rough cut of your set and listen to it like a podcast.
- Keep your notebook, pen (and even this handbook) in your bag so you can always look over ideas, add new ones and keep creative ideas flowing. Five minutes at a bus stop could give you a breakthrough moment.
- Singers should sing-along to everything on the radio. Keep learning what fits your voice, or how you can adapt to make a song work for you.
- Every morning do a vocal warm-up in the shower.
- Line learning, lyric learning is like a muscle. Don't only do it when you have to. Always be working at learning a new song, a new comedy set, etc. And lip-syncers, remember you need to learn the lyrcis too!
- Hang your washing whilst you practice an opening monologue. Tell a joke whilst making a sandwich. Sing whilst you vacuum.
- Use voice notes – at every point of rehearsal and development. Grab your phone and take a few seconds to record an idea, thought, or development you might come back to late. When inspiration strikes, record a memo and come back to it when you can.
- Learn to not care what other people think; your roommate will hear you rehearsing through the wall, people on the bus may see you muttering lines under your breath as you learn your tracks. Who cares?

> Rehearsal is, I suppose, part of my everyday life. There's no real separation – it could pop up anywhere, anytime!
>
> Son Of A Tutu[2]

Creating A Rehearsal Space

When you are having a more structured rehearsal, you don't need access to a dance studio or stage. Cabaret stages aren't usually big, you should be able to work with what you have! Create a space, and atmosphere, where you can get up, move and focus on the task in hand.

Rehearsal and Development

- Clear a practical space. Move furniture in your lounge/bedroom – go into the garden or a park!
- Turn your phone and wifi off. Anything else that beeps or alerts you – turn it off! Act as if you are in an important meeting.
- Mentally mark out your rehearsal space; where is the audience? Can the door be the entrance from the dressing room? Where's the bar? Where's the tech box? What is a good eye-line for an *anchor* (see *Chapter 8: Basic Drag*)?
- Grab a drink and go to the bathroom before you begin. Have less excuses to leave the rehearsal process once you are up and running.
- Call what you are doing a rehearsal and treat it like work. You wouldn't expect a teacher to break mid-class to take phone call or hang the washing! Get into that focused headspace: when rehearsing you are at work!

Writing, Researching, Editing, Developing

Not every rehearsal is on your feet. When you are at the computer, or notebook, developing or editing your act, it is still worth finding ways to keep focused and having a 'work' mentality.

- Turn your Wifi and phone off. If you need the internet – use it, but then toggle the Wifi back off after!
- Set a timer and a goal of what you are hoping to achieve in that time. Be realistic.
- Write at the top of a page what you are aiming to achieve in this session. (E.g. *Rewrite a specific part of a parody. Smooth out all edits in this track.*) Then stick to the plan!
- If easily distracted, find a way to hold yourself accountable. Tell a friend you will send them a new track or new script later. (They do not need to read it but can sign off that you did it!)
- If working at home: stay focused. The household jobs can wait!

A Fresh Start – Every Day

When developing a script, editing a track or writing new material on a computer, keep organised. Each time you begin work on a file: duplicate it, rename it, save it! Name the new version with todays date and then carry on with the editing and developing. It is too easy on a computer to delete or undo yesterdays work: intentionally or accidentally. You always want to be able to step back to an older version if something about todays development wasn't right!

A Research Log

Research is a vital part of the rehearsal and development process. Finding different versions of a song, looking for interesting quotes, interviews or researching a specific subject is an ongoing process. Manage time well by not letting the parameters of what you are researching spread too wide. One video will lead to another, and that to another, and before you know it you are off topic! A simple approach to staying on target is to keep a research log.

After each video, track, or article you read – add it to a research log with a brief note of why it was useful, or what it could bring to your current area of development. It doesn't need to be a full review but ideally the title (a hyperlink so you can re-find it) and a time stamp or page/paragraph number of any specific detail. If you feel there's no point in logging it down – <u>you have gone too far</u>. Don't click into the next article, video or song: tighten up the research parameters, avoid falling down the YouTube wormhole!

Rehearsing Alone

When rehearsing alone it's easy to get distracted and not hold yourself accountable to achieving much. Set a target and a schedule. Voice record, video and review what you've achieved at the end of the session. In almost every exercise in this handbook doing this will make the creative process stronger. Evaluate the success of what you rehearsed, set a goal for the next rehearsal, or is the piece stage ready? Also review the rehearsal process; are there ways you could use your time better and move your work forward further? Setting a goal for the *next* rehearsal is a good way to end a rehearsal period. It gives a feeling of trajectory and something to mull over in the back of your mind between sessions. *I know what needs to be done next!*

Find Your Family

As I've said, it can be a lonely process and you will be working alone, a lot. Find your family, your people; a few like minded performers, producers, promoters, directors or friends. Knock ideas around with them. Arrange a day to turn up early to the next show and before the tech begins maybe walk through a new piece on the stage to get some feedback. Often these relationships evolve naturally, possibly even a drag family is created. But it is essential to have other voices in the creative process to keep you sane and make the process fun. You might also find colleagues to do skill trades with – they might finesse the editing of a track and you help them make their comedy a bit snappier. Share your strengths and let others help you!

Allow Time

When learning and rehearsing material always give yourself time. It reduces stress, allows the body to absorb the work you are doing and gives your mind space to reflect. The body can only do so much in a few days; the more time you can give yourself to get familiar with your set, and let it sink into your body, the better. Doing two hours a day for two weeks will be much more successful than cramming all the rehearsal into two full days before a performance. When things aren't working – have a break, walk outside, run around the block or even sleep on it. You aren't in a rush – some time away will help!

Rehearsal Repertoire List

In *Chapter 6: Building A Set, Range and Repertoire*, we will look at collating and categorising your repertoire. The content which is *Performance Ready* can be incorporated into your daily practice. After you've done your stretches, or vocal warm up – run through a few pieces. Sometimes full out, sometimes testing yourself on lyrics, or using it as an articulation exercise.

Going over familiar, performance-ready material, will get you into the right headspace to enter a rehearsal too. It will help you remember – *"this is the energy level I need, this is how to pace my work, this is how well I need to know it!"* Use one of your *greatest hits* that you can run with your eyes shut as a way of waking yourself up and making sure you are in performance mode at the beginning of a practical rehearsal.

The benefits are three fold. Firstly it gets you in the right headspace to rehearse and develop your new set. Secondly it *keeps* your existing repertoire performance ready, and lets it sink further into your subconscious and muscle memory. Do not assume because you have successfully performed something once it will be as good next time. You need to keep running it and refreshing. Finally, it is improving all your technical performance skills, it's like a trip to the gym for your stage muscles – you want to use them every day!

As part of my vocal practice I warm up in the shower every day (See *Chapter 14: Vocal and Singing Techniques*). I will usually then sing a couple of songs from my repertoire as I do odd jobs around the house getting ready for my day. Sometimes just muttering along to myself to test lyrics, other times singing full out with a track.

My *Stonewall* piece (see *Chapter 7: Research and Further Reading*) was written in 2008, I have performed it hundreds of times. It is eight minutes of very fast spoken word; I have to work my lips, teeth and tip of the tongue to ensure every word is crisp and clear. Running it frequently benefits my articulation, rather than having a traditional articulation exercise in my warm up routine – I use that! I am simultaneously revising it, making certain that I know it inside out and working my vocal technique. All the time making sure my performance skills aren't getting lazy.

This process happens almost everyday, it's my routine and has become habitual. I don't always notice I'm doing it! if I'm not rehearsing anything further then it's just a warm up getting me ready for the day. If there's something new I'm working on I start working on that next feeling fresh, focused and knowing how well I need to know my content before I feel it's stage ready!

EXERCISE 1: CHALLENGE YOURSELF IN REHEARSAL

From this chapter (and *Chapter 6: Building a Set, Range and Repertoire*) you should be able to build up a small rehearsal routine. You'll find exercises specific to you skill set further into the book that you can add to your routine. Frequently running material from your repertoire will help you hone your craft: whether its improvisation, physicality, articulation or vocal range. But if you always use the same backing tracks, songs, piece of writing, etc. your skills will eventually stop being challenged. How can you stretch yourself? Take things a little further in rehearsal to help improve you techniques.

This exercise is really just a few fun ideas you could incorporate into rehearsal to extend your range, improve your skills and maybe find some new material. Not all of them will apply to you but why not give them a try? Remember this a *rehearsal* technique, there's no expectation for you to take this to the stage.

- **Talking Off-Script:** One of the hardest skills to develop in rehearsal is to confidently talk to an audience off-script. Practice by narrating your life. Pretend there is an audience whilst doing a mundane job, try to make it entertaining or funny. Make a sandwich and try and get a few laughs. Voice note this. Do it every day for a week, then change the topic to narrating making your bed, cleaning your make-up brushes, keep playing! As a cabaret host the biggest challenge is to talk confidently and dynamically about anything and everything.

- **Singers:** If there is repertoire you feel very comfortable with, find a backing track a semitone higher or lower. Try to make that work, how does it change your interpretation? Can you hit those notes? This is a simple exercise to slowly build your vocal range but it can also help you confirm you are using the best key for you.

- **For Comedy:** Twitter (now X) is a brilliant playground to test a quick one-liner or a witty gag. Set a challenge to do a witty tweet a day for a month. Rely on the words – not images or gifs. See what material works, gets engagement and makes you laugh. Can any of this be brought into your live material?

- **For Lip-Sync:** It's easy online (or on YouTube) to play a track sped up or slowed down. Try and keep up with your tracks at 1.5x speed without losing any clarity or technique.

- **Characters/Impersonators:** Be bold and go into a shop 'in' character (not dressed up!) but just try and live as that character for five minutes, use their voice, mannerisms, etc. Interact with a few people. It will help you fill out the living person you are embodying. Do the general public notice?
- **Step Outside Your Comfort Zone:** Rehearse material outside of your usual range or style. You don't need to publicly perform the pieces, but in rehearsal what happens when you stretch yourself out of your comfort zone? If you do upbeat lip-syncs – try a ballad or even spoken word, sing! If you write long comic stories – try your hand at one liners. Comedians could take those skills and apply them to a parody (see *Chapter 19: Parody*).

> I am not a rapper, but for articulation, versatility and breath control I often rehearse Nicki Minaj's *Super Bass* or Raye's *Escapism*. I can't imagine I will perform either of the original songs in a set. But they get my mouth working overtime, challenge breath control and are helping me feel confident an audience hears every words when I am onstage.

You might be thinking this is too soon! You haven't done your first performance and I am already challenging you to stretch yourself and rehearse outside of you comfort zone! That's because if you can get comfortable working outside of your comfort zone when you return to your best pieces, well rehearsed and on-stage it will feel comfortable and relaxed. It is also important to talk from the outset about making the most of rehearsing, documenting ideas and constantly stretching yourself from the beginning so it becomes a habit rather than something you need to find time for.

Learning Lines

Whether it's a lip-sync or song lyrics; a script or comedy bit; learning lines is something many struggle with. A few tips:

- **Little And Often.** A few times a day find ways to run through what you are learning. This will be more successful than assigning half a day where you *must learn it*.
- **Bite Sized Pieces.** If you have a ten minute set to learn, don't take the whole set in one go. Try one paragraph the first day. Then the next day the next two. The third day bring the them all together. Keep adding small sections and building up.
- **Vary Techniques.** Read over the lines a few times, other times listen to them on your headphones (it's easy to record you just reading them out). Another time get someone to test you.
- **Write It Out:** Using paper and pen copy out the full text. There is something magical in the process of taking the time to focus on each word which helps them go in. Many people are better visual than auditory learners. Find what works for you.
- **Multi-Tasking.** Again, when doing mundane jobs – run those lines at the same time.
- **A Final Read before Bed.** As you are relaxing and unwinding, just before going to sleep, have a final read or listen to what you are learning. Not a *test* simply a relaxing read. Sleep on it, you'll be amazed what your mind can do over night.
- **Cheat Sheets.** Copy the first letter of each word of the script onto some paper. Use each letter as a prompt for what you are saying. Use this technique to see how well you actually know the lines. Once you've mastered that and can perform it with ease. Do the same technique for the first letter of each sentence.

"I didn't do that! Did you?" becomes *"IDDT! DY?"*

And once you've mastered that it simply becomes *"ID"* as a prompt for each sentence. Eventually you won't need the prompts.

Off Script

A common theme in the handbook is that each gig is freshly created for the audience in the moment. This does not mean it has not previously been rehearsed, but rigorous rehearsal and development is what allows a drag act to perform their set, almost on a technical autopilot, allowing the freedom to engage an audience, play in the live space and react to what is going on.

> That's the joy of live performance, right? It's not just endless repetition. We do the same things a lot, but it isn't the same, because it's always about the audience.
>
> Ada Campe[4]

Performers of all disciplines rehearse the core of their set, the pieces, the songs, the lip-syncs – fastidiously. The linking moments, the talking, is usually more organic: not strictly improvised but pulling on sections of tried and tested material which can be selected for what will best serve this audience. For the audience it should feel organic, natural and that the performer is live, present, with them. That is the skill, the craft and the pay off of rehearsal and experience.

> It's all to do with confidence. People would say *"just do it"*…Do you have any idea how much hard work *"just do it"* is! How much you have to learn, how much you have to overcome, how much you have to prepare, how much you have to rehearse to *"just do it"*.
>
> Adam All[3]

Many acts begin having a full script for their seemingly 'off the cuff' remarks and patter. Eventually, the script becomes a rolling repertoire of lines, or stories, creating the much sought after drag illusion of having a quick response or a line for everything.

On-stage is where a lot of the audience interaction is learnt, but rehearsal should be where the polish of your set pieces, your script or your movement is honed. Rehearse everything you possibly can in advance.

To the Stage!

Debuting new work on-stage may feel challenging. Showing new work to an audience is the next phase of the rehearsal process, then you come back to the rehearsal room and keep working. *"Why didn't it get the laughs that you expected? Why did they cheer at that moment?"* When trying out new work always try and record it so you can listen back to yourself *and* the audience reaction and then review the work at your own time after the gig.

> You think of it in your head a lot, but until you put it in front of an audience, you just don't know what the beats are, what people find funny, what works on-stage, the logistics of what you're going to do, the sight-lines, any of that stuff.
>
> Ada Campe[4]

A Risk Sandwich

Introduce new work, or new skills, slowly. Hide the new bits in amongst existing work that you feel comfortable and confident with; I call it A Risk Sandwich. A drag act who sings as their bread and butter might aspire to do comedy; choose two songs and slide a couple of test jokes in the middle. Then you have two things you are confident with, and a small risk in the middle. *If* it doesn't get the desired response you have a strong follow up. Initially a couple of lines, or jokes to link two songs, but it can evolve a small comedy bit. Slowly and surely you can expand your skills set and repertoire. Maybe you don't need that second song at all because one song and a mini-set of comedy has a better flow?

Performance as Development

Many acts, especially experienced acts, go out on-stage with a framework rather than a script. They have their set pieces they are linking between. In between they are constantly testing new material, drawing on lines or jokes that have previously worked. Initially being tightly scripted can help you establish who you are, give confidence. From that you'll find bits that work, and bits that could work better. Slowly you develop a range of go-to lines and phrases. (Build your *Language* and *Lexicon* in *Chapter 13: Talking On Stage*.) But through performance, and the direct feedback of an audience, you will create your own bank of options to use in live performance.

Overview: Rehearsal and Development

Make rehearsal a habitual part of your every day routine. If you can do that from the beginning your drag journey should go far! You should always be aiming to improve your skills and technique as an intrinsic part of that process. Your skills will develop if you keep challenging yourself: stretch yourself further in rehearsal so that on-stage feels technically easy and then you can put more focus on the live experience.

- You can rehearse anywhere, every time you are doing a mundane job – run some lines or lyrics.
- Performing is not about proving you've learnt your set! It is about using what you learnt to create a live experience: you need to know your content inside and out so that you can focus on the live moment on-stage.
- Run your repertoire as part of your ongoing mission to improve your performance skills and technique.
- Add challenges to the way you run familiar material to help you step outside of your comfort zone and challenge yourself to improve your performance skills and technique.
- Learn from stage experience and bring those findings back to rehearsal to keep improving your work.

As you rehearse you will slowly build options of repertoire that you can bring to the stage. Throughout the rest of this book you will be coming up with ideas, completing exercises and then moving on to the next exercise. Finding order by documenting ideas and repertoire is essential for any performer. To have a masterlist of what you can perform right now, what you are working on as well as ideas that are still in development! It's time to look at building a set, your range and repertoire!

Notes

1. *Adam All* in interview with *Michael Twaits*, July 2024. See Part IV for full interview.
2. *Son Of A Tutu* in interview with *Michael Twaits*, July 2024. See Part IV for full interview.
3. *Adam All* in interview with *Michael Twaits*, July 2024. See Part IV for full interview.
4. *Ada Campe* in interview with *Michael Twaits*, July 2024. See Part IV for full interview.

Bunny Darko photographed backstage at the Royal Vauxhall Tavern by Fox Al Rajim

6
Why Did I Choose You?: Building a Set, Range and Repertoire

Drag performers go on stage armed with their metaphorical bag of tricks, to create a set, a seemingly fresh, live performance the audience feels is a bespoke experience. Most of this handbook is ways to develop the different tools to put into the bag, but there needs to be a little organisation behind the scenes. The goal is not to perform something once and forget it, but to build a bank of usable material that can be used throughout an entire career. A treasure trove of content to choose from to create and curate varied sets and shows.

As you work through the handbook, each piece you create, each line you learn, each concept you pitch is added to your *repertoire*. This chapter is dedicated to giving structure and rigour in how you hang onto all your repertoire and ideas. If you work through this handbook, cover to cover, doing every exercise, you will have over one hundred ideas, pitches and pieces! Of course they will need rehearsal and development (see *Chapter 5: Rehearsal and Development*) but they are ideas you can bring to a stage and will eventually form your on-stage repertoire. However, without structure, ideas will get lost; you need to create an orderly way of logging ideas, building repertoire and making sure you are stage ready at every opportunity. For novices, the exercises here might leave you with three pretty empty spreadsheets, but as you carry on through the book they will be populated with fabulous ideas. For the more experienced these pages will help tidy your repertoire and give you a shorthand for preparing and structuring any set.

Repertoire

Repertoire (or rep) is simply all the components of a set you develop and can perform on stage: songs, one liners, lip-syncs, parodies, etc. Initially you may only have a few pieces for your set, but after a few sets you'll start building options, and start seeing different ways you might structure a set; slowly forming longer sets, and who knows, eventually a full-length show!

With so many creative ideas floating around it is easy for a piece to be rehearsed, performed and forgotten about. Or worse, semi-developed, and then over-looked before it gets to the stage. Classifying your rep and keeping a log of the ideas is a simple way of staying organised. These lists will help you come back to a piece you may have forgotten about, and see straight away what use they could be and why now might be the time to choose to develop them. By the end of this chapter you will have created a *Repertoire List* which all of your rep can be organised into. I break down repertoire into three catagories: *Performance Ready Repertoire*, *Rehearsal Repertoire* and *In Development*.

Most performers consider their songs, or pieces, their repertoire but don't forget to be just as fastidious in documenting and building the repertoire of your chat; any patter, any good lines, or links as part of your set are also rep. Performers build a wide range of nicely rehearsed lines that they can draw on in performance to

DOI: 10.4324/9781003498797-7

suit the correct moment. If it's a *bit* you do, or have done successfully, on-stage, no matter how small – log it, rehearse it and keep it stage ready!

> A lot of my work is quick reactions. I have things in the arsenal for structured spontaneity; where you have this treasure trove of one-liners or responses that you deploy depending on what somebody in the audience gives you.
>
> Son Of A Tutu

A Set

A set is the term for the material you perform in your section of the show. A set can be any length 5, 10, 30 minutes or more. You might be offered a split set where you do one piece (a song, a lip sync) and then a second piece later in the same show, this is very common for lip-sync and burlesque acts. Different shows will require different lengths of set. This variety means, even when getting the early gigs, you need to find ways to adapt and change your material to structure sets of different formats. Sometimes your set is walking on, doing one lip-sync and leaving. A longer set might have some patter either side, or two pieces linked by some comedy chat. The options of how to structure a set are almost endless – aim for variety and aim to structure things to present you at your best.

When offered a booking, if you think the set time is too long/too short for what you want to achieve don't be afraid to mention that to the booker. For example; say you have two great pieces but they don't flow into each other so a split set would be best. Or the opposite, there is momentum to comedy and splitting a set breaks the flow; ask for one longer set. As ever, establish timings and expectations in advance of the gig so everyone knows what they are expecting in the show. (See pre-show communication in *Chapter 2: The Business of Drag*.)

Creating a Set

If you have a ten minute set it's not best practice to do similar tempo songs back to back – think variety! Choose things from within your repertoire that you are confident with and see which pieces when put together make a coherent set. Usually a set has a through line, a journey or a theme that at least loosely ties the pieces within it together. A short set could be two contrasting songs with a tiny bit of talking between, to move from one piece to another (this will be covered with the *Monkey Bar* technique in *Chapter 13: Talking On Stage*). Don't over complicate it, a simple line or two is enough to link a set together. There should just be a thread guiding the audience from one idea to the next, taking them on a journey and letting them know why you chose the material you have chosen.

Organising Your Repertoire

Using your repertoire spreadsheets is a simple way of seeing all the options you could bring to a set, you can find work which fits tighter nicely for the gig you have been booked for. Working through the upcoming sections will give you an overview of what rep is stage ready, what is nearly there and what ideas you have bubbling away behind the scenes. You will also have the knowledge of how to use your rep to build a strong, varied set.

Performance Ready Repertoire

If you get a call to do a gig tonight, anything on your *Performance Ready Repertoire* list is an option: it is ready, you don't have time to rehearse anything new! You have rehearsed every piece, know every move and every word! All you need to do is select a few pieces that structurally will make a suitable set.

As a career develops it is very easy to forget pieces you have rehearsed, developed and performed. Anything and everything you perform successfully should be added to your *Performance Ready Repertoire* list because you never know when it may come in handy!

All of the content that is on your *Performance Ready Repertoire* list should also be added to your *performers drive* (see Chapter 2: The Business of Drag) so if you are at a gig and suddenly need an additional piece or number you are ready. It's a back up (as well as having your planned content all with you).

> **EXERCISE 1: CREATE YOUR PERFORMANCE READY REPERTOIRE LIST**
>
> **You will need: Your notebook or a spreadsheet.**
>
> Create a spreadsheet named *Repertoire List*. Create a tab with a table the example shown in Table 6.1, this is your *Performance Ready Repertoire*. Everything that you can perform right now can go on the list!
>
> **Piece:** The name of the piece, hopefully self explanatory.
>
> **Skill/Style:** What type of performance is it, ideally put the base skill first, then any extra details.
>
> **Category:** Categorise your rep to give a simple overview: opener, ballad, upbeat, showstopper, finale, audience interaction, improvisation, get them dancing, sing-along and any other categories that might apply to your style(s) of performance.
>
> **Notes:** These are optional extras, reminders so you don't forget a key prop or technical requirement. After a performance it is useful to note if a song felt dated, a joke less relevant or there is a set-up you have to do prior to the specific piece. (Does it need to go back into rehearsal and be freshened up?)
>
> | Piece | Skill/Style | Category | Notes | Running Time |
> | --- | --- | --- | --- | --- |
> | One Night Only | Straight Song | Opener | Ballad into disco! | 3.45 |
> | Madonna Medley | Lip-sync medley | Upbeat | Cone bra! | 5–6 |
> | Love Yourself | Parody Song | Comedy | Audience sing-along | 3.30 |
> | Living For Love | Clowning | Comedy/Slapstick | Wear the cape! | 3.40 |
>
> Table 6.1 An Example of a Varied Performance Ready Repertoire List.

The listed examples are set pieces and songs. However, as you develop comedy bits, script and/or one-liners that work add those in too. It's easy to overlook spoken parts of your set which are well rehearsed. In the notes you can link to a full script if needed.

Piece	Skill/Style	Category	Notes	Time
Burlesque Intro	Warm Up	Audience Interaction	Bognor Regis Story – *Butlins*/ make some noise.	2 minutes
Someone's Late	One Liner	Live Moment	The drag queen was ready but you weren't…	10 seconds
Loud Individual	One Liner	Audience Control	I could have guessed she's wearing *leopard print/ sequins*	10 seconds
Set up Sing-along	Comedy	Audience Interaction	Cast them as dancers, singers, etc.	1 minute

Table 6.2 Example of Patter and One-liners in a Performance Ready Repertoire List.

Repertoire and Variety

Categorsing your rep and understanding its use within a set is essential. Not every song within a set or show has the same role; an opening song can establish the performer, set the tone for a set (or an evening) or welcome an audience. An end of set number may have a few show-stopping moments; a final trick before the performer exits the stage. Within your set you don't want to have three songs that essentially do the same thing. Always look for variety (see *peaks and troughs* in *Chapter 8: Basic Drag*). You can order the spreadsheet by *Skill* or *Category* to find the options quickly to fill a specific space in your set.

> If I've been booked for a ten-minute set for a gig, with no particular theme, I can simply look at my *Performance Ready Repertoire List* and thread together a set list.
>
> I can open with *One Night Only* (3.45) and then close with a comedy lip-sync *Living For Love* (3.40). Now I know I have around two and a half minutes I can use for patter. I don't need to talk before *One Night Only* or after *Living For Love*. So I need to simply look at my Chat/Comedy sections and choose some bits that would be fun but also make sense moving from one song to the other.

Rehearsal Repertoire List

The *Rehearsal Repertoire List* is about the ongoing finessing of, fairly well developed, ideas. Your rep which needs some attention, and time, before you could perform it. Either you don't know it well enough or it needs to be structured a little more, brought to life. You *think* it's going to work but it isn't quite stage ready! It may also feature some pieces you have performed but still need a bit of work. Perhaps you didn't know the words as well as you thought, or the audience didn't engage in it the way you hoped. This doesn't mean that you abandon it: it just needs more rehearsal! (How you rehearse it is what *Chapter 5: Rehearsal & Development* is all about, can you slip it into your morning routine to finesse the lines?)

> **EXERCISE 2: REHEARSAL REPERTOIRE LIST**
>
> **You will need: Your notebook and your *Repertoire List* spreadsheet.**
>
> With your *Repertoire List* spreadsheet create a new tab and a table for your *Rehearsal Repertoire List* with exactly the same categories as Table 6.1 and Table 6.2. The only difference is rather than populating with pieces you could perform instantly, this time it is pieces you need to rehearse before they are performance ready. The notes section now becomes the area to put what it is you need to work on before it is stage ready. (e.g learn the lyrics, finesse the choreography, keep developing in a practical space, bringing the jokes out, etc.)
>
> This spreadsheet now becomes your rehearsal guide. When you rehearse look at your *Rehearsal Repertoire List* and choose which piece you are going to move forward. If a booking comes in for a gig and you need an extra piece to add to an existing set – look at the categories to try and choose the right piece to develop. Something complimentary to the set you're planning, or something that provides a nice contrast to your existing *Performance Ready Repertoire*. And then most satisfyingly of all: when a piece is rehearsed, and stage ready, cut and paste it into your *Performance Ready Repertoire List*.

New Performers Can Play It Safe

New performers might be worrying there is nothing on either of their lists as they haven't performed yet – that's fine! At the beginning of your journey, when establishing yourself as an artist, I advise choosing the strongest performance skill you have and start by rehearsing some *straight* pieces in that style using the relevant chapters in *Part III*. If you've previously sung – do some songs. If you were an actor – perform some comedy. A dancer – apply that to a crowd pleasing lip-sync! Then slowly expand on the same skill set to find a few pieces you are rehearsing that fall into a slightly different category, something that could give variety within a short set. If you did one party track, add a ballad: one moment of audience interaction, add a funny anecdote about your day, or a run of one-liners, etc.

Keep adding new pieces using your existing, strong, skill set because it's likely that is where the majority of your bookings will come from. Initially you may only be booked to do one piece so don't focus on the quantity of your rep, focus on the quality!

The Oldies Are the Goodies

Audiences love hearing songs they know. They like singing, or dancing, to the classics; you do not always need to be reinventing the wheel! Comedians: audiences love hearing traditional structures – you don't need to be outrageous. Use existing structures and well known content to help you gain stage experience and master the basics of stage craft. Half the drag queens in the Western World seem to perform The Little Mermaid – *Part Of Your World*. If you want to do it – do it! Just make sure you put a little spin on it, find your point of view, see *Chapter 10: Making Choices and Finding A Voice*. Don't just go through the motions – make it your own and then an audience will love it!

Building Repertoire

As you become more established and your repertoire lists are expanding you can approach creating, or learning, a new piece due to the need for them to fulfil a role within your set – for example: new opening number, a big finish or even a new skill to add variety!

If it's something that you're new to, go to classes, find teachers who know what they're on about. There can be group classes, there can be one on ones, so many people out there with amazing skills that you can go and learn from. Put time into that.

Me The Drag Queen

If you always open with a song, how could you approach opening with a comedy bit? Keep finding variations, trying new skills. Drag is a beautifully varied art form so don't be afraid to dip your toe into something new! As you work through this handbook you will find exercises for performance styles well outside of your wheelhouse. Keep a note of them all and challenge yourself to bring some of them into a full rehearsal, and who knows maybe even take them on-stage! Don't let the good ideas get away!

In Development Repertoire

As you move forward through the handbook you will work through exercises giving you a huge selection of tiny ideas. The embryo of a live performance piece. Something to note down, think through and then spend time researching, developing and rehearsing. You have need to keep track of these ideas too. Of course some will be silly things you never return to, but in amongst the silly thoughts will be some absolute gold! Give yourself permission to have stupid ideas that probably won't work, but still write them down! The development process is about playing, seeing what fits where and if you always limit your creativity you will find yourself always delivering very similar performances. Throw some crazy ideas out, mull them over, test them out in a rehearsal and see what works before writing them off!

Don't allow under-developed ideas to get lost! It's time for a third spreadsheet: a place for all your crazy ideas! Somewhere they can stew, be mulled over but not forgotten!

EXERCISE 3: IN DEVELOPMENT LIST

You will need: Your notebook and your *Repertoire List spreadsheet*.

Create a third tab on your *Repertoire List* worksheet. The nature of a handbook like this is you end up with hundreds of half baked ideas that may get developed! After a creative moment has happened, take one minute to add it to the *In Development Repertoire List* (Table 6.3). You want to give enough clarity in the *Notes* that you can remember what that idea was, and hopefully continue its development. Make it part of your practice; every exercise you complete or act you begin to develop from this handbook can go into a spreadsheet. Silly ideas that come to you in the middle of the night – they can all go in here! You don't need to be certain, or committed to them; if you had an idea and you thought "*maybe*" – add it to the list.

Piece	Skill/Style	Description	Notes	Running Time
Victoria Beckham	Impersonation	Parody of VB.	Silly viral videos?	?
Bad Guy	Lip-sync edit	Prop based lip-sync; football, beer, etc.	Bad at being a guy	4 mins
Losing My Mind	Parody re-write	Opening number?	More draggy references.	4 mins
Opening Monolgue	Comedy	Set up who I am.	Needs more laughs!	3 mins

Table 6.3 Example of In Development Repertoire List.

I know many arty types don't like this level of organisation but it will really help hold your creative process together. Think of this as a creative teapot – let the ideas brew in here until you are ready to bring them to life! Putting them on the list doesn't mean they will ever actually be developed, but in the future it's a way to jog your memory for an idea you *could* pursue. If you decide one afternoon you need to create a new piece rather than starting with a blank page you have a full selection of ideas to start playing with.

Don't Be Afraid to Sit on It

Sometimes you have a great idea or find a great song, that you think is perfect for you, but you are busy so can't develop it: put it *In Development*. Keep thinking about it, as it develops a little add it to your rehearsal repertoire so you can try it on its feet. An occasion may arise for it at some point and it hopefully will be halfway ready. Sometimes a booking comes in and you panic "*I have nothing prepared*". Come and look at all these brilliant ideas you have previously had, what's brewed and ready for the next stage of development? Does anything fit?

Discarding an idea because you can't see an immediate use for it, or it's too similar to something you currently do, will end up limiting your repertoire. Sometimes two ideas on the *In Development List* evolve and become one much more dynamic idea. So be disciplined. Be patient. Keep working up new material, new repertoire and new ideas.

A Repertoire Progression

The dream is that ideas enter your *Repertoire List* and slowly make their way from *In Development* to *Rehearsal Repertoire* to *Performance Ready*. Occasionally you will need to demote a piece from *Performance Ready* to *Rehearsal* because you don't know the lyrics, or haven't got the rhythms right yet. That's fine. Occasionally you might be rehearsing something and think it needs a little longer stewing *In Development* so you move it down and think about it a little more, research, re-write a little until it's ready for you to get up and rehearse again. This is all part of the process! But documenting them and keeping ideas organised will help you to feel prepared and not lose any of the brilliant ideas you have stumbled across.

Overview: Building Range and Repertoire

- Create a *Rehearsal Repertoire List* – pieces you know that you can consistently run and use to practice performance skills whilst also reaffirming that you know them well enough.
- Make it habitual. Every time you do an exercise and develop an idea, or create a pitch for an idea, add it to your *In Development Repertoire List*.
- After performing material, if it needs some time in rehearsal make sure you update your *Repertoire List*.

Your *Repertoire List* will be the foundation from which you move forward and will give you options to choose from for every potential gig. Keep it up-to-date and use it as part of your rehearsal and development! We've addressed the business, economics and the trajectory of your drag journey, we have looked at how you're going to rehearse and keep organised, but there is one last *to-do* before turning your attention to your stage craft and performance: You need to be inspired!

Vulgaire photographed backstage at the Royal Vauxhall Tavern by Fox Al Rajim

7
Sweet Inspiration: Research and Further Reading

Before working on stage craft, all drag performers can benefit from taking a moment to research and revisit the possibilities of what they *might* do in drag. Dig deep, be pulled in different directions, open your eyes and see where you could find inspiration. There is always more to see, more to learn, more to read and new styles of work to explore.

Creative juices are already flowing and I'm sure you're itching to dive into *Part II* and start working on your performance skills! But first, there's time to reflect. Before starting each course, The Art of Drag, I share a playlist of videos with the students; it's a simple way of opening up preconceived ideas, exploring different approaches, styles and thoughts of drag before they start thinking of themselves. Some come to the course having overdosed on *Drag Race*, others only have experience from pantomime – everyone can benefit from finding further inspiration. I would encourage every performer to do this before turning their focus onto their own performance practice. It's a jumping-off point to find out what is out there, what is possible: what could you do in drag?

> EXERCISE: WATCH!
>
> You will need: A computer with internet access, your notebook and pen (and treat yourself to snacks and a drink? Get comfortable.)
>
> It's time to sit big and dive into a world full of fabulous drag. Watching these videos is like entering a research period, or beginning to draw up a mood board that will shape your work going forward. This is not a tick sheet for you to watch and complete: each video may lead you to more by that artist, or related artists, or perhaps a similar style. Allow yourself to go down a video rabbit hole; dig deep into the wonderland of drag performance and see what inspires you.
>
> Most readers will have dabbled into *Drag Race* so I avoided referring directly to the show, but there are a few acts mentioned who have now been on the series. If you've never watched the show – try a few episodes. Or if you have, maybe try *The Boules Brothers' Dragula*[1] or *House of Drag*.[2]
>
> I could write another book on drag inspirations and why I have pointed you in the direction of the following performances. Some of the performers may not label themselves as *drag acts* but they definitely use *The Art of Drag*. A few of the suggestions aren't actually performances but artists talking about drag, their process, their inspirations and how they approach drag from different perspectives. Not all videos will feed into your work but they will give you a stronger sense of the wider community, and the wider scene.
>
> At the time of going to print all of these are available through a simple search on the internet. (I have collated them into a YouTube playlist you can find in *The Art Of Drag* section of my website www.michaeltwaits.com.) Some are recent, some 'old school' and some are what the people you identify as 'old school' would call 'old school'. Relax, enjoy and allow yourself to be inspired.

DOI: 10.4324/9781003498797-8

Dickie Beau
Judy Speaks/Blackouts – Twilight of an Idol

Landon Cider
Enjoy the Silence – at Sasha Velour's Nightgowns

Le Gateau Chocolat
Echoes – lates at the V&A

Cleopantha
WAP

Drag Kings, Explained By Drag Kings
A short video for Vox featuring interviews with Mo B. Dick, Maxxx Pleasure, Sigi Moonlight, Johnny Gentleman and King Molasses

Norman Evans
As Fanny Lawton – Over the Garden Wall

Regina Fong
The Typewriter

Murray Hill
101 Murray: The Life and Times of Mr Showbiz

David Hoyle
David Hoyle on "Melancholic Youth" at Dave's Drop in Centre

Kiki And Herb
Kiki & Herb – Will Die for You[3]

Danny La Rue
The Royal Variety Performance 1969

Meet London's Female Drag Queens
A short documentary on London's Female Drag Queens by Vice Asia

Sasha Velour
Love Song for a Vampire – Nightgowns

Shell Suit Cher
Character comedian Tracey Collins sings 'Shell Suit in Memphis'

Split Britches
Belle Repeive[4]

Ted Talks
Many brilliant drag acts have held ted talks – start with Cheddar Gaw-jus, Miss Toto, Adam All & Apple Derrieres, Marti Gould Cummings or RuPaul

Virgin X

Shame – music video

La Voix

Britain's Got Talent with The London Gay Big Band

Sin Wai Kin

'I want people to exist in my world' (Turner Prize Nominee 2022)

I have also selected a performance of my own, and of each of my interviewees from *Part V* for inspiration but also to contextualise us for those who haven't come across our work.

Adam All

A Cup of Tea

Simply Barbra

Niagara[5]

Ada Campe

Unexpected Pleasures Story

Le Fil

This Is My Culture

Hugo Grrrl

The Man Behind the King: Hugo Grrrl

Me The Drag Queen

Roar[6]

Son Of A Tutu

Living Legends – Son Of A Tutu Interviewed by Alfie Ordinary

Michael Twaits

Stonewall

Finding Inspiration

Drag should not be the only reference point or inspiration for a drag act. The above list is not so you can create work like it, but to ensure you haven't blinkered your own view on what drag can do or how it should look.

Artists inspire me when they are talking about their art, about their process and about the way they want it to be received. My inspiration is a huge mix of references, and the older I get the more I want to research, read to inform myself and inform my work. Some inspiration is academic, some is disposable pop-culture; I could be inspired by Paloma Faith or Pinter, Pina Bausch or Paris Hilton! It does not mean I directly reference them, or try to replicate them, but their existence feeds into the world I am creating my work from. An artist's job is to reflect the richness of life back at an audience; the more you know, the richer that reflection can be.

Harbour a desire for knowledge, reading is fundamental; so pick up a book, find a reference. There is so little time and so much out there – immerse yourself in the rich culture of the world and allow it to feed into your work. You may have left school, but you will never finish learning.

Homogenised Drag

As a golden rule drag should not be solely referencing other drag as cultural reference points; because usually that drag act is referencing other cultural reference points. Performers should strive to find their own reference points from the world of politics, fashion, music, literature and more. Try and avoid being a homogenised drag act who comes on-stage and says the latest go-to catchphrase from reality TV and performs the latest hit song *the gays* are loving. Inject your unique personality into everything you do! Have the courage to be different and stand by your own convictions.

If all your opinions seem exactly the same as every other act you are on-stage with – what'a making you unique? Why have I come to see you? Don't always stick in the same ground as others; find your own voice.

> If you're coming from a place of authenticity, then the audience will feel that and latch on to it. As opposed to me going; 'oh, I should do this because this is what's on the television!'
>
> Me The Drag Queen[7]

Drag should draw inspiration from the world at large from politics, literature, film, exhibitions, history and more. Train yourself to find inspiration everywhere. Enter a research period. If there's a gap in your camp queer history – watch *Mommie Dearest*, *Paris Is Burning* or *Whatever Happened to Baby Jane*. Look through some archival *Vogues*. Listen to some interesting podcasts (I can't get enough of *French and Saunders – Titting About*[8] at the moment). Get lost in a Carol Channing deep dive on YouTube. Listen to the latest album from Chappell Roan, then deep dive into Nina Simone, Joni Mitchell or David Bowie.

Often the first time people watch *Paris Is Burning* there is a moment that they realise half the catchphrases from *Drag Race* are actually quotes from the documentary. Others are *Mommie Dearest*, the films of *John Waters* and even from Lisa Kudrow in *The Comeback*. The show is littered with queer cultural references, that are often repeated by a generation who don't know the original source.

Nurture a Hunger for Knowledge

When you discover a gap in your knowledge, don't be afraid to acknowledge that and inform yourself. Perhaps you don't understand how local elections affect national ones. We all now live in a world where you can find a blog, an article or a podcast on almost any subject to help you become more informed. As a performer, expressing opinions on-stage to others, the more informed you are the more varied topics you can explore through your work.

Many of my performer colleagues are the most informed people I know, but also some of the least *traditionally* educated. Having a capacity to excel in a traditional education system is not what I am encouraging. Even as you go through the handbook there might be words you don't know – look them up. There'll be artists mentioned you don't know, take a moment to investigate them. If this handbook brings more people to Carol Channing, Kate Bornstein or LoUis CYpher I'll be delighted!

Bibliography

My publishers might tell me to move it but I'm putting my *Bibliography* here! Firstly because I like breaking the rules and formats, secondly because this reading has shaped how I see the world, drag and performance. It's not an afterthought to add to the end of a book; it is a huge part of my journey into writing the handbook. I'm not expecting many to dig-in and read all these books but the breadth and range of reading should show how many different influences from the world of theatre, gender, performance, queer-theory *and* drag one can draw from.

Throughout this handbook I have tried to use quotes from colleagues, performers and practical examples from my own practice to illustrate and elaborate on ideas. I don't wish for this book to become bogged down in academic referencing, I want the advice to come from a practical place, advice from someone who has stood in the spotlight and forgotten their words, or been alone in a rehearsal room trying to develop a character. That's the advice I couldn't find in writing when I needed support in my career.

My queer life, and my performing life, and that of my colleagues, is where the experience comes from. But the knowledge has come from being, or attempting to be, well read. My issue is – the more I read, the more I see, the less I feel I know.

It was hard to know where to draw the line with a bibliography. I feel I was more inspired by Margaret Atwood's *The Handmaid's Tale* than I was by some academic texts directly on the subject of drag. As artists you find inspiration everywhere, reading for pleasure could still influence your work. A kitsch holiday read could help inspiration strike. But here are a few broad strokes of books that have been key to me, and hopefully the connection to my practice is fairly obvious.

Barker, C. (2010). *Theatre Games: A New Approach to Drama Training*. Methuen Drama.
Bloomfield, J. (2024). *Drag*. University of California Press.
Boal, A. (1992). *Games for Actors and Non-Actors*. Routledge.
Bond, J. (2011). *Tango: My Childhood, Backwards and in High Heels*. Feminist.
Bornstein, K. (1998). *How to Become a Real Man, a Real Woman, or Something Else Entirely*. Routledge.
Bornstein, K. (2011). *Hello Cruel World*. Seven Stories Press.
Bornstein, K. (2013a). *Gender Outlaw*. Routledge.
Bornstein, K. (2013b). *My New Gender Workbook*. Routledge.
Brecht, B., & Willet, J. (1964). *Brecht on Theatre: The Development of an Aesthetic*. Methuen.
Busch, C. (2023) *Leading Lady*. Smart Pop.
Butler, J. (1990). *Gender Trouble: Feminism and the Subversion of Identity*. Routledge.
Case, S.-E. (2013). *Split Britches*. Routledge.
Cleto, F. (2002). *Camp: Queer Aesthetics and the Performing Subject: A Reader*. University Of Michigan Press.
Donnellan, D. (2002). *The Actor and the Target*.
Double, O. (1997). *Stand Up on Being a Comedian*. Bloomsbury Publishing.
Double, O. (2013). *Getting the Joke*. A&C Black.
Edward, M., & Farrier, S. (2020). *Contemporary Drag Practices and Performers*. Bloomsbury Publishing.
Edward, M., & Farrier, S. (2021). *Drag Histories, Herstories and Hairstories: Drag in a Changing Scene* (Vol. 2). Methuen Drama.
Ewan, V. & Sagovsky, K. (2018). *Laban's Efforts in Action*. Bloomsbury Publishing.
Felix Le Freak. (2020). *Serving Face*. Penguin.
Fernandes, C. (2005). *Pina Bausch and the Wuppertal Dance Theater: The Aesthetics of Repetition and Transformation*. P. Lang.
Frost, D. (2016). *Night Flowers: From Avant-drag to Extreme Haute Couture*. Merrell.
Hall, J., Sofie Birkin, Li, H., & Hans, J. S. (2020). *The Art of Drag*. Nobrow Press.
Harrop, J. (1994). *Acting*. Routledge.
Hastings, M. (2016). *Why Drag?* Chronicle Books.
Hughes, H. (2005). *Clit Notes*. Grove Press.
Hughes, H., & Román, D. (2007). *O Solo Homo*. Grove/Atlantic, Inc.

Margolin, D. (1999). *Of All the Nerve*. A&C Black.
Miller, T. (1997). *Shirts & Skin*. Alyson Books.
Miller, T. (2002). *Body Blows*. University of Wisconsin Press.
Morris, J. (2024). *Be Funny or Die*. Unbound Publishing.
Parslow, J. (2019). *When the Lights are Shining on Them: Drag Performance and Queer Communities in London* – (A thesis submitted for the degree of Doctor of Philosophy, University of London, Royal Central School of Speech and Drama, October 2019).
Parslow, J. (2024). *Their Majesty*. Taylor & Francis.
RuPaul. (2024). *The House of Hidden Meanings*. HarperCollins.
Rupaul & Fonda, J. (2018). *GuRu: By Fixing Only One Piece of the Jigsaw Puzzle, You'll Miss Seeing the Whole Picture*. An Imprint Of William Morrow.
Senelick, L. (2000). *The Changing Room: Sex, Drag, and Theatre*. Routledge.
Sontag, S. (2018). *Notes on Camp*. Penguin Classics
Stanislavsk S.I. (1989). *An Actor Prepares*. Routledge.
Streisand, B. (2010). *My Passion for Design*. Penguin.
Streisand, B. (2023). *My Name is Barbra*. Penguin.
Tom, T., & Marquez, L. (2020). *Legendary Children: The First Decade of RuPaul's Drag Race and the Last Century of Queer Life*. Penguin Books.
Velour, S. (2023). *The Big Reveal*. HarperCollins.
Volcano, D.L., Halberstam, J., & Halberstam, J. (1999). *The Drag King Book*. Serpent's.
Von Glow, V. (2023). *Letter on Liberty: In Defence of Drag*. Academy of Ideas.
Wang, B. (24 August 2019). *Kings of Drag: A Detailed Look at London Drag Kings*. Bruce Wang; Illustrated edition.

Overview: Inspiration, Research and Further Reading

The big take away from this chapter will be to find inspiration everywhere. Don't limit yourself, or your creative process to only creating work which matches someone else's preconceived ideas of what drag would be.

- Watch: go and see live work, also research historic work. Regularly spend an afternoon on YouTube deep diving into old drag shows and see where it leads you. Watch films, camp classics, documentaries connected to drag and its history or development.
- Listen: to the news, to podcasts, the radio, audiobooks, iconic albums that you haven't previously spent time with.
- Read: anything and everything. if there's subject you are interested in, investigate, keep reading. If you liked one book, pick up the next by that author.
- Know what's out there: You may not like *Drag Race* but watch a few episodes. It's part of current drag culture and your work will be, consciously or unconsciously compared by some audiences.
- Bring yourself: Your references, your experience and your field of knowledge is what makes you unique. Bring that to your work and to the stage.
- You don't have to like everything, or agree with everything: watching, reading and learning about a subject does not mean you have to enjoy everything. But it puts you as a performer in an informed position to build an opinion and possibly develop work from

It's easy when talking about research to become quite bogged down in theory, but this is drag: you should have fun watching it! And that fun, dare I say passion, is what you should carry onto the stage. It's now time to start looking at your performance work. **Part II** gives an overview of specific stage craft that can be applied to almost all drag performance, before we move on to **Part III** looking in detail at a variety of go-to drag performance styles and skills. Get up! Let's find out what you can do on-stage, and how you can make it your best.

Notes

1. *Dragula* television series produced by Boulet Brothers Productions *Hey Qween Network (U.S.; S1)/Amazon Prime (U.S.; S2–3/U.K.)/Netflix (U.S.; S3)/Shudder (U.S.; S4–present)/OutTV (Canada)/SBS Viceland (Australia)*.
2. The New Zealand reality competition television series produced by Warner Bros – *TVNZ OnDemand/OutTV*.
3. The whole album from their Carnegie Hall concert is available on most streaming platforms.
4. *Split Britches (Peggy Shaw and Lois Weaver are "two of the foremost figures in queer performance art and lesbian identity")* have archived their work on their website. I don't wish to label them as drag but the art of drag is undeniably connected. I've suggested starting with their take on *A Street Car Named Desire* (also featuring my old mentor Bette Bourne) but you could easily spend days absorbing and exploring their back catalogue from the last 40 plus years. http://www.split-britches.com
5. Audio available on most streaming platforms.
6. Most performances of this piece are listed under their former performance name "Meth".
7. Me in interview with *Michael Twaits*, July 2024. See Part IV for full interview.
8. *An Audible Original podcast.*

Part II

Stage Craft for All Drag Acts

Lola Del Fuego photographed backstage at the Royal Vauxhall Tavern by Fox Al Rajim

8
Where Do You Start?: Basic Drag

Sometimes performers spend too much time on the big moments and forget to walk before they can run. All performers need the reminders: face forward, slow down, speak up! An audience won't care about a performance that they can't see or hear. Our first step into the craft of performance is basic drag!

You're feeling ready! You have done your prep and research. You've considered the variety of possibilities of what you are going to do on stage, and how you're going to make this journey a professional, long-lasting one! You are ready to create exciting, dramatic, dynamic work. This chapter is ten quick-fire tips to consider every time you walk onto a stage: sight lines, structures, pacing and placement. Whatever set are performing: work through these pointers to make sure you are remembering the basics and delivering your best.

Structurally these ten points could have been a *final thoughts* style chapter, a list to double check through before heading to the stage. However, each pointer is consistently referred to in subsequent chapters because they are so fundamental. It's the most basic craft of communication, being dynamic and taking an audience on an interesting journey. These will become second nature as you refine your craft and gain experience. Often, novice performers have incredible ideas but the stage craft of communicating with an audience has not yet been honed. Clear communication with the audience is essential. The more you practice, the more natural it will all become.

> It's like any other skill, you can't suddenly play a Beethoven sonata until you first learn to play *Twinkle Twinkle Little Star*. So practising the skills can get a simple thing to work, then you can start with the variations. With any skill, with any craft it's hands on learning by doing, but it's also seeing what other people have done. So, what are their skill sets, how did they do it? What are my skill sets. What am I up for doing, right now, today?
>
> Margaret Atwood – *Masterclass on Creative Writing* (Section 4)[1]

At times these may seem ridiculous in their simplicity, but mastering these exercises will help any performer feel more grounded, in control and in a position to communicate clearly with their audience. Initially you could work through these applying them to a simple song or lip-sync you know. However, they will still apply to any performance you create.

1) Can You Hear Me? See Me?

The golden rule of performance: face forward and speak up! In the back of your mind, at every point of a performance, think about sight-lines, volume and how you are directly communicating to the audience. When you are speaking, the audience need to hear every word: speak clearly, slow down and talk to them – not at them. (We'll get to in detail in *Chapter 11: Audience Experience*.)

Use the stage: the room will be designed for that to be the spot where everyone can see you. Don't make your life harder than it needs to be, if you are drifting around the room out of the light and half the room can't

DOI: 10.4324/9781003498797-10

see you they will lose the structure of your set, and possibly lose interest. *If you go off stage, find powerful spots in the room with the best sight-lines available.* Speak to the technical team in advance, ask where the good alternative spots are for you to perform around the room (Again we'll expand on this in *Chapter 12: Stages and Spaces*).

Elevate yourself over the audience; if they are sat down, stay standing. If they are standing – climb on some furniture! Make sure you are performing to the whole room. Even when having a more private moment with a smaller group try to be visible to the whole room and ensure the whole room can hear you.

2) Make an Entrance

Every performer has to get on stage, and it's the moment the audience will make most judgements and assumptions about what they are going to see. It's when you will establish your dynamic, your relationship to them and how you captivate them. That moment, however, is often thought about the least by performers. The energy and enthusiasm you walk on stage with send signals to the audience about who you are and what you are going to do. Be physically dynamic: walk (run, dance, hop) on with purpose! Those opening seconds can create interest and intrigue for the audience. They establish who you are, your status, and hold the focus of the entire room.

EXERCISE 1: GETTING ON STAGE

You Will Need: A space to rehearse. Ideally with a door.

A strong entrance sets up a strong set. Have a play with some of these ideas and see how much the impetus behind your entrance can change your act.

Imagine: It is the start of your set, a host has introduced you, all you need to do is walk through the door and get to the centre of the stage whilst the audience applaud. Find some space so you can get up and do a few different versions. It may help to visualise a specific venue. If you wish you can even give yourself some walk on music. Make the entrance your own.

Using the suggestions below, play with different energies and objectives as you walk on. Focus on the *intention* and see what your body naturally does. Allow yourself the freedom to play.

- *Surprised and delighted that the audience are there and clapping.*
- *You haven't got time for applause there's a show to do.*
- *"Well of course you're applauding look at me!"*
- *Milk it.*
- *Bored.*
- *"I'm late"*
- *Backwards: find a way and reason to walk on backwards.*
- *Head down, all business, you don't want them to see your eyes until the song/set begins.*
- *Hyped – this is the most exciting gig of your life.*
- *Chaos – crash on to the stage.*
- *As if you've been thrown onstage mid-conversation with someone backstage. Try to signal you'll finish the conversation later.*

- *The grand dame! Come past the mic stand, take a bow, take in the audience and then go to the mic stand.*
- *Punk – fuck it up a bit! Fall over.*
- *Royalty. Think Disney Princess.*
- *Panto Villain.*

What felt good? How did it affect the start of your set? Which suited your persona or character the most? Can you create your own list of ones to try? Find a couple of go-to energies to walk onto a stage with. This is not about adding a 'bit' to your set, it's literally just giving you a dynamic intention during those first few steps as the audience are looking at you.

The takeaway from this exercise should be that it's impossible to walk on-stage and do nothing. *Everything you do is a clue to the audience as to what's going to happen, who you are and where this might go.* Rather than letting the audience try to come to their own conclusion – decide what you are saying and make sure they get it!

Whatever entrance you are making: Give it an intention! Start your set strong.

> That journey on to the stage, before you even say *"hello"*, the audience has made myriad decisions; what the expectations are, what you'll sound like, what you look like, what you can do, what your personality is, what energy you're bringing to the room. So for me, it starts right from that first moment they see you, not the first moment you go, *"hello"*. All those first physical choices are really important.
>
> Ada Campe[2]

3) Take a Moment – Take a Breath

Usually, when a drag act walks on-stage there is a round of applause to welcome them, to thank them for the amazing look they have put together and show the appreciation for the craft. Enjoy that moment. Breathe. You have probably spent over an hour getting ready; carefully chosen costuming, make up and hair. Let the audience take it in; let them look at you, let them enjoy the craft of what you have created before you begin the set. Rushing out of the dressing room and doing an instant reveal before the audience have even had a chance to look at you defeats the point. Pace yourself.

Slow down. Breathe. Give the audience a moment to look at you, visually take in your drag, decode you and feel the anticipation of what they are about to experience. They are intrigued and want to see more! You've got them right where you want them to deliver a killer set.

4) Know Who You Are Performing To

The audience always come first; think of yourself as providing a service. These individuals have all left their house, parted with their time, and money, to see you. How are you fulfilling your part? You have rehearsed and planned a set. Have you thought about them when doing that?

A band wouldn't play a funeral march at a wedding. Drag acts need to be aware of the event they are performing at, and choose the most suitable content for their audience. If you know the venue, the producer, the show you are performing in then there are clues in advance as to who may be in the audience: Saturday night gays? Hen parties? Theatre crowds? Brunch girlies? People who want to dance along or an audience who want to sit and watch every detail of your polished work?

Thinking about this in advance will always help you to curate a set that best suits the moment. Ask yourself: *"is the set I've planned right for the audience I'm expecting?"* And if it isn't – how could you adapt it? This does not mean you can't challenge an audience with interesting ideas or go against their expectation, but you need to know you are doing that.

5) What Is Your Part in This Show?

Drag and cabaret shows have a shape and flow to them, audiences want variety. It's always worth asking: what is your act adding to this show? How has the set you've selected improved the night as a whole? Do you know who else is on the bill? Will you be the fourth lip-sync act they've seen? How are you standing out? On a variety night you may be the only drag act so know you need to bring the colour and drama. What's the reason you've been booked?

The audience have all decided to come and see this show, but not necessarily you. What are you adding to the mix to make this evening the best it can be? Is there any way you can ensure your set is *adding* to the show rather than repeating or reinforcing something they may have already seen? Not every show is perfectly curated with diversity so as a performer try to make sure you are still providing something that doesn't feel repetitive.

If possible; watch, or listen, to the rest of the show and let that inform your performance. Has a particular table already been picked on, then choose another. Did another comedian's jokes get too crass for the crowd? Or did their jokes tread similar ground to part of your set? How could you adapt? Could you tone yours down to hit the right level?

> **Watch the other acts, particularly the ones before you go on. They will give you a feeling of what the audience is like and what to do!**
>
> Ada Camp[3]

6) Never Assume

Your relationship to an audience is important, it's very easy to accidentally patronise, alienate or misread them. Never assume that everyone in the room has the same lived experience or knowledge that you have. It's very easy to perform a song that you love and assume everyone will join in with, only to realise whilst performing – no one else knows it! The same is true with humour.

Lip-sync edits is an area where this can happen a lot. A pop-cultural moment, or current meme, being cut into an edit that you find hilarious won't resinate with everyone in the same way. Is it hilarious to everyone if they don't get the reference? They may end up feeling they are missing out on a joke.

Reference points to a crowd of 20-year-olds will be different to a crowd of 30-year-olds, or 40s, or 50s, etc. Not everyone needs to get everything, but you want to bring everyone along on the journey, so try to make work accessible and work on some level whether or not the audience get the reference point.

Take a moment to look over your set. Have you made any assumptions? Does the song work if they don't know it? Are there ways you can make the work more accessible, more relevant to those that may not get the references?

There are many ways around this:

- Do some research, ask some friends, ask on social media etc. – "*do you get this*".
- If you're an act who talks then you can reference the point upfront. Set it up for the audience so they come along on the journey.
- Make sure the piece still works if someone does not know the original reference.

> I have an act which is a Juke Box Musical parody; it includes four popular songs turned into a musical theatre quartet, a ballad. One of the songs is Nicki Minaj's *Super Bass* which I know, if I'm working a musical theatre audience, some people may not know very well. In the introduction I drop a few hints that I'm including Nicki Minaj as a way of letting a few more people in. If they still don't know the song I set up she's a rapper and they will find it funny when I sing *Super Bass* as if it's a musical theatre ballad.
>
> Conversely, if I'm performing to a pop crowd who may get the pop references but not understand necessarily what a quartet is – then I'll explain that as part of my set up. It is about framing the work so everyone understands what I'm up to. If an audience doesn't know *Super Bass* or what a quartet is my, introduction lets them come along on the journey and still enjoy the piece.

7) Peaks and Troughs

A song has to have more than one note. An interior designer will use a variety of colours and texture. And drag acts, when structuring a set, need to consider *peaks and troughs*. Different acts will use various terminology but finding ways of creating texture, variety and depth within your work is essential for keeping an audience engaged and entertained.

This can be done through structuring a set. (For example; performing one up beat number and then one ballad.) But also moment to moment performers should always be looking for ways to add variety and interest. Visualise a sound wave, and play with the ups and downs, the contrast, in any of the following fields:

- *Pacing*
- *Volume*
- *Tone*
- *Physicality*
- *Emotion*
- *Performance zones (see point 8)*
- *Staging/positioning/proxemics*

This isn't a challenge; you don't have to hit top speed when delivering one line and then slow motion the next. Performers have a natural cadence, or pattern, to the way they perform, as you become aware of yours look at ways of adding variety. A change of pace can wake the audience up, a change of tone may draw an audience in. Consider them as sliding scales and find little ways to keep adjusting, playing to create a set with rich and interesting contrasts.

You can play with *peaks and troughs* in all forms of performance – song (suddenly speaking or shouting a line might be a dynamic change), lip-sync (cutting the track and having a moment of silence, or breath, slow movements, fast movements), in comedy doing a long story followed by a run of one-liners. The ways of creating a dynamic set are endless but the key is to create interest and avoid anything close to monotony.

8) Performance Zones

An audience is a collection of individuals, not one mass. As a performer you are trying to communicate to them all whilst simultaneously building separate relationships and making them all feel included. It's a complicated dynamic; focus too much on one group and you can lose the rest of the room. But talk generally at the whole room for too long and a set can begin to feel too theatrical as if you are performing *at* the audience, rather than *to* them.

A shorthand I use is *performance zones*: a way of creating a dynamic environment where the audience feel you are speaking to all of them collectively, and to them as individuals, including them in the progression of your set. Zones help you perform to the entire room but also find *peaks and troughs* within your performance.

Comic asides, or little moments where you engage with a specific person, rather than the whole room are the magic that help the audience to feel they are part of the evening. They are involved in a unique *live* experience, rather than passive spectators with no agency in the show.

There are three Zones performers can play in.

Zone 1 – The General

Talking to the room as a whole. It is commanding and the *performance zone* the majority of a drag act is performed in.

Zone 2 – The Specific

Talking to a specific member, or section, of the audience or a performer on-stage with you. A conversation on-stage between a performer and a member of the audience is not a private conversation. The whole room needs to hear and they are all reminded they are individuals in a live space with you. To use the theatrical term you are breaking the fourth wall and reminding the audience they're present in a shared space with you. When you talk directly to individuals or group, you remind them they are present and a key part of the show - not a passive observer.

Zone 3 – The Faux Private

There are no private moments on-stage; everything said or done is for the audience to see and enjoy. These are moments which are not directed to the audience; seemingly private moments that can add colour to your set (A note to yourself, an aside to a co-performer, the technician, the host, etc.) This is a Zone that should only be entered into knowingly and confidently. It is not a zone be in for to long, but to drop into and then bounce back out of to create texture, sometimes to comic effect with the juxtaposition.

> I take a lot of song requests in my shows: I often pretend to the audience I've never heard of a very famous artist and play quickly within all three zones performance zones. In just a couple of lines I can talk to the individual, the whole room and a colleague to create a comic effect. A specific audience member (Zone 2) requests Lady Gaga and I might *"Yes! I love her"*, I then say to the room (Zone 1) *"Gaga? Who? Never heard of her!"* And then look at my pianist (entering Zone 3) *"Do Poker*

> *Face"* and then jump back into a Zone 1 to start the song. I know the room can hear everything I'm saying but play with the dramatic irony that they can't.
>
> It's all about playing with different zones of the room to keep an audience engaged and on their toes. I don't need to tell my pianist to play *Poker Face,* she knows, but the journey the audience go on from a couple of simple lines adds energy and texture to the set.

Performance zones are not just for speaking. You can sing, or lip-sync, in each zone to create different relationships to the audience. The majority of the time drag acts are in Zone 1: dipping into Zone 2 sometimes and using Zone 3 as a bit of a wild card.

9) Anchors

Eye-contact is key to connecting and performing to an audience but if there are 100 people within a bar – where should you look? You may have a spotlight shining in your face so half the room is in silhouette and you may only see the front row. Placing *anchors,* visual hooks around the room that you can focus on, will help you connect specifically to a variety of areas in the room. *Anchors* are simply visual points you can fix your eyes to and talk to *as if* you are making eye contact with someone. In most venues Fire Exit signs will be positioned as good *anchors* at the back of the room, or perhaps a light in the tech box. It needs to be something you can actually see and talk to as if a specific audience member. It sounds ridiculous but it works!

Vary where *anchors* are around the room to keep the audience feeling engaged and included, not always speaking to the same person. A couple of *anchors* at the back of the room are essential. It is a strange audience rule; if you perform over their heads to reach the back of the room, the front of the room still feel included. It is as if you are scooping the focus from the back of the room and pulling it back to you on-stage, including each member of the audience on the way. However, if you put your *anchor* constantly at the front of the room it can build a wall stopping your energy going any farther back and cutting off the rest of the room. Always place *anchors* at the back of the room to help keep including the whole room in your set.

Place a range of *anchors* around the room, switch between them frequently to help make the audience feel you are talking to them all. Pretending that each *anchor* is someone who's loving the show, laughing at your jokes gives a performer somewhere to send their energy. Mentally cast them as some fabulous friends that are responding well to your set. This sounds like an elaborate illusion but it's a very simple trick to help the entire audience feel included. If you only perform to the people who you can make eye contact with, the rest of the audience will feel cut off: they will lose interest, they may start talking or even leave. No matter how big, or small, a crowd is, use anchors to help make it feel you are including everyone.

> As the host of *Pride In London* at Trafalgar Square I would place *anchors* around the square. I would look up at one of the windows of the National Portrait Gallery over the heads of 15,000 and imagine I was sharing a little joke with one individual back there. I placed another at the Canadian Embassy (stage left) and another at St Martins (stage right) and then used actual audience members or groups that I could see. It helped me speak to everyone gathered to watch and keep it varied and engaged with them. This technique pulls the whole audience in and can be applied to any space.

10) Ooze Confidence

Whatever happens on-stage. You meant it to happen! Relax into the moment and, as the kids say, *"sell the garment"*. The audience always want to feel that you are in complete control, even amongst the chaos. Look confident: eyes up, big smile, secure on your feet. If you can sell it with your eyes and face then people don't notice as much when you miss a step or forget a word. And when things do go wrong, shake it off, *act* as if that is exactly how you meant it to happen.

Hold yourself in a confident manner. Chest up, shoulders back. You own the room. Everyone is here to see you. Take a breath, calm your heart. And perform to the whole room. It's also worth remembering: confidence is incredibly sexy.

Bonus Point: Are You Having Fun Yet?

Whatever set you are performing. Hunt through the piece to make sure there is a some fun, humour, joy or mischief in there. Drag is a competitive industry and you have to love doing it. Make sure whatever you are doing sparks joy for you and the audience! It doesn't matter how serious the theme of a piece is, the audience want to see a moment of queer joy. A twinkle in the eye.

> Drag isn't about excellence, it's about having a good time.
> Vanity Von Glow *Letter on Liberty: In Defence of Drag*[4]

Overview: Basic Drag

After passing your driving test you no longer reminde yourself to "*mirror, signal, manoeuvre*": it becomes second nature. That is how you will feel about these basic tips. Initially every time a piece, or set, is stage ready – get the handbook out and work through the list. Check you've chosen the right material for the booking and you know how to deliver you best. Eventually it will become superfluous, but for now make sure you are setting yourself up for success by ensuring you have considered each point:

- Be seen and be heard: at all times.
- Make an entrance, everything you are doing is seen so make a choice from the outset.
- Breathe. Let the audience see you, before you jump into your set.
- Know your audience. Do a little research and let that reflect the choices you make in your set.
- Know how you fit into the show you are part of. What are you adding?
- Make your work accessible by not assuming everyone has the same reference points as you.
- Create a set with texture and variety with interesting *peaks and troughs*.
- Use *performance zones* to connect with the audience in dynamic, varied ways that make them feel included.
- Use *anchors* to talk directly to the whole room, keep audiences included and engaged, even when you can't see them.
- Be confident! Have fun!

These pointers will help you instantly build a dynamic relationship with an audience, a connection to the whole room and the live experience. They can also all be applied to those vital, first few seconds you are on-stage: giving an audience a quick overview of who you are as a performer. So, when you walk on stage, who are you going to be? And how are you going to let the audience know?

Notes

1. *Margaret Atwood* during section four of her Masterclass: Teaching Creative Writing. www.masterclass.com
2. *Ada Campe* in interview with *Michael Twaits*, July 2024. See Part IV for full interview.
3. *Ada Campe* in interview with *Michael Twaits*, July 2024. See Part IV for full interview.
4. Von Glow, Vanity – *Letter on Liberty: In Defence of Drag* – Academy Of Ideas 2023

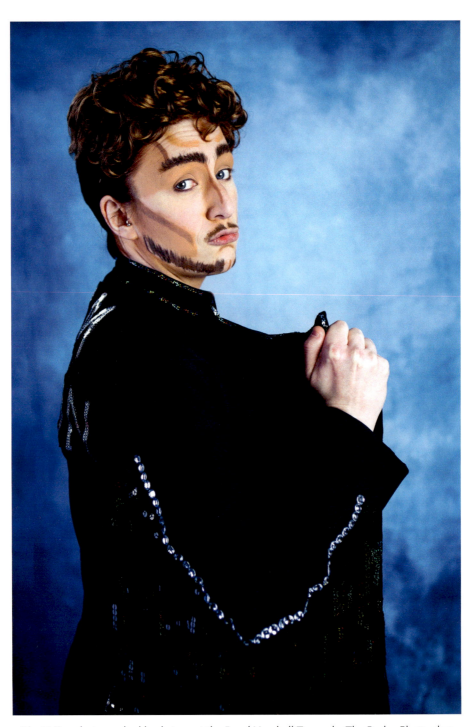

Tim Tation photographed backstage at the Royal Vauxhall Tavern by The Burley Photgraher

9
It Had to Be You: Alter-Ego

It's arguably the biggest question a performer can ask themselves – *"who am I?"* On-stage drag acts can be presenting as themself, a heightened version of themself or a character far removed from themself. This decision will affect almost every element of the craft and how they interact with an audience. It's time to think about on-stage identity!

Your alter-ego is simply the person you present as on-stage. Every performer has a different approach, or journey, to structuring and finding their alter-ego (look at the interviews in *Part IV*). Many use different language to describe it, for clarity these are definitions for the terms as I am using them:

Alter-ego: The umbrella term for who you present as on-stage.

Self: The person you are in your day to day life, off-stage. Also the physical body you are in.

Persona: A heightened version of yourself, edited to be more dynamic, theatrical or engaging but rooted in your history and truth.

Character: Adopting an identity completely outside the self, who may have completely different views and lived experiences to the performer.

> My alter-ego is a persona, a heightened or edited version of myself. I put on my costume and walk on-stage without overly changing the way I move, speak or interact with people. I am a more dynamic and performative version of myself but I am not creating an illusion that I am a completely different person.
>
> I have colleagues who completely re-tool their voice, physicality and way of being for their character, whom they use to explore and make commentary on the world. And I have many colleagues who straddle the grey areas in-between.

One thing is for certain: how you act, interact and present yourself to an audience frames everything you do on-stage. You won't read this chapter, complete a couple of exercises and know *exactly* who you are going to be on-stage. This chapter is planting seeds of thought that will grow and evolve, probably throughout your entire drag journey. The best way to water those seeds is through thought, rehearsal and stage time; you need to get up, explore and play!

Alter-Ego vs. the Self

Many believe *the self* is an onstage option; I argue as soon a performer is on-stage they are editing in one-way or another and therefore they are always presenting an *alter-ego*. You are physically on the stage, so *the self* is

DOI: 10.4324/9781003498797-11

ever present but you are performing as an *alter-ego*. This gives you the freedom to go further, be louder, push boundaries like never before – because it is never fully, authentically you, it's your *alter-ego*. The question is: how much of your ego is altered? A *persona* which is just a small side step from reality or a *character* where you are jumping into a new reality, or sliding on the scale between?

As the self is inescapable for performers, being aware of your physical self: how you look, your proportions, your size is a tricky but essential part of the drag process. Whenever possible try to develop an alter-ego who works with what you are working with. If you're tall – why not celebrate the height, rather than apologising for it and trying to be petite. If you are able to celebrate yourself on-stage through drag (especially celebrating things that historically weren't celebrated about you) there is a huge amount of joy to be found in that. It may be that as a performer you are using drag to release yourself, your truth, in a way you feel you haven't been able to before. Great! But it is still an *alter-ego* on-stage as you are editing and making choices as to which elements to reveal.

> She is parts of me, but also parts of the characters and women that I've either known in my life.
>
> Me The Drag Queen, discussing self and character[1]

Persona

The simplest place to start creating an alter-ego from is the truth – slightly adjusting yourself to be stage ready. With a persona you are using yourself, your lived experiences, as the backbone. You may not show the audience everything about yourself, not everything said is an *absolute* truth – but your personal lived experience is the rudder that guides you. Off-stage everyone has moments where they are dynamic and loud, they also have moments where they are quiet and shy. The persona is generally the entertaining, heightened version of you. The inner dinner party host.

> He's the louder, floppier, flashier, more feathery version of myself!
>
> Hugo Grrrl[2]

For drag performers, a persona may have a different name, look, energy but usually they are aware they are a drag act, they are a performer and they don't exist in the same way off-stage. Adopting a persona helps to make you more charismatic, dynamic, confident and a stage performer needs to be all of those things. You can be the version of you that you want to be. A quick way to think dynamic is to avoid neutrality at all costs; make a choice – indifference is not an exciting platform to work from. We'll dig into this more in *Chapter 10: Making Choices and Finding Your Voice*.

Autobiocrapical

I use this term to give performers the freedom to make their persona as dynamic and interesting as possible. Facts and stories are rooted in truth, but you have license to step outside of reality and chronology. Perhaps two slightly interesting things happened to you, and when placed together they become one stage-ready anecdote. You might add a slight character to people within your existing world: make your mother more disapproving, your husband more useless, your best friend more of a bitch. You might also drop some of the smaller detail from a story to get to the meat, the bit of a story or set up that audience will latch onto.

> My persona is very close to my truth, however, if I weren't in drag I would not say or do a lot of the things that I do on-stage. In drag, I have stronger opinions, more confidence and very rarely remain neutral. I use the base facts of my reality as a launch pad but have a license to bend the truth. I come from a small village near Bognor Regis on the South Coast of England, but the audience don't need the details of "a small village just outside Bognor Regis". Does the specific detail

> add anything? Bognor Regis is the joke, so I use that. The town is synonymous with Butlins, retro-seaside holidays, and sets the scene for comedy. More details, the truth, would lose the impact.

Contradiction

Having a persona gives you a license, not everything always needs to add up or match perfectly. Drag acts are: story tellers, comedians, wearing fabulous costumes – the audience are aware that some of what is said should be taken with a pinch of salt. To represent, or say something on-stage, is not always to condone or agree with it. There's room to play devil's advocate.

> My persona is quite flirty with the audience but I also discuss the fact I'm monogamous, married and have a child. I can switch between both modes depending on what I feel the moment needs – whether it's for a gag interacting with an audience member, or a sincere lead in to a specific song. One night I might be very flirty (dare I say 'thirsty') but then undercut the previous humour by discussing my loving husband. Both moments work independently but the audience laugh at the anachronism of me playing both sides. It's drag – they know not to take it too seriously, that's part of the fun.

Physicality and Voice

As a persona is based on you, there is no pre-requisite that the physicality and voice have to change. However, you may add an extra flourish, a deeper vocal tone, whatever you want that makes the version of yourself you are presenting on-stage someone who commands the room. A drag performer is rarely low status. Don't fall into the trap that the persona needs to be so authentic that you can't have some fun, release inhibitions and take things slightly away from reality! The exercises that follow in this chapter can be used to help you shape your persona, open up options of physicality and voice for your persona. And it's important to remember how much drag can automatically alter your movements – a corset, binding, heels, wigs, padding, etc. It can all hugely change our physicality, and have knock-on effect to our voice. However, before shaping your persona we should spend some time looking at the other end of the alter-ego spectrum – a character!

Character

Character is a way to explore the world on-stage through someone else's lived experience. It may be someone of a different age, political belief, outlook or ideology. They may be factual, fictional or fantastical. It may be reimagining someone you know as a parody or impersonation. But as the performer you are *acting* as if you are this person, completely removed from yourself. Where a persona has your biography, attitudes and lived experience as a backbone, a character has their own curated history, biography and world they come from.

Biography

To successfully perform as character you need to build their world and history to create depth, and to allow you as a performer the knowledge of how to perform them. Some character performers can tell you what their character has been up to since they were last on-stage. The character fully exists in the world when not on-stage and that can provide inspiration for what they might discuss on-stage.

A biography for a character can include: family background, age, work experience, relationship history, education, places they've eaten, travelled to, films they've seen, life experiences, defining moments and much more. All the facts from their biography shape who this person is. Creating a character biography is a way of fleshing out the character so the person you inhabit on-stage is fully rounded. This is not to say you need to tell the audience all of the detail every time you are on-stage! It is there for you, to inform you and give support to all the choices you make.

Impersonators have a short hand for this in that they can take the existing biography of the character, or icon, and then take what is useful and ignore the rest depending on how earnest their impression is supposed to be – more on this in *Chapter 20: Impersonation: Tribute and Parody*.

Development and Play

The biography is the backbone that shapes how a character became who they are, their experiences will give them a range of attitudes, beliefs and ideals. Knowing what your character thinks about any given issue is essential for understanding who they are and allows you to play in the live moment. Often in a character's development one choice you make can have a knock-on effect for other choices, and the character takes a life of its own which simply makes sense – don't be afraid to run with that instinct, let the character evolve in the way that they wish to. If it goes far in one direction, you can always adapt again and move in another direction the next time.

> I found that there was a beast in me that had been waiting to come out!
>
> Ada Campe[3]

Consistency

Consistency of character is important within a show: between shows, and over time, a character can evolve. If you want the audience to buy into that world it needs to be authentic in the moment. Consistency is key in the logic of what you are saying within one show, but over time allow yourself the freedom to keep playing – let go of what is no longer serving you as a performer. Maybe having a wife was funny for one set but now you wish to explore them being a spinster. As a performer you are creating the world of the character, keep evolving that world to create the best place for you to perform from, if something isn't working, move on. In the same way as a singer may not repeat a song as it didn't work in performance, a character trait can be adapted or cut.

> If you watch the first few episodes of *Will & Grace*[4] you can see the character of Karen Walker evolving on-screen. A few laughs come from the funny voice in the first episode, so the second they crank it up, then it simply becomes her permanent voice. There's a natural progression as the actress, the writers and the audience get to know the character.

Physicality and Voice

The physical and vocal choices a performer makes in creating a character can often tell you more about who a character is than the actual script. The pronunciation of a word can tell an audience all they need to know about someone's status, or deluded view of their own status, for example. A character movement can betray everything that the script is saying to undercut the character and let the audience laugh *at* the character, whilst laughing *with* the performer. Exploration of both is essential in the evolution of your character.

Which Is Best?

There is no set answer to which is best; it's horses for courses. I think having an open approach and letting your alter-ego evolve is the best. Initially reviewing how each performance has gone, did the alter-ego work, did you feel held back or liberated by the choices you've made. Putting on drag often helps some acts feel they are more of a character as generally the drag they wear is far removed from their off-stage aesthetic. However, other performers use drag to explore their gender, their personal politics or queerness and, despite not looking like their off-stage self, are very much presenting a persona that's near to their truth.

> I don't see my drag as female impersonation. Even though I adopt a lot of those things, I wear breasts, I pad, but my intention is never to impersonate a woman. Why can't a man paint with all these colors and use these things.
> Me The Drag Queen[5]

Having a fairly neutral and flexible persona allows you to jump around styles, forms and themes in a much simpler way than a character might. Often character acts near the beginning of their career hold on too tightly to their character's world so that they can't always take all the work they wish to. If you've decided to be *Tilly The Transphobic Teacher from Tottenham* and a booking comes in to host an awards show it might be quite hard to make that jump. But if *Tilly* who is perhaps just a little bit matronly, slightly above her station, and has opinions on everyone could have a riot hosting an awards show. Sometimes a very specific direction for a character is just a jumping off point, a place to play, to and create the backbone and then it's about evolution slowly chipping away what doesn't serve you and heightening what is working well.

Duality

A character can be driving the narrative of a set, giving a premise, a set-up, a reason the audience are watching. But the performer can still be present, almost laughing with the audience about how ridiculous the character they have created is. It's a *nudge, nudge, wink, wink* approach to character that lets the audience know, you know, how silly this all is. Almost reassuring the audience that we are all in on the joke, it's fun, it's drag – *"Don't take it too seriously, we know this person isn't real!"*

> Tracey Collins[6] is a cabaret character comedian who performs as Elvis Lesley, Audrey Heartburn, Shell Suit Cher, among many others. The characters are parodies; they all create moments of live chaos and are heavily improvised, interactive sets. Despite playing the characters throughout Tracy (herself) is also present. Metaphorically lifting up a wig and winking at the audience, even at times laughing herself, at the silliness of her characters and her audience. This gives license to the audience to relax, they realise this is in no way a serious moment. As a result they embrace the chaos and end up playing with Tracy in character because they understand the game and feel they've been invited in on the joke with her. It's magic to watch and creates an atmosphere of communal joy.

Playing Is Practice

You will learn so much about yourself through performance and also from mistakes you make. If you decide your persona or character is becoming a bit too bitchy, or a bit too serious, that's fine adjust those dials before you get on-stage next time. If a particular moment got a strong laugh – how can you bring more of that out? In the early days of rehearsal and performance – record whenever possible so you have a document of the gig that you can debrief and analyse later. Don't let the details you put in place become blocks for development of the alter-ego. Use what is of use and let go of what you don't need. After a gig return to your *Repertoire List* (see *Chapter 6: Building a Set, Range and Repertoire*) and update which character moments are working (add to *Performance Ready Repertoire*), which need work or fine-tuning (*Rehearsal Repertoire*) and perhaps any new ideas you had (*In Developement*) from just playing as your character in the live space. Performers learn from performing, but the challenge is to remember the lessons learnt and apply them to all future work!

Fake It 'til You Make It

For most performers the portrayal of their alter-ego is a constant evolution. Every gig is another small learning curve. Acknowledge that in the freedom of the performing you may take it too far or not far enough. It may sound like a cop-out but until you are certain who you are and what you are doing: fake it. Go on stage and show the audience you are confident in who you are, even when you are not! Smile through it. Be big, be bold and be confident.

It's Time to Play

The ideas discussed so far can seem quite daunting, it may feel like semantics as to where a persona ends and a character begins. But exploring, playing around and trying ideas out – and then possibly starting all over again–will provide you with a range of options. If you have an idea of who you wish to present on-stage hopefully these pages have given some clarity and opened up some areas to investigate further.

Working through the rest of this chapter it's time to get specific, get exploring and get up on your feet! Have some fun playing with where you could take your alter-ego. But also thinking about how your alter-ego can best serve you as a performer – what do you want to get out of being a drag performer? Because the alter-ego you adopt will have a huge impact on that. You may not have a clue yet, and that's fine. If you have an established alter-ego consider this an opportunity for a tune up. Don't expect instant answers. See where the journey takes you! Practice breeds prosperity.

> I really hated people saying: just be yourself. It is what you need to do within your character. But it takes a hell of a lot of work to get to the point.
>
> Adam All[7]

EXERCISE 1: ASK YOURSELF WHY?

You will need: Your notebook and pen.

Knowing why you are doing drag, what you want to get out of it, will give guidance to what type of alter-ego would serve you best and help you achieve. Where might you be able improve and take performance to the next level? Logic dictates you should create a character or persona that can do the type of work, portray the message and shape the career that you want to have. So let's return to that question: *Why?*

This a five-minute free writing exercise to try and answer the question – *Why am I doing this?*

Commit pen to paper and try to use the full time. You might write about *why* you love drag, *what* you can bring to drag, *who* inspired you, *what* you wish to achieve or even *where* do you see drag taking you? (If you've been working chronologically through the book refer back to your notes from *Exercise 1* in *Chapter 5: Measuring Success*)

It may be a stream of consciousness, a free writing essay, an unusual brainstorm or even just scattered notes. All are good options!

Once done, apply a little self analysis: re-read what you wrote, any ideas or concepts that you like highlight them or create a little list. In amongst the initial scribbles you might stumble across a nugget of gold which could become your drag raison d'être.

EXERCISE 2: DRAG MANIFESTO

You will need: Your notebook and pen and the notes from *Exercise 1*.

You are going to create your own drag manifesto! Having a manifesto will help guide you as to how you wish, or need, to perform on-stage. How best you can shape your alter-ego to create the work you wish to create. It sounds very grand to have a manifesto; performers don't often refer to it as a manifesto but most do have a framework of ideas that shape their ethos for being on-stage and creating work. It's a wish list. A guide so you know you are being true to yourself.

Structuring each point as an *"I want..."* helps make the manifesto aspirational and personal. Rather than a list of rules or restrictions to hold others, or yourself to. This isn't about how you want to measure success and set goals (see *Chapter 4: Measuring Success*) this is an artistic manifesto, reflecting the type of act you wish to be and the experience you might have with an audience. You may be able to clarify:

- *What is your unique selling point?*
- *Why do people come to see you as opposed to any other drag act?*
- *What do you want to offer an audience?*
- *Why drag and not stand-up, or singing or acting?*
- *What sort of performance do you want to create?*
- *What sort of audience experience? Immersive, theatrical, interactive, etc.*
- *What sort of atmosphere?*

A manifesto might only have five strong bullet points. More experienced, or aspirational, act perhaps ten. But as you grow as a performer you will find more and more points you can add to shape your approach.

> My manifesto is ever growing. I have been working a long time and it has evolved. But it helps me know what type of work I want to create, what type of bookings and offers I want to accept and find a way to be authentic to myself on-stage through my persona.
>
> - *I want to have fun!*
> - *I want my shows to be entertaining and engaging.*
> - *I want the stage to be my home and the audience my guests.*
> - *I want to create work that provokes not pacifies (but without always preaching).*
> - *I want my drag to be live, present in the moment.*
> - *I want audiences to watch my performance throughout, be fully attentive, rather than viewing me as background entertainment.*
> - *I want to make choices and have a point of view!*
> - *I want the audience to join me on the adventure.*
>
> None of these are ground breaking statements but a rudder that can give me clarity to know what I want to be doing and achieving, and also what type of alter-ego might best serve the

> manifesto. Even when outside of my comfort zone, performing in an unusual environment, I can still be true to myself by hanging onto my manifesto. Of course there are times where I have to let go of a few to the points and take the money, that's the business of drag, but I will always come back to these core beliefs. And whenever possible lean into them.
>
> There's a lot to unpick in my manifesto, but most of this is dealt with throughout the handbook. And I hope your manifesto will similarly be supported by the handbook.

But How?

Both our manifestos, as you and I both have one now, will probably have you asking – HOW?

Worry not. That is what the rest of this chapter, and indeed the handbook, is for. Creating your unique approach to: alter-ego, structuring a set, choosing a song, creating a backing track, engaging with an audience, etc.! Your manifesto will be reinforced through the choices you make moving forward; keep it to hand!. First, let's play and make some initial decision and give shape to your alter-ego. Some upcoming exercises are to encourage you to take things too far, it's much easier to go too far and come back – so don't be shy and remember, you are *testing* things out: if it doesn't fit or feel right, try something else, edit, adapt!

So Who Am I?

It's time to play and explore, have some fun and start creating your alter-ego. You may not know whether you'll be closer to a persona or character and that's fine, but using your manifesto for guidance, it's time to start exploring as hopefully you know what you want to achieve with them on-stage.

> She expresses the hopes, desires, dreams, challenges, fears, challenges of the human emotion, and human desires, and human aspiration that's contained within the queerness.
>
> Son Of A Tutu[8]

What's in a Name?

Audiences make judgements before they have even seen you walk on-stage, a host introduces you and already assumptions are made as to what type of act you will be. Drag has a long history of *punny* names, play on words. British drag especially has a strong connection to the tongue being firmly in cheek with a drag name. American acts often have an element of glamour to them. And drag families often use their name to demonstrate legacy. Is there an obvious direction you'll take your name?

> **EXERCISE 3: THE NAME GAME**
>
> **You will need: Your notebook and pen.**
>
> Find a fresh page in your notebook and jot down all the ideas that have come to mind for a possible drag name. Play with puns, with glamour, legacy if you like. Aim for a range of ideas and this is simply a place to keep a note of them. No decision needs to be made at this point, you can keep coming back and adding names to the list, and possibly removing names too.

Alter-Ego

This exercise is coming too early in the order, it makes much more sense to start creating a character, or persona, and then seeing what sort of name would fit them. However, I know novice drag acts and they always have at least an inkling of a drag name that they wish to use for one reason or another. And if you have the name in place it can be a great springboard for seeing where the alter-ego should go.

What do you want your name to say about you? I would explore a few names whilst your drag is being developed and rehearsed, see which fits. Sometimes it may sound great on paper but doesn't quite fit how you evolve moving forward.

> Often audiences have asked me to explain my name. Is it a pun they don't get? No, it's just my given name: Michael Twaits. Not having a drag name fitted well with my brand of being 'a man in a dress' and not necessarily someone aiming to create a full character or gender illusion. I always wanted the audience to know what, or who, they were watching.

I would advise against using anything which is slightly 'of the moment' or a joke you may not remember the reference to in a few years time. That said Jodie Harsh is a super-star drag act and in many ways more successful than her UK celebrity namesake Jodie Marsh, who was famous in the early 2000s but now not so much.

EXERCISE 4: CHARACTER BIOGRAPHY

You will need: Your notebook and pen.

The next step to creating your alter-ego is to know a bit about them. Building their biography is the backbone to who they are on-stage. There may be areas here you leave blank, there are no wrong answers, you may have multiple answers and wish to play around. That's great. The more you can put down on paper the more you have to explore and play with onstage. If you are planning on playing with persona are there any areas of your life you don't wish to bring on-stage? Or perhaps you wish to adapt or edit?

Name:

Age:

Gender:

Occupation:

Class/Status:

Family Information:

Education:

Aspirations:

Likes:

Dislikes:

Once you have established the basics above you can go off any level of details and maybe even a few tangents. I also think it's useful, if you know to answer the following.

- *Do they believe, or know they are a drag act?*
- *What type of performing do they do?*

- *Why are they on stage?*
- *Who are they to the audience?*

> My alter-ego uses my personal history as the backbone; I walk on stage knowing I am a drag act, that's my occupation but also my reason for being on stage, I am here to entertain, educate and inform. The audience are here as my guests and I'm going to make sure they have fun.
>
> I choose to keep a few personal details private: my son and my husband for example don't have their names revealed. I can pick and choose what to share as my persona and what I wish to remain private. This privacy is for their sake but also the anonymity means I can use them as theatrical versions of themselves if there's a joke or story where I need them to react in a specific way. It puts them slightly more into the world of fiction.

How Do I Show the Audience Who I Am?

Everything you say or do on stage tells an audience something about who you are. Our character is revealed through our actions, in life and on stage. The first thing to do is to get up on your feet and just try to *be* your alter-ego. The following exercise contains just some broad-strokes that can help. Experiment with who they are and let their biography, and attitudes, inform the way they speak and move.

For a persona, you do not *need* to change anything but some physical touchstones can help you feel stage ready (often, putting on the drag does enough). For a character, you could take them anywhere but usually from the biography you can find clues; from their age, history, or assumptions one makes about them due to their job or nature. For example: a young aerobics instructor would have a very different assumed physicality than an aging undertaker. However, there could be comedy in playing either against the obvious assumptions.

It's time to get up and play. For many it will be too soon to be fixing decisions: have a play now and then come back as your ideas being to solidify and you are becoming more aware of what you wish to bring to the stage. Don't get too fixated on a finished product but hopefully you'll find a starting point from which you can move forward.

> **EXERCISES 5: PHYSICALITY**
>
> **You will need: A pack of playing cards and some space.**
>
> Shuffle the playing cards. For each of the following options – Ace (or one) is the left-hand option and King is the right. The other cards are all at the sliding scale between the two. Take the top card and make an entrance onto a stage, walk up to the central stage spot ready to start a set but letting the card tell you how to move. Take as long as you need and feel free to embellish in any way you wish, to justify the way you are moving. Interact with the audience, ignore them. Does a specific emotion come out when you are moving in that way? This is an exploration exercise, not an exact science, don't take it too seriously.
>
> ### *Slow/Fast*
>
> How slowly can you physically move? How fast? How might this affect the audience.

Open/Closed

Body language is very telling. Open people (Aces) could be approachable, warm, kind. Closed people (Kings) are often perceived as anxious or insecure. The arms are an easy place to demonstrate being open or closed, but explore about others: the space between your legs, or your chin and neck, etc.

Light/Heavy

One could assume that a cis-man performing as a drag queen will lighten their moves and a cis-woman becoming a king may become heavier. But the obvious/assumed options are not always the interesting ones. Play around. Aces are light, Kings are heavy.

Direct/Indirect

Do you take the quickest path or the most interesting? A straight line or a wiggly one?

If this exercise is useful try creating new sliding scales: Status, Energy, Focus, etc. You might also like to investigate Laban Efforts as an exploration of physical movement through space. *Laban's Efforts in Action: A Movement Handbook for Actors* by Vanessa Ewan and Kate Sagovsky[9] is a useful resource for practical exploration and a great starting point.

COMBINATIONS

All of these sliding scales can be played with simultaneously to create your physicality. Visualise the dials on a sound technician's board trying to get the perfect sound mix. They can all go up and down by varying degrees to create that balance. And over time you will learn to adjust the dials in the live moment to create the perfect alter-ego for the space, audience or show you are doing. But for now, you do need to keep playing, experiment and review with each performance! Be brave!

> My alter-ego almost skips onto a stage, much lighter, much more open and indirect than I move normally. In life I am quite physically closed, but in drag I am all arms and legs. There are moments of restraint, pauses, slowness but overall the big adjustments I make are; opening up, lightening my weight and being a little more indirect.
>
> If I'm hosting a formal occasion I could adapt a little and bring the dials down a touch to be more sophisticated. If it's an upbeat brunch or club gig I can take the dials up to match the atmosphere. Not change who I am, but adapt to the environment I'm working in.

EXERCISE 6: SIGNATURE POSES

You will need: A little space, some performance shoes and a mirror.

On-stage you are not always in motion so finding a few static ways to stand still on-stage is gold for creating a sustained alter-ego and sustaining stage energy. Where do you place your hands? How are your feet positioned? Where's your weight? And what is this telling an audience?

Have a play around at different ways of standing still and simply look at yourself in a mirror. It can be very useful to do this exercise in full drag – so perhaps if the opportunity arises at a gig, get ready early and have a play around.

See if you can find two or three 'go-to' ways of standing still whilst staying present, alive and in the room.

> I've spent a lot of time on Pride stages stood behind speakers from charities, activists and political figures. I quickly learnt a couple of poses and where to put my focus so I still looked like me but not undermining serious issues or drawing focus from a speaker. If someone looked at me; my focus was on the speaker and giving them my full attention, present, poised and listening ready to spring into action once they were done. In the early days I saw a few pictures where I looked like I was bored, de-energised, as I listened on. I was giving them focus but I lost some of my stage energy, I needed to 'perform' listening a little. I learnt I needed a half smile, a slow nod and to make sure my eyes were on the speaker.

EXERCISE 7: LEADING BODY PARTS

You will need: A space to move about - away from breakables!

This is a fun, exercise for finding a physicality for your alter-ego. Which part of their body is in charge? Visualise that you are a puppet being held up by a string and there is someone above controlling you. Where the string is attached will affect the way in which you move; walk around the room experimenting with being led by a different part of your body. You can take this as far as you wish: be big, be bold, be ridiculous.

Points that may lead: nose, chest, groin, pouting lips, hips, knees, the left knee, the right shoulder… Let yourself go wild and play with all the different options you can think of.

To take this further you may explore the direction with which the string is pulling, from in-front, from above, or is it somehow pushing you, or pulling you into the ground?

EXERCISE 8: BORROW A BIT OF THEM

You will need: A space to move in.

Some performers find creating a physicality or voice a tricky process. Many performers, however, find doing an impersonation very simple: use impersonation as a short-hand, a new way *in* to your character physicality. No one needs to *know* who the impersonation is, but having someone in-mind can give guide: speed, weight, status, etc., quickly creating an outline for a character.

Think: old teachers, Grandma, Nicole Kidman, the man at the bus stop…

I hope some of these physicalities may have had you being ridiculous! Often, when creating an alter-ego, performers feel they have taken things too far but as you go around your daily life, start observing people: their habits, mannerisms, ways of moving, etc. People are peculiar, bring that to the stage. Some of the creations you've come up with probably aren't as far removed from reality as you first thought. Keep your eyes open, if you see anything unique, is it something you could borrow or incorporate into your stage craft?

Alter-Ego

> **EXERCISE 9: VOCAL**
>
> **You will need: A pack of cards and some text.**
>
> Much like you played with physicality on various sliding scales, you can do the same with your voice. It's useful to find a little bit of text to use for this: a script, poem or perhaps you have a character intro you could use: *"Hello I'm..."*
>
> Using the cards again play on the sliding scale (Ace being the left to King being the right) for the following qualities:
>
> **Low Pitch/High Pitch**
>
> **Quiet/Loud**
>
> **Slow/Fast**
>
> **Fluid/Staccato**
>
> How do these affect the way your alter-ego comes across? Which seem to be a good fit for you? Are there any which aren't appropriate for a base vocal quality but might be a fun *peak and trough* (see *Chapter 8: Basic Drag*) to use when surprised, or shocked? Finding a base level is useful – but all of the colours around are equally useful for creating a dynamic performance that keeps the audience engaged.

Further Exploration

How you speak and talk to the audience is a huge contribution to our character. As your on-stage persona develops you will build your own way of using language. We'll tackle this later in *Chapter 11:– Talking On Stage* but the manifesto and alter-ego choices you have made will feed into that.

If you have dived into the world of a character, take a look at some of the hot-seating exercises in *Chapter 20: Impersonation: Tribute and Parody*. With a slight adaptation all of these exercises could be wonderful ways to explore and pad out the world for the character you are creating.

You Know, so Let the Audience Know

The quicker an audience know who you are the quicker they will relax into what you are presenting on-stage. Whenever possible find ways to introduce yourself quickly and concisely.

> *"Hello my name's Michael Twaits, I'm a man in a dress."*

What has this told the audience? My name, I'm a man, I'm aware I'm a drag act, I don't take myself too seriously, I'm quite straight to the point. The quicker they can *get* who I am the quicker they will settle into the performance.

As well as literally introducing yourself there are many quick ways to tell the audience a lot about yourself. How do you enter the stage? What's the first thing you do? Say? Do you have a catchphrase?

If the first thing the audience see is you tripping over, it sets a specific tone. Those opening few seconds are crucial (remember *Chapter 8: Basic Drag?* Make an entrance, let them drink it in, etc.). Make sure these moments are thought through and rehearsed just as much as the rest of your set.

What Album Have You Put on?

Knowing who you are onstage does not stop you having a range of performance modes under one alter-ego. I like to think of myself as being a musician who covers many genres, each gig I choose a suitable album to put on: ballads, pop, greatest hits, avant guard, etc. The same alter-ego can do a family-friendly function one day and an adult pantomime the next, they just adapt, lean in to the environment they are in and make it work for them!

When you know where you are performing, or who you are performing to, it gives clues as to what version of yourself to bring to the stage. Again throwing back to *Chapter 8: Basic Drag* know who you are performing to and what your role is within the show.

Overview: Alter-Ego

Artists never finish developing, playing or evolving: keep letting your alter-ego grow as you move forward through the handbook. I am sure you'll come back and rework the alter-ego as you have a clearer idea of what you are doing on stage.

- Being aware of your alter-ego, knowing exactly who they are, allows you to feel secure on-stage.
- Your alter-ego can give trajectory as to why you are on stage, and why an audience is watching you.
- Create a *drag manifesto* to guide you towards what type of work you wish to create and the type of alter-ego best suited to you.
- Explore the options for how far away from your self your alter-ego can go. Both physically and vocally they may be very different to you. Play with the exercises and explore.
- If you are exploring a character, especially a comic one, take a look at *Chapter 20: Impersonation: Tribute and Parody* as a lot of the world building exercises could have huge benefit to a true character!

The views and opinions your alter-ego has will be key to how an audience will interact with them. A character might have wildly opposing views to you which can provide a great comic dynamic. Alternatively, you may adopt a persona which remains very close to the self. Either way using your *drag manifesto* as a starting point, it's time to start taking a look at how you curate your voice, your point of view and make interesting choices that will keep an audience engaged and wanting to come back for more.

Notes

1. *Me* in interview with *Michael Twaits*, July 2024. See Part IV for full interview.
2. *Hugo Grrrl* in interview with *Michael Twaits*, July 2024. See Part IV for full interview.
3. *Ada Campe* in interview with *Michael Twaits*, July 2024. See Part IV for full interview.
4. *Will & Grace* NBC Season 1, 1998.
5. *Me* in interview with *Michael Twaits*, July 2024. See Part IV for full interview.
6. *Find more about Tracey online at @traceycollinsss*
7. *Adam All* in interview with *Michael Twaits*, July 2024. See Part IV for full interview.
8. *Son Of A Tutu* in interview with *Michael Twaits*, July 2024. See Part IV for full interview.
9. Ewan, Vanessa & Sagovsky, Kate – *Laban's Efforts in Action: A Movement Handbook for Actors* – Methuen Drama (18 October 2018).

Conkers photographed backstage at the Royal Vauxhall Tavern by Fox Al Rajim

10
Being Alive: Making Choices and Finding A Voice

There's a famous idiom about opinions and everyone having one; for performers, having an opinion and making it known isn't a negative, it is an essential. On-stage ambivalence can be death, an audience lose interest and starts to think *"who cares"*. Nobody wants to hear a song someone thinks is just 'OK' or an indecisive, low-stakes, debate on who to vote for. Audiences engage with dynamic performers whose choices demonstrate a point of view and use their voice. It's time to get off the fence.

Not every drag act needs to be hugely political, inspirational or radical but every drag act needs to be present and share something of interest with the audience. Without making choices a singing drag act can become karaoke in a costume. A lip-sync can become a poor impersonation. A unique point of view, a twist on the expected, a well placed objective, can help create a dynamic performance of familiar material. It is not about dramatic reinterpretations, but letting the audience know why a song is chosen, what a lip-sync means to you or why that joke today. Which is what this chapter is all about: making a choice and developing a voice.

A lot of drag involves renditions of material that the audience already know. It seems every singing drag queen has performed *Part Of Your World* from *The Little Mermaid*. It's a classic crowd pleaser, has themes that can ring true to the queer community, space to add a few jokes and even a sing-along moment for the audience. So why not? But each act has to ask themselves: *"How am I using this song? What do I bring to it to make it fresh? What are the audience getting from my rendition?"*

A performer's opinions and beliefs shape the content they choose. In *Chapter 9: Alter-Ego* you created your *Drag Manifesto*: this can be a rudder to help you make choices – from the way you structure a set, to the way you interact with an audience. Why you do drag, what you want an audience to get out of sharing a live experience with you, what you want to say politically, what you find funny, etc. These are all choices that will shape you into a unique drag act.

Having an Opinion

As a performer, I want to share my point of view, my belief system, my personal moral code with the audience. I don't assume they will agree with me, but I invite them to listen and I hope they are interested in hearing someone else's opinion. I might even change their opinion, I might make them see things from a different point of view. I might move them to action but I am not alienating them for having a different opinion. I want to have a conversation.

Make It Your Own

I have seen *Part Of Your World* transformed into a camp sing along, a trans-rights call to alms, an attack on Disney's fat-phobia and much more. But choices don't have to be this extreme. The choice could be a

DOI: 10.4324/9781003498797-12

collective moment of queer joy, a sing-along to let the audience feel involved, to have a shared laugh at something camp! As long as the audience see you doing *something* that connects to them, sheds some new light, new meaning on the moment or a new shared experience for the audience – then you have made a choice.

Choices.

Tatiana, *RuPaul's Drag Race* Season 2, All Stars 2[1]

Opinions within Your Repertoire

A well-loved song can be part of your repertoire, but it is stronger if you have a *take* on it. This does not need to be a dramatic reinterpretation or a full rewrite (we'll get these with *Chapter 19: Parody*). Choices can be subtle, you do not need to be performing suspended from the ceiling dressed as Humpty Dumpty. But each piece you choose should have a purpose within the structure of your set, an objective you are trying to achieve with it; create interest and variation against the rest of your set. If your set doesn't have choices then the audience might as well be at a karaoke night.

I am not expecting you to reinvent every song you cover, or dramatically mash-up every lip-sync, just to know what it is adding to the audience experience. It could be as simple as – "*this is a Saturday night anthem, let's get everyone up and dancing!*" Many people come to a drag show wanting to hear their favourite songs, to dance and sing-along, to whoop, cheer and have fun! However, your set will become slightly one note if you use that choice on every piece you perform. How are you raising the stakes, creating theatrical *peaks and troughs*, this bounces back to *Chapter 8: Basic Drag*. Maybe have one to get them dancing, another is a sing-along, etc. Little variations on the choices you are making about how and way you are performing.

Keep on asking: "*What am I doing with this song? What am I adding to the audience's live experience? How can I make it my own? How does it reflect who I am?*"

Not every drag act sings or lip-syncs. However, it is often the place the least choices are made; there is often the idea "*I've chosen the song isn't that enough?*" When strong choices are made a set comes to life, moments of magic happen as the audience hear, or interpret a song afresh. Otherwise the song may become a moment they choose to go to the bar, the bathroom or outside for a cigarette!

EXERCISE 1: A MOMENT OF MAGIC

You will need: Your *Repertoire List.* **Perhaps a streaming service to find some musical inspiration.**

This is a simple exercise I would recommend you apply to every single item on your *Performance Ready Repertoire List*. (Curating a repertoire list is something we began in *Chapter 6: Building A Set, Range and Repertoire*.) It may be too soon and you don't have anything there yet, no problem, choose a couple of songs that you think you might perform. As you build your repertoire and add things to your *Repertoire List* come back here and repeat the exercise to be sure you're sprinkling a little unique magic on every piece you choose to perform.

Answer at least one of these questions as a way of justifying your decision to include this number:

- *What am I adding to this?*
- *Why am I performing this?*
- *What's my take or twist on the material?*
- *What am I doing with the audience?*
- *How will I introduce the track to clarify my intentions?*

> The answer could be the role it's playing within your set, the reaction you want from the audience, the little twist you have added, a moment to enter the audience or interact with someone, etc. What is elevating this song or lip-sync from just being a straight cover?

This exercise may seem daunting, here are a few examples from my repertoire list to show quite how simple a choice can be. I am under no illusion that I am the only drag act performing these tracks, but I add a little moment of magic which is a unique live moment for the audience, or give momentum within my set.

- *Chandelier* (Sia) – The pre-chorus becomes a drinking game using the existing lyrics to count the audience down to drink. Pointing and laughing at those who are doing it. During the instrumental moments saying *"I knew you'd love a drinking song"*.
- *Do It Like A Dude* (Jessie J) – Bringing comedy by reframing with an introduction that it could have been written by/for a drag queen. It reframes lyrics throughout and gives plenty of laughs.
- *Proud Mary* (Tina Turner) – I want the audience singing! And maybe even dancing out of their seats. I conduct them and keep encouraging them to join in.
- *One Night Only* (Dreamgirls) – An opening song, so I prove I can sing but then play the clown when the song goes disco to get the audience laughing. Establish I don't take myself too seriously and that anything may happen.
- *Toxic* (Britney Spears) – I'm adding comedy. I sing the string crescendo in falsetto. Act almost surprised it's come out of me. A beast possessed by the song.

My Mantra

Often students get frustrated when I tell them to *"make a choice, show some personality"*. They believe singing the song, or performing the lip-sync, is enough. And that's when I share my mantra with them: *"I am not Beyoncé!"*

What I mean by this is, as a performer, I need to acknowledge:

- There are more beautiful people in the world than me.
- There are better vocalists than me.
- There are better dancers than me.
- There are acts with bigger budgets for production and costuming than me.

I can not go on stage to try and recreate what Beyoncé does and realistically succeed; I am setting myself up to fail. The skill for a drag act is in creating a moment, communicating with an audience and putting a unique stamp on existing material. That's what I to bring to every piece I perform. No one has come to my show expecting to see Beyonce, they want to see me!

To expand on the pop diva analogy: I channel Madonna, she has always admitted she isn't the best singer or dancer, but her *opinion*, her unique point of view, is what makes her dynamic. Constant evolution: growing, challenging and stepping outside of her comfort zone is what makes her Madonna. Going against the grain, her public persona simply doesn't give a fuck; she thinks it, she says it, she believes it, she supports it. Even presenting her own songs at a live concert Madonna updates them, adds a twist and creates a fresh live experience for her audience.

Choosing the right material, making a choice with it and framing it to fit your purposes can create a magical experience. I am by no means saying don't perform Beyoncé's material: A drag king singing *If I Were A Boy* could be phenomenal, simply choosing that song as a king is a big choice and brings new meaning to a familiar lyric… With everything you perform, make a choice, show a connection and show the audience who you are rather than aspiring to replicate someone else's interpretation.

Leave the Middle Ground

If a topic is important enough to be discussed, or performed, on-stage, have an opinion on it. Never be neutral. If you have only a slight opinion on an issue, exaggerate it, lean in one direction or the other! Heighten it for the moment: to be entertaining, funny, irreverent or simply to shoehorn in the next song.

The simplest way to create, and curate, a point of view on-stage is to leave the middle ground; refuse to be indifferent. This doesn't just apply to pieces, or repertoire, within your set, it applies to everything going on in the live space: every linking line, every chat with the audience and every aspect of your performance. (For the *Drag Race* fans out there – it comes down to a *Toot* or a *Boot*.) It can be more dynamic if your opinion is slightly against the expected, to not always choose the popular option. Every drag queen seems to love Lady Gaga – I dare you to hate her! Find a reason to and run with it. See what happens!

Non-Verbal Acts

Forming opinions, shaping pieces and having a point of view is just as important, and achievable, for non-verbal acts. If you are delivering a lip-sync mix of bangers that you love – how does it affect the shape of the piece if you throw in a song you hate, or is really silly, or has a completely different feel. Or a piece of text from a news report, film or interview. There are many ways to express your opinion without speaking.

Serious about the Frivolous, Frivolous about the Serious

This chapter can make one feel they need to be informed and engaged on every hot issue; this isn't the case at all. A drag act can be very entertaining if they are giving an impassioned speech about something inconsequential – a speech about drug store mascara that is delivered like the State of the Union address! Equally, performers can be entertaining if they are dismissive of the big issues. Referencing one of the most quoted pieces of writing on Camp:

> One can be serious about the frivolous, frivolous about the serious.
>
> Susan Sontag [2]

Drag is fun, and an audience have often come to a show to escape from the woes of reality. Inverting expectation is a wonderful shared experience for an audience.

Being in the Room

An audience interact with you and give prompts throughout a drag show. They give live, and unplannable, prompts for you to interact with. Both literal prompts (by talking to you) and found prompts (where you notice something: an item of clothing someone is wearing, someone arriving late, an odd laugh). These are the types of *live* moments where you interact with them in the live space, acknowledging them, and adding an opinion to help build a unique live event for the audience which they feel is totally bespoke! *Chapter*

11:The Audience Experience will expand on this but these are all opportunities to show the audience your unique point of view, your opinion. Always be listening and looking for moments to pounce on. And always have opinions ready!

EXERCISE 2: IMPROVISED OPINIONS

You will need: Your notepad, something to record yourself or perhaps a rehearsal partner.

Flex your muscles with some quick fire responses from the list below; read the prompt and then give an opinion out loud without pausing! Remember to try and leave the middle ground, sometimes go against the grain, don't be afraid to be camp – take something super seriously, brush off a recent political conflict.

Answers can be: brutally honest, reworking of facts, subversion, excitement, quoting/misquoting a famous connection. Through practice you will be able to build up a bank of responses that will help you feel confident to give suitable, opinionated answers to anything. If something seems funny, witty or interesting to you – note it down!

Example Prompts

- *A loud audience member.*
- *Madonna.*
- *A gin & tonic.*
- *New York City.*
- *Meryl Streep.*
- *A handsome man.*
- *Donald Trump.*
- *A leopard print top.*

This is just a starter list. Now you know the exercise, look for prompts that might suit your style or performance or the spaces you'll be at. What's trending on social media, who's in the Top 10, guests at the Met Gala, Oscar Nominations, Top 10 props to take to a drag brunch etc. If you have a rehearsal partner get them to fire random prompts at you.

Keep practicing – read it out loud, pass an opinion, move on. Or even better play devil's advocate – if you loved Meryl Streep: try another response where you hate her. See what happens! Play!

Record the exercise and then listen back. Was there any comedy gold, were there any phrases which could work for various prompts that you can hang onto? Make notes of the best bits in your notebook. This is the beginning of building your language and lexicon which will dig into further in *Chapter 13: Talking On Stage*.

I do a form of this exercise on stage every week at my *Saturday Supershow* because I take requests. As the audience shout out artists and musicals I respond briefly to each one. I never just say – "ok". I share something about myself, or imply something about the requestor, make a joke about the artist or a song. It's part of the live experience.

Some are silly, some are me demonstrating knowledge on the subject, some are cheeky, others are ambivalent because I know the audience will hate me for that…There's a lot of misdirection comedy and playing against expectation which is fun.

For example – the requests:

Barbra Streisand – *"My people are here! Thank you"*.

Lady Gaga – *"Never heard of her"*.

Depeche Mode – *PAUSE "Did you enjoy that silence?"*

Elaine Paige – *"Ah the singing potato"*.

Oasis – *"Who?"*

Chappel Roan – *"Good luck, babe"*.

Taylor Swift – *"Meh!"*

Sometimes I even just say a simple and impassioned *"Love it"*, *"Hate it"*, *"Toot"*, *"Boot"* and move on. But I have always an opinion. I have around 30 go-to responses that I will impose on different requests each week. For example: one week I've *"never heard of"* Gaga the next week it's Judy Garland. Within the context of one show I try to perform the same narrative but the audience know there is a slight irreverence to the responses I'm sharing.

How to Find a Point of View

Develop a hunger for knowledge; nothing gives you a sharper point of view than being informed. Interesting people are interesting to talk to; informed people are interesting to talk to. At a show an audience wants to feel like they are spending time with an interesting person. This doesn't mean you need to change who you are. But keep striving to become more informed and let that feed into your work; there is always more to see, more to know and more to read! Revisit *Chapter 7: Inspiration* if you don't know a reference pick up a book, listen to an album, watch a film or google it! When a new album comes out that you know will be popular, give it a listen. Keep being connected to what is going on.

> The fool doth think he is wise, but the wise man knows himself to be a fool.
> *As You Like It,* William Shakespeare

Be Unique

There are many expected, or assumed, views people have around drag and drag artists. There's an assumed liberal/leftism. However, our views should not be homogenised: we should be able to have differing views to each other, to be able to hear different perspectives and opinions without always taking offence or 'cancelling' someone. You can become more informed on a subject by listening, and even debating, an opposing perspective.

Performers have the privilege of being able to talk to an audience, to try to move them to action. This can be for them to have a fun night out, but can also be to show them things from another perspective, to be an instigator of political change. You are much more likely to have effect on an audience if you can show you are informed and passionate about something.

Echo Chambers

Social media creates echo chambers full of like-minded individuals. I look through my news feed and see: mothers breastfeeding whilst bejewelling a corset, drag queens doing their make-up at the back of a bus, fundraisers for top-surgery, trans couples exploring how to have children, and plenty of memes about cats or nostalgic cartoons. My interests, my circles and my political outlook shine back at me.

This has normalised all of the above to me, none of my opinions seem extreme as the echo chamber shows me similar life stories. I have connected with like-minded individuals to create a safe space. But there will be conservative counterparts who see fundraisers for their local homophobic church, petitions to get LGBT+ books out of schools, parents teaching their children how to fire guns and more. And their world view is reinforced back to them. Opinions become amplified because we all see in our own echo chamber that we are not alone, which gives us courage in our convictions.

I personally think the most interesting, and informed opinions are those that can understand *an element* of both sides. If you have an opinion, as a form of research, try and understand why someone thinks the opposite. Play devil's advocate. Can you see from their perspective for a moment?

It's very easy to allow social media to reinforce our opinion and to reduce big debates into being polarised sides: *"you are with us or against us"*. Looking from alternative angles can be an interesting opinion, it can make you more informed or bring you back to your original stance with more conviction.

Subtle Politics: Charm and Disarm

When discussing political change, or social injustices, many think about impassioned monologues, dramatic protests, placards and pleas for change: these are all effective performance techniques. However, a well-rounded performer can still represent their political voice whilst hosting a brunch or karaoke party. Your point of view can shine through every time you are on stage – not just when you are *trying* to get a message across. Remember a softer touch can often have a bigger effect.

> I often get men after a show wanting to say *"hello"*, shake my hand and say something along the lines of: *"I didn't expect to enjoy that"*. I used to find that a real insult, but now I take it as a huge compliment. Because they have been impacted by my performance, a small change in their opinions can feed into the rest of their lives. They enjoyed sharing a space with me, laughing along. Possibly they previously saw drag, or queerness, as a threat but they related to me and therefore have readdressed their opinions slightly.
>
> As a performer, I believe I have a duty to make everyone feel welcome and fulfil the transaction that has taken place: they bought a ticket, I provide the show. Rather than attacking an audience who disagree with me politically I welcome them in, I have enough love for everybody. If they feel safe, and are enjoying the show, they can hopefully listen and broaden their views. Remember, audiences may have never met a drag act, or in my case an LGBT+ parent, before. I want them to have a fun night with me, to open their eyes a little.
>
> I show them a different perspective of the world, and because they are having fun they are listening to me: how am I going to do that if I instantly enter attack mode? If they are laughing with me during the show, when I express an opinion they don't agree with they can at least see it from my perspective. I am in some ways relatable to them. I call the approach *Charm and Disarm*. People connect with me because I'm charming, so they relax, they listen and then they realise that perhaps they should, or could, reconsider some of their former opinions. They can see we are not so different, who I sleep with does not have to be the headline of my life, we can all exist happily in the same world.

Obviously, this example is about my practice but I hope it illustrates that sometimes a soft touch can have a big effect. As you develop your voice it does not always need to be shouted from the rooftops, it can just be baked in to the performance so it's inescapably present. The work we have already started (in *Chapter 9: Alter-ego*) with drawing up a *Drag Manifesto* and ways of shaping your *alter-ego* are ways of letting your opinions and attitudes flow through all of your work.

Overview: Making Choices and Finding a Voice

Having a point of view and making choices will shape the way audiences engage with you. It's what will build your brand, shape your repertoire and provide direction for your drag journey.

- Always know why you are performing something. What are you adding or bringing to the live experience? If the answer is nothing, then ask why are an audience watching it?
- Choices can be small, subtle. It is not always about shouting and shocking, just knowing who you are, why you are there and telling the audience that.
- Explore things from a different point of view. You don't need to change your own opinions but research why someone else has an opposing opinion can help strengthen your own arguments.
- Get off the fence. If you are neutral, or ambivalent, towards something why are you discussing it? Always bring passion to the stage.
- There is an artistic license. You, or your alter-ego, can exaggerate how you feel to make a moment dynamic.
- Have opinions. Be informed and keep learning!

You've begun the journey of shaping your opinion and sharpening your views, that will carry on throughout your career. Revisit these exercises as you grow in confidence on-stage. Your point of view is what will make you stand out to an audience, and producers, who will want to see you again and again because you are offering them something dynamic and interesting. You now need to think about how you connect to the audience, how you present your opinions, your work, to them. You need to be able to share moments with them and give them that unique live experience that will keep them coming back for more.

Notes

1 This is Tatiana's catchphrase and you would find her saying it in any episodes of *Drag Race* she is featured in Season 2, *All Stars 2*.
2 Sontag, S. (2018). *Notes on Camp*. Penguin Classics.

Pussy Kat Bangkok photographed backstage at the Royal Vauxhall Tavern by Carol J Moir

11
People: Audience Experience

Many drag acts come on stage and perform a well-rehearsed set *at* the audience. That should be reframed to performing *with* them, *to* them and *for* them. The audience have entered a contract with you; they have paid their money for a ticket, given up their time and want to be entertained. They want to enjoy every moment and have a good time. What are you doing to fulfil your side of the contract?

A drag brunch, a cabaret bar, a Pride stage, a piano bar: they all have an audience, and every audience is different. As a performer always think of the audience as a room full of individuals rather than a singular audience. Each person within the audience is an individual, each will have a different lived experience, a different interpretation of your performance. They will have also come to the show with a different expectation, a different mood and different hopes. These variables are why each performance is a unique occasion and why, as a performer, you need to keep thinking about the *audience experience*.

Drag shows aren't generally formal; they may have some background chatter, people moving to the bar, phones going off, creeping to the bathrooms, etc. The etiquette is less formal than a theatre audience and less raucous than a concert. A relaxed, social atmosphere with fabulous moments is often what people have come out for. As a performer it's wonderful to be part of a social night out but it's also a challenge; there is a skill to holding an audience, trying to consistently keep yourself the focus: keep being captivating, keep being dynamic but let the audience enjoy themselves.

As a performer I have been on festival stages with 15,000 people in the audience and then the next week playing to a quiet night in a 20 seater bar. The approach and the skill needed when communicating with an audience doesn't alter, it adapts. This chapter is all about building the skills and knowledge to connect to any audience, to conduct their experience to give them exactly what they wanted and achieve your best performance.

The Cycle

Visualise communicating with the audience as a cycle. The audience reactions, however subtle, should be affecting your actions on-stage. And your actions on-stage are what generate their reactions. It doesn't matter how big or small the audience, or space is, the transference of giving and taking, acting and reacting, is always there.

Imagine you are talking to a friend over lunch: Whilst you are telling a story they are eating, nodding, occasionally '*uhuhing*', but they aren't technically *adding* anything further to your story. But their slight reactions are making you carry on, they help you craft the story and give you the impetus to carry on. You can tell when they are really engaged and can perhaps embellish the story a little, or when they are bored and you need to wrap the anecdote up. You are reading all of their micro-reactions and that's exactly what you need to do with an audience! A laugh, a smile, a sigh, a yawn, some chatter, a round of applause – these are all their parts of the conversation. Look out and listen, let them affect you. Create the cycle.

> I'm listening to them. I'm not listening to me.
>
> Ada Campe

This cycle applies both to the room as a whole and to an individual. When someone gives you something – take it, acknowledge it. If you see a particular person laughing hard at a joke – "*she knows, she gets it, thank you*". You are in the live space together and the more you can be present, reacting off of the audience's reactions, the more they will feel the magic of a live, unique experience. Highlighting people giving good reactions can also encourage others to get more involved. (This works for non-verbal acts too – if someone is clapping, clicking or giving a "*yasss girl*" during a lip-sync, point a finger at them, give them eye contact, a wink, etc. Communication does not need to be verbal.) A good host will have set the expectation for the audience, either implicitly or explicitly, in terms of them getting involved, answering back, clapping and cheering. But sometimes an audience need a few pats on the back for giving good reactions to help them keep going! It's a way of giving them permission to be involved.

The Live Experience

There's magic in the air at a drag show; performers and the audience share the space, breathe the same air and embark on adventure together. This isn't theatre where performers carry on with what they were going to say regardless of the audience, drag shows are inescapably a one off, live experience. If a glass smashed on the ground I want to know what drink was spilt – "*Can the bar top up that red wine for her!?*"

This does not mean you need to stop performing to comment on *every* cough, phone ringing or toilet trip. But the audience need to know you have clocked it, and it might be used. You learn to always have one eye on the room during your set; you know, see and hear everything, it's a sixth sense performers develop on-stage. Acknowledging something live in the space reminds the audience that you are all sharing this one off night with them, it ups the excitement, sustains their attention and builds a sense that anything might happen. These unplanned moments are happening on top of your rehearsed set, this is why we keep coming back to the idea of rehearsing and knowing your repertoire so well it's just muscle memory. It's not possible to be trying to remember lyrics to a song at the same time as being fully present in the space.

The Love Experience

Not every stage persona has to be nice or warm. However, until your alter-ego is really established, and you are very comfortable on-stage, the easiest way to win an audience over is to come at them with love. Want to be their friend, want to get to know them. Even when insulting them, congratulate them on being bold enough to wear that outfit. ("*I wish I was brave enough to wear leopard print on a Tuesday!*") You will still get the laugh, but the individual will not feel as bullied as if you were to shame them for wearing it.

> Even when the claws come out, it's always done with love.
>
> Me the Drag Queen[1]

Drag queens, specifically, have a reputation for coming out on stage and being rude to everyone. And if you are the master of insult-comedy (or reading, wait for *Chapter 18:Comedy, Reading and Roasting*) perhaps you can make it work without turning a room against you! *Perhaps*. Most acts when they take an attacking, or belittling, approach have less laughs and audiences can shut-down or even become afraid they will be picked on. As the performer you lose *the cycle* because they are too scared to give you anything.

> There are a few very successful drag acts who when I go to see them I want them to be rude or to pick on me; Myra Dubois, Bianca Del Rio, Jinkx Monsoon, come to mind. But these are world class acts who have honed their craft and comedy. It often becomes cringeworthy when acts *'have a go'* at being shady for no reason. It's one of the quickest ways to alienate an audience and for a show to lose momentum.

Give Guidance

When on-stage you are *conducting* the audience, guiding them to getting the best out of your performance. A good host will have warmed the audience up and set the tone for the evening. But if you come on-stage and feel the audience aren't where you need them to be – try and set your own rules and encourage the responses you want. Giving guidance is a simple trick to help navigate the audience and give them clues as to how to behave. Throughout the set pepper in suggestions, both subtle and blatant, to let the audience know if they can sing-along, answer back, suggest ideas *or* the opposite if you want a moment of calm.

- *"Are we ready for a sing-a-long?"*
- *"I know we've had a lot of fun but I'm going to calm things down – listen to this…"*
- *"Would you like to hear a story?"*
- *"I know it's Megan's hen night – but for the next five minutes, it's all about me! Eye's this way please!"*
- *"Don't leave me hanging on the chorus – I want to hear you!"*
- *"It's up to you all now – are we doing the clean version, or the dirty?"*

Remember, if you don't get the full response you were hoping for, or if it's a lukewarm reception it's easy to pull more out from the audience with a request for more:

- *"Are you sure?"*
- *"Sorry, I can't hear you?"*
- *"You'll have to do better than that!"*
- *"I'm not convinced…"*

Depending on the structure and style of your set your set there are different forms of guidance you might give. A non-verbal act can mime *"give me more"* or *"make some noise"* gestures before doing a reveal or a dramatic move. Simply pausing for a beat and putting your hand up to your ear. Think of the guidance as an invitation, rather than an order or ultimatum. It's not about telling a group of people, who aren't having fun, that they *"must have fun"*: it's inviting them along on a journey, letting them express themselves. For some it's the first time they've seen an act like this, how are they to know what they can do if you don't let then know?

Leave Your Day in the Dressing Room

A professional performer needs to walk on-stage and aim to deliver their best every single time. No excuses. Leave any baggage you bought in from your personal life in the dressing room. If you had a tough journey in, if you had an argument with a partner – find a way to leave it in the dressing room. You don't need that negative energy hanging over your set. Find a way to shake it off!

Easier said than done, I know! One simple approach is to remember how lucky you are that you have been booked, hopefully paid, to be a performer at this show. Focus on those positive things, and on wanting to do your best as a professional so you are invited back. Another technique I find useful is to put my phone on airplane mode! The outside world doesn't exist for the next few hours, focus on the job at hand.

I also find not talking about it helps. I often talk about personal things after the show as I de-drag with friends. But in the build up I like the distraction of dressing room banter if possible, and if I'm on my own I might pop on a funny, comfortable, podcast.

A final suggestion: sneak into the space pre-show and listen to who's there! Is it Bob's first time at a drag show? Jane's birthday? This is a special occasion for them. They may have saved up for tickets. Or a babysitter? Listen to the audience and remember that each individual in that room has paid their money, given up their time and are here for this event. You *are* the event so get in the head space of doing your best.

I Love *This* Audience

As a young performer I would often get annoyed with an audience for small reasons and feel they were working against me because they were too drunk or too quiet. I wanted to perform to them and they weren't returning the response I wanted. It's important to get out of that mentality: Celebrate the audience that you have with you. Find a positive to approach to walk into your set with:

- Are there less people in tonight? *Great! I can try and create some intimate moments!*
- The bar is full of drunk hen parties. *Great! They will lap up the upbeat mix I've prepared.*
- They are all very quiet. *Great! They are really listening, they will love that long story I have...*

You don't need to adapt your planned set to fit the audience, but find those moments in a set to celebrate who *is* in the audience and work with the energy they are giving you.

Get to Know the Audience

In *Chapter 8: Basic Drag* you learnt to try and research who your audience might be. With longer sets, or heavily chatty sets, it's possible to learn more specifics in the first few moments, especially with where an audience's taste and energy level is. What they find funny, even what they need from you: listen to them and react to it. If you are onstage with options (perhaps a few jokes, or a story, or a song) – then give them what you think is the best for them, rather than what *you* want to do.

> I use one story to get a measure of what audience find funny, because I know the story so well, so it helps me to work out what they laugh at. *This* is funny for you. *That* not so much.
>
> Ada Campe[2]

Pockets

There are always different pockets within an audience: a group who've never seen a drag act before, a birthday party or some quiet theatre goers branching into cabaret for the first time. Some will be attentive, others are trying to chat subtly, and of course some are trying to get the drinks in! Never treat the whole room as one area, try and work out what each pocket needs or is after and use different techniques to pull them all in, or thank them for interacting the way you want them to.

If you're heading into an upbeat track – find a way to dedicate it to the hens in the corner. Engage with them as a subgroup of the audience. If you can see another group is becoming a bit chatty or possibly looking like they are losing interest, is there a way you can pull them back in? Chat to them for a moment? How can you shake them up, or give them a bit of love?

Simple Tricks

If you ever feel you are *losing* the audience, or a section of the audience, there are a selection of simple tricks that can help pull them back in. It's easy to feel you are failing when an audience is not giving 100% focus. See it is a challenge to conquer! Try not to attack or go on the offensive; find ways to pull focus back and remind them how brilliant you are!

Ask a Question: There is a reason pop stars always ask *"are you having a good time?"* It gives the audience a chance to interact, to shout back and feel part of the event. A simple call and response or raising a glass for a communal *cheers*. If you are leading into a song: *"Are you ready for a banger? Is it too early for a sing-a-long?"*

Make Eye Contact: if there's a specific group or individual you feel is drifting. Use eye contact. Make them one of your *anchors* for a while (see *Chapter 8: Basic Drag*). Usually if someone's drifting it's because they don't feel included.

Check You Haven't Ignored Them: It's possible you have ignored the back of the room, or one corner. Think of the *anchors* in *Chapter 8: Basic Drag*. Drop an *anchor* in their area and keep throwing some focus their way.

Bring It Forward: Physically come down-stage; the closer you are to the audience the easier it is to hold their focus.

Get Rid of the Fourth Wall: Enter their space. When a drag act is in amongst the audience it is amazing how focus and atmosphere can shift. If there's a table of people making a lot of noise. Go up to them, have a look. Without mentioning it you are physically saying: *"I'm watching you"* and a noisy pocket will generally get the message.

If this isn't enough combine the approach with a question: *"What's going on? What's so entertaining over here? What are we celebrating?"* Again, it's not attacking them, it's an invitation for them to come back in. It should bring the focus back, and you can carry that back to the stage. There are ways to do this mid-song, during a lip-sync routine or during the set up of your next number or piece.

A Private Moment: A wink or a cheeky smile at an individual can make the world of difference to how they are engaging with you.

Touch Them (Consensually/Gently): Audiences are generally well trained in theatre rules. When performers break the fourth wall it can make them sit up and pay more attention. When performers physically touch them it is a heightened version of the same technique. A gentle hand on a shoulder as you walk past can have a huge effect.

Have a Chat: If there's a particular table or group you feel you are drifting. Check in with them; ask a few questions, compliment an outfit, ask them what they're drinking. Something that feels unrehearsed, a moment that says – *I can see you and you can see me*.

Peaks and Trough: Mix it up. (Again, look at the *peaks and troughs* in *Chapter 8: Basic Drag*.) Find some variety to wake the audience up, or calm them down! Have a moment to be still, silly, scream! A moment of change in a room can bring an audience's attention back in line very simply.

Name Them: Audiences like to feel seen and understood. A game I play is naming the pockets or individuals without asking them for names:

> **Group Names:** *"Jim's Stags, the birthday girls, my south Londoners, my gays."*
>
> **Assumed Names:** Making up a name for an audience member usually gets a laugh: *"Sally here, I don't know why but you look like a Sally. It's the bob. Anyway…Sally – how are you?"*
>
> **Comparisons:** There's humour in finding a good comparison but there's also humour in the comparison being well off: *"Gorgeous, like a young Catherine Zeta-Jones"* or If there's five ladies on a table: *"the Spice Girls here"*. A group of straights feeling out of their depth could become *"Ed Sheeran's Fan Club."*
>
> **Brands:** Hen Nights for me are usually *"Claire's Accessories"*, a gruff group of bears as *"My Fire Boys."*
>
> **Reward Good Behaviour:** If you do a sing-along and the audience do well: Thank them, tell them how brilliant they are. With a longer set, dangle a carrot for them: *"Maybe we'll have a sing-song together again, if those hens are well behaved."*

A Terrible Audience

There is no such thing as a terrible audience. They may be flat, quiet, but during a show never give up on them. Sometimes the quietest audiences during a set give the loudest reaction at the end. Some audiences don't feel confident in how to react, or interact, with a drag act. They are like a baby eating ice cream for the first time – until it's finished they didn't know what to make of it!

There are, of course, terrible *members* of the audience but in amongst them are those who really want to enjoy the show. Focus on them, and giving them the best you can. Invite everyone along but don't let one person in a bad mood ruin the experience for the whole audience. Someone there has paid to see you at your best, so give them that. Someone needed the fun, that release, of the show you planned to give – so make sure they get it!

The biggest mistake a performer can make is to blame the audience for a bad show. A defeated attitude will drain the energy of a set, or even a whole show. Focus on the positive audience members, try to spread their positivity. If the negative members of the audience are really ruining the show, get them out. Especially for a ticketed show, if someone is too drunk, too disruptive or worse, unsafe: you are fully within your rights to ask them to leave. It has only happened a few times in my career but when one person is ruining the evening for other members of the audience, it is absolutely the right thing to do. Your duty is to deliver the best show for the majority of the room. Signal to the host, to the bar staff, to security; they will support you because they want what is best for the show and the best for the audience.

Hecklers

Before digging too deep into the concept of hecklers there are a few points to clarify:

- Heckling rarely happens.
- Hecklers think they are '*improving*' and '*adding*' to a show.
- Hecklers are often drunk.
- You, as the performer, always have the power.

Not every drag act is a comedian and not every act needs to have razor-sharp comebacks for a heckle. Depending on the situation there are many approaches to dealing with a heckler. I find going in too strong, or attacking, doesn't help. It becomes fuel to the fire, even if you feel in the moment that you *won* the atmosphere can turn sour.

Here are six go-to approaches for dealing with a heckler as an act who is not a comedian. I am definitely not an insult comic but I've provided an example of things that I have used in the past to illustrate each point.

1) Do Not Accept the Premise of Their Question/Statement

A heckler usually thinks what they are saying is funny or is adding to what you are doing. By not accepting the premise you starve their moment of oxygen. Simply don't engage with the content they have offered into the room. Engage with them, and the fact that they have interrupted the night, possibly sarcastically affirm them as a vitally important person. But don't respond to their question/statement, an answer signals that you are having a conversation and they will respond again, they will try to keep going. Take ownership of the moment by only engaging with them as someone who interrupts and, to be honest, is quite selfish.

> *"I don't mind a heckle my love, but I do take umbrage with poor diction. I'm sure what you said was hilarious to you but to the rest of us it just sounded like a dog barking at the back of the room. Think cut-glass-diction, give it some Dame Judi Dench!"*

2) Give Them Enough Rope and They'll Tie Themselves in Knots

The opposite approach is to throw them into the spotlight for a moment. Give them a little airtime and watch them flounder:

> *"Someone has something to say...please. I'm sure the paying audience will be delighted and riveted by your vital contribution to their evening...we're waiting..."*

3) Be Blatantly Honest

Avoiding humour can help you move on quicker. If you throw a joke, it *can* again make them think this a battle of wits and they'll keep going on. It's usually someone who has overdosed on a few episodes of *Drag Race* and thinks they could do your job. Much like not accepting the premise, withholding humour can starve them of their moment and makes everyone else in the audience want them to shut up.

> *"I don't wish to be rude, but please do shut up. People have paid for a show, not for you."*

Once the moment's over you can use a joke or a humorous line to move on and come back to where you were.

4) Facts Are Facts

Use facts to make a point. The point is usually that no-one has come to the venue to hear from this heckler.

> *"The audience have parted with their money, arranged their evening to see me perform on-stage. Can I just check, did anyone come here desperate to hear an unsolicited opinion from someone wearing (insert description/read)? No? There we go."*

5) Kill Them with Kindness

This can be done genuinely or sarcastically but it always works. Just check in with them.

> *I will approach them like a mother picking up a child whose fallen off their bike way: "Where are you? Did you want a moment? Oh take my hand. Did you need a little bit of attention? Did your parents not teach you the etiquette of how to enjoy a show in the audience? I'm so sorry. Poor you. Do you need a hug?"*

6) Ready-to-Go One Liners

If you are a funny drag act. Having a couple of good remarks ready is gold. Apply the previous rules of not accepting the premise of their question. But a sharp retort can just send a clear signal that you're ready to play, and you know you will win.

> *"Who's said that? Where are you? I'm toilet training my son at the moment, so I'm very used to dealing with unwanted shits."*

EXERCISE 1: HECKLE HACKS

You will need: Your notebook and pen.

For each piece of guidance brainstorm, or role play, how you could use them to handle a heckler. Some approaches will fit your alter-ego more than others. Try to write three responses from each of the six styles. Despite not knowing when you might need them these can be planned in advance because remember – you are not going to engage with the premise of their question!

If you are a novice act this is a back up for when you need it. More experienced performers, you know your style and presence on-stage and what works for you. Perhaps you've had experience with a heckler. What do you wish you had prepared?

Hopefully you won't need them but working up a number of responses is a great security blanket to have on-stage!

Stage-Time Is the Best Rehearsal

A lot of the skills needed to build and sustain an audience relationship are developed in performance. Through working on-stage you will hone skills and learn how to read the room, connect to an audience and keep them consistently engaged throughout our set. Learn from each experience – if there was a nice moment in a show, make a note, is there a way to add that to your repertoire so you can recreate it? If you discover a funny line in the live moment add it to your notes. Slowly you will build a bank of witty ways of working with an audience and have lines for every occasion. It will feel like an off the cuff reaction to the audience but it can be your go-to line for a specific reaction, or group of people. Eventually you build up enough content that you can dip in and out it's like a randomised script – you never know what's going to happen next, but you know there's a line for everything.

> I have bits, but it's not from anything that I've sat down and consciously written or workshopped and rehearsed. They've fallen out of my mouth without me thinking. I've gone, *oh, that's quite nice*. And sometimes I'll have that bit of my brain that goes: *well, that was fun. Try to remember that?*
>
> Me the Drag Queen

Overview: Audience Experience

The audience always needs to come first. What are you giving them, where are you taking them and how can you make the performance a success.

- Learn to listen to the audience and respond. The give and take between performers and an audience is not one way, it's a cycle.
- It is a live experience. Whenever possible demonstrate you are in the live space with them, not just running through your material on autopilot.
- Love the audience. Find ways to have fun with each audience member, celebrate their unique qualities.
- Conduct the audience. Give them pointers for where you are going, if you want noise ask for it, if you need calm bring their focus in.
- Listen to the individuals, and the pockets, in an audience. It's a constant juggling act of keeping everyone focused, engaged and entertained. Use some of the simple tricks to make sure you pull back focus as needed.
- Hecklers rarely happen, but always be prepared.
- Learn from every experience. Even though live performance is a unique, one-off occasion, it does not mean you can't use the same lines every time an audience is loud, quiet, raucous. Build your own repertoire of reactions to their reactions!

You will keep learning how to interact with an audience from every performance – because the audience is always slightly different. The other variable drag acts need to be ready for is that every performance space is different and that has a huge knock-on effect to the way you can structure a set and the audience experience. It's time to look at performance spaces!

Notes

1. *Me* in interview with *Michael Twaits*, July 2024. See Part IV for full interview.
2. *Ada Campe* in interview with *Michael Twaits*, July 2024. See Part IV for full interview.

Sally Slowcook photographed backstage at the Royal Vauxhall Tavern by Fox Al Rajim

12
Anywhere I Hang My Hat Is Home: Stages and Spaces

The size of the stage, the technical support available, even the shape of a room will all affect the way in which a drag act performs. Even when in a new space, to the audience, an experienced drag act always looks at home, as if they are exactly where they are meant to be. This can be achieved by allowing time to get to know a space and familiarising yourself with it before performing.

You will arrive with a suitcase at a new venue and usually have a matter of hours to get ready, to move from being a stranger in the space to appearing to be the master of it. The space may be a bar, a Pride stage, a restaurant or a theatre but the same rules apply; learn to adapt to the space you are in. Drag acts work in a wider range of venues than most performers, often with less technical support and with a more transient audience, so honing the skills of knowing how best to use a space is key to continued success. This chapter is full of pointers so you can plan in advance how best to use a space for your performance.

Take Your Time

When new to a venue it always helps to arrive early; see if you can sneak an extra five minutes on-stage before everyone else arrives, mark out a good area to get ready in the dressing room, say '*hello*' to the staff and possibly the person who booked you. Be friendly, try and learn the teams' names and let people know you are here, ready to work when they are. If you have had a chance in advance to see a performance in the space before – even better as you come armed with a little knowledge and probably a few questions.

Technical Rehearsal

A technical rehearsal (or tech) is not about rehearsing your act, you should have done that. It's about preparing the technician, and team, to help make your act the best it can be. And preparing you to perform in this specific space. It is up to the tech team what bits they feel they need to check, how long they need to sound and light check. It's rare to get to run your entire set.

The rest of the technical rehearsal is also for you to let everyone know anything unexpected or to see how they can best support you. Ask the right questions:

- "*Can I be seen here?*"
- "*Is there a specific good spot to stand in the audience?*"
- "*Where can I be lit in amongst the audience?*"

DOI: 10.4324/9781003498797-14

Preparation and Communication

Hopefully you have spoken to a technician (or again, tech) in advance and provided your *Performers Drive* (see *Chapter 2: The Business of Drag*) link to them so they know exactly what you are needing and when you need it. Be very clear in all communications, both in advance and during the tech rehearsal, say exactly what you need: "*I need a mic, a stand and the tracks to be played on these cues! Lots of reverb on the song but not when chatting between*". Never assume the technician knows your material, the songs, or what you are trying to achieve in the set. Always try and give simple, concise instructions i.e. "*3 minutes into the poem I say the word 'black' loudly – play the track then, nice and loud*".

> I have to lay it all out with tech. We've had some great tech crews, but a lot of them are so different to artists. It's just work, and you know. "*Oh, you wanted a mic?*"... But I'm always calm, and I rarely ever get upset outwardly. Because I just don't feel it's worth it. And people are trying to do their best.
>
> Simply Barbra[1]

Mic Technique and Rehearsal

A technical rehearsal is not a time to mark through a song roughly. If you are belting loud in performance, do that in rehearsal so the tech knows. Can you hear yourself? How's the sound quality. Prepare the technician for your performance by performing full out. Remember if speaking, or rapping, it's always worth letting the technician see some of this so they know to remove any reverb as words will lose clarity. Reverb is a drag act's best friend when churning out the sing-along hits: it fills the voice out and gives a lovely rounded quality to the sound. But if you rap with reverb, or delay, the audience won't hear any of the articulation and therefore struggle with the lyrics!

Microphones work best if you keep it as close to your chin as possible and let the technician alter the volume as needed. Talk or sing into them, rather than over them. If you provide a constant level for the technician, they can ride out the volume to make you sound your best. Drag acts love the visual of a Mariah moment moving the microphone arms length away from them but this is rarely necessary. Let the technician do their job. There is a reason a drag bars microphone always has lipstick stains on it – that's how close it needs to be! For hygiene you can bring disinfectants or even a microphone cover (a muff!) if that suits – although they can affect the vocal quality.

Feedback

Most drag bars are used to acts working around the room, not just the stage. But there is often a speaker in one corner of the room you may not have noticed that can give some unpleasant feedback if you get too close to a microphone. Always walk around the area you plan to use during the tech rehearsal *whilst* talking into the microphone. Feedback happens when the microphone picks up its own sound through the speakers and loops around in a continuous cycle.

If you ever are performing and you hear feedback – nine out of ten times it's because you've moved a microphone too close to a speaker. Calmly step back, give the speaker space and let the technician do their job. Usually it happens because you didn't work the room during your tech time. Don't assume it will be fine because you've seen someone else do it: speak to the technician and make sure they know what you plan to do in advance. Then they can support you and make it work.

Technicians

During your set a technician is doing everything you need them to do. However, they may not be watching if you have told them you don't need anything. They might be prepping for the next act, downloading a track, setting something up. Remember to always tell them everything you can in advance, anything to look out for. There's nothing wrong with saying *"depending on the atmosphere I might come out and talk to the audience at this point"*. There are issues if you haven't told the technician you are doing that because odds are on you won't be well lit and could get feedback.

Know the Space

Most of the things you need to know about a space can be established during a technical rehearsal. Even though you are confident in your set, physically standing on-stage with the lights on will help you prepare for this specific performance. It will inform you about audience sight lines which are essential when keeping a connection to the audience.

It will also help with your own visual sight lines: how much will *you* be able to see? How much will you need to 'cheat' being able to see people at the back of the room. Are there obvious points in the room you can spot to be your *anchors*. (Remember *Chapter 8: Basic Drag*. Always look for those Fire Exit signs.)

As we've said, most shows will provide an opportunity for you to have a tech rehearsal. Use that time to get to know the space, feel the room, what does the floor feel like under your shoes? During a tech always try to wear your performance shoes and bring any props that you will use so you can sort logistics; *"where will you put that once you've used it? Where will you get it from? Where does the mic stand come from? Who tidies up at the end?"*

Audience Sight Lines

If you have time (which you should because you planned to arrive early!) watch other performers do a tech run. Sit in the audience, maybe in a few different spots and see what it feels like. Others' tech rehearsals will teach you about working the space and what the audience experience.

Drag acts often want to enter from the audience. This is fine – but not every venue has a follow spot or sight lines that make this easy. Breaking the fourth wall is great but make sure you have worked out the logistics and informed the host and tech. Watching someone else attempt it can help you make the best decisions for your set.

You may have marked it through in the tech run but imagine adding 200 people to the space. Will it still be as easy? Will it work with your costume? Is there any way you the tech team can support this?

Where Do I Start

The opening seconds of an act are when the audience make the most judgements. You want to be able to walk onto the stage with confidence, an air of belonging, being at home and knowing where you are. Work out the logistics of how you get from A to B during your tech.

Some bars have dressing rooms in a separate area to the stage, sometimes you *have* to come through the audience to get to the stage. Whatever the set up is in each venue, practice the route to the stage and confirm at what point you will come on-stage. If working to tracks, when should they be played: is it entrance music, or to start when you are centre stage, or wait until a cue from you? Make sure that first moment is finessed to give you the best start possible.

Be Everybody's Friends

Simply shouting *"DJ"* or *"Music please"* into the void gives a very different sense of you as a performer compared to using the technicians name. This may work for your alter-ego but as a rule of thumb, audiences will warm to you quicker if you treat everyone with warmth and respect.

When signalling a tech operator to queue your track use their name, thank them. Obviously, drag alter-egos may have delusions of grandeur and you may have your own flamboyant phrase – *"maestro please"* – but always speak to the team with love. There's plenty of comedy to be had playing off the staff as comic stooges but first establish a working warm relationship so the audience feel you are joking with a team member rather than bullying a minion. This can be extended to door staff, bar staff, security, waiters and anyone else working in the room with you.

Everyone in the venue is a professional and a skilled person at their job. Don't be a diva telling people how you want things done: be a professional asking how collectively you can do the set justice. They will know their venue and what will work well – so listen to what they are saying.

> **Don't be a dick. Respect expertise. Don't cover the stage with shit and expect other people to clear up. Don't be rude. Don't chat the way through other acts. Don't drink heavily at the bar. Don't clatter around making noise. And thank people, I suppose! But that's just: don't be a dick.**
>
> Ada Campe[2]

Returning to the business of getting bookings (covered in *Chapter 2: The Business of Drag*); if you leave a venue and the staff that work there thought you were good to work with, you are much more likely to be rebooked! Nobody invites back a performer who was rude and hard to work with.

Any Specials

Every venue has a few tricks in its repertoire a piano to perch on, a bar to lean on, a central area in the audience where there's a well-placed spotlight. To help create dynamic *peaks and troughs* (*Chapter 8: Basic Drag*) acts want to use the room to its full capacity. In a new space – make sure you ask! There are no stupid questions: *Where can you light me? Where best to stand in the audience? Do you have any tricks or specials?*

> If I'm on a new stage I will always ask what tricks there might be! If I know it has a trick I always ask if I am able to use it. I often host variety shows in West End Theatres: at His Majesty's Theatre (where *Phantom of the Opera* is resident) I asked about the balcony above the stage, when we were at the Adelphi I asked about the trap door, The Gillian Lynne I asked about the revolve. They usually say *'no'* but imagine the drag potential of using a revolve midway through a song! You have to ask!

Taxi for One

All of these points may seem small fry compared to the actual set you are going to perform, but knowing the space, how to command it and how best to keep an audience engaged can elevate a performance from good to showstopping.

Allow yourself time to get to know the space, the team, ask some questions, be inquisitive and see if there are any small adaptions you could make to your set which will create some unique drag magic for the audience.

A few years ago I was working in a bar in Manchester, one wall was floor-to-ceiling glass looking onto a busy street. During the tech rehearsal I asked how far the signal for the microphone goes. They weren't sure but were happy for me to test it; so I went into the street, then across the street and down the road a little with someone in the window giving me a 'thumbs up' when they could hear me. Throughout my set I joked about being excited for a big night out in Manchester after the show. During the last number in my set I went out on the street (during *Don't Rain on My Parade*) and as I finished the song I hailed a passing taxi and jumped in. The last thing the audience heard, and saw, was me clambering in the back and asking the driver to take me to Canal Street (the gay district). I never reappeared they just saw me disappearing into the night with gay abandon…

Obviously, I did not go to Canal Street, I turned the mic off, went round the block and handed the taxi driver a few pounds which I had in my bra. Knowing the room, knowing the space and having had time to plan for what might happen with the host and the tech team I was able to have a wild improvised moment. We all knew something chaotic might happen (assuming the atmosphere was right) but these are the moments you can't precisely plan. Everyone was prepared, ready to expect the unexpected. It was only the final moment of a half-hour set but it is still a moment people talk about and is the perfect example of being fully prepared to utilise a space to the best of its ability.

Overview: Stages and Spaces

The most important part of utilising a space is being prepared – both in advance of the gig, when being booked, and before the gig when doing a tech. Allowing yourself time to get to know the venue so it feels to the audience you are on-stage in a place where you belong.

- Arrive early. You can never have too much time.
- Prepare the technician in advance with clear, concise notes to cover your set.
- Try to watch a technical rehearsal of another performer so you get to see things from the audience's perspective.
- Ask questions about what's achievable. How can the technical team elevate your set?

Remember, a technical rehearsal is not about *rehearsing* your set, it is about making your set the best it can possibly be in this specific location. You will have already worked on your performance; using *Part III* you'll have created and crafted some dynamic pieces, which you'll have rehearsed and structured within your set in the best way possible! It's time to get crafting those pieces! What are you going to do on-stage?

Notes

1. *Simply Barbra* in interview with *Michael Twaits*, July 2024. See Part IV for full interview.
2. *Ada Campe* in interview with *Michael Twaits*, July 2024. See Part IV for full interview.

Part III

Specific Drag Performance Skills and Styles

Katastofa Chernobyl photographed backstage at the Royal Vauxhall Tavern by Fox Al Rajim

13
Tell Him: Talking On Stage

Whether it's a couple of lines between lip-syncs or a ten-minute monologue setting up an evening, talking naturally to an audience is one of the most important skills a drag act can develop. A few words can pull disparate parts of a set together, shape an evening and keep an audience fully engaged. Without this ability, performance options and opportunities will be limited.

Many performers find linking between pieces the hardest part of a set, both to rehearse and execute. There is an assumption that *something* will come out of their mouth at the right moment. Do not underestimate how important these small moments of talking are, they need to be planned and rehearsed whilst feeling organic. A mistake many make is assuming because they can talk at ease *off-stage*, these skills will naturally translate *on-stage*. This chapter is going to look at the basics of why, how and when to speak on-stage and have some top tips on what to do and what not to! Making you feel prepared to talk on-stage for any length of time, seeming at ease and in control.

Who Is Your Audience?

In both *Chapter 6: Basic Drag* and *Chapter 9: The Audience Experience* knowing, or at least investigating, who your audience might be is crucial to delivering a strong performance. With talking it will help you to know the style of language, energy, tone and subjects you can discuss and reference. This part isn't rocket science: naturally, people adapt to who they are talking to (most people wouldn't swear in front of Grandparents).

You do not need to change who you are, but lean into the room you are in.

> I often getting bookings at more formal, corporate, events where it is obvious they booked a drag queen to mix things up, to be a bit outrageous. However, we are still at a formal occasion so I need to find the balance. I give them a bit of camp; saying the straight, male, CEO is *"goooorgeous"* and making his employees laugh, rather than dropping f-bombs. The evening is stuffy, I've been booked for a few laughs, to loosen things up, but not to offend or upset people. This comes back to *Chapter 5: Basic Drag*, knowing who the audience is and what my part of the show is. Then applying it to the way I talk to the audience.

Speak to Them Slowly and Clearly

Always remember the basic stage craft of ensuring the audience hear *every* word. (Most novice performers need that reminder to slow down from *Chapter 8: Basic Drag*.) Speak clearly, hit every letter in every word. Carry the energy through to the end of every sentence. This is part of why I recommend doing vocal warm

DOI: 10.4324/9781003498797-16

ups every day – it's not just for singers. Your mouth is a tool, and key to your communication – all of the exercises in *Chapter 14: Vocal and Singing Techniques* can benefit your speaking skills.

This has been addressed already but I'm highlighting it one more time: talk *to* your audience. You are having a conversation with them rather than talking at them or running off a script. (Revisit *Chapter 9: Audience Experience* for ways to bring this to life.)

Say It Once, Say It Clearly

Audiences watching a drag show often have distractions around them – drinks at the bar, friends arriving late, someone they are flirting with. It isn't theatre where performers can leave a few breadcrumbs for the audience to follow the trail of a narrative: leave a clear path, full slices, occasionally a loaf! Always make it very clear when you are dropping a clue for them to follow.

However, don't keep repeating yourself or over labouring a point: once an idea has been established, move on. Often novice performers can't believe an audience is keeping up with them so spend minutes paraphrasing a point they established in 30 seconds. Have confidence that if you speak clearly to the audience they will understand. And if you are really unsure – ask them! "*Did you get that? Are you ready? Shall we do this?*" Again, throwing a few questions at the audience is a great way to ensure they are on-board but also maintaining *the cycle* relationship (from *Chapter 9: Audience Experience*).

> We're working in the informal, alcohol ridden industry. It's a pretty safe assumption to assume that they've either got a short attention span or they're drunk.
>
> Me The Drag Queen[1]

Framing, or Re-Framing, a Piece

Many acts are only talking to an audience briefly to introduce a song, or a piece. Getting this right is essential as it frames the way the audience will perceive everything you are about to do. I often talk about how performers *frame* an act because like any piece of art, how it is presented will affect the way in which an audience interprets and appreciates it. A simple introduction can hugely change the way the audience react to something you do. A simple frame is how you can let the audience know your specific point of view, how you want them to interpret the piece you're presenting and how to communicate some of the ideas that came out in *Chapter 10: Making Choices and Finding A Voice*.

> There is a story, possibly an urban myth, that when the Tate Modern first opened in 2000 that a cleaner left a mop and bucket on the side of a gallery. In a room full of modern art, gallery visitors stood around the mop and bucket to admire the *art*, to question it and look for meaning. "*Was it a statement on servitude? The futility of cleaning a large space with such simple items?*" "*Or had a cleaner just left a mop and bucket out?*" The audience framed happened objects as art – "*This is in a museum therefore it's a work of art*". As a performer you can achieve that with the way in which you frame your own live performances.

A Simple Frame, but Not Too Simple

How you introduce your work is vital, you are telling an audience how to interpret it, how to respect it, what world it falls into, how to analyse it. It may be simple, it may be complex, but the framing will guide your audience because it guides them how to engage with what you are doing, and may add layers or humour. Often a host will be framing the work for you, but if the set up isn't right you need to be confident enough to talk to the audience so they are ready to receive your work as you intended! There's a range of approaches for framing a song, or piece, that will help keep an audience interested and engaged. The following are examples that would work for any performer delivering a straight song – a simple frame to bring the audience in, get a laugh or keep them engaged. This is by no means an extensive list but often performers think framing only matters if you're performing something with a message, these tips will work for Saturday night bangers, ballads and sing-alongs:

Don't Tell Them What It Is: Leave them in suspense. Listening to every word to pick up what the song is. Tell a story, or frame what the song means to you – but let them have the moment of realisation of what the song is as you perform it.

Drop Clues: It can be fun to drop some clues as to what you are going to do so the audience become investigators trying to be the first to work out what the next number is.

Tell Them Who You Are Singing It To: Why not dedicate the song to a lover, someone in the front row or someone you hate! How does that effect how you interpret the song? This can be sincere or comic.

Sing-Along: Create a choir in the room. Give them the green light before you start singing so they know they can join in. "*I want those backing vocals loud and proud!*"

Get Dancing: If you want them on their feet – let them know! Get the party started. "*I want you up and dancing to this one*", "*you remember the moves*", etc.

Mis-Direction: When singing a classic, why not pretend it's a niche choice? "*An avant-guard moment – a drag act singing... ABBA!*".

Recreate a Moment: Ask the technician to light you in a specific way. Or find a spot in the room to perform it as the original artist: hop on the bar, a staircase, a table. Adjust your costuming to faux recreate an iconic moment. Cast a member of the audience as your onscreen partner.

Talk Into It: Sometimes the first line of a song can be the last line of the story. An easy example is to discuss a scary experience and then lead into Gloria Gaynor's *I Will Survive*. I can think of at least three acts I've seen do this exact example – it always works and always gets a good laugh as the audience *get* where the act is going. Even before you are doing a song, they know you are doing a song and what song it is.

Tie It to Your Alter-Ego: Why is your alter-ego singing this song? I play up on-stage that I am a failed actor, I can act like it's an audition that I'm obviously wrong for: "*I'm perfect for this role – a sexy sixteen-year-old seducing an older man*".

Blame the Audience: "*I wasn't going to do this number, but this person down here has been begging for it all night*" They obviously haven't. "*You've twisted my arm*".

I try to avoid negative examples, but to my mind there is no worse frame than a frame that does nothing:

"*This song is by Dusty Springfield, it's called* Son of a Preacher Man, *I hope you enjoy it.*"

This does *nothing*: They don't even have conviction that the audience *will* like it. To me, this is an announcement that the performer has made no choices about their performance, has no take on the song, and will do nothing with it. They are almost inviting the audience to lose interest and chat over the song. This could work for a function or background singer, but as a drag act I never want to be background! And I hope you don't, get centre stage!

> **EXERCISE 1: FRAMING**
>
> **You will need: Your notebook, pen and audio recorder.**
>
> One of the simplest tasks I do on the first week of *The Art of Drag Course* is to ask the students to pick a song (to sing or lip-sync) and introduce it. It's your turn! Look at some of the songs/numbers you are considering doing in your set, if you haven't already got some then for now just choose a song you might like to do or a drag classic (*Part of Your World*, *ABBA*, *My Way*, *Don't Stop Believin'*, etc.). Choosing well-used songs is good practice for breathing fresh life into well-trodden ground!
>
> Pick three songs and write at least two different introduction options for them. Use the points above as inspiration. Initially write notes but then when you've found enough try performing them out loud, voice recording so you can hear back how they sound. Later, when rehearsing your songs/lip-sync try to include the introduction as an integral piece of the rehearsal, not something added on last minute! Could some of the framing be over the introduction of the music…?
>
> For more experienced performers: is there an instrumental section to the song where you might say something that throws back to the way you framed the song?

Monkey Bars

I use the visual of *Monkey Bars* when talking to the audience: they are all about momentum, getting from one place to another, if you can reach the next bar you aren't going to fall. As a drag performer your rehearsed pieces within your set (be it a song, a lip-sync, a stand-up bit, etc.) are the bars and the talking between is the momentum. The bars are strong, and you know they make sense, work and stand alone. The momentum is your way of moving from one bar to the next: what you are saying is the driving force of moving through your set, or show.

When wondering "*what should I say next*" (when writing, rehearsing or on-stage) think about the two monkey bars you are between. You are at Point A and need to get to Point B. What are the changes, what are the points in common? You know how to frame the piece you're going into, so all you need to do is find a way to move from your last piece, to the next frame. When you master this you can structure you swing between your pieces whilst talking to the audience to guide them along the way.

> As an experienced performer I do not plan every word between my pieces, I use the monkey bars! I guide the audience through the set, talk to them to ensure they see the progression: "*we were here, and now I'm taking us over here. Come with me!*"
>
> It doesn't need to be a monologue, a couple of lines is plenty. From a ballad to a sing-along moment I may simply say: "*You listened beautifully to that, thank you. But some of you, I can tell, I can feel it, some are itching to show me your own skills. Your vocal talents. Are we ready for a sing-along?*"
>
> It's subtle, but those few linking words also throwback to *Chapter 11: Audience Experience*. I make the audience feel the set is being planned for them, because I am listening to them, it's our shared experience. I'm using questions to keep them engaged but not picking on them. And it all feels quite natural, not a scripted moment but a shared moment; where we are and where we are going together – as audience and performer. However, if it was a quiet audience, or they were too raucous, I could easily adapt the phrase to fit their mood but still invite them in on a sing-along!

Get Somewhere

When talking on-stage it does not have to be funny, but it does need to *get* somewhere. A performer should always know why they are speaking: a story, a few lines, a set up, building an audience connection, etc. In the early days the balance of ad-libing and working off bits of script, there will be occasions you get lost in the darkness! If you find yourself talking without an end goal – it's a problem! It happens to the best of us when filling, or getting thrown by an unexpected live moment, but learn to prepare for it. Don't keep digging, desperately trying to find a point or a punch line; pull the emergency release chord and move on to the next piece! Ok, you fell off *the monkey bars*: it may not be elegant but jump back on with energy and keep going.

Keep the energy in the room, keep the show moving.

Me The Drag Queen[2]

EXERCISE 2: EMERGENCY EXIT

You will need: Your notebook and pen, possibly audio record to hear them out loud.

You want to be prepared for the worst. Write three short lines to help you cut a rambling story short and jump into the next piece without a clever lead in. Be prepared that sometimes talking off-script can go wrong – so have a tiny bit of script ready to steer you back on track!

This is an insurance policy for you when talking on-stage. Ideally with speed and wit, it's ok to undermine yourself or be self-deprecating, your alter-ego will provide a framework possibly for the best way for you to do this. Below are a few of my go-to emergency phrases for inspiration, that suit my persona.

Try to keep the energy in the room. Try and keep that live connection with the room. Is there someone you can comically blame? The bar staff for too many drinks? Or welcome the audience to the world of live entertainment – stuff happens!

> If this happens to me I have a few go-to phrases:
>
> *"I can see some of you looking for a punchline as if this is a joke, but this isn't comedy – it's just the life of a gentleman, in his early mid-late-twenties, wearing a dress for a living – shall we have a song?"*
>
> I might blame an audience member: *"I'm so sorry, I was going somewhere but I got distracted by your sequins – where is this from? Well done you!"*
>
> *"This isn't comedy, it's just my life!"*
>
> In all cases I will then move on with panache and energy: *"Right! I feel a song coming on – let's do it"*.

Quick Fills

Often performers need to talk to the audience for practical reasons, there's a moment of dead stage-time between two set pieces. Maybe a track hasn't played, you need to catch your breath, allow the stage manager to set up the next prop, etc. It's always best to not literally tell the audience that is what you are waiting for. It looks amateur. It's a moment to carry on talking to them and connecting with them. Lean into the moment by all means but don't explicitly say "*I need to wait a moment before carrying on*". If out of breath – "*whose been the to gym today?*" If you need a drink – "*This isn't a gin, it's a vocal warm up, I'm a professional*". If the stage manager is tidying up for you perhaps – "*I'd offer to help it's above my pay grade, thank you James!*" When filling you need to keep the energy up so, when ready, you can carry on the momentum. Again, if you know this is likely to happen due to big transitions in your set – plan a little material that fits the moment. Have a little bit of patter ready – a thought on a recent pop album, a TV show, a political movement – whatever suits your alter-ego.

Blur the Lines

When a drag act is at home on-stage and talking naturally to an audience the lines between a set piece and the patter become blurred. When you have truly mastered the craft of talking to an audience what initially was a quick objective to move from one song to another, can become a small stand-up set in its own right. The gold of an accomplished performer is to seamlessly link all these areas so the audience can't see where one set piece ends and another begins. *Was that a link or a quick comedy set?*

This comes from practice: the more you perform, the more you find a rhythm and way of interacting with the audience. You will also learn what works for you, and what doesn't. You are constantly evolving your set and building a repertoire of small objectives, little phrases that you can add to your armoury. I recommend, especially at first, adding all of these into your *Repertoir List* from *Chapter 6: Building a Set, Range and Repertoire*. Note down any moments of gold that happened so they remain with you. If you didn't record the whole set make notes, voice note yourself, because you won't remember everything the next day! Slowly you will build a bank of go-to lines to use for different audience types in different situations.

Language and Lexicon

Your alter-ego will develop their own way of speaking, a certain heightened use of language. This is something that builds and evolves through on-stage experience but being prepared, rehearsing and working off-stage will help immensely! Words matter! A few words can make all the difference in setting up an audience's expectation. Imagine the atmosphere difference between "*Good evening you beautiful humans*" and "*Right bitches, who's ready to get fucked up!?*" Both are a welcome (of sorts) and could have huge effect in telling the audience where this show might be going and who you are!

EXERCISE 3: OPENING MOMENTS

You will need: Your notebook and pen. Voice recorder so you can try ideas out loud when ready.

Below is a list of essential things that most acts need to say on-stage. For each point brainstorm a few options that you can try out in rehearsal and on-stage.

1) The First Word

Nothing sets the tone as much as the first word(s) you say. The audience have seen the gorgeous visual drag creation you have made, you have reached centre stage and are ready to talk. That first word, noise or sentence will set up the rest of your set.

What will you say? How will you phrase it? *Hello? Good evening? Welcome? What are you doing here?*

> For me, the more glamorous I look the more 'blokey' I make my initial *"Hello"*. It instantly makes it clear: I don't take myself too seriously. There's rarely an H on the *"'ello"*. It juxtaposes with the aesthetic and quickly engages an audience. It's direct, it's friendly, it's simple!

2) Introduce Yourself

How can you establish who you are, why you are here, what can an audience expect in a quick sentence or two? What's your name?

> *"I'm Michael Twaits, I am a man in a dress…That's right, very trendy, very down with the kids"*.
>
> It's very blunt but contextualises where I sit on the character–persona scale. It relaxes the audience as I slightly undermine the gender illusion created visually. Anyone who says they are *"down with the kids"* clearly isn't which makes me relatable, allowing the audience to laugh with, and at, me.

3) Name the Audience

As a general rule society is moving past the binary of *Ladies and Gentlemen*. Find your own take on a fully inclusive phrase for the audience. Simple ones include: "*people, beautiful humans, my lovelies, friends, chums,*" etc! There are some casually gendered phrases still used on the scene that do cut some people out such as "*Guys*" and "*Chaps*", so try to think inclusively. It may be short ("*Everyone*") or overly specific ("My *avant-garde-cabaret-glitterati*").

> I tend to stick with *"Everybody"*.

Find your own language and phrasing to make everyone in the room feel included when you address them, so they come with you on the journey of your set, they are part of the adventure.

I have a theory that if you get your audience onside for the first five minutes, you have got them for the whole thing.

Hugo Grrrl[3]

EXERCISE 4: ONGOING LANGUAGE

You will need: Your notebook and pen. Voice recorder so you can try ideas out loud when ready

You have established your *opening moments* with your choice of words but throughout an entire set, or show, there are opportunities to have a unique take on how you speak to an audience. Keep your pen busy and use some voice notes to see how they sound out loud as you carry on building your lexicon. After you've tried some out at a gig, come back and review – maybe try some others and make notes of which were a good fit for you. Drag is all about personality, being interesting, heightened. So take some of the simple things we all say on stage and find *your* way of doing it – drag them up a bit!

1) "Yes, Dear"

You need to find ways to talk to individuals within the audience, drag has a long traditions of "*Dear*", "*Darling*", etc. More modern acts might use "*Girls*", "*Hun*", etc. Kings might take the masculine lads approach: "*Mate*", "*Bro*", etc.

How are you going to generically refer to an individual without knowing their name? What does that say about your alter-ego?

2) Name Them

As well as "*Dear*" or the like, there is a whole host of names you can give individuals that can make them feel included, feel seen and of course be hilarious. Remember in *Chapter 11: Audience Experience* it was to hold their focus and keep them included. Revisit and brainstorm a few examples for *Group Names, Assumed Names, Comparisons* or "*Brands*". Find What works for your alter-ego (page 122).

3) Positives and Negatives

Positives and negatives are important because you want the audience to feel the love coming from the *Love Experience* (*Chapter 11: Audience Experience*) but if everything is "*fabulous*", it loses meaning. You need *peaks and troughs* (*Chapter 8: Basic Drag*) so find how you are going to deal with negatives too!

> These can be incredibly simple. Don't over think it, but with the negatives, remember these aren't words to attack an audience with, just a small disagreement – try to keep them playful.
>
> **Positives:** *gorgeous, wonderful, beautiful, sexy, macho…*
>
> **Negatives:** *interesting, that's a choice, vile, hideous, each to their own, awful…*

4) Rename the Basics

There is a lot of comedy to be found in renaming, or even reinterpreting the pronunciation, of things everyone knows. What might you call:

The Venue You're In

The Bar

The Bathrooms

The Technician

The Stage

These don't need to be belly laughs; just little witty, or camp, ways of saying things. As a drag act making everything more extravagant builds a world, and an atmosphere, for the audience. It's not about telling jokes, but being a bit silly and playful with an audience.

> My dressing room is often "*the glamorous spa and sauna area*".
>
> A sip of my drink is "*a professional vocal warm up*".
>
> Sarah Rose, my pianist, is "*the busiest fingers in London's glittering West End*".

5) Get Them Going

Phrase such as *"are you ready?"* are a go-to for any drag act trying to build a bit of excitement and interaction between themselves and an audience. *"Put your hands together"*. What could your versions be?

6) *"I'm Done"*

At the end of a set, as the applause happens, it is a real skill to get off the stage smoothly without ruining the moment. Sometimes acts say too much and lose the feeling of a big finish. Others run off before the audience has finished appreciating them.

> I tend to keep it simple and let the work do the talking, rather than going for an extra laugh: *"Thank you so much"*, *"You've been fabulous"*, etc.
>
> If it's a regular gig, or a local gig, I'll often add *"see you soon"* making it clear I've enjoyed their company and I expect them to be back again!

If you are a lip-sync, burlesque or circus act – be specific about the physical actions you do at the end to say you are done. Don't be afraid to just hold your final pose for an extra second or two, then turn to the audience and bow, curtsey, wave, give a cheeky wink or flash them before you get off stage! Try to avoid nodding or seemingly agreeing with the applause as it reads as arrogant.

Evolution

Hopefully you have pages overflowing with hilarious and silly words and phrases. Nothing is set in stone; try them out on-stage and in rehearsal. Keep the ones that work well; evolve, or cut the ones that don't work for you. Depending on the gig you are doing, the set, the atmosphere in the room, you will have options – try them all out.

You always want the language you use to feel natural, to feel that it's the way you communicate instinctively rather than it feeling like a script, or a *bit*. It's why practising out loud and using voice notes is essential with these exercises – it helps you find the rhythms of the language and how they work for you. The more naturally you can talk to the audience the more they will connect with you, despite watching drag they want to create an authentic connection to a performer.

You don't always need a laugh from these. It's about building your on-stage presence and audience relationship. However, when you listen back to voice notes you might find some bits you thought were funny don't get a laugh. Don't panic, but look at the rhythms, was it too wordy, does it need another word or two, a beat before you say it! With new material it needs to be run in front of an audience numerous times before you can definitively see how it's going to work. Keep performing, reviewing and trying again!

Don't Do It!

As an act you always need to show respect for the show as a whole, the venue, the host, the other performers etc. Let everyone do the job they were booked to do and don't (intentionally or not) undermine them. Here is a quick list of things to avoid when talking to an audience.

- ***"Welcome To My Show"/"Thanks for coming out to see me"***. You are one act, possibly midway through a show. It's not your show, remove your ego. Unless you are a character who wishes to come across as an arrogant, egotist and that's part of your humour. Avoid doing this!

- **Don't Start Hosting.** You may be an accomplished drag host, but if you aren't the host tonight, don't start hosting. Do your set and let the host do the hosting. Don't reintroduce the host at the end of your set – take your applause and get out of the way, let them do their job!
- **Joke About Other Acts.** Unless it's a roast, or there's a very specific reason, don't do it! Focus on yourself, your set and the audience. If you're having a great night watching the others, fine, mention that but don't do any jokes about them. Get on with what you've been booked to do.
- **Don't Repeat Things.** It's often hard on a line-up show to know what everyone else is up to. But try and keep an eye on the show as a whole. If someone has done a comedy set on The President, for example, try and cut your joke rather than paraphrasing and repeating already trodden ground. Be aware of the night as a whole! (Back to *Chapter 8: Basic Drag.*) If you are singling out an audience member or using a volunteer, try and find out if anyone else has earlier and make sure you have picked a different person.
- **Don't Plug Your Socials.** It's become an epidemic where acts seem to think saying the names of their socials on-stage will get people to follow them. It won't. Being a good act will get people to follow you! Be the best you can be and try to find ways to use your name within your set. Your socials should be your name and easily findable so just say *"I've been XXX"* as you finish if you need to!

Final Thoughts

Respect the Venue and Producer: Love the venue you are in. Throwing back to *Chapter 2: The Business Of Drag* you want to be rebooked – so make sure they know you love being there and respect them. Don't talk the venue down, and despite your being a busy act don't start promoting shows in other venues on-stage – both venues may book you but they are direct competition!

Faux Bespoke: Audiences love people to know where they are performing, and an act who seems to be in the live moment. Always look for ways to <insert name here> for cities, venues, hosts, colleagues or even news stories. A phrase can be slightly adapted to feel bespoke to where and when you are despite being used in every gig you do. As you expand your experience keep an eye out for opportunities like this.

Little Lies: Talking genuinely to an audience doesn't always mean being truthful. Many drag acts play on having delusions of grandeur, and perhaps they are slightly disappointed with tonight's venue or audience (Myra Dubois, Kiki & Herb, Lily Savage, etc.). The audience know the performer is joking with them; the tongue is firmly in the cheek. The lies are preamble, building a relationship with the audience and helping them to 'get' the acts point of view and humour.

Overview: Talking On Stage

Aiming to feel natural, unscripted, in the live moment and still having trajectory is a balancing act which takes years of experience to truly conquer. Keep rehearsing and trying out ideas on-stage! At first try short, rehearsed, scripted lines but as it builds you may find the confidence to try new material in the moment on-stage. When something works, make a note of it!

- Always talk *to* the audience. Invite them along on the journey of your set.
- Know who your audience are. Research beforehand and use the first moments to gauge their reactions, learn where their taste and energy levels are at.
- Try to speak clearly, not be repetitive and always have a point you are getting to – think of *Monkey Bars*. You have to keep the momentum.
- One line of dialogue can completely change the way an audience interprets a three-minute song. Work on framing of your pieces, see how it changes the reactions to it.

- Prepare yourself for failure. When a moment goes wrong, or you get lost, have a go-to phrase to pull you back.
- Build your language and lexicon. Everything act needs to say the same things at some point or another – so give it your unique spin.
- If you can connect to the audience in the opening moments, and show them who you are, it makes the rest of the set much easier as you have them on side.
- Write, rehearse, try out, evaluate, re-write, rehearse, try out. And keep doing it!
- Work on your vocal technique, every day, warm ups will hugely benefit your skill set. It's not just for a show day! (Examples are coming up in *Chapter 14: Vocal and Singing Techniques*.)

The more stage-time you have the more the craft of talking to an audience will improve (many of our interviewees in *Part IV* discuss how this was one of the hardest parts of their development). But prepare yourself as much as you can; write, rehearse, review! Remember, if an audience can't clearly hear and understand you, it doesn't matter how good the writing is, they can't hear it! Work on your vocal technique – the next chapter is all about that! Don't think because you aren't a singer you don't need to work on vocal technique – every performer who speaks on stage needs to work on their vocal technique.

Notes

1 *Me The Drag Queen* in interview with *Michael Twaits*, July 2024. See Part IV for full interview.
2 *Me The Drag Queen* in interview with *Michael Twaits*, July 2024. See Part IV for full interview.
3 *Hugo Grrrl* in interview with *Michael Twaits*, July 2024. See Part IV for full interview.

Lorelai Spera photographed backstage at the Royal Vauxhall Tavern by Fox Al Rajim

14
Make Your Own Kind of Music: Vocal and Singing Techniques

A performer's body is their instrument, and this chapter is to encourage all drag acts to get to know their instrument! And rehearse with it. Like any instrument, the more the voice is used the more sophisticated the music can be. All drag acts need to get familiar with their voice, and build a routine that allows them to practice and improve everyday!

This chapter has exercises, techniques and ideas throughout to help you find your own approach to singing. To build vocal confidence which will help both in speech and song. As a performer knowing your voice, knowing your range and knowing what you are capable of is essential. For many jobbing drag acts, talking and singing are quite hard to avoid. Many consider a bread-and-butter drag set to be: sing a song, have a chat with the audience, tell a few jokes, sing another song and repeat. The two have a natural flow together, singing can move into talking and back; a story can just segue simply into a song. The two parts of the set become almost seamless as you move from introducing the song into performing it – or vice-versa. (See more details on framing in *Chapter 13: Talking On Stage*.)

Don't be under the illusion you need to be a technically brilliant singer to sing in drag. There are many drag acts out there who use their instrument like a wrecking-ball! The most important aspect of learning to sing, to my mind, is finding the *confidence*, to sing with conviction on-stage, unapologetically.

> Whilst training at drama school I hated singing. I was terrible at it; I was anxious, I cried in class, I never knew what to do with my hands and had no control of my technique. However, once in drag I realised that I did have all the tools to perform a song well. Drag gave me something to hide behind, an excuse – *"I didn't sing that, the wig did!"* Once again I found drag a way to shake off my inner doubts and release the best performer within me. The confidence it gave me allowed me to improve my vocal technique exponentially.
>
> Initially I used singing for comedy: a quirky take on a song or a parody. But slowly my voice became stronger and I became more confident using it. It was a long process, I wish I knew sooner that I didn't need the drag to find that confidence, I just needed to practice!

Throughout this chapter I have provided simple, dare I say dumbed-down, ways to access your best vocal ability. This is a shorthand to get you confident on-stage and singing and speaking clearly! If you wish to be a classically trained singer – there are conservatoires for training, academic books and plenty of tutors out there. Invest in your craft and take a class! This is a short hand to brush up your skill set and improve the tools you have!

DOI: 10.4324/9781003498797-17

Experienced Singers

Those reading who are established singers or musical theatre graduates, you may feel you already have the skills and don't need this section. Don't let pride, or your ego, stop you from working on your technique. Maybe explore some of the journey I'm sending less experienced singers on. Your vocal range, style and technique can always be expanded. And the goals of singing in drag could be very different to a polished Broadway show. How you personally sing may not be how your alter-ego does? Play with us!

Novice and Anxious Singers

There's no such thing as a *new* singer; everyone has attempted to sing at some point. I like the word novice as it implies inexperienced but with aspirations to be better. The biggest task, if you want to be able to sing on-stage is to get comfortable singing. And the best way to do that is practise.

EXERCISE 1: GAINING CONFIDENCE

You will need: To head to a karaoke bar! Take a friend, make a night of it.

If you are an anxious singer, or feel self conscious this is an essential exercise to do, and repeat, until you start to become comfortable singing publicly. It is arguably the *dirtiest* drag secret ever written: go to a karaoke bar.

Ideally a bar with a stage rather than a private booth. You need the audience to hear you sing, to experience the feeling of fear and potential public shame! Pick a simple song that you think you know and just do it. You might rehearse the chosen song at home in advance to help get a confidence boost. The words are on the screen in front of you and you are given a microphone which means you don't have to do *anything* whilst performing; hold the microphone and look at the screen. There's no need to interact with people or make a show, simply sing the song on the stage.

If there's an instrumental moment and you feel awkward, lean over and have a sip of your drink to give you a bit of *'business'* before returning to the usual position of looking at the screen. If the thought of singing publicly is what is stopping you from singing – *get to a karaoke bar!* Build your confidence, learn to relax and, dare I say, have fun!

> I couldn't sing! When I started singing I used to get muscle cramps across my lower back and spine. I was incredibly anxious. I didn't know how to use the voice that I had. I went to karaoke night with friends and trained myself to get over the fear. I sang *Sweet Transvestite* from *The Rocky Horror Show* once a week for the best part of a year. As my confidence grew I put in a second song (usually *You Had Me* by Joss Stone).
>
> *Sweet Transvestite* was a great choice – you can *speak-sing* the majority of the song. A few sung notes are needed in the chorus but really if you can speak in time to the music, you can perform it. It's an actor's song. Slowly as I became more comfortable I added more *'singing'* rather than just speak singing. I kept working on it, and for the majority of the time, despite singing it every week I simply stared at the screen pretending I was reading the words because it gave me something to do and I didn't need to *perform* too much to an audience.
>
> The next step was arguably the hardest. I asked a friend to sit near the front and I looked at them rather than the screen for some of the song. Instantly a performance, of sorts, came

> out. Slowly I started moving between the screen, performing a bit, grabbing my drink for a quick sip and this combination made me loosen up. Eventually I was brave enough to try more songs.
>
> I grew more as a singer through this process than a year at drama school standing by a piano doing scales, being told where to breathe from and how to correct my posture. Before I could tackle any kind of feedback from others I needed to find a place where I was comfortable singing in front of others.

Finding the Animation in Your Voice

Performers need to know what their voice can and can't do. Vocal dexterity can help in creating your alter-ego, communicating with an audience and finding an interesting range of songs to sing. Drag acts are visually playing with perceived gender and character. You *can* play with vocals as much should you wish to: sing deep, sing high! Shout or whisper! And use all the colours in between!

Being a bit silly and playing with your voice in rehearsal is a great way to loosen up an anxious singer, and discover interesting varieties within your voice. It will help you work out how best you can perform a song, what songs will suit your voice.

> EXERCISE 2: HAVING FUN WITH BRUNO
>
> **You will need: The track and a copy of the lyrics for** *We Don't Talk About Bruno* **from Encanto.**
>
> This is a simple and effective exercise that works with many songs but we'll use: *We Don't Talk About Bruno* from *Encanto*. An ensemble song originally performed by voice-actors meaning all the character voices are distinctive, varied and animated. Being an ensemble song there is **no way you can sing it all!** You have to play around, jump in and out of bits, be a little ridiculous. This is an easy *in* to finding vocal agility, variety, light and shade in a song – always remember variety will help keep an audience engaged! (These are vocal *peaks and troughs* – Chapter 8: Basic Drag.)
>
> Try and sing along with the entire song, jump in and out of characters, try using different elements of your voice. There are around ten characters singing separately, and together, at different points of the song. You probably won't be able to do them all at first. How can you make each section work for you? How can you make each character sound distinct? (These characters are all Colombian – but this is not an *accent* exercise – sing in your native accent.) Focus on the variety of vocal qualities. Have fun – no one else needs to hear you! Get it wrong! Take things too far! And then do it again!
>
> There are numerous vocal qualities at work here: speech quality, lyrical singing, low bassy notes, twang, operatic, breathy/jazzy and some belting to name a few. A technical vocal coach would guide through what part of your vocal tract to use for which ones. But instinctively performers are good at replicating a sound, and quality that they hear. Investigate and find out what your voice can do. Which character is closest to your 'comfortable' singing style? Which ones do you think you could incorporate? Get to learn your instrument and challenge your vocal abilities.

> This is a vocal exercise to come back to consistently. Add it into your warm up. In a way it's a bit like a tongue twister: run it a lot to learn it at first, then add it into your regular warm up routine to keep developing and improving your vocal dexterity and trying to take it further. Initially try keeping up with the singers, then maybe invest in a backing track and see how you can do on your own. If you have mastered, or got bored, with *Bruno*, find a similar song – the opening *Belle* in *Beauty & the Beast* for example is full of characters and fun vocal variety.
>
> The goal is to explore different colours to your voice. Which ways of singing could you use for a whole song? Which could you play with for one line or one moment?

Putting Animation into Other Songs

If you can successfully sing various parts of *Bruno* then you have successfully introduced yourself to your own singing short-hand. A quick way to find interesting vocal ranges that you can play between. Now find ways to apply it! Naming different lines in a song as different characters/voices from *Bruno* will help you find moments of variety within songs that previously you've been singing in one style.

Let's take *Cabaret*: Sally quotes her friend Elsie within the song. Try giving Elsie different character vocals from *Bruno* and see what it does to the meaning, the comedy, the rhythm of the song.

Sally: *"I remember, how she'd smile at me and say:"*

Elsie: *"What good is sitting alone in your room..."*[1]

Why not get a laugh for playing with and exaggerating vocal range? It's these types of choices which will help make the song your own, add comedy and variety and keep the audience engaged. It isn't only in musical theatre songs this would work: In pop songs, an easy example is Lady Gaga's *Poker Face*, there are plenty of opportunities to jump into different ranges. With *Poker Face* the third verse rap section could be really fun. What happens if you do this as Dolores? Or Louisa? Or Pepe? How does each character's vocal quality from *Bruno* change the song for you?

> **EXERCISE 3: ADD ANIMATION TO YOUR REPERTOIRE**
>
> **You will need: Backing tracks and ideally a print-out of lyrics for songs in your repertoire.**
>
> Pick a song from your *Repertoire List*, or that you are considering using, and try to assign at least three different singing qualities (or characters from *Bruno*) into it. Possibly highlight on your lyrics where you're changing vocal qualities. What effect does it add? Does it give the song variety, dimension, can it add in any humour? It might be for a couple of words or a full chorus, there are no rules! Just find vocal variety.
>
> You can return to this exercise after *Chapter 15: Sing a Song* once you have looked at textual analysis and see if specific vocal qualities match with different sections of the lyric.

Invest in Yourself, Everyday

The best way to improve at anything is to practice, little and often so that it becomes habit. Everyone can find a few minutes in their day to do a vocal warm up and train their voice to be stronger, clearer and more dexterous. Like any system of muscles the more you use it the stronger and more agile it becomes.

If you can spend around two minutes on each of the areas below – you will see progress. *Exercise 4* covers seven areas, which is under 15 minutes a day. You could easily do this whilst having a shower and getting ready in the morning; before you know it you will have habitually built it into your daily routine. Don't think a vocal warm up is only needed before a show or rehearsal.

> When I'm backstage, I get ready really early…I don't like to be rushed! I like to stretch, there'll be some sort of physical warm up, some sort of vocal warm up, some sort of lubrication and pacing.
>
> Adam All[2]

EXERCISE 4: VOCAL WARM UP

The below seven areas all have example exercises and different ways to warm up parts of the vocal tract, the various areas of your body that produce your voice. There are countless books, YouTube playlists and more that you can dive into to move forward and find variation, you might already have a few of your own. These are just starting suggestions and you should keep exploring which work best for you, and which are helping your voice the most.

Through exploration you will structure your own vocal warm up: something you might use pre-show to get warm but more importantly something that you do every single day.

1) Breath

Take a moment before you start working your voice to take some deep breaths. Try breathing in for a slow four count, out for slow four count expelling all the air over that four count. Then do an in for four, out for eight. Then in for four, out for 12…

The goal is to keep expelling all the air from your body on the breath out but keeping the breath coming out at a consistent pace. Supported. Once you master that – can you do 16, or 20? (This helps build you breathe support for a long line or lyric in the middle of a song.)

2) Facial Warm Ups

Chew Toffee: Imagine you are chewing a very sticky piece of toffee. As you chew it gets larger and larger then smaller and smaller. Work the small piece all around your mouth. Slowly it gets larger again. Maybe it gets tougher and chewier so you have to work slower – or softer so you can chew at double speed. Work the imaginary toffee all around your entire mouth and it will wake up your jaw, lips and most of your face!

Big Face/Little Face: Make your face as big, open and wide as possible on an inhale. As if you are hugely surprised. Then as compressed and small as possible on an exhale. Repeat five times. You should be able to feel the stretching and loosening along your jaw, brow, around your eyes and nose. A full facial warm up.

Tongue Circles: Stick out your tongue and point up, down, left, right. Stretching the tongue opens the voice and sound qualities up a lot. A fun take on this one is to 'sing' with your tongue out the *Mission Impossible* theme and move tongue direction on each note. If you don't need to wipe your lips at the end you haven't stuck your tongue far enough out.

3) Humming

Without getting too technical, singing and speaking use resonators. This humming exercise is a simple way of warming the front of the face, the soft palette, the body and then the voice up. It's fun to explore where you can place a hum in your body to feel it resonate.

On one long breath work through the three stages below – *Hmmm-Ng-Ah!*

1) *Hm* – The hum should be vibrating almost to the point it tickles the areas it's resonating in. Note wise the lower you place the hum the lower in your body you should feel it.
2) *Ng* – Then move the hum to the soft palette (that's the Ng noise at the back of your throat) I find I put the tip of my tongue on the roof of my mouth to open it up.
3) *Ah* – Finally slowly open the mouth for a nice clear, open *Aaaah*.

Slowly work up and down your range. Again there are plenty of YouTube tutorials on humming and waking up resonators – so dive in and see what resonators you can get buzzing.

4) Sirens:

A siren is sliding through your entire vocal range using an open vowel sound (*ahh*, *ooo*, etc.). Start as low vocally as you can and slide up high as you can. Work up and down on different sounds – but it's called a *Siren* because that's how you should sound!

Early in the morning the sirens may be smaller, or have a few vocal cracks or breaks. But as you warm up and the voice warms up you will find a wider range and a more supported range. Again, the more frequently you do this the wider the range and the smoother the journey will be.

5) Horse Flutters/Lip Trills/Tongue Rolls

With all three of these do a few initially to loosen up your cheeks and lips. Then return to voicing a Siren and working up and down your range whilst doing the action.

Horse Flutters: Blow out your cheeks and lips and let the relaxed lower half of your face vibrate. It isn't an attractive or easy action to explain but the horse flutter is a great name for it as it does sound like a horse!

Lip Trills: This is exactly the same action as above but with only the lips loose. The cheeks are not fluttering at this point. It can tickle a little on the tip of your lips as you do it fast.

Tongue Rolls: Opening your mouth and relaxing your tongue roll an 'r' on a note. This isn't quite a tongue pop, it's softer, repeated and much faster.

6) Tongue Twisters

Clearly, and slowly recite the following tongue twisters a few times each. Gradually speed up as you gain more confidence. These are all famous tongue twisters and many more can be easily tracked down. If you have vocal ticks of troubles (sibilant S's or trouble with 'TH's) then find some that work on your specific sound issues to work through them

- *She sells sea shells on the sea shore. The sea shells that she sells are sea shells for sure.*
- *Gabby Gardners Gather Together to Gossip in Garrulous Groups.*
- *Peter Piper Picked a Peck of Pickled Peppers.*
- *Unique New York.*

7) Tone

Try to sing these tongue twisters on one note, take a breath and go up one note. See how high and low you can confidently go.

- *Mummy Made Me Mash My M&M's.*
- *Floppy Fluffy Puppy.*
- *Pineapple Caterpillar.*

These exercises, used regularly will help your singing and speaking voice on-stage: improving diction, clarity of communication and your vocal range. Keep adapting and improving your *Vocal Warm Up* and push yourself a little bit further (reach a little higher on the *Sirens*, go faster on the *Tongue Twisters*). At the end of my daily *Vocal Warm Up* I always jump into a couple of songs I'm learning or are on my *Repertoire List*. It's a natural progression to improving my vocal technique but also getting to know my repertoire better. An informal rehearsal!

Overview: Singing and Vocal Techniques

Audiences need to hear every word so diction is important, variety is important for them to keep engaged and performers should aim to constantly improve their craft. What's the point of good jokes if an audience can't clearly here the punchline?

- Explore and learn what your voice can do! Play. Be silly. Keep finding variety.
- Build confidence, especially for singing on-stage. Practice makes progress: So sing as much as you can.
- Play with your voice, find interesting variety, colour and character in your voice. Sing different songs, not just ones you know you can. Sing as different characters.
- Develop your own *Vocal Warm Up* and build it into your daily routine and pre-show routine!

All of these vocal exercises and knowledge will help your vocal clarity on-stage. But now it's time to look at acting through song and choosing the right material as you get ready to sing!

Note

1. Cabaret by Fred Ebb and John Kander – © 1966 Alley Music Corp (BMI)/Trio Music Company (BMI)/Carlin Music.
2. *Adam All* in interview with *Michael Twaits*, July 2024. See Part IV for full interview.

Princess Eva After photographed backstage at the Royal Vauxhall Tavern by The Burley Photographer

15
Sing: Sing a Song

Performing a song is about much more than just singing the notes or remembering the lyrics. It is about telling a story, creating a moment, shedding new light on familiar material and communicating with the audience. A beautifully sung song can be boring, or even worse feel like a second-rate impersonator. It's time to look at the craft of singing a song and preparing it for the stage!

In a singing contest, the best singer will usually win: in a drag contest, the best singer rarely does! In drag, singing does not necessarily need to sound beautiful, or even be in time to the music. You can tackle a song in numerous ways to create a unique audience experience. This chapter will look at: acting through song, building a structure, finding the jokes and creating your unique interpretation.

Every time you approach a new song for your repertoire, follow the next few pages as a way of giving yourself options. Ways to open up ideas that will create a dynamic, structured and unique interpretation. If you have jumped straight into this chapter – welcome – first visit *Chapter 10: Making Choices and Finding a Voice* and *Chapter 12: Audience Experience*. The interpretations you make, your choices and the way you connect to an audience are vital tools for any drag act when singing!

When singing a song do you ever feel the audience switching off? Then you possibly haven't worked the song enough to find the moments of gold. Or, perhaps, you are singing the wrong songs?

Picking the Right Song

Choosing the right song can be a game of trial and error. Often you'll hear a song and think – "*I want to do that*". You may have an idea for a specific concept or interpretation you could explore. Before working too much on the song it's best to test the song out and see if it's something that can work for you. You don't want to invest rehearsal time on a song to then find you can't get close to the finishing notes.

EXERCISE 1: TEST DRIVE A SONG

You will need: The original song, hopefully a backing track and somewhere you can sing out!

Before deciding to add a song to your repertoire it is always useful to take it for a quick test drive.

Can you sing it? What might you do with it? How will the audience connect to it?

- **Can you sing the song?** If the song is consistently a little too high or too low that isn't a problem. You can find an accompaniment which is transposed up or down to suit your range. However, if you find at times it is too high and other times too low, then the range is too wide for you. Leave that song for now and start looking for another. If your technical singing improves through

---

DOI: 10.4324/9781003498797-18

- **Is this song of use to you?** Could it be an opener, closer, sing-along moment? Is there somewhere you can see yourself using it in a set? Is it adding something new or varied to your repertoire (See more in *Chapter 6 :Building A Set, Range and Repertoire*)

- **Is the song interesting?** When you take out all the vocal production does it still sound good? Pop songs often aren't very varied if production is removed, make sure you still think the song sounds good. Musical theatre songs were written to be sung, pop songs often have many layered voices, backing vocals, voice effects that once removed can leave a very simple tune that isn't worthy of a live performance.

- **Are you just indulging yourself?** I *love* Tori Amos but her music doesn't generally fit my style of performance. It's not familiar or crowd pleasing. It's great to listen to at home with a glass of wine, but generally drag is on-stage in front of people wanting a big night out. Choose material that works for the show you are booked for, not just songs you happen to like.

- **Is it well known?** Audiences love to feel *in the know*. There's a reason the popular songs are popular. Don't be afraid to choose a classic and make it your own. There are gigs where rare, unheard songs, are very rewarding for an audience. But generally, especially at the start of your career, you want to have familiar, bookable, crowd pleasing material.

> I love Kate Bush, but for most shows I would only choose to do *Running Up That Hill* or *Wuthering Heights*. However, I do an annual Kate Bush themed night and that's when I can bring out an album track or B-side that I know will be appreciated because I know the audience are all fans of Kate Bush.

The answers may not be *positive* for all these areas straight away! A song may need to be cut down to be more interesting, transposed up to fit your voice better. That is all very achievable as you shall see in *Chapter 16: Creating and Editing a Track*. You might even need to do some writing to have the right introduction, or *frame*, to make the song work (see *Chapter 13: Talking On Stage*).

How to Successfully Perform a Song

There are a range of techniques and exercises which will help you successfully perform a song. All of these are to do with connecting with the song and using that to connect with an audience. Rather than focusing on replicating a beautiful sound step back and think about what affect this song is having on the audience. A vocal coach can bring out the best of your voice if needed, but these exercises will help you find interesting options of how to perform, act and interact with the chosen song.

Cabaret from the musical *Cabaret* will be our example song to work with for the rest of this chapter.[1] It has a rich text to explore, with lots interesting and options. However, the exploration and exercises coming up will work when applied to *any* song. Each exercise will provide a different '*in*', a way of unlocking something interesting in a song. Some will work better for one song than another song, and for one performer than another.

As performers, if you are ever midway through a song and feel you are slightly *checking out*, or going through the motions, then your audience will be too. If you experience that on-stage, come back and have another look. Find more interest, more variety, more fun! Digging deep will help you find the gold to keep the audience engaged from beginning to end.

Acting through Song

The role of an actor is to take the audience on a journey, a development or adjustment from where the mood or atmosphere was before they started performing. As a drag act you can aim to do that with every song. Audiences do not want to *just* sit and watch someone be fabulous: they want to be engaged, provoked, surprised and delighted. A song isn't only a journey for the audience, with acting through song it can be a transformational journey for your alter-ego. It may change you, or it may change the audience or the atmosphere. But each song is a little story, a little transformation and a shift in the room. When the song is over something has changed.

Analysing the Text

Analysis will help elevate your performance, find the key ways to connect with a song, the audience and create some live magic. Analysis can make the difference between the song feeling like a possible *filler* moment and help the audience see they are watching a world-class act. I can almost hear some readers thinking – "*Too much! Just give the gays what they want – a camp number!*" But believe me, it's worth the investment in your material! The more experienced you become as a performer the easier it becomes to add songs to your *Repertoire List.* You'll develop your own shorthand from these exercises but the goal is to be able to craft a song audiences will actually listen to as much as they listen to a story, or a joke – rather than going to the bar or chatting to their friend!

The Truth of the Text

I love Dame Sheila Hancock: I saw her in *Cabaret* in 2006 with Anna Maxwell Martin as Sally Bowles. Dame Sheila became an icon to me when she judged the BBC reality TV contest *Over the Rainbow*. Most judges go for soundbites and cliche whilst giving feedback to the contestants. Dame Sheila was critiquing as if she was back at the Royal Shakespeare Company – analysing cadence, connection to the text, rhythm, vocal variety and interest. Her catchphrase was "*the truth of the text*".

> I do musicals, but I come at them as an actor…I haven't got a great voice but I can sell a number but I'm not a singer.
>
> Shiela Hancock in interview with Terry Wogan, BBC[2]

Whether singing Sondheim or Britney Spears she would encourage the performers to keep looking for the "*truth of the text*". How can you sing a song, connect to an audience, use the lyrics to tell the story? As a drag act you have chosen that song – tell a story using those lyrics! A story doesn't mean a literal narrative every time, but show us something new, dynamic, reinterpret the expected, make us laugh, dance or cry – just do *something!*

With pop songs acts often ignore this approach but by analysing the text you may un-tap new meaning, comedy or progression through the song that will make an audience sit up and engage with you.

Research: What's Been Done?

Investigate what's been done before: listen to as many different versions of the song as you can, live versions, acoustic versions, choral versions? Was there a *Glee* version? The *Post-Modern Juke Box*? A heavy metal version? As always, the internet is your friend – explore!

For *Cabaret* it's easy to find a huge range of performances: Liza Minelli, Jessie Buckley, Kelly Hunter, Natasha Richardson, Judi Dench, Louis Armstrong and more. Do any of them jump out to you as unique, odd, different, interesting? Which do you connect to?

The Liza, film, version has a very glossy, big-finish feel to it. Liza belts beautifully and gives a smaller, more controlled performance which is suitable for the screen. Compare it to Jessie Buckley who has an almost unhinged, primitive take on it. Some performers manage comic moments, others bring you to tears; they are all connecting to the text in a different way to tell their story. But they are all using the same text – the lyrics!

Research: Context

Once you've immersed yourself in what is out there, the next level of research is to know the context of the song. Narratively, if it is from a musical, what happened before? Who is *meant* to sing this song? How does that character's journey affect how you interpret the song.

For a pop song, context is everything! Was this a career high or low? Is this song associated with anything? Many songs are about personal relationships: think about Britney Spears and Justin Timberlake. Was it a breakout single? The research isn't about finding definitive answers, it's about providing context and possible options for exploration as you move forward. Anything even vaguely related – make a note of it! You could use this knowledge implicitly or explicitly to frame the work, get some laughs or contextualise the song for the audience.

Cabaret has some great context: Sally has just been asked by her lover to move to America to escape wartime Germany to raise her baby with him. She's decided to stay in the decadent *Cabaret* world she knows and loves. Is she upset her lover left her? Delighted that this is her life? Is she drunk? As a performer when singing this song I could be Sally, and do a musical theatre performance, or myself and engage with the *Cabaret* space I am in? There are options!

There is also plenty of context with Liza Minelli that suits my camp sensibility! Liza winning an Oscar for the performance and arguably fully stepping out of her parents' shadow. I found a story about Liza at the Oscars noticing Diana Ross (also nominated that year) had a costume change just before the Best Actress announcement which led Liza to assume Diana would win. This is why Liza was so shocked and dramatic as she accepts the award. It's exactly the kind of camp story I might tell, even re-enact, at my shows! Already I am armed with lots of options to explore! Stories to share and laughs to have.

EXERCISE 2: RESEARCH YOUR OWN SONG

You will need: Your notebook and something with access to the internet – streaming services, YouTube (or similar) and Google.

If you haven't chosen a song yet, or it feels too soon, then use *Cabaret*: listen to the versions I found and see what other bits of camp trivia you can find that might be fitting to develop into an anecdote for you. Immersing yourself in the research should become a habitual process for you. You don't want to be singing a song and realise you didn't know the backstory in it. If you have a great song in your rep – then do the research now and bring that song with you over the upcoming exercises too! Get on the internet and do a deep dive; find everything you can – you never know what will end up being useful! For every song in your *Repertoire List – Stage Ready, In Rehearsal* or *In Development* – you should have a dedicated page of research in your notebook!

EXERCISE 3: TEXTUAL ANALYSIS

You will need: A copy of your lyrics printed out and a selection of coloured highlighters and a pen.

Find a reliable version of the lyrics: you need to be confident punctuation, spelling and spacing are all correct. If you are able to double space the lyrics to have space for notes – even better. Print them out, or handwrite if needed, and then work through the lyrics, focusing on each of the following points separately:

Meaning: What is the song about? Literally, the surface meaning? Make sure you understand every word and reference in the song. Use a dictionary and the internet if needed.

Subtext: Do you see options for subtext, the meaning behind the lyrics? The subtext is usually what changes most in each artist's interpretation

Language Choices: Sometimes a lyricist uses particular words or phrases which can lead you in a certain direction or open up ideas for development. Does anything stand out as distinctive, unusual or interesting?

Punctuation: This can help us see the intention of the lyricist(s). Check for the full stops, exclamations, questions, colons, etc. What performance options do they give us? They give breaks, a moment to breathe, a change in intention.

Rhythm: Is there a set rhythm, is it consistent, does it change, does this tell you anything in the narrative of the story or the journey of the song?

Rhyme: Is there any? Is it consistent? Are the rhymes at moments of change, development, juxtaposition?

Questions: They are a gift for drag performers; a chance to engage directly with the audience or maybe to try to get a response.

Speech/Character: Many songs have a change of character, or a quote from someone else. Again a moment to easily add colour and variety to your performance.

Repetition: When a key word or lyric is repeated it's useful to break down what that means, why do they keep repeating it?

There won't be gold in every area for every song. Sometimes you'll find a word that just gives you a fun idea you could play with in performance. Other times an entire new way of interpreting the song. But you won't know until you start digging!

These are a few notes and thoughts I had during analysis for *Cabaret*. These are exactly the types of notes I would write for myself as I work through any song. Lots of questions, lots of options and lots of things to explore but very few definitive answers!

Meaning: The opening line could be a call to arms; telling everyone to stop being boring and live life to the fullest!

The story of Elsie shows that we all die in the end, at least she made some good memories.

The through line could be *don't just watch the Cabaret – be part of it.*

Subtext: The song is frequently performed with a feeling of "*I'm fabulous – come and be more like me*". I wonder if a more interesting choice is: "*None of this matters, it's all bullshit!*"

Language Choices: There are many, but two that really interest me are:

"*Old Chum*" – This could be Sally's take on *my dear*. She's fabulous, everyone is made to feel special but often it is a very shallow relationship, perhaps she can't even remember their names. Is Sally drunk?

"*Happiest…Corpse*" – The juxtaposition of these two words is brilliant. (A possible laugh? Or great sadness. Again, options!)

Punctuation: The punctuation is fairly standard. However:

The '…' after "*blushing flower…*" and "*happiest…. Corpse…*" imply pauses, is she searching for the right words? Or drunk and lost her train of thought?

"*Come to the Cabaret!*" Has an exclamation mark sometimes, but not always! This is interesting that they have repeated lyrics but different punctuation. Is it asking for different interpretations as the song progresses? Is Sally thinking out loud through the song so by the end has changed how she feels? Initially my Subtext 1 of being happy but arriving at Subtext 2 of "*this is bullshit*"! That could be a great through line.

(After further research I found another version of the lyrics that had all of the *Cabarets* get an exclamation mark. So once again, options!)

Rhythm: Everyone knows the rhythm of the song; it's actually hard to read the lyric and not fall into the sung rhythm. Therefore, if/when it gets broken it will be quite striking. A dramatic pause or two could make interesting moments and bring focus to my interpretation.

The opening verse rhythm: "*What good's permitting…*" is structurally the same as "*Start by admitting…*" The first is about the mundane life and the second about the longevity, or lack of longervity, in life. Could *that* be the journey of the song?

Rhyme: The structure is fairly formulaic: couplets matching up. I don't see anything particularly unusual to work with here – and that's ok!

Questions: There is only one question – "*What good is sitting alone in your room?*" That could be the quest of the song: to make sense of this question.

Most singers will cheerfully sing the song not even realising it's a question. They slide straight into "*Come hear the music play*". Could I *really* ask the audience the question? Add a pause before carrying on? Is it an accusation? Self reflection?

Speech/Character: There is Elsie, Sally's friend who died, in death Sally sees a happy soul who was proud of the life she lived.

We also have the neighbours at the funeral/wake: "*that's what comes from too many pills and liquor*". This one needs to be acted out as it is clearly not what Sally thinks herself – fun additional character or vocal style to play with.

Repetition: There are plenty of repeats within the chorus. Opportunities for development or to change interpretation.

Sally saying "*What good is sitting…*" and then later Elsie saying to Sally "*What good is sitting…*" could be fun to contrast in performance as it's two different voices/people.

From Analysis to Performance

The analysis above has done very little to actually move a performance on physically or structurally. But it has given a wealth of options to play with in rehearsal! Now it's time to start exploring, seeing what suits and move towards performing the song. Try things out in rehearsal and see what happens.

What Is Your Goal for the Song?

When structuring your set: *Cabaret* – it could be a barnstorming opener, welcoming the audience into the room with you, a mid-show change of pace or, as it is in the film, a great closer! What you want to use it for may well affect which interpretation you pursue. Sometimes you will develop the song and see where it fits in a set. Other times you may aim for a song to be used in a specific way so can develop it with that in mind.

It's time to get on our feet and explore. The chances are you have already seen a direction you are thinking of going in. But before committing and bringing in the music, work through the exercises below to see if any unlock anything further.

EXERCISE 4: PLAY WITH THE TEXT

You will need: Your annotated lyrics and some space. A voice recorder.

It's now time to get on your feet and work with the text, the lyrics. Hear it aloud. Each suggestion below is about opening up ideas rather than completely curating a song, lifting analysis off the page and seeing how it could be explored in performance. The different ways in which you look at the lyrics through these exercises can add colour and depth to your performance. Who knows, a full concept may emerge. And as an added bonus: you may find by the end of this exercise you have actually learnt the majority of the lyrics simply through repetition. For some, it's reading the full song aloud seeing how your notes affect the piece. For others, you might just have a few lines you wish to play with over again. It will be useful to voice record any or all of the following and listen back to them, sometimes you will pick up on something new from listening back after that you didn't notice in performance.

1) Free Flow

Re-read aloud, on your feet, let yourself move around a bit. Try not to impose too much, let it flow naturally and see what happens! Does anything of interest start to emerge? Allow yourself to be led by what comes organically, trust your instincts. You aren't committing to anything but experimenting with various options. Jot down anything noteworthy! Simply read a few times like a speech or monolgue.

2) New Line, New Movement

This is an old acting exercise for finding meaning and subtext, through physicalising where punctuation is. Usually indicating a change of thought for the performer. Read the lyrics aloud again this time purposely moving throughout the space. Walk in straight lines (space allowing) and change direction at every sentence end. Physicalising these changes may help you realise where the big changes are.

This is not how you will end up performing the song. But you could bring it down to a performable level: set two poses and switch between them on the punctuation, or two points of focus points – two *anchors* in the room or two different *zones* in the audience (from *Chapter 8: Basic Drag*). Instantly you have choreographed some movement to the song which physicalises the meaning of the lyrics.

3) Never the Same Twice

Look at the repetitions in your analysis. Set the challenge of trying to say the line in a different way every time you come to it. Which words do you emphasise? Change of tempo? Volume? Play around changing the emotion, speed, focus or intention behind the line.

> "*Life Is a Cabaret*" – is the frequently repeated line. There are so many ways to play with it. It opens and, nearly, closes the song. To transition from the first "*Life Is a Cabaret*" being a joke to the final one bringing you to tears – that could be a Tony Award winning moment!

4) Make a Moment

Is there an area of the lyric you had previously overlooked but now find interesting: how could you highlight it? What would happen if you shout that line? Break the natural rhythm of it – throw in a pause? Redirect it to just one person as an aside?

> I hadn't noticed "*What good is sitting…?*" was a question. I was too familiar with the song. In performance I want the audience to have that moment. They know the song, even from the intro they semi-relax because they know what is coming – *Cabaret*. If I were to really shout it out, that would create a slightly awkward moment and stop them relaxing. It's indicating from the outset: "*this isn't the song you think it is!*"

5) Where Are the Jokes?

Not everything a drag act does on-stage needs to be funny but it's always worth scanning through to see if there are any moments that *could* be jokes. Or if you could add humour through your interpretation.

> I flagged "*happiest…corpse…I'd ever seen*" as joke. How can I get the laugh? What word needs emphasis for that to be funny?

> Another option is a prop-based gag? Lots of my notes questioned if Sally was drunk; could I have a glass and do a *cheers* or have a drink, every time I say "*Life Is a Cabaret*" and slowly get more drunk? Or cheers a different member of the audience every time?

6) Remember It's Drag

A lot of the analysis can seem quite dry and technical. Have a think now about putting it into the context of a drag bar! Think about where, when and how you are performing this song. What comes out when you connect the performance to your drag (clothes, make-up, etc), your alter-ego and the shared space. Are there any ironies that a drag performer is singing this? Does it add new meaning? Do the lyrics apply to the evening, or show, you are performing in?

> *Cabaret* is very easy to connect to drag! I will be in a cabaret venue talking to an audience about coming to the cabaret! Job done.

> There might be a band – "*come here the band*". Do I have a band, or is it a technician in the tech box playing the track? Is there a gag there?

> "*Queen*" – In the original song Sally interprets Elsie as looking regal in her coffin, but I could imagine that she's implying "Drag Queen"! Did the funeral home give her a bit too much make up, hair and bling so she looked like a Drag Queen? Or was Elsie actually a drag queen?
>
> **7) Who Are You Talking To?**
>
> Returning to the performance *Zones* (*Chapter 8: Basic Drag*) think about who you are talking to.
>
> Are there obvious shifts in the lyrics? Play with delivering different lines to different *Zones*. How does who you are talking to change the intention of the song? Can it bring out humour, interpretation – and of course create *peaks and troughs*?
>
> The difference between performing the line "Life Is a Cabaret" to Zone 1 and Zone 3 is huge. Is this a rallying cry for everyone or a personal journey of discovery? Moving from one to another is a wonderful transition and journey for the song.

Bringing In the Music

You should have found plenty of options to play with in performance, possibly little moments to get a laugh, perhaps a whole concept to run through the song. Whatever your analysis has brought up it's now time to see if you can make that work for the song. It's time to bring back in the music, hopefully you have a working track that you *think* suits you as a performer and for the style you wish to do the song in. If it's not perfect you can make cuts and edits (that's coming next *Chapter 16: Creating and Editing a Track*). But for now, work with what you have and if a track seems a bit long, or a slightly off key, that can be sorted.

> **EXERCISE 5: GET SINGING**
>
> **You will need: A backing track, your annotated lyrics and some space.**
>
> You've done your research, you've done your analysis and you've played around with the interpretation, it's time to sing! Revisit *Exercise 4: Playing with the Text* but singing rather than speaking for each of the seven points. Sing through your track with that at the forefront of your mind and see what happens, play, explore; the only wrong answer would be to sing the song through without thinking or engaging in the analysis you made. Make some notes of what worked, what surprised you, what was fun? Try bringing a few of them in at the same time. You can do them all or just the ones that had interesting choices for you.
>
> Remember, you are looking for *your* version of the song. Introducing a couple of interesting choices can be enough to make something feel special to an audience, hold them captivated, surprise and delight them.

Existing Iconic Moments

Some songs have iconic moments an audience are waiting for. When singing *Le Jazz Hot* from *Victor/Victoria* the audience will be waiting for the long note at the end. You **cannot** cut the iconic moment, *but* you could replace it with your own moment, with a strong choice, something dynamic. Maybe some audience interaction, down a drink, find a joke or play against the expected performance.

There may be an associated dance to the song? How could you reference or parody that? You can't sing *The Macarena* and not acknowledge the dance. Can you…?

Where Are the Breaks?

Musically in a song there are often instrumental breaks, a guitar solo, a build to a key change etc. These could be moments to drop out of the song and reconnect with the audience, either through a conversation, a joke, a quick interaction, move around the space…or is this some dead space that could be cut from your track? (See *Chapter 16: Creating and Editing a Track*.)

The joy of live singing is that you have the ability to drop out of the song, say something, and jump back in. To move from singing, to talking and back to singing in a song is a simple way of creating *Peaks and Troughs* (see *Chapter 8: Basic Drag*). This as a way of creating and acknowledging the live experience or to simply drop in a joke.

- In an instrumental moment saying "*choreography*" and then doing a dance (silly or serious).
- Comparing yourself to the original artist – "*Liza wishes she had these legs!*"
- Encouraging the audience to sing, dance or swing along to the song.

Staging and Choreography

If you aren't a dancer, don't stress about the choreography: the song will tell you if choreography is needed. And if you aren't a dancer, be a mover! *Movement* can tell the story.

How are you staging the piece? Are you using a mic stand or holding the mic? Or moving the mic stand once the song gets going? Thinking about your movement and doing some basic blocking will stop you from pacing around the stage looking lost. Always move with intention. A simple exercise I do is to mark up lyrics with a suggested *mode* of movement – note I didn't say dance!

EXERCISE 6: MOVEMENT

You will need: Your lyrics.

Having a loose plot to your movements throughout a song can help build momentum, and give clarity to the story telling. A song is usually broken up into verses, choruses and maybe a bridge. Assign something to each one and see how that shapes your performance.

- *Mic in stand centre stage/take mic out of stand.*
- *Come down stage.*
- *Move/pace across the stage.*
- *Enter the audience/return to the stage.*
- *Bring in simple hand movements or full on choreography.*
- *Start sitting down, find the moment to stand up.*
- *Big finish! (See below.)*

Don't over think the movement. A progression could simply be mic in stand, remove mic from stand, come down stage and final pose. Spread over three minutes that doesn't sound like much but that could easily be the progression of a ballad. Especially if your analysis has led to a dynamic, interesting interpretation of the song.

Top and Tail

Strong Openings: The audience want to relax; once you have sung a few notes *well* they relax and trust you, they don't critique your singing as much once you've made it clear that you can sing! (If you can.) Come out and do some clear, strong singing at the start. Lead with your strengths – if you are a fabulous singer let them see it. If you are a comic, lead with a comedy song so they know not to over analyse the vocals – they're here for a laugh.

Finish It: A key to moment to any song, or set, is the end. An audience like to know you have finished. Striking a pose and holding it is a visual cue for applause. Find your own version of the Freddie Mercury dramatic stance with one hand in the air to clearly say to an audience – *"applaud now"*.

Back To Basics: Revisit *Chapter 8:Basic Drag* working through each point using this song. Think about making sure you can be seen and heard, making an entrance or an impact at the top of the song. It's also worth thinking about *Chapter 13: Talking On Stage* – what's the set up or framing of the song – what are you going to say to bring the audience in on the journey.

It's now time to start running the song. Over, and over again to make it really solid.

EXERCISE 7: RUN IT, AGAIN AND AGAIN

You will need: Your tracks, your lyrics, some space and an audio recorder.

Run your song: over and over again! As you do this you'll keep finding new levels, new moments and fresh ideas. Keep playing with it, refer back to your notes, see what else you could pull out of it. When you perform a song live it will be a little different each time, so don't worry about locking things in. Lock in the lyrics, and your analysis of the song should bring a seemingly fresh retelling of the song every time you do sing it:

- Make sure you know it, inside and out, every single word.
- Make sure you have some interpretation coming through that makes it interesting from your analysis. What are you bringing to this song?
- Know, roughly, what you are doing physically, have a plan, an outline or any physical movement.
- Know how you are introducing it, and finishing it. Rehearse this as part of the song so it becomes a natural flow in and out. It may change from gig to gig, but have fun finding ways to start and finish it.

The last part of this process is probably the part you are probably most anxious about. Record the song as you run it, then listen back and be honest with yourself. How does it sound? Have you bitten off more than you can chew vocally? Or does your interpretation carry the performance to make it something unique?

Once you start performing the song you may want to bring it back to rehearsal, go over your notes, what worked, what didn't. From rehearsal to the stage isn't a one-way street, it's a back and forth as pieces are always going to keep developing. (See *Chapter 5: Rehearsal and Development*.) Sing through it every day for a while after your *Vocal Warm Up* (see *Chapter 14: Vocal and Singing Techniques*).

Uses of Song in Performance

This chapter is written with the approach to a whole song but there are no rules for how to use song in performance: sometimes a cut-down version (one verse, one chorus big finish) is enough!

Cuts: Not every song in performance needs to be performed in full. If you feel the song is serving it's role but is a little long – see if you can cut some of it out.

Snippets: Through analysing your song you may have found *a* moment, or *a* joke, that really works but won't sustain for a whole song. Working with a pianist or band it's easy to offer up a snippet and then stop. However, if you are based on tracks you can still edit together a snippet, or a selection of snippets as a short set in its own right.

Sing-Along: Drag shows are often raucous and audiences love to sing-along to songs. Sometimes they perform backing vocals and you remain the lead, other times they do the full song. Making the right choice of song and conduct the audience in the right way can create a live moment of gold.

As much as you can analyse a text looking for meaning and acting choices, you can return to these exercises looking for call and response opportunities. The singer becomes a conductor encouraging backing vocals, preparing them for key changes, shaping the choreography, etc. There is an art to getting a sing-along to work and staying in control of the moment. You want to remain the focus: never relinquish the power of the microphone and always try and remain in a powerful visual position in the room.

Overview: Singing a Song

Very little of this chapter focused on the technical aspects of singing. Drag is about bringing a performance to life, unlocking interesting choices, creating moments and making a unique audience experience. If you are keen to improve your vocals – practise is the best thing to do. You can always explore singing lessons. But a drag act does not have to sing beautifully, they just need to make choices and have conviction.

- Test drive a song before getting too attached: if the vocal is too big, or doesn't fit your voice, see if there are alterations you can make. Or find a new song.
- Research your song: what's been done with it, when was it released, any specific context that could add some interest to your performance of it.
- Work through the lyrics like an actor would work a text: Keep digging for interesting perspectives even if they are familiar lyrics.
- Run it, run it, run it!
- Be honest with yourself: If it doesn't sound vocally great – how could you improve it.

There are many ways to use song in a drag performance. Above I mentioned making cuts, editing together snippets of different tracks. Even if you think you are an accomplished singer who can sing anything it is still a required skill to be able to edit a backing track. Whether it's to change the key, cut a verse or even make a medley – every drag act needs to be able to do the basics of sound editing!

Notes

1. *Cabaret* by Fred Ebb and John Kander – © 1966 Alley Music Corp (BMI)/Trio Music Company (BMI)/Carlin Music.
2. Shiela Hancock in interview with Terry Wogan, BBC. March 2010, https://www.bbc.co.uk/programmes/p0073cqn

Glimour photographed backstage at the Royal Vauxhall Tavern by The Burley Photgrapher

16
Putting It Together: Creating and Editing a Track

It's rare for a drag act not to use music in any way within a set: a song, a lip-sync, a burlesque act or even some simple entrance music. Learning how to smoothly edit and creatively shape a track is an essential skill in the drag tool box!

You may think – "*this doesn't apply to me!*" – however, even acts performing to a *straight* song need to be able to edit a track. It may be too long, the wrong key or, as many backing tracks do, have dead space at the beginning, etc. If you are performing to any form of track, check the structure is serving you the best it can. Some acts cut a verse out of a song to make it work, others use audio from film, audiobooks, the news, podcasts, TV and more, the skill is that the finished track feels like one, fluid track.

This is a chapter of two halves: firstly discussing editing basics, tips and ways to get the best out of an existing track. Secondly moving on to mix tracks for lip-syncs, burlesque, mash-ups and more. As a singer I edit every single backing track I use, to make sure it is suited to me, simply using the editing basics. A mix edit is a much more involved, creative process. Think of the pieces shared by *Dickie Beau*, *Regina Fong* and *Me The Drag Queen* from the suggestions in *Chapter 7: Research and Further Reading*. Whatever style of drag you are doing – spend some time mastering the editing basics.

Editing Basics

Equip yourself with the basic skills so you are able to easily, and simply, update your set with new content. There are a range of free, or affordable, editing software options: *GarageBand*, *Adobe Audition* or *Audacity* are current go-to's for the industry. Technology and software will change faster than the publication of a book, so I am not detailing specifics '*how to*' guides for each software but there are numerous YouTube tutorials on which software can do what. Depending on your needs, one piece of software may be better than another but with a little exploring and experimenting you'll find one that feels intuitive to you.

The skills everyone should master are:

- *Cut and paste sections of track.*
- *Edit volume/levels of specific moments.*
- *Change the key.*
- *Add/decrease reverb/bass/treble.*
- *Fade in/out a track.*
- *Export a finished edit to a usable format.*

The software examples above have *thousands* of other elements you can explore in the future but master these skills first as it covers 99% of what a drag act needs. Invest some time getting to know how to achieve these basics: in a few hours you can develop the skill set to edit a killer track!

The Highest Quality

Before editing a track, always source the highest quality original version of the audio. Every time something is edited, reformatted and compressed it loses quality. To ensure the best quality buy a digital copy of a track, there are many ways to rip sound off of a video but you sacrifice the quality. When played over a professional speaker system, low-quality tracks are noticeable and often distracting. Technicians may even limit how loud they play the track as they don't want poor-quality sound to reflect on them or the venue's equipment. So aim high!

Mastering and Levelling

When cutting tracks, or adding multiple sources into one track, it is common for the sound levels to vary and be jarring. Pay attention to balancing, the volumes, learning to mix and balance the sound level is fairly simple. Aim for the level of the track to be consistent from beginning to end. During the editing/creative stage things move around so it's best to wait until a track is structured before smoothing out every join.

Once levelled export the track, again in the highest quality format possible, and then have a *break* from it. When you return, listen to the track with fresh ears on a variety of devices: different speakers pick up different sound qualities. Turn the volume up loud and listen for cuts, odd levels or jarring moments. Make notes: then return to the edit to finesse.

Levelling Your Set

If you are performing a set/show, especially if you know there isn't a technician, or you are just playing the tracks yourself through a PA System, then level all your tracks. This means setting them all to one standard volume level so you don't need to adjust the playback for each new song. Simply play your set on speakers and listen out for moments where things get too quiet or too loud, then adjust each track accordingly.

Teching a Newly Edited Track

At a technical rehearsal with a new track always ask for a full play-through. Don't be afraid to ask a technician for feedback on the track: are they doing any live levelling, altering the volume, bass or treble? If so, return to your edit and re-work before you use it again.

Naming Tracks

When editing tracks, it is common to have multiple versions and it's easy to get confused! Many artists send over tracks named ridiculous things such as *"BEST FINAL FINAL 2 TO USE"* because they keep editing what they thought was the final version. It's easy to mistakenly use the wrong version, have a logic to what you name the tracks which are performance ready and double check in the tech it is the correct *cut* of your track. Delete the drafts you no longer need, and rename the best track as something suitable!

It's always good practice to keep a history of the workable versions of previous edits so you can adjust after feedback from a performance or rehearsal. But you don't need to save every export of every draft. *Try* to keep things organised.

Editing a Straight Track

A straight track is exactly as it sounds – a track that plays straight through. A lip-sync, a song, a burlesque act performing from beginning to end of one song. An audience will feel by the end that they've heard the whole track: the beginning, middle and end are all there. However, you may have trimmed a section to make the track service you best as a performer.

Shorten the Track

It's ok shorten a track, some songs are just too long: don't be afraid to cut a verse or two. During rehearsal it's important to ask the question – *"what does the repeat of this verse/chorus add to my performance?"* Maybe as a singer the vocal builds, the audience will join in the second time around or perhaps, for a lip-sync act, the choreography intensifies. Great! But if you feel you are just repeating ground you've already covered – cut it down! In a ten-minute set three short songs may work better than two long ones!

Shortening a track usually involves cutting a verse and/or chorus *near the middle* of the original song and editing it back together to sound seamless. Avoid cutting the end of a track as most songs build to have key changes, ad-libs and crescendos – you want to keep that build so your performance can benefit from it.

Different Cuts for Different Gigs

It's useful to have a couple of cuts of a song that you like performing. Sometimes you know you need to be snappy, use a short version; other times you know the audience will love this track so use the full version. When structuring your set (see *Chapter 6: Building A Set, Range and Repertoire*) you can select the best version of each song to fit that set.

Key Change

Vocalists, being able to edit the key of a song to fit your voice is gold! Not every song suits being sung in a different key, but with many songs, an audience won't even notice. There are backing track websites where you can edit the track before purchasing it to create a track in the right key for you. If you have time and ability, learning to do this yourself will open up an infinite amount of songs for you to perform.

A Sharp Start

Backing tracks often have a few seconds of silence, or a metronome, at the beginning, these aren't meant to be used in performance! They are used to help a singer come in at the right point, or in the right key. However, these should not be left on the track for performances as, quite simply, it sounds awful. If you are using an in-ear monitor the tech can play it to you in-ear before opening the track into the whole space – but drag acts aren't usually working with this sort of high-tech support! Dead time on a track can also cause issues for a technician who may think they haven't started the track correctly; they'll hit play again which actually pauses the track making the dead time even longer. Always edit out any preamble prior to submitting your track.

A Cold Start

If a track has a cold start – meaning the vocal comes in right at the top of the track – there are a few ways you can *cheat* this:

Create Your Own Intro: Often the first 8 or 16 bars can be looped so you can treat them as an intro. So add a short repeat at the top of the track.

Have a Fanfare: If the track you are using doesn't have a usable loop, explore a fanfare or camp flourish before the track begins. Add this as an attention-grabbing moment opening the track, have a timed pause, and then you will start at exactly the right moment. The audience hear two tracks but you know it's one track and when the fanfare finishes you have, for example, one breath and start singing/lip-synching.

Too Much Intro

The opposite can also be a problem, a track has a long introduction leaving you uncertain when to start. This gets more complicated if you are trying to chat over the intro to keep an audience engaged. An easy trick is to add a tiny but distinctive noise to the track four counts before you begin: a bell, a note, a drum. Possibly a noise used later in the track. If well blended, no one else will notice but you will know it's time. It needs to be subtle and suit the style of the track but noticeable enough for you.

Commissioned Tracks

Another option, if you have a budget, is to commission backing tracks with the cut, key and edit exactly how you wish them to be. If it's a lesser-known song this may be the only option for getting a professional-sounding backing track. This can cost anywhere from around £50 to £250 depending on the level of your requirements, length of track and the number of instruments involved. However, when tracks are delivered you usually are able to provide feedback and get the track edited a few times to make it exactly how you wish it to be. There are also technical services online that can do this for a lip-sync edit too, but again these cost. You also lose a certain amount of creative control that most lip-sync artists want to have.

Creating a Mix Track

The editing basics for a mix media track are exactly the same as editing a straight track. However, in a mix edit you may have hundreds of cuts to finesse and balance rather than just one or two. It is more work but the skills and the techniques are the same.

Editing of a mix track is a much more artistic and creative process than tidying up a straight track. There are limitless ways to craft a mix. Where you look for sources completely depends on the type of work you wish to create. If you know there is a theme you want to explore – dive into a research period and see where you can find interesting quotes, opinions, songs, old TV shows on that theme, etc.

A mistake novice acts can make is to choose a range of funny sound clips, memes and a few songs they like and try to create an act. All of these components will work in a mix but there needs to be a theme or structure to bring things together. Like structuring a script, a comedy set or spoken word piece, there is no one way to create a mix track but there does need to be a level of cohesion. I have broken options down into six styles, this is by no means definitive, but it is a good place to start thinking about ways to edit. For each style I've listed an easily findable performance to help illustrate (many of which were previously shared in *Chapter 7: Research and Further Reading*).

Creating and Editing a Track

1) One Song as a Through Line

Any piece you present needs to feel cohesive, less is often more when it comes to how many sources to pull into a lip-sync otherwise it can become very confusing for an audience, an information overload. Choosing one song as the backbone of the lip-sync, that you cut away from but consistently come back to, gives the piece structure. Thematically the additional media edited in (quotes, sound-bites, sound-effects, etc.) will usually elaborate, explore or juxtapose the themes of the existing song. Adding comedy, drama or a political point.

> Me The Drag Queen performs *Roar* by Katy Perry and edits in famous battle scenes from various films – *Braveheart*, *Lord of the Rings*, etc. Taking the theme of *Roar*[3] as a battle cry.

2) A Strong Theme

Creating a through line with a strong theme; this could be songs all on the same subject, the same genre or the same artist. Through choosing songs on the same theme you may find ways to show many artists have similar opinions, or comically that one artist contradicts themselves. Points can be made by adding contrasting material or spoken word into the edit at key moments – or it could simply be a party track of bangers on a theme.

> The burlesque artist Cleopantha,[2] with her piece *WAP*, uses the theme of *"bad ass females who have changed the face of rap"*. It is a party track, a crowd pleaser that reaches a crescendo with Megan Thee Stallion and Cardi B. The structure has a narrative for the audience, a journey; Cleo edits songs by female rap artists and clips of the outspoken men, trying, to disempower the women. Rather than playing tracks one after another Cleo structures the piece as a search, bringing the audience on the journey. As she investigates the artists she uses *The Pink Panther Theme* as a fun investigator motif. As each song plays she embodies the artist as she then brings their energy to the stage building to a crescendo with a mop and a bucket!

3) A Simple Joke

Sometimes, simple is best. Making a small addition, reinterpretation or change to a track can be all that is needed to make it your own interpretation. This could be using physicality to reinterpret the meaning of the song or it could be just taking a lyric as a simple instruction. (Many an act has found themselves turning around in unusual ways thanks to Bonnie Tyler.) A track, or tracks, can be edited to provide that simple joke for you.

> Me The Drag Queen's version of *You Haven't Seen the Last of Me*,[3] by Cher, is a strong example of this. The beginning is a straight rendition with no edits. However, at the crescendo when the song seems to finish and she goes to leaves the stage – *"You haven't seen the last of me"* is the line as she goes to leave but the track kicks off again pulling her back centre stage. Again…and again…after a while she physically becomes out of breath, frustrated and stuck in the endless loop of trying to finish the seemingly never-ending song.
>
> To throwback to the point of having different edits for different gigs, Me has two or three different cuts of this track; it can be anything between a four and seven-minute piece depending on what she thinks fits the gig best.

4) Channelling an Artist

There are many reasons to lip-sync, and embodying someone else's voice is an important one. There may be a particular artist who you focus on for your piece where you use extracts from interviews, performances and/or songs they released to create a tapestry which explores a specific moment/theme of their life. A simple choice would just be to pick the artist's best-known tracks and edit together your own mega-mix for a crowd-pleasing, fun number.

> To this day Dickie Beau's[4] *Judy Speaks Blackout*[5] is one of the greatest performance pieces I've ever experienced live. It is certainly the greatest mix edited track I've seen. Embodying and performing the words of the artist at different points in their career to explore the development of their career and how the industry and the fandom treated her.

5) Word Play

A strong motif for an edit is to take one word that you link to through various songs. There are so many songs with the word *love*, *girl*, *boy*, *dance*, etc. Every time it gets to that word link it to the next song for comic effect, juxtaposition or to get the audience playing the guessing game of *"what's next"*.

> Adam All[6] performs his *Knight Act* using a series of more and more ridiculous 'Night'/'Knight', related songs and puns. The style, tempo and feel of each song develops, becoming more varied and comic as the track evolves. The variety of songs linked together through one pun provide plenty of clowning and choreographic moments. Songs include: *One Night Only, Oh What a Night, Marry the Night*, etc. He performs the piece dressed as a medieval knight.

6) Medley with More

There are of course simpler, less developed ways of editing a track. Sometimes a performer just wants a medley of bangers, or showtunes, for the audience to enjoy. Even when doing what might be considered a *simple* crowd pleaser why not try and give it little link. A reason as to why you are performing these particular tracks. A joke, a theme, a pun, revisiting an era: it doesn't need to be sophisticated, but show the audience some thought has gone into the set and its structure. Often a medley/mash-up edit can feel too random, framing the piece helps the audience know what's happening – and often engages them in guessing what might come in next.

> Welsh Drag Queen Wilma Ballsdrop has a medley of great songs: George Michael, Dead Or Alive and Amy Winehouse. On the surface there is no link but when she cues the track she says: *"it's time for my dead mix – they've all gone"*. It's dark humour, but the audience love the selection of songs and also love guessing which lost icon might be performed next. And it is always evolving – if someone else dies, chances are Wilma will edit them in!

Trajectory

All edited tracks need trajectory; like an empowered speech, or a good song, there should be a build as the edit goes on. Build to a crescendo, *a moment*. Each time something is added it should feel it is elaborating or enriching the theme, taking a joke further, building the tension, furthering the journey or taking the audience somewhere new: adding to the overall piece, not just repeating. Throughout the development, research and rehearsal of your piece ask yourself – *"how does this move my performance forward?"*

EXERCISE 1: A STARTING POINT

You will need: Your notebook, access to the below songs and the internet.

Below are six classic songs. For each of our six edit styles, above, use one song to create an initial idea you *could* expand on. Don't worry whether or not it's a piece you would want to perform – the exercise here is to find various ways to create *a concept* for an edit. Get the creative juices flowing; some will be fun ideas that will only live in your notebook, others might be the start of a piece you add to your repertoire. There are no bad ideas at this point. Keep writing them down, and review later. And if you have too many ideas – even better!

ABBA – *Thank You for the Music*

Billie Eilish – *Bad Guy*

Britney Spears – *Oops!... I Did It Again*

Blur – *Girls and Boys*

Diana Ross – *I'm Coming Out*

Madonna – *Like a Virgin*

Moving forward you can do this with any song that you choose; I've picked these as I think they all have a variety of directions with which they could be taken – comedy, camp or political. Once you've an idea for all six you can bring them with your to the development stage with *Exercise 2*.

EXERCISE 2: DEVELOPMENT

You will need: Your notebook, your chosen song, a computer and internet access for possible additional media.

Now you have various short ideas, or pitches, pick *one* to develop. Choose your favourite, or the one that seems most on-brand for you, and work through the following steps to bring it to life!

Research Period: Listen to the track, and other related tracks. See if there are any other famous versions of the track? Has anyone else done this? Brainstorm all the possible sources you could draw on. Look for quotes, sound bites and speeches that might be useful too not just music. What are themes of the song – are there famous interviews, books, podcasts or films that mention this theme?

Collate Your Sources: With all the sources you wish to use find the highest quality version, keep them all in a named folder for this mix.

Edit a Draft Track: Start drafting the track using the details from the first half of this chapter. Which track(s) is the through line, which are the best clips to add in, which might work, which are wild cards. It's all about playing around and seeing what may develop.

Listening to a track and performing a track are two different things. Often as you start editing tracks together the concept comes together and finds a life of its own. Keep the track in a rough editable mode as there will be a lot of back and forth during development period. Save and date each versions so you can return to a predecessor if things go wrong! Wait until you are close to finished before mastering each join, things will keep shifting around and you may waste time finessing a join that isn't needed.

Rehearse, Rehearse, Rehearse: You might feel a track feels the right length but then on your feet realise it's all moving too quickly, or too slowly. Even when the track is in development try and play around with it physically. Keep jumping back and forth from editing the track to rehearsing the track and seeing what feels right. (We will address rehearsing a lip-syn in our next chapter!)

Edit, Edit, Edit: The tighter the edit on the track the more professional your piece will come across. When adding quotes and speech over music you may wish to underscore them by keeping the track running. Using a karaoke version of your through line song is a great way to cheat the track slightly. You can keep the music going, include the quote, but not have it over the lyrics. This can also be useful when mastering the joins of tracks if you need to add in a few counts of music to make a transition less jarring.

Deeper Rehearsal: However you are performing use the relevant chapter(s) of the handbook to work through the piece as rigorously as you would anything else. An edited track or mash up still needs to have the same level of textual analysis, physical exploration and vocal exploration. Dig deep into the different exercises and see how it can help inform your edit and bring it to life in the space. (Return to *Chapter 15: Singing a Song* or turn the page to look at *Chapter 17: Rehearsing and Performing a Lip-Sync*)

Finesse the Track: Once you are happy with your performance and the track that's the time to master, level and finesse the track. Make sure the cuts are smooth, well-timed and that the flow of the track fits with the way you are performing it. Is it the right length? Does the piece feel too long? Too short? Is there any dead space? Do you need to return your collated sources and find a few extra moments to build a crescendo? Or edit the track down – sometimes less is more!

Overview: Editing and Creating a Track

- Every drag act needs the basic editing skills: to cut, copy, shorten, level, master and finesse their tracks.
- Strive for the highest-quality audio. Always.
- With mix tracks always aim for a piece with clarity and progression.
- Explore different ways of creatively mixing songs and media to create dynamic mix tracks.
- Keep developing the track, even after performances, come back and fine tune it as with any other performance. Just because you have rendered the track doesn't mean you can't keep improving it.

There are many creative ways of mixing a track to create an entertaining piece for your audience. These small ideas you've explored for potential pieces are a great starting point. Once you've begun developing them into a piece singers can take their edited medley back to *Chapter 15: Sing a Song*. Lip-sync acts you might some killer-tracks you now wish to make and bring to the stage. Bring those ideas with you now – *Performing and Rehearsing a Lip-Sync*.

Notes

1. *Me* discusses this further in interview with *Michael Twaits*, July 2024. See Part IV for full interview.
2. You can find Cleopantha on socials at @cleopantha. Her edit for *WAP* was polished and had sound effects added by @jfbDJ
3. *Me* discusses this further in interview with *Michael Twaits*, July 2024. See Part IV for full interview.
4. Find Dickie Beau at @dickiebeau
5. Currently available within *The Art Of Drag* playlist at www.michaeltwaits.com
6. *Adam All* discusses further in interview with *Michael Twaits*, July 2024. See Part IV for full interview.

Bryan Air photographed backstage at the Royal Vauxhall Tavern by The Burley Photgrapher

17
Gotta Move: Rehearsing and Performing a Lip-Sync

The time has come…for us to take a look at the performance skill of lip-sync. There are many different styles and skills within lip-sync: acting, dancing, gymnastics, comedy and more. But beyond learning the words – how does one rehearse a lip-sync act?

With the mainstream status of *Drag Race* and the finale of each episode being a *Lip-Sync for Your Life* it is often assumed that lip-sync is a main staple of *all* drag acts skill set. Lip-sync provides an artist with the opportunity to embody another performer in a live space, reinterpret work or create a soundscape to perform against. This chapter will look at approaches to lip-sync, the types of track you might use, how to embody, rehearse and build a lip-sync. You need to make sure you are using your whole being on stage – not just your lips!

> I have been performing in drag for over 15 years, I have never lip-synced on stage as part of my set or show. I have on film sets (for technical reasons it's rare to sing live on a film set) and in a couple of plays where I played the role of someone who lip-synced. However, as a host I have watched thousands of lip-syncs and as a facilitator shaped many. I need to give a nod to Me The Drag Queen,[1] to my mind one of the UK's greatest lip-sync acts, as I've had the privilege of sitting in their lip-sync workshops on *The Art of Drag* course twice a year for the last decade. Their skills, knowledge and wisdom have undoubtedly shaped my thoughts and approach to lip-sync and I'm sure she'll disagree with so much of it!

Approaches to Lip-Sync Performance

Within all styles of lip-sync there are different energies, or an ethos, a performer might adopt; some acts pick one and remain constant for the whole act, others will start in one and adapt, or yoyo, into others. Here are just some of the main areas to consider as styles of lip-sync:

Acting through Song: In the same way as you act through song when singing (see *Chapter 15: Sing a Song*) a lip-sync act delivering a song can act through the song, connecting emotionally to the song and the audience. Do not pass over a bit of textual analysis to find a deeper connection to a song.

Dance and Tricks: Popular due to *Drag Race* where the embodiment of the song, and the communication to the audience, becomes slightly secondary to the technical *wow factor* or splits, kicks and dance moves. It's crowd pleasing and usually high energy! Often a mixture of choreography, improvisation and well-rehearsed trademark moves to get the audience cheering.

Bring the Song to You: As drag acts we all have our own style. Just because you are performing a lip-sync to a song by an artist doesn't mean you have to move, look or even have the attitude of that artist. You can bring your take, your style to the song. Look at Naomi Smalls lip-sync to *Come Rain or Come Shine*[2]

DOI: 10.4324/9781003498797-20

Judy would never move or act like that, but the energy is contagious and the interpretation is wild and unique. How could you bring a song to you?

Bring You to the Song: The opposite can also be true and a great experience for an audience. Seeing an artist who usually does pop songs taking on a musical theatre song (or vice versa) can be fascinating. Seeing Monet X Change in the lip-sync to *Come Rain Or Come Shine* against Naomi was a revelation. Despite Monet not winning, her interpretation, bringing a more controlled and grounded side of herself, was wonderful and showed great range.

Tribute: Taking this idea of bringing yourself to the song a step further, you can step into the world of a tribute act. Lip-syncing a performance can simply be to recreate the magic of a live performance as if truly singing. You could borrow facial expressions, trademark choreography or elements of the aesthetic from the original artist. The UK drag troupe *Gals Aloud* have seen great success with recreating the magic of *Girls Aloud*'s classic routines. The tribute could be sincere, or could be a comic parody.

Parody: Performing a song but bringing a new, possibly unintended meaning, to the original lyrics through actions, props or costuming. Much of the upcoming *Chapter 19: Parody* can be applied to a lip-sync performance and interpretation.

Types of Lip-Sync Track

On-stage, lip-sync can be used in numerous ways to create a live act; in *Chapter 16: Creating and Editing a Track* there are thoughts on creating and editing a track and finding different ways of mixing media together to make a dynamic track. The following five areas are ways in which a lip-sync may be performed aren't exclusive, many merge different forms of lip-sync in performance.

A Straight Track

A track that plays through as an entire song with the artist performing along to it. There are no mix edits, no additions. It's arguably the most straightforward style of lip-sync but the simpler the act seems the tighter the technique needs to be to truly shine and hold an audience. As performers we all need to return to those key questions: *"what am I bringing to this performance, what's my point of view, my twist or my technical skill I'm showcasing?"*

> I'm a real fucking sucker for technique these days. If I know that you've really worked at your craft. That's enough for me.
>
> Me The Drag Queen[3]

An Edit

A track, or multiple tracks, edited on a theme or as the backbone for other audio clips. The drag act performs the edit as one piece and uses cuts to create dynamic moments of comedy, dramatic moments. You can play along as if you are surprised/confused as the edits come through or deliver the piece like a well-rehearsed monologue showcasing excellent technique and command of the moment. You could create different physicalities, or characters, for each of the voices. A common theme with an edit is the performer playing a game of '*who is in charge*' – the artist or the track?

As an act approaching this style of performance; technique and accuracy that comes from strong rehearsal is unavoidable. The wittier, more clever the edit seems, the more the piece needs to be impeccably rehearsed. Timing is everything.

A Skill *AND* a Lip-Sync

Artists who work in different performance mediums (burlesque, pole dancing, circus, fire, etc.) may also use lip-sync *on top* of their base skill set to create a more dynamic performance piece. The essential thing to remember here is that the lip-sync can't be secondary or feel like an afterthought. The lip-sync still needs accurate rehearsal, it needs to become second nature as the other skill is often dangerous and therefore choreographed to perfection. A performer who is lip-syncing does not want to casually look like they are singing along; if you are going to lip-sync – LIP-SYNC!

The Wild Cards

Many artists are using lip-sync as a base for new styles of performance and audience interaction. It is important as an artist to think outside the box and give the audience a new, live experience. Some ideas I've recently seen include: lip-syncing to live singers, to unknown tracks, combining lip-sync with videos, with projection, live relay and even AI. The possibilities are near endless, a lip-sync act is anything but a one-trick pony. What could you bring to your lip-sync?

A Lip-Sync Battle

Thanks to *Drag Race* and *Comedy Central's Lip Sync Battle*, the concept is universally familiar. On the drag scene many competition nights adopt this, in one way or another, as part of the event. The *battle* adds a dimension of improvisation as performers have not usually rehearsed together, are jostling for attention and the stakes are usually pretty high.

The two performers may have rehearsed the track solo and then perform side by side, but in a 'battle' scenario, audiences are looking for the magic live moments: interaction, one-upmanship and, dare I say, a fight. Remember to aim for a *sporting* battle, only consensual touching or interaction! Think about sight-lines; try not to block each other. If you can't be seen – you gotta move!

Despite the performance not being rehearsed it is usually judged on the craft, so, again, technical accuracy is vital. Due to the nature of the battle, an act will still be able to prepare; learn the lyrics, find their own concept and a range of options for where they may take the performance to in the live moment.

> I won't dwell too much on a lip-sync battle other than to remind you that you need to be prepared: knowing words and having some trajectory in mind. All of the craft from the rest of the chapter applies. However, if you are new to the concept of a lip-sync battle I've selected a few from *Drag Race* which I believe are well executed and have a variety of different approaches. The episodes have been cited and at the time of publication, all of these episodes are easily available on streaming platforms.
>
> **Coco Montrose vs. Alyssa Edwards – Season 5 Episode 9** – *Cold Hearted* **by Paula Abdul**
>
> *Drama*. The backstory and 'drama' being played out is almost pantomime. It has built all season for these two performers and the lip-sync and not disappoint.
>
> **Valentina vs. Monet X Change – All Stars 4** – *Into You* **by Ariana Grande**
>
> *Dancing excellence*. Valentina embodies Selina and J-Lo giving the ultimate Latina drag experience. It's very sexy, no real comedy or twists but a performer who knows exactly what their body can do showcasing technical excellence.

Raven vs. Jujubee – *All Stars Season 1* – *Dancing on My Own* by Robyn

Emotion. It's useful to see a different pace and an emotional tone within a lip-sync battle. Technically, it is not the tightest, but the emotion and connection actually make it very memorable.

Monét X Change vs. Shea Couleé's – *All Stars Season 7* – *Old McDonald* by Ella FitzGerald

Attention to Details. A battle with something that isn't modern or trendy. Analyse the use of eyes, costuming, breath and poise. Shea knows exactly how to move to have flourishes accentuated by her costume from both lyrics and instrumentation.

BenDelaCreme vs. Aja – *All Stars Season 7* – *Anaconda* by Nicki Minaj

Camp/Comedy. Nicki Minaj is not an obvious match for Dela but she plays the comedy, facial expressions and overt sexuality to huge comic effect and out lip-syncs Aja (who does an excellent performance full of moves and tricks more authentic or expected for the song.)

Naomi Smalls vs. Monet X Change – *All Stars Season 4* – *Come Rain or Come Shine* by Judy Garland

Contrast. Monet channels Judy bringing control to her performance. Naomi brings all the modern tricks and flicks with a slightly manic performance. She throws in some Judy-isms but takes it to the greatest of extremes. Two completely different but brilliant interpretations.

For each of these examples the act, especially the winning act, has a concept and trajectory for their interpretation. They aren't standing up proving they know the words, they are bringing the track to life in their own, unique way – A generic choice, gives a generic performance. Try to dig deeper than "I'm going to be feirce". Sometimes a tiny choice can give a drive for an entire performance (think Roxy Anderws with a nail file on *All Stars* Season 9.)

Know Your Lyrics

Many novice acts who lip-sync use a performance to showcase that they know their lyrics. This is the absolute bare minimum you can do. A true performer is barely thinking about the lyrics, they come naturally, after much rehearsal, it's a muscle memory, it's physically in their body, they are focusing on bringing the piece to life, connecting to the track, to the audience and the live experience. Never think – "*I know my lyrics, it will be fine*".

Much More Than Just the Lyrics

When working on a lip-sync act it is essential to consider every noise which is on the track. Things that can be easily overlooked, but when included, or brought to life, give lip-sync a real finesse and sell the illusion that you are doing the vocal or add comic dimension to the performance.

- **Breath:** Especially on the long notes – show the big breath, are you running out of air?
- **Coughs, Laughs, Vocal Ticks:** The moments on the track which seem insignificant when you listen are the moments that can best convince an audience you are embodying the track. Again look at *Dickie Beau's* embodiment of the minute details within the tracks in *Judy Speaks*.[4]
- **Big Band Moments:** Dramatic musical drum rolls, fanfares, crescendos and builds where you can use your arms, or whole body, to punctuate, if not conduct the orchestra as if they are with you, live! The final seconds of *Don't Rain on My Parade*, or the final build to a close of *Moving the Line* from *Smash* are great examples.

- **Quirky Instrumentation:** Pop songs, especially disco songs, often have odd instruments and noises. Hear them, play with them, ask the audience did you hear that? Conduct them? Add comic choreography just for that noise. Have fun!
- **Sound Effects:** If you have used an audio clip in an edit and it sounds like someone is walking, slamming doors – use those noises. Don't ignore them – embody them. Bring them to life. The creaking door at the start of *Thriller*. Typewriters in *9 to 5*. The violent noises (drills, smashing glass, etc) in *Bury a Friend*.
- **Pauses:** Use them! Make eye contact, dare the audience to ask – *"where are we going next?"* Demonstrate that you know the track so well you can relax into the pause for the exact required length of time. A classic Britney Spears *"stop"* moment.

Bringing Basic Performance Technique to Lip-Sync

Every point in *Chapter 8: Basic Drag* can be applied to every lip-sync. Rather than asking you to go and re-read I am going to give a bullet point here for each pointer because too often lip-sync acts are performing tricks that get a round of applause but have often forgotten the performer basics. Here's a few big pointers for getting your lip-sync stage ready.

Be Seen: Without having your own voice to command a stage – sight lines are essential. Especially making sure the audience can see your lips. (Top tip: a lip-sync is rarely a time to choose a nude lipstick.) Find the focal points in the space to make sure you are being seen by everyone! Have a conversation with the technician to ensure you have light on your face throughout. (Top tip: White/bright light is best for drag so the audience can see the make-up illusion you've created.)

Making an Entrance: What the audience see either side will adapt the way they perceive your piece. If you are non-verbal, that's fine, but you can still show a range of personality for the few seconds you are on-stage. The attitude and intention you bring to the stage can tell the audience everything they need to know! On *Drag Race* Georgeous is a master of entering and leaving the space as their alter-ego but then dropping into a lip-sync in the required style. Show your range and highlight your skill set.

Let Them Drink It In: Can you let the audience have a moment with you before you do too much; let them see what you're wearing, setting up how the piece is going to go. Do a move, hold the pose. Let the audience enjoy each aspect of your routine and its build. Avoid doing too much too soon: splits, back flip, cartwheel, straight into a roll off the stage isn't giving the audience time to react or engage. Get the reward from each element of your set: do something, get your response and *then* move on!

Planning: This is a combination of points three, four and five in *Chapter 8: Basic Drag*. Knowing who you are performing to and how you fit into the show should help you choose the best material for each gig; don't assume all audiences want the same thing. If you are at a high-end awards show, try and match the atmosphere. If you are one of eight lip-sync acts on the bill what are you bringing which is distinctive and will make you stand out?

Peaks and Troughs: Three minutes for a track can be a long time: make sure there is some light and shade within the lip-sync. Play with the speed you move, how closed/open you are physically, moving or not moving, even where you place your eye contact (*see Zones/Anchors* below). For an audience to stay engaged a lip-sync needs structure, development and variation. This does not mean tricks and kicks every few seconds; aim to have a trajectory, keep leaving yourself somewhere further to go until the final, crescendo, moment.

Zones of Performance: With lip-sync these are more important than ever. Using zones within the audience to keep them engaged but for you to seem like you are communicating, interacting and responding to them. Highlighting sections of the song where it refers to specific people or characters – cast them in the room: eye contact, pointing, moving directly towards individuals or groups.

Anchors: Eye-level for lip-sync is vital: keep pulling the whole audience in! Play to the back, the front, and keep the whole room engaged. If your performance is general rather than specifically placed it may feel like you are ignoring the audience, which can make you seem nervous or arrogant. Make eye-contact, fake eye-contact and keep working to every corner of the room.

Ooze Confidence: An audience want a lip-sync to feel every bit as live and unpredictable as if you were singing or talking. You need to convincingly create the illusion that the voice (or voices) are coming from you. Confidence and commitment are the two best ways to sell that to an audience. Own the stage. Own the song. The best way to achieve this is to be well-rehearsed and master the craft.

Are You Having Fun Yet: Can you inject a fun little into the track: a cheeky look, a fake-out teasing a particular move or even just a wink to the audience. Taking something too seriously, and not having fun can become one level. Find a moment of stupidity or fun in everything.

Rehearsing a Lip-Sync Act

You cannot know your track too well, whatever style of lip-sync you are performing: rehearse, rehearse, rehearse. As ever, this doesn't always mean full-out performance: But constantly listening, mouthing along, dancing around to the track so it's *in* your body. Often novice acts will present lip-sync which feels more like a technical exercise to prove they have learnt the words. Learning the words is only the first part. You now need to bring it to life!

Some performers think lip-syncing is easier than singing. But if a singer forgets a word in a song they can replace it with another word, if a lip-sync act forgets the words, or rhythm, it just looks messy. Learn your words! Below are five simple ways to rehearse and open up your lip-sync no matter what style of track you are creating or performing to.

EXERCISE 1: ALWAYS REHEARSING

Your will need: Your track, on your headphones – wherever you go!

You have edited or created your track, undoubtedly you know the majority of the words already from how many times you listened to it in the edit. However, it's not possible to listen to the track too much. You can *semi*-rehearse simply by listening to the track and running the words along with it, or the breathing or visualising your physicality. On public transport, at the gym or even doing the dishes. Listen to the track, run the track, all the time. Even though you aren't singing – sing along with the track to practice the articulation, what does your mouth need to achieve? Acknowledge the breathing! Knowing where the singer, or speaker, breathes and pauses is vital for creating a living lip-sync which sells the illusion to the audience.

Running tracks, to ensure every line is exact and the timing is finessed, is a daily part of drag life. Much like a singer does a vocal warm up and marks through a song incorporate going over your tracks as part of your daily routine; make it habitual rather than something you need to 'make time for'.

For further ideas revisit *Chapter 5: Rehearsal and Development* for ways to incorporate mini-rehearsal into everyday life, make it habitual.

> The amount of time I spend in GarageBand, in many ways, is a big part of the rehearsal. That's all about the structure, about timing of things. And again, that's a stage at which things start seeping into my brain.
> Me The Drag Queen[5]

EXERCISE 2: ISOLATIONS

You will need: Your track and some space.

Lip-sync is a whole-body activity. Many acts will focus on learning the words, the lips, and then rely on instinct and improvisation in the performance. As performers become more experienced they can rely more and more on this. But spend some time isolating your body parts, and experimenting with different areas of the body and how they can bring your track to life. What are the options? What are the potential moments for comedy, contrast or dynamic use of your body on stage?

Play the track through from beginning to end, only moving with the following body parts and see what you can create. Some performers find this works better in front of a mirror, but others find that inhibits them. Go big, play and see what you can unlock. If there are any moments that feel right, or feel good, make a note and see if you can bring them in when you bring it all together. Run the track, try to perform the full track, but exclusively using the following body parts:

- *Your eyes.*
- *Your arms.*
- *Your hips and butt.*
- *Your legs.*
- *Your upper body.*
- *Your lower body.*

Keep playing around with different parts of your body and see what you can find within the track. If there are different voices within the track could each be informed by a different body part? your lips are not the only part of your body bringing the performance to life, don't overlook any aspect of your body on stage! You may add an extra part of your body as the track progresses – each verse or chorus brings in another part of the body so you move from near static to full body involvement.

The take away is to use the whole body – not just your lips.

EXERCISE 3: THE BODY IN THE SPACE

You will need: Your track, a printed breakdown of the lyrics/text and some space.

How you use the stage, or space, you perform in is a vital consideration in creaying a dynamic lipsync. Play with proxemics,: how close you are to the audience and your body in the stage space. Some of the options to explore include: on stage vs. off stage, moving vs. still, upstage vs. down stage, stage left vs. right, levels – high vs. low.

A simple way to structure a routine with a build and with variety is to take each verse or chorus and give it a rule, or dynamic you are going to play. It's a simple system of making sure you don't peak too soon. If you have a very involved mixed track each time a source material changes find a different way of moving, or set one dynamic stage movement for each source. Keep playing and seeing what can be brought to life.

This is a very simple structure that would just bring a little dynamic structure and build to most straight songs. This technique would work for more involved mixes too: Each change of track, source, voice - find a different dynamic or proxemic to play with to create a planned build throughout the performance.

Verse 1: Centre stage on the spot. Establish the song, the style the alter-ego or person adopted to the track.

Chorus 1: Start to move in the space. Approach the audience, a few simple steps.

Verse 2: Bring in interesting levels – go high, go low. Strike a dynamic pose.

Chorus 2: Start using the whole space.

Onwards: Bring out everything you planned – any tricks, entering the audience, etc. Building to a crescendo.

Finale: Return to the opening position but with the added drama of achievement.

This isn't fixed choreography but a way in which to perform which allows a natural build and for you to play with the audience.

EXERCISE 4: JUST BREATHE

You will need: Your track, a printed breakdown of the lyrics/text and some space.

It's easy to fixate on the big moves and the lyrics as a lip-sync performer. Don't forget about the little moments, the details are what can really help shape the performance and sell the illusion that you are singing the song, or actually speaking the text. Have a run through where you focus on *performing* the breaths. Overly act each one so they are clearly pronounced to the audience. It's usually clearer in musical theatre where the breathing comes, pop music can be multiple takes and layers edited into one track. But still try and find those breaths! If you can't hear them, try and sing it yourself and see where you need them.

This isn't giving you a version you would perform, but physicalising and focusing on the breath will help you learn exactly where the singer needs to breathe. You can then work those moments into any further rehearsals of the track to convincingly convey a physical connection to the song.

EXERCISE 5: REHEARSE, REHEARSE, REHEARSE

You will need: Your track and some space. Something to record yourself with should you choose.

A lot of the magic moments in a performance aren't realised until you are on your feet performing the piece. The previous exercises were ways to open you up, make sure you know the track, know where your body might go, what you might do in performance. Now it's time to rehearse the piece numerous times and keep exploring. See what develops.

> For each run through set yourself objectives of what you want to get out of this one. Find a little more humour, channel more of the diva, tighten up the technical aspect of breathing, find more varied use of the arms. Without having a goal a rehearsal can lose energy and become more of a mark through to prove you know it. These are valuable (see *Exercise 1*) but now you are getting ready to bring it to the stage – go big! You want to clear some space, get on your feet and rehearse full throttle.
>
> Some acts love to record themselves at this point, analyse the performance and keep working on it. Others need to take it to a stage and get the audience feedback. Either way make sure you have prepared yourself for every eventuality. Before taking the piece to the stage rehearse with anything practically needed: hats, heels, a gown with a train – make sure you have factored that into your planned movements and choreography! Your drag will affect the way in which you perform so don't let that come as a surprise.

Overview: Rehearsing and Performing a Lip-Sync

A lip-sync is by no means an easy way to perform. Audiences are eagle-eyed looking for how you have embodied the track and how you are bringing it to life in the shared space. If you've seen lots of *Drag Race* you will know that a few well-placed tricks and kicks can get a good reaction – but they are rarely enough to carry you all the way to the end. A detailed, technically accurate lip-sync full of colour, variety and trajectory is always king.

- There are various approaches to a lip-sync. Within your repertoire look for a range of edits, straight songs, upbeat, down beat, comedy.
- Revisit the second half of *Chapter 16: Creating and Editing a Track* for ideas on how to create interesting tracks to perform to.
- Immerse yourself in your tracks, listen to them all the time. Every sound which is on the track is something you can incorporate, know every second of the track.
- Rehearse, rehearse, rehearse. Play with different approaches to rehearsing the piece to open up dynamic physicalities, an accurate lip-sync and an exciting live experience for the audience.
- As you rehearse, and perform your track, don't be afraid to return to edit the track to further improve it and subsequently improve your performance. Both elements are in constant development.

I referenced how an act may use their introduction, or outro, to frame a lip-sync and share something with the audience. Many lip-sync acts, especially near the beginning of their career stay away from talking and using a microphone. But when you are ready to branch out – finding a couple of jokes, a few easy lines that you can use time and again, to introduce yourself and your work is great start. When you're ready – turn the page for a simple introduction to *Comedy, Reading & Roasting!*

Notes

1. See Part IV for full interview with *Me*.
2. *RuPaul's Drag Race All Stars* – Season 4 Episode 8.
3. Me in interview with *Michael Twaits*, July 2024. See Part IV for full interview.
4. See *Chapter 7: Research and Further Reading*.
5. Me in interview with *Michael Twaits*, July 2024. See Part IV for full interview.

Eddie East photographed backstage at the Royal Vauxhall Tavern by The Burley Photgrapher

18
Send in the Clowns: Comedy, Reading and Roasting

Some argue comedy cannot be taught, but I definitely think it can be learnt! Knowing the type of humour which suits your alter-ego, and audience, is crucial to developing your comedy skills. Through practice, building experience, stage time and growing in confidence – everybody can get a few laughs on-stage!

This chapter is exploring the basics of comedy that work with drag and looks at the types of comedy formats an act might need to be familiar with. The *drag essentials:* comedy, reading and roasting. It will be useful for all drag acts, drag hosts (more of that to come in *Chapter 22: Hosting and Solo Shows*) and to be honest, anyone speaking on stage for entertainment! Pay close attention if you are especially anxious about comedy or consider yourself to be of another discipline: Everyone can benefit from a few lines to link pieces together, or a cheeky laugh as they introduce themselves. It isn't always about full-on belly laughs; some acts just wish to be witty and warm.

There are many books on stand-up comedy that can help a performer who really wishes to be a comedy act, there's a *Further Reading* list towards the end if you want to dig deeper. The focus here is to keep it light, funny and arm you with a comedy overview that's easy to include within your performances.

Stand-Up vs. Comedy in Drag

I want to put this out there from the top of the chapter as I know many get worried, even anxious, about comedy. Many drag acts are funny, but are not comedians, and that's okay! You won't read one chapter and be a stand-up king. (This isn't to say there aren't drag acts who do stand-up: Myra Dubois, Bianca Del Rio or Kate Butch.)

A stand-up walks on stage and delivers a comedy set that is written, structured and will usually be fairly similar at their next gig. The structure is arguably closer to the theatre in that they repeat the written pieces in order, show after show. In development they will edit, re-work and find the rhythm and the beats to get the best laughs. The majority of drag acts who use comedy are actually less structured: They work off the room more, they are funny, quick-witted and seemingly have a line for everyone. Often, rather than running one set, or script, they are pulling on countless options they have brought on stage with them. Finding the best line to use, or re-use, for that moment. They can structure, or re-structure, their set in the moment, bespoke for the audience they are playing to. Feeding off the room and living in the live moment, but actually being prompted by the room and drawing on a wealth of lines, bits and ideas that have already been developed and rehearsed. If you can master that, you are a master of live drag comedy.

Initially, you only need to find a few funny lines, a few options you can draw to establish yourself, set up any other material you're performing and possibly a few one-liners for live moments. Slowly allow that bank of options to build. As experience grows you will find confidence in simply listening to the room and then pulling out the best material to suit that moment.

DOI: 10.4324/9781003498797-21

I have bits, but it's not from anything that I've sat down and consciously written or workshopped and rehearsed. They've just sort of fallen out of my mouth without me thinking. I've gone, oh, that's quite nice. And sometimes I'll have that bit of my brain that goes, well, that was fun. Remember that?

Me the Drag Queen[1]

What's in a Name?

Out of all the drag skills I feel comedy is the one that people get most in anxious about. There are simple techniques to relieve the pressure. The first is not to label yourself as a comedian, think witty, light-entertainment, charismatic. Whatever term suits your style. But ensure a host doesn't introduce you as a comedian, because that sets expectation!

> As a performer, I never use the label of being a comedian. I know I am funny and people will laugh as I talk. I often use phrases such as *"This isn't comedy, it's just my life"* to reinforce I'm just having a gossip, I'm their funny friend, not a stand-up. I feel people are smiling throughout my set, laughing at times and enjoying time in my company. I think this was a big break through for me as a performer: taking the pressure off by simply not labelling myself as a comedian allows me to push comedy further without the pressure.
>
> I'm not a comedian, but I am funny.
>
> Me The Drag Queen[2]

The second is to be prepared. Write, rehearse, refine, perform, re-write, rehearse, perform, and so on! Find the sense of humour that suits your needs and style and keep finessing it.

Building a Comic Repertoire

Just like you have a *Repertoire List* of songs or lip-syncs, you should have a *Repertoire List* of comedy lines, bits, even short comedy sets that they can draw on at different points. Aim as a performer to build up a bank of short sets to suit occasions you will frequently need them for. Always keep notes of bits you've developed, what worked in performance, what needs re-working, etc. (There's more on this in *Chapter 5: Rehearsal and Development* and *Chapter 6: Building a Set, Range and Repertoire*.) There are plenty of exercises and ideas to explore in this chapter to help create a simple repertoire to start you off, but first let's look at some different styles and approaches to comedy. What is funny? And why?

Find Your Comedy Heroes

If you are serious about using comedy, in or out of drag, do your research and find your references. Find *your* heroes, study the greats and what makes you laugh. Then find their heroes who they studied. Know the lineage of where your sense of humour comes from. Analyse the timing in their humour, the use of language, the use of structure, the rhythm. How do they physicalise a joke, how do they keep you engaged? Do not try and *copy* their humour but allow it to inform you and clarify where you think you could get laughs.

> I am far removed from Victoria Wood – a British Southerner, cis-male and a different age bracket – but her humble, honest, self-deprecating style is baked into my drag persona. The glee and silliness

of French & Saunders is equally in my stage DNA. I don't use their jokes (NEVER USE SOMEONE ELSE'S MATERIAL). But I am funny on-stage because I laughed at them, and then I worked out why I laughed!

I use lots of real-life observational humour, camp references and being a bit outrageous. I observed from *Absolutely Fabulous* the joy of watching someone say or do things that audiences *wish* they had the confidence to do. So I create that for my audiences.

Jokes, Structures and Styles

A good joke has a structure and a good set needs variety. Below is a short introduction to various *types* of joke, set-up and structure that can help you to play with comedy on stage and create varied material to keep an audience engaged. Many will be familiar, although labelling them as a *type* may be unfamiliar. Think about what makes you laugh and what type of humour you wish to bring to the stage: which techniques do your comedy heroes tend to use? If you already have some comic repertoire you use on stage – where does that fit? The variety and craft of comedy comes from finding the balance and the range in set-ups, punchline and language used. Let's look at some of the big ones.

A Traditional Joke: A set-up and then a punchline. The set-up might feature details, locations, characters and the punchline is the twist, surprise or the resolve intended to make the audience laugh. Simple, right?

One Liner: A one liner is exactly as it sounds. A joke which is set-up and then delivers a punch all within one line.

A Topper: This is a short one liner, or extra punchline, to deliver on top of an existing punchline to ride the laugh out a little longer.

A Shaggy-Dog Story: A long story, usually humorous and ridiculous all the way through, hopefully with a nice punchline that makes the journey worthwhile. But peppered with smaller laughs along the way. The biggest laugh, the pay off, should be the end, the final punchline.

Flips or Reverses: Taking the audience down an expected joke path but the punchline being unexpected and reframing the whole set-up.

> I was in my car driving back from work. A police officer pulled me over and knocked on my window. I said, "One minute I'm on the phone".
>
> Alan Carr

Puns: A play on words. Exploiting the similarity/duality of two words. There is something unifying about a pun, a little bit like a cracker joke at Christmas. The audience do a little bit of an eye roll together whilst laughing.

> Miss Fame, Don-a-tell-a me that was your best celebrity impersonation.
> RuPaul critiquing Miss Fames impression of Donatella Versace[3]

Double Entendres: Arguably a pun but where one of the meanings has a risqué or sexual meaning. Drag names are often double entendres (*Iva Dong*, *Lucinda Rear*, etc.).

Observational Humour: Shining a comic light on the details of everyday life. Remember, comedy can be about simple things: a toaster, a lampshade, a camp clutch bag. Victoria Wood was a master of this.

> The Italians have got opera, the Spanish have got flamenco dancing. What have we got? Weight Watchers.
>
> Victoria Wood

Compare and Contrast: The above quote is observation but also a compare and contrast. It's a very familiar comic structure. The humour usually comes when two things that aren't in any way related are compared but this can be inverted.

> Foreplay is like beef burgers – three minutes on each side.
>
> Victoria Wood

Wit: Clever, intelligent humour.

Folly: The joy of laughing at someone who, possibly unintentionally, shows themselves to not understand something fully. Folly is a wonderful place to play because drag acts are often seen as *others* or *otherworldly*. For example: a drag act trying to *understand* heterosexual mating rules is pure folly.

Slapstick: Physical comedy. Acting out a scene or a skit. Tripping on a banana peel. You may be talking but the physicality while you are talking is where the humour comes.

Self-Deprecation: Making yourself the butt of the joke. If an audience know you don't take yourself too seriously, and that you can laugh at yourself, it's a leveller in the room; you're not presenting yourself as flawless, you're just as messed up and ridiculous as the rest of the world. It can be charming and gives you the license to throw jokes at everyone else later.

Dramatic Irony: The audience knowing a fact that the performer is unaware of. Olaf's song from Frozen – *In Summer* – is full of humour. It's dramatic irony because the audience know something he doesn't – he will melt!

The Rule of Three: This isn't a style of joke, more a structure for keeping a set varied or observations within a joke. If you use one style of comedy, one style of set-up repeatedly it gets familiar. Do it once, fine. Twice, fine. The third time you have to mix it up. (In *Chapter 1: A New Beginning* you had three brainstorms: Brainstorm One, analysis and exercises; Brainstorm Two, analysis and exercises; Brainstorm Three – here's a whole chapter to explore it.) Breaking a rhythm keeps people engaged!

Malapropism: The mistaken use of one word with another. I once coined a malapropism myself when trying to encourage a young act to find some "self-defeating humour" [deprecating]. Officially a malapropism is used unknowingly, or by accident. Which can work brilliantly for a character-based act or impersonation (Remember that for *Chapter 20: Impersonation: Tribute and Parody*) because the character you are playing doesn't know they are using the wrong word.

> I guess I'm gonna fade into Bolivian. [oblivion]
>
> Boxer, Mike Tyson, June 2002[4]

Combinations

No styles from above needs exist in isolation. You can hit more than one mode at a time. One of my favourite Victoria Wood *one-liners* is also *self-deprecating* with a *double entendre*:

> I thought *Coq au Vin* was love in a lorry.
>
> Victoria Wood

Language, Rhythm and Phrasing

If the concept for a joke is funny but at first it isn't getting the right laugh, play with the language and rhythm of the delivery. If the concept feels right exploring, through rehearsal and performance, can unlock the bigger laugh. Language and rhythm is hugely important in comedy; certain words are funny, combinations of words give interesting rhythms. Sometimes the structure of a joke is correct but the laugh isn't as big because the wrong word has been used. When honing and developing your set/bit – play with the language, the order, which word to emphasise, etc. Are there too many words distracting from the joke, or too few? Sometimes using a thesaurus to find a word which flows better, or sounds punchier can make all the difference. Sometimes adding alliteration, or a rhyme can just highlight the wit of what you are saying to an audience. Other times it can make the joke seem too structured.

Comic Rules

It's important to bear these things in mind when branching into comedy for the first time.

Never Use Someone Else's Material

With singing and lip-sync acts are often reinterpreting what someone else has written. In comedy – by all means be inspired – but do not use another performers jokes.

Where Are You Punching?

A lot of drag comedy is aimed at other people – pop culture figures, political figures, the audience, other acts on stage: everyone is fair game. But a comic should never be punching down. Anything that makes the person in the frame of the joke a minority, compared to you as the performer, is off limits. That doesn't mean it can't be referenced, but it shouldn't be the punchline of the joke!

> **Now, just a recap on pronouns for the room here, now, out of drag, Etcetera uses they/them pronouns, so for example: "They" haven't been in the top, so we won't be seeing "them" in the final.**
>
> **Art Simone** *reads* Etcetera Etcetera In *Drag Race Down Under Season 1*

This was a great read because it was brutal about Etcetera Etcetera. It also acknowledged correctly their pronouns, supporting their identity and actually using them to frame the punchline. A non-binary identity being a punchline wouldn't be funny. Correctly using their pronouns to put them down, twice, was a good read!

Know What You Are Booked For

If you are booked for a roast then you need to have some savagely written one liners and reads. If you are at a fundraiser for a charity savaging the CEO, the volunteers and the cause is not a good idea. Similarly, if you are at a comedy show, bring a comedy set but don't start roasting the other people on the bill if that isn't the gig! Always think of *Chapter 8: Basic Drag* – know the gig you have been booked for and prepare material that suits the occasion the best!

Reading the Room

This is not the drag definition of *reading*; this is being aware of how jokes are landing, getting a sense of if you are too crude, too bitchy or too much for the audience. There are moments on stage where you might say an expletive and can feel the audience wince. Other times a throwaway read/comment to an audience member can get a huge laugh and the rest of the room perk up "*do me, pick on me!*" Respond to these moments and try to give them what they want. For the cabaret environment it is absolutely essential to be able to read a room and adapt your set to fit. That doesn't mean change what you are presenting or who you are, but take your foot off the accelerator, or crank it up a gear. Listen to their reactions and respond accordingly.

For most experienced performers the material that makes it out of their mouth on stage is only a fraction of the material they had prepared. Always have a few options in your pocket, with experience and stage time you will develop the skill of selecting the right joke for the right moment.

Respect the Audience

Don't over explain the joke or punchline. The audience want the jokes to hit them, not to get to the punchline before you have. If you feel they know the punchline already, don't deliver it – the punchline becomes that they've already got it and you giving them the knowing look. Over explaining a joke is the death of comedy.

Show Don't Tell

Don't tell them you're going to be funny; just make them laugh. If you're a character who is really zany don't tell them – *show* them. Telling an audience something about yourself and then having to prove it makes life much harder as a performer. In many ways this throws back the point above (*What's in a Name?*), if I don't tell them I'm funny the laughs come easier. Setting up that they're going to laugh only gets the audience thinking "*I'll be the judge of that*". Don't put that pressure on yourself until you feel you have really honed your craft.

EXERCISE 1: BUILD THE BANK

You will need: Your notepad and pen. A voice recorder to help hear them out loud.

It's time to attempt to write some comedy bits: not a full set, probably not a shaggy-dog story, simply a few lines. For each of the below try to make the audience laugh whilst telling them something practical. Often acts struggle with knowing what to tell a joke about: don't look for inspiration elsewhere, look at what you need to tell them anyway and make it funny! This an expansion of the *Capital on Language Lexicon* exercises in *Chapter 13: Talking On Stage*, bring those notes back out! Previously the goal was to build your relationship with the audience, to be unique, now aim for laughs!

The themes below are all common moments within a drag set or bit – how can you make them funny and unique? Choose the ones you think you would use as a performer. Use the *Joke Structures and Styles* for inspiration and for different directions to explore. Try to write three options that you *might* use for each of these areas:

- *Tell the audience your name.*
- *Why are you on stage?*
- *Share some personal details; love life, work life, journey here, etc.*
- *See who's in the room.*
- *Interact with the audience.*
- *Order a drink from the bar.*

Comedy, Reading and Roasting

- *Do you like my outfit?*
- *How did you get here tonight?*
- *You need to finish your set?*
- *Are you ready for my next piece?*
- *Thank you and goodbye!*

What you've created are starter phrases which can go into your on-stage comedy repertoire. Test them out, some will become go-to phrases. Some won't work and can be discarded, others will be saved just for specific occasions, others will be useful at almost every gig!

From these ideas you might be able to structure a few jokes back to back and have a small introductory set – which leads nicely to forming a mini set.

EXERCISE 2: A MINI SET

You will need: Your notepad and pen.

Most comedy sets start with a bit, or a mini-set, small segments that slowly build. Below is a list of mini objectives that a small set might be used for, again all things you would probably need to say any one on-stage. If you're new to comedy you might want to get comfortable having a segment at first, a run of lines that move your set on but not relying on comedy throughout. These should be very short – three to four lines. Under a minute of material. But it is the beginning of seeing how a few lines next to each other can work, build and shape into a set.

- Introduce/establish yourself (*name, reason for being on stage, personal detail*).
- Set up the next song (*why've you chosen it, why do you like it, what the audience might get out of it, tell a story, humour about the original artist, how've you improved the song*).
- Get interactive (*ask the audience some questions, play off them, ask them what they think of you, your outfit, ask them why they are here, who's single, etc*).
- Set up the rules (*this is more for a host; but explaining when to make noise, when to laugh, the structure of the evening or the set*).

These two exercises should arm you with something you can start rehearsing and exploring. Try a few lines on stage, introduce things slowly. Remember the *Risk Sandwich* (from *Chapter 5: Rehearsal and Development*). If you have a *lead* skill as a performer, such as lip-sync, try doing a lip-sync, then introduce yourself with a small comedy segment, a mini set, that leads into your next lip-sync. At first, a few lines, and as confidence builds you can do more and more.

Reading and Roasting

I'm sorry to say but it is a recurring pattern that people who consider themselves funny underperform at reading and roasts. It's also common a dark horse slips in and seems to *win* the occasion. The reason is, funny people who can get a few laughs off a crowd when chatting think that skill will translate: it will not!

Light entertainment, stand-up and reading/roasting are all very different skill sets. If you are going to read someone, or join a roast, work hard – it is an art form!

> As drag queens we shrug off a lot of insults. So when we get our chance to throw an insult we turn it into a high art form. We call it reading, or throwing shade. And it's part of our culture.
>
> RuPaul's Drag Race – Season 2[5]

Reading and Shade

I don't wish to get caught in the semantics of language but it feels remiss not throw a little light on the subject of shade. *Reading* is simply a well-executed, insult based, *one liner* aimed at a specific individual or group. Often an in joke or something based on at least a fragment of truth. Many believe it was something that originated backstage in ballroom culture between gay men, trans and drag performers, as a way of sharpening claws and comedic skills before taking to the stage.

Shade on the other hand is a little less performative and arguably more honest. Shade is more subtle, side-eye, or a sneering comment. With shade you don't need to always finish the insult because…

> shade should have an element of plausible deniability, so that the shade-thrower can pretend that he or she didn't actually mean to behave with incivility, making it all the more delicious.
>
> Anna Holmes – *The Underground Art of Insult*[6]

Telling someone their dress is hideous is a simple *read*, asking someone if the dress is new might be *shade*.

> *Read*: Michael's make-up? Crayola sent a 'cease and desist'.
>
> *Shade*: Michael's make-up? I didn't know she wore make-up?

The distinction is subtle, with both humour, or wit, has to be there. If you *read* me I want to laughing and outraged – both at the same time! If you lose the laugh, you will just come off as a bitch. You have to be funny.

Comedy Not Savagery

Novice performers often take reading too far down the insult route and forget to put in wit, humour or a punchline. The essence of a *read* is that it fits into a *one liner* format: everyone laughs, even if the read is on us. So, make us laugh!

Roast

All the rules of reading apply to a roast. However, a roast is a string of jokes, or reads, strung together and over a longer set: you have time to tell a little story, build to a joke, add a couple of *toppers*. A good roaster can keep the laughter rolling throughout, the next punchline can hit before the laughter has fully died from the previous one! There should be very little dead time in a roast. (There may be *shade* thrown into a roast, usually that's the rebuttal or interactions between roasters. For example; thanking/congratulating the act before you when it was evident their roast bombed – *shade*.)

Usually a roast celebrates a legend of the community: a birthday, an anniversary, a fundraiser for their chosen charity. You have been invited as a guest. Always top and tail with love before dishing out the insults! Treat it like being in someone's house; thank them for the invite and take your shoes off before you start drinking all their wine, and at the end of the night thank them for a lovely evening! At a roast anyone, and everyone, stepping near the stage can be *read*!

Four golden rules for a successful roast are:

- *Show some form of love/respect set-up.*
- *Always find a moment of self-deprecation.*
- *Open the jokes up enough that everyone can all laugh along, feel in on the joke. In jokes don't work as an audience will feel excluded.*
- *Make sure everyone is laughing!*

Research, Again

Roasts, and reading, have many familiar patterns and it's worth doing some serious deep diving into successful and unsuccessful roasts. If your only reference is a *Drag Race* roast watch Martha Stewart or Nikki Glaser on *Comedy Central*, find some videos with Lady Bunny reading and then go back down the YouTube wormhole! Watch, learn, find rhythms you like, but remember, never directly use someone else's material.

Familiar Formats for a Read

There are many familiar themes and structures for a read. Watching just a few episodes of *Drag Race* can make some of the reads seem repetitive because the structure is so familiar. The skill is to take the expected but make it your own, and as much as possible, specific to the person you are reading.

Use Their Work against Them

When making jokes about people in the wider world, famous people, it's common to take the things they are known for and rephrase or repurpose it against them for comedy. Make a pun based on their name, or their latest product. (Next time I'm at a roast I expect this handbook to be used as a weapon against me!)

Self-Deprecation

I cannot stress enough the importance of including some self-deprecating humour in a roast. Jinkx Monsoon is a master of this, audiences end up laughing with her as she savages everyone and anyone! *"If you can't make fun of yourself…"*

Misdirection

This is a reading take on a *flip or reverse*; lead them down a path and then have a punchline that twists.

> Ginger Minge – in my eyes the true winner of season seven…of TLC's *I Didn't Know I Was Pregnant.*
> Katya, All Stars – Season 2 Episode 1[7]

With Love

The audience want to see the love. See that you are all peers/colleagues/friends and therefore have a license to make fun of each other! Start with a compliment, or defending them against someone else's read, only to deliver the savage punchline yourself.

> Trinity: so kind and compassionate and caring! She even let her last boyfriend down easily…she said *"let's just be cousins"*.
>
> Jinkx Monsoon, *All Stars* – Season 7 Episode 10[8]

Puns

Making a pun based off of someone's name or an achievement in their career.

> **Manila Luzon!** Emphasis on lose. Twice.
>
> Monet X Change, *All Stars* – Season 4 Episode 1[9]

> I do a lot of gardening…but you are without a doubt the dirtiest, used up hoe I've ever seen.
>
> Martha Stewart[10]

Two For One

Much like a compare and contrast joke: if you can compare one performer to another in the room you may be able to insult both with one read.

> Jessica Wild is so full of shit she makes RuPaul's diaper jealous!
>
> Jimbo, *All Stars* – Season 8 Episode 9[11]

Three and One

Another common structure is to give three, quick mini insults which might be outrageous but that you frame yourself as not agreeing with, to then deliver a bigger insult.

> Initially your make-up was kind of busted, your outfits were a mess and your personality was super grating. But look how far you've come now. You're much older.
>
> BenDeLaCreme, *All Stars* – Season 3 Episode 1[12]

Rephrase Classic Phrases

Taking a popular or well-known idiom and repurposing it as a read.

- *"The host with the most…most _____"* (most whats?)
- *"Time flies when you having fun…which is why at her shows…"*
- *"You can take a horse to water, but you can't make it…"*

> You can take the girl out of New Jersey, but you can't keep the girl from giving blowjobs to homeless men along the New Jersey Turnpike…
>
> Alaska on Michelle Visage, *Drag Race* – Season 5 Episode 7[13]

Rephrase Modern/Drag Phrases

There are many drag catchphrases that can be reworked in the same way as classic phrases if it suits the show you are part of.

- "If you're not wearing _____, you're not doing drag".
- "If you can't love yourself, how the hell are you going _____ ".
- "No T, No Shade, No_____".

On stage, and on TV, reads all seem fresh and specific to the exact moment. But like most stage work they are structured, rehearsed and then drawn on from a wide repertoire when needed. It's time to start developing your own range of reads.

EXERCISE 3: READING IS FUNDAMENTAL

You will need: Your notepad and pen.

You need to write some reads for specific people. Without knowing who you might be on stage with it's hard to prepare. But sharpening your skills is the best place to start and it will become easy to adapt a strong read to a different specific person or situation, for now pick a favourite TV show (*Friends, Buffy, Game of Thrones* or a specific season of *Drag Race*) and write down the top five featured characters.

Write a minimum of three reads for each of them. If you happen to find a two-for-one read by comparing and contrasting them to each other – great! Really you want a unique selection of reads where you can just change a few adjectives/specifics to hopefully make them specific to a whole new group of people!

Once written, play around with performing them. Try to avoid using the *Drag Race* robot-read voice that many slip into on the show, you want to do this from the perspective of your existing on-stage alter-ego. As ever, voice recording can be a useful evaluation tool.

Familiar Formats for a Roast

All of the formats for reading may be put into a roast. But most of the formats below are a little too long winded to fit in as a quick read OR aren't quite cutting enough to stand alone. When doing a roast an easy way to build up some reads and jokes is to bring your own take to some classic approaches. You don't need to reinvent the wheel – be specific, fresh and in the moment! Remember a roast gives you more time to set up a joke, more time to build on a joke, or add a *topper* to keep the laughs coming – but it all needs to be funny!

How Old Is He?

Take a well-known fact about the person you are reading (so old, so gay, so camp, so dumb, etc.) and then tell us how old, for example, they are with three quick reads. You may apply the *Rule of Three* from above and give a twist on the third one, or save the funniest for last.

I'm the Nice One

Building someone up, being the good friend, but actually burying a strong read in amongst the kindness. It's killing with kindness. As a read these aren't the most savage but a couple of these in the build of roasting one individual before giving them a tougher read can be a strong structure.

They are such a inspiration to the community, over the past five years their work has been seen by literally ten's of people.

You give so much to our community. Thank you. Crueler voices might say it's because you have nothing else going on in your life. (Dramatic pause to say "*I'm saying nothing...*")

Mis-Reading

At a roast acts often have notes; if you do then incorporate a mis-read into your roast. It's a simple gag that justifies you having your notes with you. You simply need to find two words that look very similar but one being kind and one being an insult.

My go-to is **Hit** and **Shit**:

Known for their *hit* show at... I'm so sorry I misread that... Known for their *shit* show.

The False Set-Up

Setting up as if you are going to do one of the classic set-ups but then actually stop and present it as fact.

Michelle Visage is so full of seamen...period.

Jinkx Monsoon, *Drag Race* – Season 5 Episode 7[14]

EXERCISE 4: ROAST YOUR FAVOURITES

You will need: Your notepad and pen.

Review your notes from *Exercise 3*, pick your favourite read for each character as a starting point and try to turn it into a short set about each person. Rather than just one read you now want to build a few together, or expand them to thirty seconds to a minute. If it helps your structure choose one person who is the honouree of the roast so you have something to build up to, aiming for a crescendo.

As an extension write a short intro (usually including an honouree to be there, a moment of self-deprecation and a general read of the group as a whole) and then of course an exit line (thanking for a great night, a moment of love to the honouree and then introduce the next roaster, with a final read).

Further (Actual) Reading

This really is an introduction to comedy and its uses within drag. If your goal is to be a fully-fledged stand-up who happens to use drag, here are a few books to help you dig deeper:

Double, O. (2013). *Getting the joke*. A&C Black.
Double, O. (1997). *Stand up on being a comedian*. Bloomsbury Publishing.
Lukas, M. (2023). *Finding your funny muscle*. Merlin Makes Publishing.
Morris, J. (2024). *Be funny or die*. Unbound Publishing
Rosenfield, S. (2018). *Mastering stand-up: The complete guide to becoming a successful comedian*. Chicago, Illinois: Chicago Review Press Incorporated.

Overview: Comedy, Reading and Roasting

The golden rule for comedy is: the audience need to laugh. At every stage of development (in rehearsal and on-stage) test material, sense the audience and check they are laughing.

- Not everyone who uses comedy needs to label themselves as a comedian.
- Play around with variety of jokes structures and comic styles addressed and see what fits you. For those new to comedy - try a line here and there between different parts of your set. See what works and slowly build on it!
- Learn to read the room: Listen to what's working, if you can't adapt in the moment learn from that gig and evolve your set before the next.
- Explore the variety of comedy approaches, audience want variety: It's rare a comic will just use one-liners. Explore the range and see which suit your alter-ego.
- Keep trying material out: Play with tone, language, pacing.
- Use the exercises to build some comic lines, and mini-sets, that you can try out between other successful material: As you grow in confidence your can keep building on them.

With reading/roasting:

- Come from a place of love, have a depreciating moment, good jokes and the audience will be on your side.
- Don't feel you have to be a bitch. Why not be the nice one and be funny!
- Use the exercise to build starter read and roasts as a way of crafting your funny bones!

Like all other styles of performance, comedy is a journey: research it, write it, rehearse it, perform it, evaluate it. Then re-write, re-rehearse and keep on going. Keep refining and reworking! Understanding the different types of joke, comic uses and language and comic timing is an art form that take experience, stage-time and hard work. The skills though will ripple through to all areas of your practice. Including our next area – Parody!

Notes

1. Me in interview with *Michael Twaits*, July 2024. See Part IV for full interview.
2. Me in interview with *Michael Twaits*, July 2024. See Part IV for full interview.
3. "Snatch Game" *RuPaul's Drag Race* Season 7 Episode, 13 April 2015, *Logo TV*.
4. Mike Tyson in interview after losing to Lennox Lewis. https://youtu.be/6tLrIkPK8kg?si=JkwKkqIE06LHZLWZ
5. *RuPaul's Drag Race* Season 2 Episode.
6. Holmes, Anna (14 May 2015). "The Underground Art of the Insult". *The New York Times*. Archived from the original on 16 May 2015.
7. "All Star Talent Extravaganza" *RuPaul's Drag Race All Stars* Season 2 Episode 1, 25 August 2016, *Logo TV & VH1*.
8. "The Kennerdy Davenport Centre Honours Hall Of Shade" *RuPaul's Drag Race All Stars* Season 7 Episode 10, 15 July 2022, *Paramount + and Wow Presents*.
9. "All Star-Spangled Variety Show" *RuPaul's Drag Race All Stars* Season 4 Episode 1, 15 December 2018, *VH1*.
10. Martha Stewart roasting Natasha Leggero – 30 March 2015, *Comedy Central*.
11. *RuPaul's Drag Race All Stars* Season 8 Episode.
12. "All-Star Variety Show" RuPaul's Drag Race All Stars Season 3 Episode 1, 25 January 2018, *VH1*.
13. "The RuPaul Roast" *RuPaul's Drag Race* Season 5 Episode 7, 11 March 2013, *Logo TV*.
14. "The RuPaul Roast" *RuPaul's Drag Race* Season 5 Episode 7, 11 March 2013, *Logo TV*.

Debbie Del Rey photographed backstage at the Royal Vauxhall Tavern by Fox Al Rajim

19
Isn't This Better: Parody

In performance drag acts are famous for their re-writes and reinterpretations of well-known material, it's time to look at that drag staple: parody song! Queering the familiar; to pull the metaphorical rug out from under the audience, throw a political punch or get a big belly laugh.

To parody is to exaggerate, imitate and reinterpret something familiar in a comic way. With parody songs performers are changing either: the words, the meaning of existing words through re-interpretation or changing the style of the song, to give the existing lyrics a new meaning. All the time keeping the original work intact *enough* that the audience know what it is being parodied. As the original is reworked, reframed or reimagined audiences laugh at the changes and new meaning. It's a simple technique for creating work which feels fresh, that can show a creative point of view, but the audience are already familiar with. This helps them engage quickly, and keeps them engaged, as they want to listen carefully for the changes. The sign of a strong parody is that when you hear the original again you laugh remembering the parody!

This chapter will look at creating, shaping and performing a parody song, a stand-alone piece which could form part of any set or show. The approaches and examples given have been written from the assumption of someone singing live, however parody can work for a lip-sync artist if they structure or edit a track in the right way. It's worth highlighting there are numerous examples of performers whose entire stage presence is a parody. If you were impersonating an icon you may decide to reimagine some of their greatest hits, catchphrases and mannerisms to shape you whole set and alter-ego, this will be explored next in *Chapter 20: Impersonation: Tribute and Parody* and in *Chapter 25: Interview with Simply Barbra* but for now the focus is one parody song!

The What vs. the How

The creative process often comes back to these two elements: *What* you are going to do/say and *how* are you going to do it. With parody it becomes *what* are you saying (the joke, the issue, the political point) and the *how* is the original song that you will adapt. Finding that initial link, or *in*, to the parody is usually the trickiest part but once a good pairing is found, the parody can often seem to write itself.

Sometimes inspiration will just strike and the connection is obvious, other times you go hunting for the perfect song to make a point with, other times you know the song is adaptable and just need to finesse how you will reinterpret it. All are valid approaches that can create a strong piece.

Knowing the Original

In simplified comedy terms: the original song is your *set up* and your reworking is the *punchline*. If the audience do not know the original song they are not getting the full joke; pick songs most people know! The quicker an audience can recognise original song, the better.

DOI: 10.4324/9781003498797-22

If an audience don't know the song, or understand that you are performing a parody, they might consider the song an original comedy track you have written and a lot of the wit, and your work, will be lost on them. Test how well known a song is before committing to it. What you think is a classic may have passed others by: do a little research. It's hard to go wrong if you choose a break-through single for an artist or something from a *Greatest Hits* Album. When the opening chords to Dolly Parton's *9 to 5* start everyone knows it. If you chose *Here You Come Again* would it be as quick? Or *Shine Like the Sun*. You want a *9 to 5* style connection for most parodies. There is always the desire to be unique but here the *what* you are doing is the unique part, the original song choice is just the *how*.

Being Bookable

You want your work to be usable, and reusable. If you re-write the lyrics to Lady Gaga's *Poker Face* with a witty welcome to the show ("*This is who I am*"), you could potential use it at every show. If you write it about a news headline this week, it might be chip paper next week as the moment has passed. I am not saying you can't write a parody on specific themes but for longevity, and to get value out of your writing, try to avoid anything too niche which might not be relevant a few weeks down the road.

> I recently did a May 4th *Star Wars* night and rewrote – *Do You Want to Build a Snowman* as *Do You Want to Be a Jedi*. It was a fun, comic number in my set, lots of specific filmic references and a few belly laughs but I will probably not perform that again. Perhaps on May 4th in a future year? The references are too specific to perform outside of a *Star Wars* context and it doesn't fit with my usual onstage persona.

Focus on creating parodies with broad appeal that you can frequently used at varied gigs. When niche or specific bookings come in and you *want* to create a parody for the occasion, that's great! The exercises here will all still work, but a parody creation is a lot of work for a one off performance. The broader themes the work has the more you can use it.

Trajectory

Often performers find a brilliant one-line replacement, or one reimagined moment, for a chorus which is the inspiration for the parody. However, one joke being repeated each chorus won't keep an audience engaged the whole time. You always need to find ways to build on a joke. Think of the comic rule of three (see *Chapter 18: Comedy, Reading and Roasting*) doing it once twice is fine but the third time you have to go somewhere new with it. Keep the audience engaged and questioning what might happen next.

Inspiration

Inspiration can strike at any point: you might get an idea on a bus, hear a song in a shop or even overhear a phrase in a restaurant and think – *that might be something!* Note it down and then come back to it when you have some time. When you have time to be creative, rehearse and write you don't want to be staring at a blank sheet of paper waiting for inspiration; you want to come to a page of notes and ideas that are in development – pick one and see where it goes. Nurture an ongoing practice: When an idea comes to you, note it down, build a bank of potential ideas that *might* develop into a piece. Always relish the ridiculous and indulge the idiotic, note each silly idea down and watch your *Repertoire Lists* keep growing (see more in *Chapter 6: Building a Set, Range and Repertoire*).

When performing parodies I'm often asked how I came up with the idea; the answer is generally from playing, exploring and not being afraid to be stupid. For every silly idea that occurs to me I probably only develop one in ten into something stage ready!.

> If I don't know what to do, but I need to make something new, the best thing [for me] is to stick the radio on. 80s and 90s music is pretty good because there were a lot of innuendos hidden in the songs. It wasn't too blatant. Today's music, it's a little bit too obvious. It's not funny. But in the 90s, there's a lot of stuff that you could misread as being about something else – which is where I like to find my little treasure trove.
>
> Adam All

The Chicken or the Egg?

When a *what* and *how* pair up the creative momentum of a parody is magic, but how can you find that match? It is a definite *chicken or egg* situation! Sometimes there's a burning desire to communicate an idea so you go hunting a song that fits that issue. Other times, there's a particular song which you feel is just asking to be played around with, and you need to work out in what way. Both approaches can yield strong results.

The best advice is to keep workshopping ideas, keep editing, play around and try to make yourself laugh! And of, course, write everything down! It's too easy to mess around with ideas, have a giggle and walk away forgetting half of what was created – so keep notes! For re-writing lyrics, singing a quick voice note of how you *might* re-work a song is a quick way to save a creative idea for later.

Modes of Parody

There are three main ways to parody a song and bring new meaning to it: *re-style*, *re-interpret* or *re-write*. None of these modes needs to exist in isolation but for clarity we shall address each mode individually. There are many ways to combine the different styles at various points within a song to help give theatrical *peaks and troughs* throughout.

1) Re-Style

Performing a song in a genre or style outside of its original form. Taking a rap song and performing it as a ballad, or turning pop into musical theatre. This is probably the one least thought about in terms of a parody but can be hugely effective and you help take songs from outside of your alter-ego's expected field of reference and make them fit your style.

For inspiration on these and to see examples take a look at *Scott Bradley's Post Modern Jukebox*, who also have officially released backing tracks to some of their greatest hits. Or look at how many times *Down The Witches Road* was re-styled within Disney's *Agatha All Along*.[1] A restyled parody is simply re-styling like these examples but aiming for a comic result.

> I often take pop songs and put them into either a musical theatre or vintage swing/jazz style. Suddenly when slowed down, and acted out a little more, pop lyrics can become hilarious. I may suit a musical theatre, up-beat pop type vibe – but I will bring Eminem, Nicki Minaj or Rage Against the Machine to the stage with my own reimagining.
>
> I perform Taylor Swift's *Blank Space* as a jazz standard and I play the flirty ingénue looking for love. During the opening lines I do some light interaction with the audience, lots of eye contact and long pauses but only using the existing lyrics. It turns disposable pop lyrics, originally delivered almost robotically, into a flirtatious, seductive hunt for love. The audience enjoy something familiar

> becoming unfamiliar and laugh harder as they realise they hadn't actually listened, or connected, with the lyrics previously.

Taking the re-styling further it is also possible to sing one song to the tune of another, rather than just in a different style. (In many ways this a *Two-for-One* gag – see *Chapter 18: Comedy, Reading and Roasting*) This is something harder to stumble upon but can give brilliant results.

> A strong example of this is Victoria Wood who on Radio 4's *I'm Sorry I Haven't a Clue* sang *Bob the Builder* as if it were *I Dreamed a Dream* from *Les Miserables*.

Re-styles don't always need to be performed in full. Sometimes the audience *get* the joke and to perform the full song, without a specific build, can feel a little too much. You may however have a few reinterpretations on a theme and wish to do a run of snippets to get a few quick laughs in succession.

> I have a set where I perform sections from a fictitious upcoming show called *"Someone's Song, Someone Else's Lyrics!"* It's a silly introduction that allows me to sing a few different snippets of re-interpreted songs. There's no deep meaning, there's no actual show! I won't ever perform the show, they are just quick parody gags. Some drag irreverence to make the audience laugh and say: *"oh those lyrics fit that tune, that's funny"*.
>
> I sing *Dear Theodosia* from *Hamilton* with the lyrics from Jessie J's *Price Tag*. Usually, I sing enough of the original so people know the song, and then drop in the second song. These two aren't the most iconic as some songs so I set them up a little bit more. Another favourite, which needs no introduction, is I perform is *Oops!...I Did It Again* which fits perfectly to the second half of *Don't Rain on My Parade*. It works! (As I'm writing this I'm wondering if that means it would work the other way round? Noting this down so I don't forget to give it a try!)

2) Re-Interpret

Taking the meaning of a known song and twisting it through the way you perform the song; this could be the way you introduce the song, move, dance, the way you act or through use of costume and props.

> I once saw a lip-sync act go around a bar gently poking the faces of the audience during the chorus of *Poker Face* – it was so stupid, I loved it! I don't think the gag lasted for the full song. But I belly laughed at the stupidity!

There are many songs that have had this treatment given to them time and time again. (Drag acts showing us what they would not do during Meatloaf – *I Would Do Anything for Love*.)

> London Drag-duo Adam All and Apple Derrieres re-interpret *Always* by Bon Jovi brilliantly. Opening as a straight power ballad but towards the crescendo they start taking sanitary towels and tampons out of their pockets, bra or wig and throwing them into the audience, and at each other. Re-interpreting the entire song to be about *Always* sanitary products and menstruation. The lyrics

actually fit amazingly well when taken in that context and there is also something incredibly powerful about Adam being a king and tackling issues of menstruation. It's actually a parody that gets better with a re-watch, the opening lyrics especially are perfect when you frame the piece as being about menstruation.

In conversation Adam All talked about vocals staying as true as possible in performance to the original vocal performance so audiences can really focus on the parody he was presenting. A re-interpretation parody isn't a time for your own jazzy riffs!

> All of the ad-libs – exactly how the original singer does it. I'm quite fastidious about not adding my own riffs. Doing it the original way.
>
> Adam All

EXERCISE 1: RE-INTERPRET THE CLASSICS

You will need: Your notepad and pen, access to the tracks and their lyrics.

From the list below brainstorm different interpretations you could give the song through performance *without* changing the lyrics. Find two options for each of the listed songs. It's the over arching premise of your re-interpretation that you want to find at this point. All these songs beg a question and you need to give us a comic answer: What will or won't you do? What might you be the winner of? What are these rules for? What do you want? What is your job?

Maybe This Time – Cabaret

Anything For Love – Meatloaf

New Rules – Dua Lipa

I Want It That Way – Backstreet Boys

9 to 5 – Dolly Parton

You might use props, hand actions, choreography, costuming or more to re-interpret these pieces! Each song – needs at least two suggestions so you have options and ideas you might come back to. Or if you are revisiting this exercise, open some pop music playlists, or greatest musical playlists, on a streaming service and find some more material!

EXERCISE 2: DEVELOPMENT

You will need: Your notepad. pen, access to your chosen song and mptes from *Exercise 1*.

From the ten ideas you have brainstormed pick one to develop further. Think about: How could you perform this on stage? How can you structure the song, build the song to sustain the joke the full length of the song? Will it work for a full song – is there a journey? At what point do you reveal your re-interpretation – it may get a bigger laugh later in the song? Or is just a snippet – a quick gag to use and move away from?

> How far can you take the joke? Is there a crescendo moment? Remember if the song is too long you might edit it down to being short (see *Chapter 16: Creating and Editing a Track*). At this point you want to start rehearsing it physically and see what comes out, move around the space, try out ideas. Try to keep the laughs, and trajectory building. How can you use the space? How far can you take something? With each repeat of a chorus ask yourself – "*what am I adding?*"
>
> It won't happen instantly, this is the first step in developing an idea from a pitch to a possible piece. It takes time, investment, rehearsal and effort. Add this piece to your *Repertoire List* (see *Chapter 5: Rehearsal and Development*) – is it *In Development* or *Rehearsal Reperoire*?

3) Re-Write

Arguably the most common, or expected, mode of parody. A solo artist can easily achieve this with a backing track, some creative thinking, a paper and pen! Simply find your comic *in* and get re-writing! (There are so many different famous examples of parody *re-writes* with artists like Weird Al Yonkovich or former drag super group DWV.) The upcoming examples and exercises will provide a few simple approaches to getting started with a re-write and help you build the tools to make this an easy go-to performance mode for you.

> One of my most used parodies is a re-write of Justin Bieber's *Love Yourself*.[2] I wanted to create an opening number for when I was hosting drag line up shows, or competitions, that told the audience "*I know you've watched drag race but that doesn't mean you know everything about drag – respect our artists*". I had noticed since the mainstream success of *Drag Race* that many audiences thought they were connoisseurs of drag and would speak to acts after the show, giving them tips despite having no technical or professional experience. Once I had worked out the main hook it was obvious that *Love Yourself* was the right option.
>
> For many reasons – legal and professional – I am not putting the re-written lyrics in here. You can find a video of me performing the parody in the playlist from *Chapter 7: Research and Further Reading*.)

The process of writing a parody is something each performer will find their own way of doing. As a way *in*, I have broken down the process into four phases, not every step within will be relevant in every case, but these are ideas of how to give some rigour to the development. As ever, it's about finding what works best for you. There are a few upcoming *Exercises* that will bring you through these Phases so they become second nature. Firstly though read through *Phases One to Four*, see examples from my creative process, and understand the options prior to creating your own re-writes.

Phase One: Clarifying What You Want to Say

Drag acts should always have something to say, or an idea to explore! A parody re-write can cover anything from the sublime to the ridiculous. It might be a political call to arms, or just a list of items you find alluring in the supermarket aisle! The concept for a parody re-write doesn't need to be a sophisticated argument or hypothesis, it can be stupid. At the beginning of your career, or working on a first parody, then choosing the *What* as being an introduction to your alter-ego, or an introduction to the show, is a great choice as it's something you can keep in your repertoire and keep evolving. (Keep this in mind for our upcoming exercises.) Often one parody can tick off a few things you wish to say around a similar theme. An introductory act you might have: *what your name is, why you are on-stage, where you come from, hints about your love life, character traits, etc.*

For my parody of *Love Yourself*, I wanted an opening number which told the audience lots of pointers that are variations on the theme:

- *Show our performers, love and respect.*
- *All drag is valid.*
- *There are no rules to drag.*
- *I'm the host.*
- *This can be scary, give them support.*
- *They only need positive feedback.*

This gave me plenty of directions to take in the re-write without being too repetitive or trying to squeeze too many themes into one parody.

Phase Two: Finding the *How* – An Original Song

At this point artists have to go fishing for a *How* (the song) here are a few ways steps to trying to find the perfect fit:

Key Statements: Writing statements that clarify your concept will form the base of where you draw your re-write lyrics. The blunter, and shorter, they are the more likely you will be able to tweak re-work them into the space of existing lyrics. Statements, phrases, keywords that clarify what you want to say. This could be a brainstorm or free-writing process depending on what works best for you.

A Simple Rhyme: From these key statements you might find key lyrics which rhyme with an existing song's lyrics. The closer the word is to the original the easier the re-write will be. (If your *Key Statements* feature *farts* then look for songs about hearts. I'm now laughing at the concept of writing *Fart Of Glass* parodying *Blondie's Heart of Glass*. The opening verse needs no rewriting other than fart and heart … a silly idea to note down in case an occasion arises!)

Thesaurus: From the key statements you can find variety on the theme and expand options simply by using a thesaurus and finding different ways of working them. Expanding the range of language will hopefully help finding an easy *in* to a song. A new word that will rhyme with a common word that is featured in songs.

I did say a parody can be ridiculous. I'm now laughing at the concept of writing *Fart Of Glass* parodying Blondie's *Heart of Glass*. The opening verse needs no rewriting other than fart and heart…

Digging for Gold: Sometimes it isn't one word, but the cadence of a phrase or sentence that makes you think of another song. Read all of the options out loud and listen carefully for any familiar phrases, sounds or rhythms. Is there a flow that sounds similar to a familiar song? One silly line connecting is often enough to help find a match that may become a full parody. At this stage I often open up playlists online and look at the titles of famous songs: *Today's Hits, 80s Dance Party, Karaoke Classics*. Do the song titles, or the song's hook, resemble one key statement? At this point every option gets noted.

Review: Has inspiration struck? Look at the song options that have come up and see if anything connects to you. I often get the sense: "*I like where this is heading*". Before I know how it will all come together. Shortlist one or two favourites, but don't discard the earlier idea.

Further Listening: Listen to any songs that have been shortlisted, pull up their lyrics. Is there a spark of inspiration, a potential to develop?

> When I was digging for gold with my *Love Yourself* parody, the moment that struck was being able to tell the audiences to *go fuck themselves*! From there the *what* and *how* had a clear tie together and something I could work off of. I could deliver various statements about what I didn't want an audience to do, and then tell them – if they did – to *"go and fuck themselves"*.
>
> My brainstorming around key statements also brought up lots of *Drag Race* phrases which audiences are familiar with but I, personally, don't use. This armed me with a rich range of options as I approached the next phase – actual re-writing!

Phase Three: The Actual Re-Writing

At this point there is a lot of trial and error, it's a balancing act of trying to change the meaning without losing the original structure or tune.

How Much to Change: The goal of a re-write is to *change* the lyrics enough to make your point, bring humour, and reinterpretation, to the piece whilst *maintaining* enough of the original material that the audience still recognise it. Change too much and you are just singing brand new lyrics over a backing track, that loses the power of a parody re-write. There is also humour in the remaining, original lyrics that may now have new meaning due to you theme or interpretation of the song.

Trust the Original Structure: Always try to maintain the original structure, rhythm and rhyme of a song. Work with the original, not against it. The song still needs to have a flow that is familiar so the audience can hear the original within the re-write.

Highlight the Rhymes: Each song has its own rhyme structure and when re-writing it's best to keep them in place. If there is a rhyme alter both parts of the rhyming pair, ensuring it still rhymes. To maintain the integrity of the original it benefits if the rhyming words aren't too far away from the original.

Keep the Rhythm: Think about the syllables and maintaining the same count; wherever possible replace like for like to keep the familiar rhythm of the song.

Be Consistent: If you substitute key words in the chorus as your hook try to follow that through the whole song. If a song about *Love* becomes *Gloves* then if there's *Love* midway through put *Gloves* in and see where that goes.

Repeats vs. Repetitive:

The chorus does not need to have different lyrics on each repeat, a chorus should be repetitive, it's the hook of your track. However, you can find ways to build it through performance to give variety, but the lyrics, and repeats, should fit the original song's structure unless you are intentionally breaking it to make a point or have a final moment.

Maintain the Story: Songs often have a story and, if possible, a parody should play into the story rather than erasing it. For example Bon Jovi's *Livin' On A Prayer* has a narrative about Tommy and Gina: what they do for work and their relationship. This can be adapted, but as an iconic song don't put a full new story into its place, and not throwback to them at the same point. Utilise the original: The audience will laugh more at how you have adapted the existing story rather than imposed another one. Recast the story, queer it, but still follow the original beats of the story.

> I perform *Livin' on a Prayer* most weeks at my show; it comes in my show just after I have used an aerial hoop for a song. The stage manager runs on and de-rigs the hoop on a step-ladder, Sarah (my pianist) is playing the music live. To cover what's going on I re-write Tommy and Gina as the people in the room. I sing about the stage manager (Tommy) – using their name – and Sarah (Gina)! Suddenly these people become characters in an 80s classic and the audience laugh along. It's a simple form of parody that gets belly laughs every time and leads into a fairly straight-foward Saturday night sing-along version of the song.

Subtle Changes: Often just the switching one word – a pronoun for example – can change the perspective of a song. For example I, we, they, you can all replace each other without altering the rhythm or flow of a song but can drastically change the message. Don't be afraid of doing small twists and leaving the rest of a line intact. Sometimes those are the funniest moments of all for an audience because you have made it so easy.

Tricky Parts: As things fall into place, print your lyrics and underline any sections of text which don't fit your concept. If small changes won't work – return to your *Key Statements* and see if there are any others phrases that might fit in. And if not – get the thesaurus out again!

> At this point in the process for *Love Yourself* I had a very strong re-write but I felt it was becoming a bit too negative. I needed to revisit ways of getting easy, lighter laughs rather than always attacking the audience. A few self-deprecating lines: I did not want to attack *Drag Race* fans (I am one), I wanted to lampoon the connoisseurs of drag it had created.
>
> There was a lot of back and forward to get the balance right between the writing, the re-writing and the way in which I performed it!

Phase Four: Shape, Structure and Rehearse

Playing with the re-write is a constant juggling act. Keep notes of previous versions as you will want to revisit them along the way. When writing a parody it's easy to get caught up in the big laughs and lose the craft of keeping the original structure. You constantly need to review: *Is it funny enough? Does it get somewhere? Or is it one joke told eight times over four-minute track?*

Cheating the Re-Writes: Sometimes when you're re-writing, the original lyrics work but are just in the wrong part of the song. It's fine to cut and paste half of verse one with half of verse two if that serves your purpose. It's your parody and the audience want some familiar lyrics, the more you can retain and reuse the better.

Breaking the Rhythm: Despite the importance of keeping rhythmically as close a possible to the original, towards a crescendo all rules are there to be broken. The audience now thinks they know where the piece is going, intentionally breaking the rhythm for a comedic reason, or dramatic emphasis can bring a piece to a solid conclusion. Only use sparingly but it can help the piece have a finale moment and give a final chance to clarify your point, or get a big laugh!

Where Are the Jokes?: Pop music producers say each song needs at least three hooks to be a hit. With a parody you want at least three good recurring jokes, or moments where the adjustment really fits and you get great laughs. Make sure you aren't relying on one joke over and over.

Checking the Flow: Occasional a parody song can feel a bit too butchered, the jokes have been shoe-horned in and it needs finessing. Is the flow of the original song there? Double check the rhythm and flow and see if you can pull it back towards the original. The best way to test this is to sing it out loud!

Rehearse, Review, Repeat: Things should be falling into place by now, so it's time to stand up, sing out loud and try to bring it to life off the page. Often what looked like it flowed on paper has a few awkward moments when performed aloud. Keep running it aloud, reviewing, rewriting and then running it again constantly aiming to find a smooth flow.

Bring It to Life: Review your piece at this stage for *Chapter 8: Basic Drag*, how you can bring the piece into the live space. Can you address some lines to specific members of the audience? Is there some interesting staging? Look at all the performance essentials that can bring the piece to life!

With *Love Yourself* I had plenty of laughs within the song, the structure was familiar and the piece came to life when I realised the chorus, or hook, was a sing-along! Where I was worried the audience might feel I was attacking them – them joining in on the chorus was their way of saying they agree with me, they were on my side of the argument. And it was the moment of live magic I needed to feel I was achieving exactly what I wanted it to!

EXERCISE 3: PARODY RE-WRITE – LOSING MY MIND

You will need: The lyrics and a backing track for *Losing My Mind* **from** *Follies***.**

This is a gift of an exercise to help sharpen your skills for re-writing lyrics, and to use to become familiar with the structure and rigour needed to write a good parody! Finding the idea and the original song is often the hardest part! Generous creature that I am, I am giving you the *what* and the *how*, a full concept for your first parody – and you are going to put your skills into practice on rewriting.

A favourite song of mine to perform is Stephen Sondheim's *Losing My Mind*.[3] It's a beautiful piece of music and wonderful lyrics. The song also has many moments with which to directly connect to an audience but no need for choreography. The twist of the parody is simply that you are losing your mind because of **drag**. Where the lyrics were originally thinking about a lover, it is now all about drag. Work through *Phases One* to *Four* re-writing the song using the concept of losing your mind over drag. You might want to be specific in the direction you are taking but you don't need to fish for an original song as it is provided. However, the *Key Statements* for each drag performer will be different.

The first move is to replace the word *you* with *drag*. Then see where you want to go, how much you want to change. As a parody this would work as a brilliant introductory song for an act: setting up what type of drag you do, why you love drag, how you interpret drag, etc. You might bring out some of your *Drag Manifesto* from *Chapter 9: Alter-Ego* for *Phase One*.

Use this as an opportunity to hone your craft and play around with the idea of re-writing. If you create something that works – use it, add it to your repertoire – a gift from me to you!

EXERCISE 4: YOUR OWN PARODY RE-WRITE

You will need: Your notepad and pen, access to track options.

This is the big one. I'm sure as you've been reading you've had a few ideas, so what are you waiting for? Using *Phases One* to *Four* above create your own parody.

Before running all the way through focus on *Phases One* and *Two* alone three times to get a few different options ready. Then mull them over, let them brew for a while. Maybe run a few ideas past a friend or a colleague and see if they laugh. The creative process is not always instant so do not feel you have to start this now and complete it in ten minutes.

When you've made a decision continue to *Phases Three* and *Four*. Add the piece to your *Rehearsal Repertoire*, add the two ideas you didn't follow to your *In Development Repertoire* (see *Chapter 6: Building a Set, Range and Repertoire*). You never know when you might come back to them and have a break through moment of how to make them work.

EXERCISE 5: SONG FIRST

It's time to go on a creative fishing expedition, but the opposite way around! Rather than having an idea and trying to make it fit. Sharpen your creative skills by taking the following songs and brainstorming a way you *could* develop them into a full parody song!

This is a quick-fire exercise to find a few concepts, ideas that you can add to your *In Development Repertoire*. One might become your trademark song, others might just put a smile on your face for a moment:

Dolly Parton – *Jolene* – Who could you turn Jolene into?

Dua Lipa – *New Rules* – What are you making these rules about?

Spice Girls – *Wannabe* – What do you really, really, want?

Vanessa Carlton – *A Thousand Miles* – Why would you walk that far?

This is a great exercise to come back to all the time. If there's a popular song, or a classic you think you could sing, why not see what you could do with it and expand your repertoire? It may be a full song, or it may just be a snippet for a joke before moving on. Get in the habit of doing this informally, on the go, when you have a few minutes and are listening to music ask yourself how you could re-write another song. Keep flexing the creative muscles!

Rehearsal

Once you have created your parody songs or concept it's important to now take that into the rehearsal process. If it's a lip-sync re-interpret parody go back through the exercise in *Chapter 17: Performing and Rehearsing a Lip-Sync*. If you are singing live work through *Chapter 15: Sing a Song*. It's easy to forget about the performative elements of your piece once you have written something you are proud of. But the funny writing is only one part of the battle: don't let the writing to do all the work – you still need to make it live, and connect with the audience. And always return to *Chapter 8: Basic Drag* and master those simple skills that bring the piece to life in a dynamic way!

Combinations

Nothing exists in isolation – a *re-style*, *re-interpret* or *re-write* approach can be combined and all overlap to create something unique!. As long as the original song is still recognisable! Breaking these modes of parody down into separate sections is a useful way of analysing and creating work. But do not be mistaken into thinking that these are the only ways to use parody or that elements from all three can't be used to create one hilarious piece. Keep exploring and see what you create! Conversely, you don't always need to do a full piece, sometimes just changing a couple of lyrics in well-known songs for a little laugh is enough to give a straight song a moment of variety.

The Legal Stuff

Parody often gets overlooked as a performance mode in TV and Film because to be recorded (or broadcast) it raises a lot of complex licensing issues and permissions that need to be granted. I've side stepped printing lyrics for my re-writes as again it's a grey area. In live performance, in a club environment, generally it is fine because a venue will have a music license (e.g. PRS). As soon as it's recorded, printed or for sale it can be dangerous, muddy waters. However, different territories have different laws, rules and regulations. Rules on 'fair use' vary greatly between different countries, and also through different mediums of performance. I am not a legal professional, I earn my living being a bit of an idiot in a dress: If you do have concerns, it is always worth seeking advice, if you are a member of a union (Equity, SAG, etc.) they would be a great starting point.

Overview: Parody

Audiences love the familiar, they also love a fresh joke. With parody they get the best of both worlds: something they know, being played with, so they feel in on the joke and laugh even harder!

- Whether a re-style, re-interpretation or a re-write always have a strong clear concept for why you are changing the original.
- Work through the four phases of re-writing to help ensure you have a rich and varied song which is more than just one repetitive joke.
- Always have a few ideas bubbling away at the back of your mind. Keep evolving them, returning to them and add the notes to your *Repertoire List*.
- Inspiration can strike at any point, always note it down!
- Don't forget you still need to rehearse and work on the performance of your piece. The writing of the parody is only the content – you need to bring it to life in the room.

From these exercises there are plenty of ways *in* to creating a parody song. But a parody song may be a way *in* to a whole set, or character that you could develop. Keep these ideas and exercises to hand as you move forward to *Impersonation: Tribute and Parody*.

Notes

1. Streaming on Disney+.
2. Used as part of the opening set up to *The Art Of Drag* Graduation Showcases at The RVT, London. available in the YouTube playlist linked to in The Art Of Drag section of my website www.michaeltwaits.com
3. Currently an old version of my parody is again in the playlist available at www.michaeltwaits.com under *The Art of Drag*

Veneer photographed backstage at the Royal Vauxhall Tavern by Fox Al Rajim

20
With a Little Help from My Friends: Impersonation: Tribute and Parody

Barbra, Liza, Judy, Cher, Frank…Trump? Everyone loves seeing an icon brought to life, reinvented or reimagined. It can be to pay tribute to a great act, recreate a magic moment or play with political satire but impersonation is a rich performance area full of laughs, possibilities and variety.

Impersonation on stage covers a vast area: some acts sincerely perform a tribute show, others create a parody for comic exploration, many reimagine their icon in ridiculous situations, others drop into the character of an icon for a few jokes, or a song, as part of a show outside of the impersonation. There are many ways to create dynamic moments using impersonation. For clarity I am using the term *icon* for the person being impersonated; an umbrella that covers celebrities, historical figures, famous fictional characters and more.

A drag impersonation can be a full show the as Simply Barbra (see more in *Chapter 25: Interview with Simply Barbra*) where the act fully exists as their take on the icon, parodying the known facts about them to the audience's delight. Or a tribute like Derrick Barry[1] as Britney Spears, where Derrick exists on stage as themselves recreating a Britney illusion and routine for the audience to enjoy the magic of Britney; a celebration of her music and artistry without really parodying or poking fun at her. Others use what we know about the icon as fact to hang their comedy on by filling in the blanks with ridiculous suggestions to parody the icon. (Tracey Collins[2] as Elvis Lesley, in this world Elvis didn't die but left show-business and now works in a *Tesco Metro*). Other drag acts adopt a voice and a physicality without creating a full costume illusion to sing one song, or deliver a couple of jokes as an icon during a short set for a quick comic moment. (La Voix[3] for example frequently brings Liza Minelli and Shirley Bassey on stage for a few short moments within a solo show.)

The audience do not need to be *tricked* into believing they are seeing the real icon. Part of their enjoyment is the craft of the performer delivering an impersonation, to see the performer's take on the icon, how close to reality are they remaining – *is it a sincere tribute or a full on parody?*

Constructing an Iconic Impersonation

Drag performers need to be able to distil an icon into a shorthand, a few key elements, to quickly tell the audience who they are and let them *in* on the joke, or style of impersonation. What are the key elements of creating *your icon*? Is there any iconography that instantly tells the audience who is being portrayed? Any iconic moment the audience are waiting to see or hear about?

Could you perform Trump without fake tan? Or Barbra without the nails? Cher without a wig? When you are deciding who to impersonate it's always worth brainstorming their iconic traits that can be a tool to tell the audience who is being impersonated, and the approach (the scale from sincere to parody). Before bringing any icon to life you need to do your research, and also know whether you are aiming at a sincere (convincing, loving, tribute of the icon) or a parody (comedy, lampooning of the icon) because it will make an enormous difference to the choices you make. Any performer can take on any icon with the right approach: Bob The Drag Queen did a brilliant Carol Channing[4] – because he took a few iconic moments and ran with them so the audience were in no doubt who he was playing. At no point was it a Carol Channing Illusion.

Dig deep into each of the following areas as a starting point, keep notes on everything:

The Look: Drag consistently plays with visual illusion, when attempting to look like another performer: Do your research and get the key points right. There are drag acts who, thanks to detailed make up and costuming, look exactly like their icon: Chad Michaels as Cher or Coco Montrese as Janet Jackson. If performing a sincere tribute, aesthetically looking like the act becomes more important, and there needs to be an element of subtly, even kindness in the interpretation. For parody however, performers can think in broad-strokes, imagine the icon as a cartoon. What are the three or four key elements one thinks of for that character? Play with those to create a visual aesthetic based on the icon but it doesn't need to be authentic. It can be taken to the extreme, in some cases almost grotesque, think of a fun-house mirror: it's all over the place but you always know who it's a reflection of, and that's why it's funny.

The Voice: The tone, speed, pitch, accent, even where they place the voice in their mouth is a huge part of creating an authentic illusion. The more specific the icon's voice, the more specific your authentic impersonation needs to be. (Of course if playing with parody it might be hilarious for *your icon* to look exactly how they should but their voice is two octaves higher or lower, that would be a choice.)

The Performance: If you are doing a sincere Britney Spears tribute act, rather than a parody, then you need to actually sound like her when you sing or look like her when you dance. The performance becomes king, the focus of what you are doing. If you are doing a Britney Spears parody however, you don't need to do any of this, there would be huge comedy in her trying to keep up with her backing dancers or not realising her microphone was on.

Language: A key indicator to creating an icon is their language and lexicon. If an act in a blonde wig says "howdy y'all" in a southern accent audiences instantly assume this is a Dolly Parton reference. But if a perfect Dolly accent and cadence said "hello everybody" the audience would be confused. *"Is it Dolly? Dolly says Howdy?"* Focus on catchphrases, key words and phrases that the icon is known for. Establish the icon with a few clichés or obvious choices early on so the audience are in no doubt of who this is.

The Physicality: How does *your icon* move? How do they hold themselves? What are there angles, classic poses and gestures? Do they have go-to facial expressions? Finding how your character listens, waits and is resting is a great way of helping create a fully rounded character for an audience. Are there iconic poses from album covers, films, campaigns, etc? If you can still look like you are embodying the character when seemingly doing nothing, then that's a real performance.

The World: Knowing the icons world is essential to creating a full character – whether a parody or a tribute. You can not impersonate someone you don't know. Immerse yourself in their world, in their references. The internet makes this very easy what are their most iconic moments?

EXERCISE 1: RESEARCH *BEFORE* DECIDING

You will need: Your notebook and pen, the internet and time.

Before fixing on an icon to impersonate shortlist two or three and work through the above six areas for some initial research. It always helps to choose people you already have a good knowledge of. Perhaps someone you have been compared to in performance before? And remember that the audience all need to know who it is, now is not a time for niche references.

> Decide upfront if you are aiming at a sincere tribute or a parody. If aiming for a sincere tribute you need to authentically be able to replicate the look, the voice or the performance to have a strong base to build an act. Be honest about whether or not that is achievable. For parody make sure you are choosing someone you feel ok making fun of and playing around with.
>
> You may not get all the way through the research before you realise that this icon isn't for you. That's fine, just move on and look for another one. You don't need to fully flesh them out as a character at this point., just find an icon you feel *could work*. Look at your research and ask – *"is there enough to work with?" "Is there somewhere I can take this?"* And if the answer's *"Yes"* you are off to a great start!

Whenever delving into the world of impersonation I would recommend drawing up a full CV on *your icon*. You don't need to constantly *prove* to an audience that you have facts but during rehearsal and development it gives you a chance to ensure you know you are being accurate, or for a parody playing against the character type for comic purposes.

Play against Type

In the world of comedy and drag, rules are there to be broken. If you wear a black quiff and a white bejewelled jumpsuit the audience will know you are being Elvis. There's potentially huge comedy in your performance if he were to have a completely different voice. Give enough signals at the beginning so everyone knows who you are, then go crazy. Parody gives a license to play against the facts as much as to play with them – as long as it is making the audience laugh!

The Combinations

An impersonation does not need to achieve well in all six areas, the performer simply needs to have an awareness of them so they know if they are being accurate in the portrayal or playing against type. If you look or sound just like the act, then usually the audience will be generous with the other areas. (There are many Adele tribute acts around the world. Many haven't kept up with Adele's weight loss but if they sound just like Adele, nobody cares.)

There's a wonderful George Michael impersonator who does the rounds in the UK who physically looks *nothing* like George. However, he has a short crop of hair, draws on a goatee and wears large sunglasses – iconic later days George Michael. His voice however, his physicality and his personality are all very accurate impersonations. The audience get on board and have a great time reliving some George Michael iconic moments – not poking fun at George but also at no point believing the performer *is* George. In theatrical terms the audience suspend their disbelief for the evening and have fun!

Creating an Icon

The following pages are framed towards creating a character to play for *The Snatch Game*[5] or a similar format of improvisation. I chose this angle as it's very familiar to many as a form for using an impersonation in live performance. However, this exploration and the exercises would be brilliant ways to build your version of an icon for: a viral video, an icon dropping into a drag roast, a snippet of a full-length set framed as you being this icon!

A performer needs to be able to live, on-stage, as their icon in the live moment, so you will need to do all of the work below, whether working in sincere tribute or parody. If steering towards a sincere tribute, try to stay as close to reality as possible and don't worry about looking for laughs, aim for accuracy. However, even within a traditional tribute show many acts have a few comic moments of parody within the flow of the performance to create dynamic *peaks and troughs*.

To perform on a stage you need to be able to improvise and live freely within the alter-ego, in this case *your icon*. The following exercises will help you make a more fully rounded performance but all of the previous work from *Chapter 9: Alter-Ego*, *Chapter 10: Making Choices and Finding a Voice* and *Chapter 11: Audience Experience*, now apply to you within the role of *your icon*. Once you've been through the exercises here and structured *your icon* you should return to previous chapters in *Part 3* to explore a song, a lip-sync, a parody, etc. as *your icon*.

The Snatch Game

The drag world currently has many nights based on some variation of *The Snatch Game*. It's a great evening of comedy that challenges performers to be masters of impersonation, comedy and improvisation on the spot. Performers are impersonating icons on a quiz show format but are aiming for laughs. (The format is a parody of TV game show *The Match Game* or *Blankety Blank*.)

Performers don't have a lot of time, they need to show their take on the icon, use quick, large broad strokes to establish who they are whilst being funny.

This is not a time to do a sincere, authentic tribute (although working through these exercises will help any performer build their icon's backstory and structure). A sincere appearance here will stop the comedy flowing, the performers need to think of their icons in the fun house mirrors – make them ridiculous. An audience want to see the parody and see the performer poking fun at the icon, if you are too respectful, or accurate, *your icon* you may be stopping a lot of comedy coming out. Always keep at the front of your mind this is *your* take on the icon, your interpretation.

Where to Start?

Before getting into the exercises creating and realising *your icon*, here are some thoughts on how to approach this type of impersonation. As ever, there is no definitive formula to what will work, but there are some definite ways to set yourself up for success, and a few pitfalls to avoid!

Icons Are Iconic

Choose the right icon for you, but remember the audience all need to get the references! There is a reason Barbra Streisand, Cher, Britney Spears, Dame Maggie Smith, Liza, Carol Channing and Caitlyn Jenner have won *The Snatch Game*: they have a very rich world to draw on that spans a very well documented career with many pop cultural references. They are acts who are easy to caricature and heighten, have catchphrases and go-to jokes an audience are waiting to laugh at! Someone who's been in three episodes of a reality TV show doesn't have the same wealth of interesting references to draw on.

Comedy Is King

Impersonation is secondary, the goal is the laughs! The impersonation is what you hang the jokes on but always remember the laughs are what matter. (Once you have fleshed out your icon it would be worth revisiting *Chapter 18: Comedy, Reading and Roasting* to see what you can bring in from there as your icon, many moments in *The Snatch Game* come close to a celebrity roast!)

Adding Comedy to Comedy?

It's a matter of taste but I believe choosing someone who is already funny, in an intentional or comedic way, is actually a hard task. There is an expectation that you will need to match, or exceed, their level of comedy. Taking an icon and then turning them into something funny is a lot easier.

> *The Vivienne* is a brilliant comic impersonator. She won *Drag Race UK Season 1*'s *Snatch Game* as Trump and it is one of the best *Snatch Game* performances in the show's history. She parodied someone who takes themselves seriously to huge comic results. On *All Stars 7* she played *Patsy Stone* from *Absolutely Fabulous* and *Nan* from *Catherine Tate*. Arguably she did the most accurate impersonations but these comic characters felt like she was *recreating* someone else's humour and she didn't *add* anything to them. If reviewed as a showcase her skills as an actress and impersonator, this was a success. But compared to her previous performance it felt like she restricted herself by her choice and didn't show any point of view with the way she impersonated the icons.

Improvisation Is Key

Having a range of options from research (*Exercise 1*) and rehearsal (below) is essential, but the challenge is to fit that into the format of the live experience, play with all those elements in the moment. The key phrase in improvisation is *"yes and…"* The idea is to accept what is offered and build on it. Don't block other people's ideas or reject them: accept them and run with them.

Know Their World

Pick someone with a wide world that you, and the audience, are familiar with so you aren't grasping at straws to remember a reference point and get laughs. It's forgivable to forget a minute detail, you can play into that in performance – *"I've done so much"*. But know the iconic moments. If playing Cher, you might forget the name of a song she released sixty years ago, but you better *Believe* she needs to know about her Oscar win, about Bob Mackie, *Turn Back Time* and *I've Got You Babe*!

The given circumstances of your character are based on the icon. But you need to have fun filling in the gaps. To carry on the Cher example – no one knows where she put the Oscar when she got home – *"I want to keep having surgery until I look like that Oscar – no wrinkles, and no facial features"*.

My Icon

Call the icon *my icon* to allow yourself freedom to have fun and step away from the original; leave reality behind because the task is not to be an exact replica but to have fun and make jokes within this framework.

Icon Plus

An easy *in* for comedy is to add a trait, or a quirk to your character that will bring comedy to everything you do, i.e. My *Cher only sings her answers*, My *Cher has narcolepsy*. Abandoning reality but upping the comic stakes. It gives you something to play in performance outside of representing your research.

Fun House Mirrors

Keep thinking of the fun house mirror: the audience can see who it is *your icon* is but at the same time it looks crazy, and ridiculous. And that's the fun of parody – exaggerating what is there!

Bring Yourself to the Role

It makes sense to play to your strengths when choosing an icon: imagine someone else is casting you in a role. How do they see you? If you're great at accents – brilliant, but don't do one if that's going to hold you back. If you are high energy and a bit manic – find a character that suits. Or if it doesn't suit you for some elements *Play against Type* (see above).

Relax

Performers can try too hard to drop in all the details to prove they know the character but then don't actually have anything funny – just facts and no sense of playing in the moment. You need to improvise rather than trying to shoe horn in your rehearsed little bits of trivia.

No Time Like the Present

There is a creative license in performance: reality is out the window. Dress as an iconic era for *your icon*, you are not locked into that time period, you can still reference their past, present and future. Again, comedy is what matters.

Be Positive

Some performers take the *"why am I here?"* approach. And it hems them into a negative space with nowhere fun to go. Again thinking *"yes and..."* is key. Would *your icon* be on a game show? Who cares! Have fun and play positively!

Find Your Catchphrases

Build the language and lexicon for *your icon*. Playing off their existing catchphrases and world but bringing them into your live performance. (To flesh out the icon, why not revisit *Chapter 10: Talking* and try to build your *Language and Lexicon* for *your icon*?) This is comedy, feel free to parody existing catchphrases for comic effect.

EXERCISE 2: PREPARE YOUR ICON

You will need: Your notebook, pen, notes from *Exercise 1* and the internet for research.

Prior to getting up and practically creating a character you need to have a range of options of where you might take *your icon*. Remember to frame them as *your icon*. Take what is useful from reality, fill in the blanks and interpret things in a way that is useful to you and think *funny first!*

Select an Icon: Shortlist using *Exercise 1*. You may want to test run them through the following areas and see which you think is best. Bring the research from there into this exercise.

Icon Plus: What are you adding on? Are they a genius, excited, tired, scared, filthy, horny, etc. The more detailed you can make it the more it will give you to play with.

Build Their World: Refine your research from *Exercise 1* into potentially usable points. Note down the things they are most famous for. What are associated they with? (Books, film, music, political movements, iconic moments, iconic outfits, feuds, iconic failures, etc.)

People: Who do they know? (Family, friends, rivals and colleagues). Having a best friend, mentor or a nemesis that is easy to drop in as a punchline is a great comic go-to.

Positive Attitude: If *your icon* is someone who is tired, bored or doesn't want to be there, it becomes a drain of energy. Find a reason they are having fun being here. It's a much easier place to perform from!

Physical Character Traits: What are the go-to gestures or actions that could help establish exactly who you are?

Catchphrases: List any existing catchphrases, can you adapt them? Create their go-to phrases. If they don't have a catchphrase could the title of their book, lyrics from their songs, films, etc.

Fun and Fantasy Facts: Is there room to fill in some flights of fancy, to send up the icon and add fun? Is there a reason that your act could have met or worked with The President, Another Drag Act, A Random Celebrity? Having some pre thought through ideas that have the <*insert name/place here*> format can help you seem to be improvising in the moment whilst actually using planned material.

Get brainstorming and keep expanding all these ideas as to where you could take *your icon*. To help open ideas up and give some illustration I have brainstormed my ideas for an icon below. Have a look through and then return to your notes padding them out. From the brainstorming and writing you do here you will create too much content for just one performance. Cherry-pick the best parts but hang onto the rest of the notes as they might be useful at another point.

Case Study: *My Victoria Beckham*

I don't envisage you will ever see me on *Drag Race* so I don't mind sharing that I would be: Victoria Beckham, *my* version of Posh Spice. These are my initial notes and thoughts that are fleshing out *my* interpretation. It's not a script, it's a framework with which to start playing from.

Select an Icon

I'm obviously a huge fan of Barbra, but don't think I could do the accent well enough. I also wouldn't want to make too much fun of her. Who else could I, quite easily, be able to look like? Sound like? Act like? I'm British, I have dark features and sound posher than I am: all things that point to Posh Spice. I'm very informed with her era of pop culture which makes the task less daunting when improvising her world. It would also be fairly simple costuming to create an iconic look: little black dress, dark straight, shoulder-length hair (or a pob – the posh bob), statement sunglasses, etc.

Icon Plus

My Victoria thinks she's far more intelligent than she is. I will deliver everything as if it's really informed and profound, even though it's probably not.

Victoria Beckham is a hugely successful woman; *My Victoria* thinks it's because she's a genius. I will play her very slow (arguably a bit thick) but thinking she's highly intelligent. Instantly that gives me levels of humour. Also, this gives the comedy option to misunderstand words and get the wrong end of the stick. (Possible malapropisms – *See Chapter 18: Comedy, Reading and Roasting.*)

Whatever other people are doing, I suspect she has done it, is about to do it, or at least thinks she has! Is she stupid, or deluded? (e.g. *"My single 'Let Your Head Go' was nominated for a Nobel Prize".*)

She has a definite disconnect to the real world and with real people.

Build Their World

She's a Spice Girl! That's enough to hang a whole interpretation on. But *My Victoria* views that as a trivial few years leading up to all her huge achievements. She thinks people know her now as a designer, UN ambassador, a philosopher, etc.

In my answers I can incorporate Spice-related references, drawing judgements on the other Spice Girls (using *Chapter 18: Comedy, Reading & Roasting's – Compare and Contrast*) without even bringing them up, and Spice-lyric puns: *"She's a Wannabe", "Zigazigahh", "I'm not very Sporty", "I don't like Scary things"*, food related questions could all lead to Spices – *"yuck Ginger!"*, etc.

People

David: Her husband, a footballer, perhaps she sees his career as a hobby? In her eyes he's a house-husband and she's the career woman. He's riding on her coat tails.

Her Children: My Victoria's eldest was famously named after being conceived in Brooklyn. What might the other children have been called? Billericay? Or DUMBO?

Brooklyn: Generally children, I feel, are off-limits for being the butt of a joke. But he is an adult now, so fair game! He is famously a nepo-baby who flits from one career to another. Possibly she thinks he's a genius too: *"a Picasso for our times"*.

Enemies: My Victoria hates Ginger and Scary, both would be easy comic punching bags that I could work in. If needed Stella McCartney is another option from the fashion world.

Positive Attitude

My Victoria is delighted to be here. It's fun for her to connect with the 'real' people. You are very lucky to have her: #yourewelcome. *"Do we win money? How novel. Oh people are getting competitive – you must be poor"*.

Physical Character Traits

She's known for being sultry. Looking slightly bored, the iconic pout, looking through her fringe/bangs. I think I could use the pout as the main physical impression, a pout also encourages a slightly whiny way of speaking. When I pout there's a slight lisp as I talk which isn't accurate for Victoria but is funny for *My Victoria*.

Victoria Beckham is known as Posh Spice but was she really posh? *My Victoria*'s voice will be less about impersonating Victoria and more about lampooning British class culture and someone aspiring to seem more upper-class than they are. Having an affected upper-class accent, overly pronouncing words to make her sound posher than she is, even her own name, e.g. *"I'm Victoria Bickham"*.

Catchphrases/Language

I don't think she has one iconic catchphrase that audiences will be waiting to hear. But I would use lyrics from the Spice Girls back catalogue and re-writes/repurposing: *"Stop right now thank you very much…", "I'll tell you what I want…"*. This is a simple opener to any answer with a Spice Girl nod.

"Hasta mañana" – she could think this means almost anything apart from *See You Tomorrow*. Possibly her equivalent of *Namaste*.

> **Fun and Fantasy Facts**
>
> The Spice Girls have had various formations at different points: why didn't *My Victoria* go back each time? Did they have understudies – did Cliff Richard cover for her one night because she was at a school parents' evening? Did anyone else used to be in the Spice Girls?
>
> Emma actually wasn't in the Spice Girls she was the make-up artist who got into a few of the music videos by accident.
>
> She thinks she's a very talented performer. Perhaps she learnt from the greats: her acting teacher was *Little Jimmy Kranekee*, her fashion mentor *Su Pollard*, etc.

Hopefully you have created a similarly rich and ridiculous selection of notes of options to explore. Keep diving into the notes, adding more as ideas come up and playing around with them. However, it's now time to get *your icon* stage-ready! But when entering the world of improvisation how can you know what you are going to be given to respond to?

I had a break-through moment at college regarding essay questions. I realised if I just adapted the opening and closing statement to an essay on a specific subject I could, in essence, write an essay I've already mastered and simply reframe it to the specifics of their question.

This is how I approach this type of improvisation. I can't have an answer prepared for every possibility, but I can have a way of framing interactions to then feed in a line, or moment I have already written/rehearsed.

Now you've decided who you are going to be and have fleshed out a world for them. It's time to create a few go-to sound bites that you can say on the following subjects/themes.

> **EXERCISE 3: PREPARING YOUR CHARACTER TO IMPROVISE**
>
> **You will need: Your notepad, pen, notes from *Exercise 1* and *2* and a voice recorder.**
>
> For each area below come up with at least two options/answers that will be your go-to responses. Try to share them to be jokes, or at least joke shaped, maybe not set up and punchline, but funny references, use of language that will get an audience laughing! Revisit *Chapter 18: Comedy, Reading and Roasting* – think *puns, double-entendres, shaggy-dog stories* that are a pure *folly* that an audience will enjoy!
>
> **Introducing/Establishing** *Your Icon*: Everyone needs to set themselves up. Having a phrase or two ready that sets up who you are but also gives the audience a nod and a wink into where you are taking the character will help set up all future laughs. Set *your icon* up from the beginning and then you are free to play. You want people to 'get' *your icon* as quickly as possible.
>
> **Thanking for the Question:** A simple preparation tool to buy yourself time to think of an answer, or slip in a pre-written joke. It may also help you stay on brand whilst stepping slightly away from your character with the answer. Not every answer has to be twisted to be *your icon's* world but the lead in, or out, should be.
>
> **Giving the Most Obvious Answer:** Often a question will have an obvious answer that you can't instantly relate to as *your icon*. Framing the answer slightly with a short intro could help you stay on brand and get a laugh. How does *your icon* know this? Or did they copy someone else's answer?

Outside the Field of Knowledge: Not every answer is funny or makes sense from *your icon's* perspective but having a premise of how, or why, they know something outside of their world will allow you to get a laugh with any answer. Answering with *"I don't know"* doesn't fit the *"Yes and..."* rule of improvisation.

Preparing to Be Around Others: There's no way to know who is going to be interacting with you. But having a few quick retorts, references and comparisons for the people around will help you stay in the moment. Think of structures with an easy <*insert name here*>.

Punchlines/Toppers: A lot of the improvised humour is funny because it's live and in the moment. Sometimes having a topper, or a punchline to one-up the answer and ride a second laugh can elevate a performance from funny to hysterical.

This is an exercise you may want to run through it a few times, some of the ideas you have will fit into more than one category which is great. The categories are simply there to get you thinking and creating easily usable phrases. As you develop ideas you may create a few more categories that would be useful to you.

Now they have been written it's worth running them aloud. Voice noting them and listening back. How can your characterisation add to the comedy to the well-structured lines? Does the rhythm and language of your written lines fit the way in which you will perform the icon? Keep playing, keep adapting and keep writing!

Once again I've done an example for some of the lines I might create, I find most of them are much funnier when I do the voice. I've written some slightly phonetically so you can see how *My Victoria* will use them.

CASE STUDY: PREPARING *MY VICTORIA* TO IMPROVISE

Introducing/Establishing Your Icon

- *"Singer, turned actress, turned model, turned fashion entrupeneer Victoria Bickham".*
- *"I'm the most successful Spice Girl. A shrewd business women, socialite, superstar and stylistisisist".*
- *"I'm a fashion eecon, a designer and of course a part-time Cliff Richard impersonator".*

Thanking for the Question

- *"I'm so pleased you asked something on par with my EQ. Often people only want to talk to me about fashion, music or pegging. But I love talking about...".*

Giving the Most Obvious Answer

My Victoria doesn't always need a Spice or Fashion reference. She's so deluded by her own intelligence: She can give the most obvious answer available whilst acting as if she's reinvented the wheel:

- *"Well. This might be a little avant-bard but as an educated woman of the world I think...".*
- *"A very old, old, old, very wise friend (Geri) once said to me...".*

> *Outside the Field Of Knowledge*
>
> - "During the filming of Spice Girls The Movie I was in a steam room with Gary Glitter and he told me...".
> - "Not a lot of people know this but before I got in the Spice Girls I worked as an ambassador in the Middle East. Handing out Ferrero Roches and solving world conflicts...".
> - "Much like my solo pop career, this probably isn't the best idea but...".
> - "As Geri once said...".
>
> *Preparing for Interactions*
>
> - "I'm sorry I don't recognise you – were you in All Saints?"
> - "Thank you. I like your dress, is that Stella McCartney for ASOS?"
> - "Who do you think you are?"
> - "You're gorgeous. You look like a young David – if David was *insult, *insult or *insult".
> - "How dare you, I'm a married woman. But I guess it wouldn't be the first infidelity in the Bickham household...I once shared a packet of crisps with Gary Lineker. It was very erotic".
>
> *Punchlines/Toppers*
>
> - "Friendship never ends" – After being savage about someone (possibly Geri).
> - "Like David says: 'Posh in the streets, Scary in the sheets'".

This is not about creating a script that will be delivered in a specific order, but fleshing out a few go-to answers and phrases to help you play as *your icon*. As a performer it's important to feel prepared but not tied down to a script. Having options to respond to any interaction, not well-written joke that only works for a specific question. From an acting point of view, having a few go-to lines ready that can establish *your icon*, help you get into the voice, rhythm and characterisation.

If the above exercise was useful and you would like to take it further try creating answers, ideas and references your character might draw on for the following subjects: sex, health and fitness, award shows, political elections, or any specific big current affairs.

Preparation and Rehearsal

The best preparation you do is to play and have fun as your character. Improvise as them to learn what's funny, what makes you laugh?

> EXERCISE 4: HOT SEATING
>
> **You will need: A rehearsal partner.**
>
> If you have someone to rehearse with do some Hot Seating. Your rehearsal partner simply throws questions at you. Simple questions at first: *"Who are you? What did you have for lunch? What's in your handbag? Favourite food?"*

Try to work in some of the material you discovered in Exercise 3, find ways to steer the conversation around to your best jokes and points. But try to stay in character the whole time.

As you become more comfortable go further. If you are developing an icon for a set with audience interaction – what questions are you asking them? What questions might they ask you? If you are preparing for a *Snatch Game* style show – ask some questions in that format.

EXERCISE 5: A SET?

You will need: Your notepad and pen.

If you've enjoyed developing this character – you might be thinking there's more mileage in this than just *The Snatch Game*. Put the game show format aside and try to place them on stage within more traditional drag show doing a short set. What could they do? Maybe start looking through previous chapters as your icon. How do they talk to the audience (revisit *Chapter 13: Talking On Stage*)? Are they going to do a parody of the icon's own song (revisit *Chapter 19: Parody*)? Etc.

Try to create a concept for a short 7–10 minute set. You can draw on any of the exercises earlier in the book to create a short set for *your icon*. Perhaps a one to two-minute opening introduction that brings *your icon* to the stage, using some of the above as a starting point but then go into a song, lip-sync, parody or any other type of performance.

> *My Victoria* is going to walk on stage doing a fundraiser for Geri (*"she doesn't get much work"*) possibly so she can afford a new wig or something silly. She'll shake a bucket trying to get donations, improvise interactions with the audience (twisting a lot of the lines from above) before building towards the big moment which is her song. She's going to do something she "never does anymore" and sing a live version of a Spice Girls song. A prolonged series of vocal warm ups, stretches etc. before the track begins. She will then stand on stage and do nothing but hold a microphone whilst a backing track plays. She will then look really pleased with herself, and her achievements, before leaving the stage.

The more you play around in rehearsal as *your icon* the more colour and variety you will find for them. I hope some of you may discover a new alter-ego you can occasionally bring to the stage. If they are something you are going to develop – revisit earlier Chapters from *Part II* and *Chapter 13: Talking On Stage* with *your icon* in mind to flesh out how they will interact with an audience, perform on-stage and get you feeling more confident in creating a live experience.

Overview: Impersonation: Tribute and Parody

Drag impersonation is a rich world to explore and there are many ways it can develop. The exercises framed toward *The Snatch Game* would make excellent icon development exercises no matter what type of impersonation you wish to do – think about the desired result and where you wish to sit on the line from sincerity to parody.

- Be realistic about your chosen icon – if you wish to be sincere in your impersonation you need to share a lot of similarities and be able to do their act justice, pay it tribute.
- Play around on the scale from full sincerity to parody.
- If aiming for parody be sure the audience know the icon well enough to get the references you're played with them. But also be sure you are comfortable poking fun at the icon.
- Research their world, build your version of it, keep playing!
- Use the exercises to flesh out your performance, develop a language and lexicon for the icon and have a few go-to phrases and comments to use in performance.
- Play, have fun. Be in the moment as *your icon* – if an audience reacts to you, reply to their reaction. Keep it live!

Doing an impersonation should not turn your performance into an *acting* exercise where you are simply delivering a script. All of the live, interactive elements of drag need to be there. As drag acts there are times you may move into the world of scripted work and acting and that's where the next chapter is heading: *acting, scripts, casting!*

Notes

1. Derrick featured on various seasons of *Drag Race* and can be found at @derrickbarry
2. Find Tracey Collins and all her characters online @traceycollinsss
3. La Voix features on Season 6 of *Drag Race UK* and has been a known face on the British drag circuit for the last decade – @lavoixtheshow
4. *RuPaul's Drag Race* Season 8 Snatch Game.
5. *The Snatch Game* is a parody of *The Match Game* used each season in *RuPaul's Drag Race*. It has become one of the most popular challenges as it forces acts outside of their usual alter-ego and to portray an icon in an improvised quiz show which has no fixed rules.

Bernie M photographed backstage at the Royal Vauxhall Tavern by The Burley Photgrapher

21
Where Is It Written?: Text, Acting and Castings

Drag acts are usually the ones controlling everything within their set: You write the jokes, re-write the songs and improvise your way through each live experience drawing on a range of quips and lines from your repertoire, discovering new bits along the way. Occasionally though, opportunities arise where you need to become actors! Performers who are interpreting someone else's words: whether professional TV or film acting, sketch comedy within a cabaret night or even a poetry reading. Having an ability to bring a text to life is a great tool in the drag treasure trove.

This chapter is essentially two quick fire introductions to the world of performing a text. Firstly a guide to how to bring a text to life and secondly some practical examples of where text work might be needed and how you can always achieve your best.

Performing a Text

There's no way to teach someone to act in half a chapter of a book, but as a drag act who has some performance skills, there are a few easy tricks to adapt existing skill you already use and apply that to a text.

Textual Analysis

The first thing to do with any text is to have a read-through (or two) and do some simple analysis. What does this scene tell you about the character you are playing? What are the objectives of the person you are being (this applies even if the text is meant to be you)? What do they want? Most of the textual analysis broken down in *Chapter 15: Sing a Song* can be applied to any text. Keep looking for the clues on paper that are there in black and white. These are the facts: *the truth of the text*.

Everything else is for you to fill in using educated choices, colour between the lines to make the text make sense for you and to give you an interesting interpretation. Visualise yourself as a drag Sherlock Holmes solving the mystery of who this character is, why they are acting the way they are and then work out how you can bring that to life.

Subtext

The text is what is printed on the page, the *sub*text is the underlying meaning of what is said. Are they being honest? Sarcastic? Seductive? Ironic? The choices you make as a performer should come from the clues in the textual analysis but the subtext is what creates your interpretation, your unique reading of the text. Think of the different ways you could say "hello" to someone if you were attracted to them, annoyed with them, surprised by them, etc. This is subtext.

DOI: 10.4324/9781003498797-24

Bring the Fun

When acting in drag, almost every time, the role is a drag act because the writer/producer wanted variety, colour, diversity and fun. If a casting director has approached a "real" drag act rather than an actor, it's because they want that authenticity and the skill set you have! Bring that level of fun to the text, of being cheeky, authentic and basically – interesting! Don't hold back or be too worried about *serious* acting, worry more about showing a bit of your alter-ego: throw in a wink, a tongue pop, a few clicks, gyrate your hips, give a comic double take, large reactions. Anything you can do to make the text become draggy fun and full of colour. Nine out of ten times they came to you for drag, so give them drag! They have come to you because they want you to be you, or at least your alter-ego: they've seen something in *you* they like and they want you to apply *you* to this text.

Add Some Business

Business is a simple acting term that means *do something*. Often a text will give a stage direction that says what you are doing but sometimes there are just lines on a page with no guidance and in those cases – think of something small to do! Especially for on-screen work.

Very rarely in life do you engage with another person 100%. Look in the text for clues, or ideas that would make sense:

- If you are in an office? Tidy the paperwork, where's the sheet you are looking for?
- In a bar? Drink your gin, stir your drink or suck on a cocktail cherry!
- Backstage? Fix your make-up in the mirror or adjust a costume!

What *business* could you do other than listen fully to what's going on in the scene? A little bit of *business* can bring a performance, and a scene, to life. It also can tell the audience the subtext for this character in the scene.

> When I first started getting castings for drag roles I was 100% taking myself too seriously as an actor and I missed out on some great jobs. I was interpreting the text, using my drama school experiences and *acting*. I was up for roles as a sassy side kick or a camp cameo but presenting them with Lady Macbeth. They wanted drag, I needed to loosen up.
>
> Now, I always find ways to be a little flirty, irreverent or cheeky in an audition. Even if its a serious scene, especially for on-screen work. Depending on the role I add an extra bit of *business* that feels draggy: tidy my make up in the mirror whilst chatting, chew some gum, have a drink, flirt with someone whilst talking, do my nails, etc. Simple, but obvious, drag-related business. I'm not reinventing the wheel here; I'm auditioning to be a drag act so I'm delivering a drag act! If they want subtlety – they'll ask for it.

Who Are You?

As drag acts we are often cast as our alter-ego rather than the performer behind them. Getting the balance right can be tricky if there's a vast difference between the two of you. You, the performer, might be a wonderful actor, but perhaps your alter-ego isn't. Is there fun in that? Probably not in a casting situation – but for a role in a play, or film, there could be options to explore. This happens a lot with the great British tradition of Pantomime where a drag act might play the Dame and they might fall out of character for the Pantomime to reveal their drag alter-ego having a wonderful time on stage.

Drag acts like Lily Savage and Myra Dubois will be cast as a character but are playing their drag character playing the character. Paul O'Grady did not play Miss Hannigan, Lily Savage did. This sounds like semantics but it's all about perspective and how far away from an established character or persona you take things.

> I worked box office when Lily Savage was playing Miss Hannigan in *Annie* at the Victoria Palace. I loved watching how playful Paul could be as Lily, because the audience had a relationship with Lily and so that was a really interesting layering standing alone from the story. The story had to be fulfilled but there was also a story going on between Lily and the audience, and I thought that was very interesting.
>
> Ada Campe[1]

Always explore which levels you are playing on. Are you approaching this as an actor outside of your drag alter-ego, possibly creating a new character or persona? Or are adapting your existing drag alter-ego to fit someone else's text?

Do They Know You? If So, Surprise Them

Often a drag act might be acting in a sketch or a scene in a club atmosphere, or a weekly competition. When the audience know you, know your persona, there is a lot of fun to be had in playing against type. Even if on the surface it is unsuccessful it could provide a great layer of humour. Think of Georgeous playing 'butch' in *Drag Race All Stars Season 9*. The performance was not convincing at all, but that's where the humour was found and it was all the more endearing due to us knowing how far removed that was from their usual persona. Again, this is not something to play with in a first appearance, or in a casting, but if you are in a series of shows – always look for variety.

Returning to the Basics of Drag Performance

With any scene – return to the basic drag choices and make sure you still try to apply them all! Even though you're using a text, or script, work back through *Chapter 8: Basic Drag*. You may not be in a traditional drag environment but you can still *make an entrance*, use *performance zones*, *anchors*, create *peaks and troughs*, *ooze confidence* and *have fun!*

What is your role in this project? A drag act is often thrown into a scene to give an injection of energy or drama. If that's the requirement then you need to fulfil it.

Types of Performance

It would be easy to think I am writing this from a prospective of acting in theatre, film and television. But all of this advice can be put into practice with any text-based work. There are various ways scripted or written text can be used in a cabaret or drag performance. Sketch shows, comic monologues, dramatic monologues and more.

Spoken Word Poetry

Unlike most of the text looked at in the chapter it is usually written by the performer. There is something personal about the performance of spoken word. A subtle baring of the soul that an audience can connect to. Stay true to the drag basics, find the variety and colour in the delivery. Connect to the audience, eye contact, *performance zones* and *anchors*. And *if* you are reading the words bring your eyes up to the audience as often as it possible don't allow a physical script to inhibit your performance.

Contests

There are countless contests on the drag scene and often text (for example; a scene, some jokes, or an acting challenge) will be on offer. In this scenario the overall objective is always to have fun and make the audience have fun. So be ridiculous, think about being more Jim Carey and less Meryl Streep. It's a bar contest so don't take it, or yourself, too seriously.

Castings for Film and TV

Each opportunity within this is so varied. You may be playing Puck in *A Midsummer Night's Dream*, or a Drag King in *Eastenders*. However, the basic rules of working with a text still apply. Use the text as your backbone for working out what is essential, fill the blanks in yourself. Remember you have been cast as a drag act and to bring that flavour and colour to the role. It's better to make an interesting choice and be asked to simplify than to make a forgettable choice and not connect to the casting director.

In a casting, as well as rehearsal and performance, if you get an opportunity, try to give different options, ideas and takes on the text. Who knows what you will discover. If you do a take one way, you can always ask a director to do another take but with a different intention – "*can I try again but take it even camper?*"

As drag acts you get used to total autonomy, but as soon as you are cast in something you become a pawn in someone else's game – and you need to accept that. You are a small cog in a much bigger machine and you need to be prepared to think of the machine as a whole, more often than not that means doing as you are told! You have been cast for who you are but that does not mean they want *all* aspects of your usual alter-ego: they may want your aesthetic or your comedy. You may need to let go of some of your usual approach to a performance, a different look, a different character backstory, even a different politic: be prepared to be as adaptive as you can. You need to be able to put your ego, and your alter-ego, to one side.

> I was cast in a small (tiny – don't blink) role in Ridley Scott's *Napoleon*. The scene is mainly on the edit room floor. However, at the costume fitting dresses were being selected by an Oscar-winning costume designer and my camp sensibility was very excited. I had visions of being a gorgeous French drag act, with fabulous frocks, Marie Antoinette hair and a gorgeous little mole! Of course the dresses were ill-fitting! As I went into hair and make-up test, they gave me the lightest make-up I have ever worn, and then smeared it all over my face to give an '*end of the night*' look. My fabulous French fantasy was not to be. I was playing a French aristocrat dabbling in drag – wearing his mother/sister's clothes that didn't fit and possibly doing his own make-up for the first time.

The Audition Is, Usually, Everything

If you are lucky enough to have an agent, or to get castings, remember the audition is 90% of the work. For the smallish, drag roles in TV, Film and Commercials, turning up on set they usually want you to just recreate what you did in the audition room, or tape, on their set for their cameras.

I was naive and used to think once cast in a TV or Film project I would have rehearsals, meet with movement directors, singing coaches and dialect coaches to finesse the finished performance – as yet this has never happened for me. Obviously, if you are the lead in a big-budget project, it may. But through my TV and Film acting experience, mainly glorious bit parts, the truth is they want the finished product from the self-tape recreated on set in the costume and lighting they have organised. They don't want someone who needs to work on the accent, they choose someone with the right accent. Or as I found out on set, the silly face I pulled was exactly what they needed me to recreate. I was on set for a project and they showed me my casting tape and literally said – *"this face please"*. That face got me the job and they just wanted it recreated on set.

Castings: You Are the Right Person for the Job

Always remember you been have asked to audition because someone has seen your work and thinks it will work for the role you are up for. Bring yourself to the role, your best self. Actors often walk into a casting expressing *"please pick me."* Instead change that attitude to *"I'm the answer to your problem"*. The casting director saw the photos, or that bit of footage, and now you are at the casting simply to confirm you are the person they need. They didn't call you in so you could turn up as a completely different person, they want you.

A Few Tips for Casting Self Tapes

TV, Film and Commercial casting is often is done with through self-tapes (at least initially). You record at home and deliver it by email for them to review. The casting director will give you a few sides of text to learn or perform and a very brief outline of what is required.

Self tapes are becoming ever popular and for drag acts that's a blessing: previously having to turn up to an office in full drag for a five-minute meeting is a hassle and an expense! A self-tape means you can get into drag and record yourself at home in your own time.

- **Do What Is Required.** Often there are a few parts to a self tape: read the scene, introduce yourself to the camera, show a few drag looks. Make sure you have included everything, but also not added in too much extra. They may be looking at 30 different applicants so want to be able to initially rush through them and see the good stuff!
- **Invest in a Ring Light.** You don't need a professional studio set-up but a little bit of front-on lighting and a tripod to hold your phone makes everything look a lot better and makes your life a lot easier. These are very affordable and are definitely worth the investment.
- **Review Footage before De-dragging.** Most performers do a couple of takes and then send the best one over. Make sure you review and select your takes *before* you get out of drag. There's nothing worse than realising it wasn't good (or you had a wonky eyelash) after you have cleaned up and then you need to do the whole process again.
- **Build a Library of Looks/Stock Footage.** Getting into drag is expensive and takes time. Save footage from every casting to build up a reusable bank of looks. When you do a new look, record yourself; close-up, a mid-shot and a long-shot of you walking into shot, possibly dance or *act* for a minute. (In commercial castings you often have a breakdown that needs reactions but no texts – *flirty, surprised, angry, shocked*, etc. Or simple actions; *walk into a room, touch up make-up in a mirror*, etc.) If every time you do a self-tape you can record and label any reusable, non-specific footage you will build a bank of drag looks, and acting, for future castings.

Often a drag casting will ask to see more than one look. Or you may only be able to share one look for the scene but you can attach a different look, or even look different for the introduction to show some range. If suitable attach a short montage, 20 seconds max, of different looks at the end to show variety of drag you can offer – especially if for the majority of the self-tape you were slightly outside of your comfort zone.

- **Profiles.** Most castings will ask for profiles. This is usually a mid and long shot of you. Look to camera, then turn your whole body, 90 degrees, looking left then looking right. There are plenty of YouTube examples on how to do these. But again, in drag doing a self tape I always do one and then save it to my footage.
- **A Neutral Background.** Self tapes are always suggested to be in front of a neutral background. This does not mean moving everything in your house to have a plain wall. It means not having any clutter, or a window, or anything distracting behind you! They want to focus on you not why you haven't put your washing away! Casting directors understand you are at home working with what you have. Just tidy up a little and find somewhere as neutral as possible.

A self-tape can take a long time to put together – getting into drag, recording, reviewing, editing. Maybe half a day, the casting might be a tight turn around. Being prepared and having options ready in advance is priceless. You can even set up a reusable template in iMovie (or whichever editing software you use) to speed up the process. Obviously this won't work if there is a full scene to read but being able to show a few looks and versatility is always a good thing.

> I have had self-tape castings where I have not even gotten into drag! I already had the footage they needed, the profiles, a few looks or comic reactions. I just recorded an introduction, which they usually want out of drag, and explained why I was right for this specific job. Then cut to pre-recorded footage. I also save a few non-specific clips of myself talking to a camera in drag and introducing myself with the facts that won't change between castings (*name, agent, height, two sentences about myself and then record profiles*). It means if a casting comes in, as they are often last minute, I can put together something that showcases a little of what they want and if they want more – they can get back to me.

Overview: Text, Acting and Castings

You may not have any desire to step outside of the bar or club scene, but you never know what opportunities may crop up for a drag performer. If you get a casting, or get handed a text you need to bring to the stage, bring it to life and make it your own.

- Never neglect a textual analysis – dig deep to see what options there are.
- Bring yourself to any text, but also bring some options – subtext, business, objectives – which can build an interesting and memorable interpretation.
- Someone else may have written the text but you can still apply your alter-ego to it, and apply the *basics of drag* to it!
- Castings are a lot of work but open up some very exciting opportunities. Be prepared, keep building a stock of usable footage and make the most out of your time in drag.

Using someone else's words can be a very odd feeling for a drag performer. As you grow in experience you may start looking towards finding ways to have more control, and more power, in shaping the performances that you are involved in. Rather than performing one set or performing someone else's work, you might be looking to perform a whole show – be it a *solo show* or *hosting* a line-up show!

Note

1 *Ada Campe* in interview with *Michael Twaits*, July 2024. See Part V for full interview.

Red Velvet photographed backstage at the Royal Vauxhall Tavern by The Burley Photgrapher

22
Move On: Hosting and Solo Shows

There comes a point when performers will set their sights on more than just one set. Rather than being part of the show you want to steer the entire show, either hosting a show or performing a full-length solo show. You have looked at the majority of the skills needed, now you need to address piecing it all together. This chapter will look at tweaking your existing performance skills to open up new opportunities as a performer.

It is a chapter of two halves but the skill set of hosting a show, and shaping a solo show, aren't as different as they might first seem. A drag host is like a dinner party host; you conduct the evening and make sure each person, or subgroup, is having fun, feeling included and ready for whatever is coming next. A terrible host tends to lead to a terrible night, a good host makes an audience feel at home, relaxed and ready for anything.

When thinking of hosting a show I often use the metaphor of a swan: elegant, calm, show-stopping, gliding around on still waters, but underneath the legs are paddling like mad. It does not matter who is in, or on, the pond – the swan still owns it and everyone else is simply a guest.

When Am I Ready to Host?

If you can master talking on stage, communicating with an audience then you are ready to host! I would recommend at this point revisiting *Chapter 11: Audience Experience* and *Chapter 13: Talking On Stage* – these skills need to be second nature and to be fully mastered. There are many technical aspects to being a host, lots going on simultaneously, so you need to have a firm hold of the basics prior to taking on a whole show.

That said, if you don't try, you won't know: if an opportunity comes up take it! So much performance craft is developed on the job, bite the bullet and give it a go! Work hard in advance to do the best you can, review how it went and learn a few lessons. Maybe you are ready?

First Things First

A strong host has honed their craft as a performer and is ready for anything to happen on stage. They have a wide repertoire they can bring with them so can find pieces that *compliment* the rest of the show, and they usually have a showstopper or two ready to guarantee a good night. As a host you have a longer time to build relationships with the audience, you need to have a range of options to draw on to talk to the audience and be present throughout the show. You need to become adept at reading an audience and giving them what they need. If they are timid, warm them up, if they are rowdy, calm them down; guide them through the show.

The Structure of Hosting

There are ten structural elements every host needs to host a show. They may be pieced together in various configurations, you may not always use them all but if you're new to hosting this is a great guide to ticking all the boxes! A host can elevate a seemingly desperate line up into a really special occasion for the audience. Master these points and you can master hosting:

1) **Opening Number:** This may be anything from your repertoire list (see *Chapter 6: Building a Set, Range and Repertoire*) that you labelled an opener. A song, lip-sync. If you are a comedian it could be your tight three minutes establishing the gig. The opening number needs to start the show with a bang and set a president for a good night.

2) **Welcome the Audience:** It sounds simple but welcoming them makes them feel included: *This is our unique show.* Invite them along on the crazy journey. Make sure they know what this specific night is, they may have just stumbled in for a drink, so signpost the route through! *What's going to happen? What should they expect? What do they need to do?*

   During the welcome establish the room you are in. Assuming it's a cabaret space you could do some light audience work, highlight a few members of the audience who might be touchstones throughout the show. (Give an early warning to the hen night, etc.) Create the atmosphere that tonight is a special, unique occasion, partly because *they* are there. (The **welcome** and **opening number** can be switched around if that suits your performance style.)

3) **Set up the Rules:** Before getting another performer on stage – set up the rules. What atmosphere are you aiming for? Theatre-style respectful silence or mosh-pit madness? Is there an interval? Is the bar open? Is it a contest? Is there variety or five similar lip-syncs back-to-back? Manage expectations, set out a plan from the outset, it will make the rest of the show easier and have trajectory.

4) **Introduce an Act:** The essential thing when introducing an act is getting their name and pronouns correct, establishing the atmosphere for their act and not accidentally giving spoilers. If you want the audience to cheer, do some warm up work. If the next act needs calm, command it before bringing them to the stage. Your introduction is instructing the audience how to watch the next act, you want it to be as successful as possible, so give it a strong set up. Always speak to an act prior to a show – how do they like to be introduced?

5) **Move from One Act to the Next:** This is exactly the same as part four but you need to make sure you are giving a guiding hand. Returning to *Chapter 13: Talking On Stage*, the two performers are the *monkey bars* and you need to build the momentum, and connection, between them so the audience are moving with you from one to the next.

   The first thing to do is thank, or congratulate, the last act. (Use their name again to help cement that with the audience, get another round of applause for the act.) Then the job is to seamlessly start changing the atmosphere ready for the next performer. If genres and moods are changing, guide that. Do not send a comedian on after a performance poetry piece about grief if you haven't reset the atmosphere – or vice versa!

   Check in with the audience, lift them back up, have a few light laughs, realign their focus and be respectful to both the act before and the act that is coming up. A simple bit of call and response can achieve this well – *"are you ready?"*

   It can happen that a performer didn't go down very well. As the host you may need to do a bit little more in between work to help bring the room back in line! Throw in a quick number or do some audience work just to cleanse the pallet before moving on.

If one vibe might be something that's super dark and intense and the next act is going to be more lighthearted, it's your job as the host to bridge that.

Me The Drag Queen[1]

6) **Be the Audience's Safe Space:** When the audience like a host, they relax. They feel safe because even if the act coming up isn't to their taste they know the host will be back in a few minutes and everything will be ok. This isn't a prompt to make yourself the star of every show, it's to make sure you deliver your best at all points. Sometimes when hosting you don't get to perform many pieces, you just get to chat and do some audience work but you are the performer the audience connect with the most. If that's not a good connection they won't enjoy the show!

7) **Keep the Audience in the Loop:** Before leaving the stage for an interval or break always reaffirm what's happening next. Let them know how long the break is, what's coming next, thank the acts they've seen so far and keep the momentum up! It sounds like a lot but it can be achieved very simply: "*Go and enjoy a drink – but first show some love the brilliant acts you've seen so far – we'll see you in ten minutes!*"

Throughout the night remind the audience of any major rules: if there's a specific act that has interactions, do you generally need more interaction, or less talking! Often audiences are getting progressively more drunk so they need reminders. In a some bars people may join midway through the night – how are they to know what they have walked into? Remind them, frequently, but in a varied way. Welcome new-comers and try to keep everyone engaged.

You are literally the host, this is your house, you are showing off all your lovely things (acts) and hoping everyone who came to your party goes home thinking you are the loveliest person alive and they are super jealous of how incredible your home (venue) is. Own it baby!

Adam All[2]

8) **Watch the Show:** As a host you need to be in the room and experiencing what is happening! What is the live experience the audience are getting? How else can you carry on from that moment of momentum? Whenever possible watch the show: be in the audience, the tech box, behind the bar; whatever works for the venue you are in. Whoop and cheer along with the audience. Act the part of someone having a good night out and enjoying the show because that energy will be infectious to the audience! It does not matter if you have seen that trick, or heard that joke before, *act* as if it's the first time it has ever happened, experience the show from the audience's perspective.

9) **Close a Show:** Line up shows sometimes have a planned finale, competitions have the results or producers may ask the host to do a closing number – which is when you look for a showstopper in amongst your repertoire. This is where a host's memory is tested: The thank you's! Ideally name all the acts, but also thank the tech team, the bar staff, the audience – and don't forget to find a way to credit yourself and take your applause too. If there's another night upcoming, make sure you mention that!

10) **Fill:** This is the easiest and hardest thing to do as a host! Just talk the to audience and make them feel it is part of the show, when actually you are filling time, distracting from things happening behind the scenes or waiting for someone else to be ready! There are some more examples of this below, but you need to have a few ideas prepared!

Guide the Audience

As a host you often need to give the audience permission to cheer, whoop or interact with performances. In others, happened gigs (where an audience is out for a drink and something *happens* to be on), you will need to do the opposite and explain that while the acts are on stage the audience listen! Do not be afraid to tell them explicitly. If suitable dangle a carrot: *"if you listen nicely we can have a sing-along in a moment!"* Tease them with forthcoming attractions so that they remain focused and hooked throughout.

No Clipboard Compare

Using a clipboard as a host sends a sign to the whole room that you don't care about this gig! Never be a *Clipboard Compare*: referring to notes on-stage advertises that you haven't done enough prep-work and that you aren't even trying to hide it. Between each act all you need to remember is the name of the last performer and the name of the next one. Why do you need a clipboard? Put a running order, and some notes if needed, wherever you will be watching the show from. When one act is on, double check who is up next. It's that simple. (Occasionally at big events you need cue-cards to help with the exact names of organisations or large groups but even then make a point of it, apologise but clarify it's because something really matters: *"I'm sorry I'm reading but I want to get this right, they donated so much to this event!"*)

Always Speak to Performers Prior to the Show

Always try to talk to each act before a show, let that help you choose what you will do during the show, but also how best to frame their work. It may turn out you have all singers on a bill so need to do more comedy. Knowing the shape of the evening will help you do the best you can do. For each act make sure you have the correct name, pronouns and know how they want to be introduced. Try and avoid getting too much information – a few bullet points to go on stage with. Ensure you know how to pronounce their name!

> One of my first experiences hosting was with a variety act who performed on a bed of nails. On the running order it said their name, and then *'bed of nails act'*. The act was running late so I didn't get to meet them prior to introducing them. It turns out the bed of nails was a surprise crescendo – so I stole their thunder by announcing it. These things happen – but that's why it's essential to be on time to a gig and try to talk to every act!

Support the Performers

Not every performer you introduce will be brilliant, or to your taste, but you need to make them feel supported and *never* turn against another performer. Help them, guide them. The host is like a mother presenting her babies to the audience. Look after them, check they are well received and remember each one is your favourite!

It's Not about Me (but It Is)

The golden point for a host is when they make the show feel like it's about all the acts but the audience leave wanting to see more of the host – because they were brilliant.

> Don't Indulge yourself too much because it's, you know, it's simultaneously a very indulgent job, but not, you know? Your responsibility is more to the cast and the room than it is to yourself.
>
> Me The Drag Queen[3]

How Lucky Am I?

My approach to hosting is to have fun with the audience. I try to make it feel that I am on a night out with them. ("*How outrageous is it that this is my job?*") A few simple tricks of language can make the audience feel you are excited for the night too and that they are in for a treat. Rather than making the audience excited, try and share your excitement with them. Energy is contagious.

Create a nurturing environment. Another wonderful trick is to use the pronouns *you*, *we* and *our* rather than *me*, *myself* and *I*.

- "This is *your* show."
- "One of *our* favourite performers."
- "*We* are all in for a treat tonight."

Build a sense of camaraderie between the performers and yourself, the venue and producers and also finally the audience and yourself. It builds the feeling of a bespoke show that they are buying into.

Audience Work

At the top of the show always include some audience work to establish the atmosphere you want. Usually I will provide a few opportunities for the audience to clap or cheer during my *Welcomes* at the top of a show. If they respond well I can move on, if not I can explain that this "*isn't theatre*" – they need to get involved and have some fun in the freedom of drag and cabaret.

This only works though if you allow space yourself to react and interact with the audience. (Think of *The Cycle* from *Chapter 10: Audience Experience*.) You say something, they respond to it and you respond back. That is how the audience feel part of the show, make sure when you ask a question – you listen to the answer.

Structural *Peaks and Troughs*

As a host you need to be flexible: always have a few extra tracks with you in case someone is doing a number you wanted to do, or everything feels a little similar. (This should be easy as you have your *Repertoire* in your *performers drive* – remember *Chapter 2: The Business of Drag*.) If you're hosting, you probably have enough rep to add a *hosting* folder in there where you can put two or three options of opener, closer, filler which you can draw on at any point!

If it's a singer-heavy night – try to balance the night out with more chat, or a lip-sync, a poem! As a host you have to look at the structure of the show as a whole. You are adept at doing this for your own set, now look at the bigger picture – including other people's material. Where would it help for you to mix things up, perform in a different way, use a different part of the room? As the host you can make a line up show feel curated, interesting and full of variety by simply using the room in interesting ways and bring in some of your own repertoire at the right moment.

Filling

Filling can be scary. It can be daunting to put the momentum of the show on pause and need to somehow keep the stage alive. A few options:

- Always have a couple of spare tracks with the tech in case you need to do a number. Let the technician know how you would cue them in – just in case.
- Write a few comic audience interaction moments. (Look for a new boyfriend/girlfriend, see who's in tonight, check-in with anyone you had an earlier bit of banter with.)
- Standard call and response. Audiences can always be entertained by being involved. *"Who's single?"*, *"Whose first time at a drag show?"*, *"Where are my gays?"*, Etc. Think of easy ways to get those who want to be involved feeling active and fill a little bit of time with light banter. It doesn't need to be one-liners, just warm and engaging.
- Have a couple of go-to conversations, stories or arguments you can draw on. A mini comedy set that can be inserted with ease to almost any show.

> Many of my stories are about when something went wrong at another live show as it's a moment an audience can relate to and understand how you are connecting it to the current one. I often use a true story, when someone accidentally flicked a whole Chicken Kiev on the stage from the audience: *"that's live performance folks"*. Depending on how long I need to fill, I can drag it out for around five minutes. I can discuss the exact moment it happened, the noise, the poise in the room. I can explore: what happened next? (*"what would you have done?"*), food allergies (*"I wouldn't have minded but I'm gluten intolerant!"*), what did it mean? (*"in some cultures perhaps that's a compliment?"*), what might be thrown at me tonight? etc.
>
> It's such a silly story that I have the freedom to play with it for as long as I need.

- Remind the audience of the rules. Maybe even critique their interactions – who's cheering the best, who got scared during the last act, who got too excited during the burlesque moment? Come from a place of love but check-in with the audience members.

> I was hosting *Pride in London* 2023, and we had a surprise performer, Rita Ora, coming on to do a half-hour set. She had done her tech rehearsal in the morning and was at the hotel across the road. However, London was so busy she couldn't get to us. I went on stage to introduce her on my own in front of 15,000 people *knowing* that she wasn't backstage yet. Due to it being a surprise and half-hour set no-one else was ready to come on. I used every audience interaction trick I had up my sleeve: getting each different group of the LGBT+ community to cheer, get flags waving, some call-and-response work, etc. The whole time a voice in my earpiece was saying *"fill Michael, fill"* on repeat. It must have been around a ten-minute improvisation of simple audience work. It was all fine, but I wish I had emailed over a couple of additional tracks so I could have just sung a song or two to fill the moment!

When hosting, always, always be prepared that you may need to fill – don't panic, just be prepared! You may find you get annoyed when you don't get the 'fill' moment because you love telling a particular story you saved for that role.

Rules and Regulations

It's sounds dramatic to lay out the rules, but what I mean is to make sure the audience know what they are in for, where the show is going and what is expected of them during the show. If you don't set things up correctly, especially for non-verbal acts, it can be really tricky! Tell the audience what's expected of them and make sure they understand.

> I host a lot of burlesque nights, at the top of the show I do a very silly *idiot's guide* to burlesque noises to ensure the audience know what to expect and what is expected of them. I pantomime doing a burlesque routine and ask them to make different noises for different parts slowly building up to me introducing the first performer.
>
> In essence, it's a five-minute comedy/slapstick bit with the target of getting the room ready. After an interval I need to bring the room back and check we are all still on the same page. I don't repeat the set. I simply say; "*Remind me…*" and then do the three key actions from the earlier burlesque warm up. Then assuming it's gone well I tell them how good, or how drunk, they are and bring out the next act. But if that doesn't quite work I can be adaptive in the moment and do a little more warm up work to settle the room after the interval.

To return to the dinner party analogy: the host has to be having a good time for the guests to be having a good time. Have you ever been at a dinner party and the host is in the kitchen doing the washing up? Guests feel abandoned, unsure if they should leave or stay; that's how the audience can feel if a host isn't being attentive. Enjoy the show with them – be seen to be laughing along! Don't dip out back to pack up your bag for a quick exit! Share your love of live performance. Showcase the best of yourself and the audience will come with you on whatever adventure you take them.

A Solo Show

Doing a mixture of sets, headline slots and hosting can be a hugely rewarding career, but sometimes a drag act wishes to create a full-length show. Before tackling a full-length show I would recommend having a bit of experience at all three gig types before pulling it all together. But what is a solo show? A piece that takes the audience on a themed creative journey, or perhaps brings all the disparate pieces from their repertoire into a full-length *best of* style show that is a calling card for all the skills the performer wishes to showcase.

If you have reached the point where you are considering creating a full-length show, the assumption is that you have honed your craft with smaller sets; you know how to work a room, connect to an audience and give a top scale professional performance. Much of the advice given in *hosting* (above) can be directly applied to curating your own full-length show. Rather than introducing different performers you are segueing into different pieces from your own repertoire. Some might be unique for the show, others might be well run in pieces you have been using within your sets. There are no definitive rules, and no one is checking. However, an audience for a solo show will often be made up of people who have seen you before and want to see more. Try to make sure there are a few unique moments in there for them as well as crowd-pleasing moments they might be hoping to see again. If I went to see Barbra and she didn't sing *Don't Rain On My Parade* I'd probably be disappointed!

Bangers Only?

For our purposes, a solo show focuses on the concept of a sit down, *an evening with* type show. Something closer to a theatre show than a club night. Many drag acts do an hour or two-hour solo set in a bar but it may not have the same license to take the audience on a journey. In a bar there is always a transient atmosphere and audiences might come and go, they are catching up with friends and drinking. The shape and structure of the set would still benefit from the same rigour but an hour, or longer, club style set is really just a long/extended set.

My definition of a solo show is that it always has an audience who are there to watch from the beginning and will follow it all the way through. The set, or structure, is the same each time the show is done (even planned improvisation comes at the same moment). The show has some form of narrative or thread which runs through holding it together so the audience can see why you chose the content you did. It may be a themed show, autobiographical or a *'best of'* review.

Structure

For all solo shows it is important to look at the structure and to create variety over the whole show. Unless you are an *incredible* singer it's hard to sustain an hour of singing piano-based ballads with no chatter, or jokes to alter the mood. Audiences need those *peaks and troughs* (back to *Chapter 8: Basic Drag* again). Changes of tempo, style, mood, volume and even audience connection are vital in crafting an engaging show.

As the star of your solo show you can create *peaks and troughs* stylistically – from jumping between live vocals, lip-sync, comedy, poetry, impersonation and more. Most acts have strengths and will play to that (I tend to do an evening of song with a couple of nods to other disciplines). However, within the structure of each set piece you can find variety of tempo, style, ways to interact with the audience and even how you use the room.

These skills and performance modes are all elements tackled in *Part II and Part III* so should be very familiar. If you created a piece or two from each chapter, and feel you have a strong stage craft, you might be in a place to start pulling together the structure of an interesting solo show.

> When structuring a show I often use coloured post-it notes: green for a song, yellow for a story, pink for a wild card moment (spoken word, a parody or improvisation), etc. It's a simple way of visualising where the dynamics are for content choices.
>
> If two green are back to back, I make sure they are contrasting or complimentary in style but not repetitive. The contrast could be the way I perform them: something as simple as sitting on the piano for one, standing centre stage for another. Backing track from one, acoustic for another. I always have variety, texture and layers in mind when structuring.
>
> If the post-its look bland or formulaic, what does that say about my show? How can I mix it up? I always aim for a pink (wild card) post-it to be two-thirds of the way through to mix the show up a little.

This is not to say that every solo show needs to be a mixture of performance styles. If you are a drag act using stand-up comedy. An hour-long show could easily be pure stand-up. But how can you inject variety: funny stories, audience interaction, one-liners, reads, a mini roast? Keep looking for variety within the structure of whatever you are shaping.

Framing/Hosting Yourself

If you have a selection of repertoire you want to perform it's quite a useful exercise to return to the *Hosting* section above and look through the basics of how to set up or introduce that type of work. Instead of introducing another performer, it's setting up your next piece but the audience still want to be guided, conducted, so as to be in the best place possible to watch it.

How can you perform one piece and then segue into the next? What do you need to do to take the audience on that journey? What do you need to tell them? What is this showing them?

Remember that whatever the show, you can still do those hosting basics of having an opening number, setting the rules and a showstopper to make sure the audience come along on the journey with you. And more importantly feel like they have got somewhere in the end.

Show Inspiration

A solo show needs something that holds it together. There are many ways to find inspiration as to what you wish to create but here are a few starting options. Many of these could also be used in conjunction.

A *Best of* Show

As experienced performers your repertoire slowly builds, some repertoire becomes a calling card the drag world knows you for, others might be brilliant but hard to pull off on a more transient, or chaotic night. Spend some time looking at your repertoire list and ask yourself which pieces you are proud of. Which pieces do you think represent you the best? If the motto for the show was *"all killer, no filler"* would that piece still be included?

A best of show does not need to be sold or marketed as that but it is a way of starting the development process of a solo show. Showcasing a collection of your best pieces being bought in a complimentary and cohesive way.

With this type of show there are usually three or four key pieces or sets a performer wants to showcase and that gives the backbone of the show. Bringing those particular pieces together may highlight a theme, or a narrative, worth discussing or exploring.

Autobiographical

This could be from an honest perspective or from the perspective of your character. An evening exploring who you are, why you are the way you are, what inspired you to become a performer, why are you on stage, etc. This isn't an ego trip, it should be exploring the world at large through your experience within the world.

A Themed Show

A themed show can in many ways be structured due to having a few showstoppers or developed sets you feel could justify a full show. It's also a nice way to market to a specific audience or group who will be interested – a Kate Bush show will bring your usual audience but also fans of Kate Bush.

However, with a themed show, the performer is usually exploring a specific point. I've seen shows of drag acts purely exploring the music of a favourite artist, or music from a certain point in time, political movements, etc.

Use Other Stories to Tell Ours

A common theme in queer storytelling is simply to queer, and retell, well known stories. To put a different twist, or perspective, on a story everyone knows. Putting yourself as the performer in the lead role – because growing up there was never a queer lead in a story! Retellings of myths, children's classics, folklore and fairytale are all very common approaches; *"You in Wonderland"*.

New Work

Not every solo show is a Frankenstein's monster of short sets being strung together. Drag performers can create an entire evening of new work through rehearsal and development to create a new piece. Many drag acts will test drive bits of the solo shows at other nights as a way of marketing a forthcoming solo show but also as a way of learning about their piece – seeing where the laughs are, how it all shapes together.

> In 2015 I was offered a show at a Central London members' bar with a nice theatre space. I was working, was established, but had not thought much about doing a full-length show yet. I looked at my *Repertoire List* (all three lists from *Chapter 6: Building a Set, Range and Repertoire*) for inspiration and started creating a *Best Of* Show. What was my best piece? What was my favourite piece? What did I love performing and didn't get to do very often? From this a setlist began to form.
>
> There were a few songs about queerness: Charles Azenvour's *What Makes a Man* for example, not a party track but I loved it. My *Stonewall* Poem – which I knew would be a closer, or a crescendo moment of variety. I had rehearsed a ballad version of *Running up That Hill* by Kate Bush for a function that got cancelled but still had it in my repertoire list. I also had *If They Could See Me Now* from *Sweet Charity*.
>
> Despite approaching from a *Best Of* Show, there was also a slight theme developing. For me this was a show about falling into drag. Putting on the heels for the first time and never really taking them off. It reminded me of folk story of *The Red Shoes* where a girl puts on some red shoes and simply can't stop dancing. This in turn led me back to Kate Bush and her song – *The Red Shoes*. I liked the idea of bookending a show with Kate Bush. I like those sorts of threads running though, pulling themes together. Kate Bush also has *Wow* which is a song about a performer being alone on the stage, again this felt thematically right so I worked with my pianist to open the show with a medley of *Wow/The Red Shoes*.
>
> Suddenly the show had a theme, a through line, new songs and linked lots of my 'best' set pieces together. I needed to simply pad it out a little and find a few ways to keep it varied. The show became *The Red Shoes* and thematically was me exploring an unexpected journey in drag performance, queer life and queer politics with some of my favourite material.

Overview: Hosting and Solo Shows

Before jumping into hosting and solo shows you need to have mastered the craft of performance. Specifically *the audience experience* and *talking on stage*.

- Structure your hosting duties using the ten pointers and you will be ready for every eventuality.
- Keep trying to be the audience's favourite – because a strong host makes everyone relax.
- Watch the show, work the room and tailor the unique live experience that is the show.

Before doing a solo show it's best to have had some experience doing sets, hosting and some headlining slots so you feel ready. The host is the one who holds a drag show together and that is what you will need to do in a solo show. Rather than preparing the room for the next act you are simply keeping the room with you.

- Structure your show like a long set, think of *peaks and troughs* and the journey you are taking an audience on.

- Try to incorporate something old and something new. Something old that is a 'greatest hit' to get the new audiences to know who you are. Something new to reward and excite your regular audience members.
- Use your *Repertoire List* as a starting point to find themes and ideas you might want to explore further.

Hopefully you are feeling ready to get out there and get gigging now! But sometimes the jump from hypothetical to actually doing it can be a challenge. It's time to get moving!

Notes

1. *Me* in interview with *Michael Twaits*, July 2024. See Part IV for full interview.
2. *Adam All* in interview with Michael Twaits, July 2024. See Part V for full interview.
3. *Me* in interview with *Michael Twaits*, July 2024. See Part IV for full interview.

Michael Twaits photographed backstage at the Royal Vauxhall Tavern by Carol J Moir – I hadn't done the course, but there was a photographer with time so...

23
Don't Rain on My Parade: Onwards

This handbook has split the art of drag down into manageable chapters hopefully giving direction, inspiration and clarity. If you're working through cover to cover – well done. But drag isn't linear and drag doesn't need to fit neatly into categories. One of the biggest rules of drag is to keep playing: fuck around with formats, find new ways of creating work and new ways of representing yourself. Don't let anyone hold you back!

This chapter is a few last pieces of advice, examples and a final exercise to help you remember to keep creating, keep working and to make your own rules! A few final thoughts to leave you with before you head to the stage. Don't let the structure of this book make you think that drag needs to be formulaically structured: put some jokes in a song; edit a track that fuses lip-sync and live vocals; create an alter-ego who does a vast range of impersonations; impersonate an icon whilst parodying another icon's songs! Why not? There are endless possibilities you can play with, none of them need to fit neatly into one category. When you need help: dip into a few relevant chapters and see what they can unlock.

Finding new material for a straight song or lip-sync can be quite straight forward: hear a song, like it, give it a go, rehearse it. For more bespoke pieces, mash-ups, spoken word, parodies and mixed discipline showstoppers they quite often take a lot of time, craft and development. Often you'll lose confidence in something along the way, that's fine, take a day or two away from it and come back with fresh eyes. (It doesn't always come easily.) Exciting work often leaves an audience asking *"where did that come from?"* The answer is usually hard work and a brave performer.

Don't Hold Yourself Back

When an idea excites you, run with it! Don't ignore some gold because you aren't *certain* how it will fit in within your style of performance. Artists often don't know what an idea is going to develop into until it has had a chance grow; with thought, working through on paper, in rehearsal and on its feet. Don't endgame and worry about who will, or won't programme it. Good work will find a place to be shown! Enjoy the journey and see what you create.

You have a notebook full of rough ideas, and hopefully a few crazy ideas amongst them. You also have your *In Development Repertoire List* (see *Chapter 6: Building a Set, Range and Repertoire*), full of varied ideas which still need development! Dip in to them! Read over them regularly, you never know what you unlock when you come back to a concept with fresh eyes. Challenge yourself to not only pick-up and run with the ideas you can already see working. Invest in crazy! Step out of your comfort zone: if you are thinking *"I've not seen anything like that before"* – great! – work on it and soon you could have an audience all saying exactly the same thing! *"I've not seen anything like that before"* is a bold and dynamic place to be working from.

DOI: 10.4324/9781003498797-26

I am best known for my hosting work and singing. However, my most well-known 'piece' is *Stonewall*. It is spoken word, poetry (dare I say rap), combined with music. Queer history, politics, flights of fancy and community connection all roll into an impassioned eight minutes. It does not fit in to every event I get booked for. But it is by far my most requested act. (I have actually had to find ways of creating sets that support it so I can turn the eight-minute piece into the crescendo of a twenty-minute or half-hour set.)

However, if I sat down to write something bookable, that was classic *Michael Twaits*, this would never have been what I envisioned. Let your creativity flow without worrying too much about the result. When I first performed *Stonewall* I was told by a producer it wasn't a very bookable act, *niche* was the word used. But good work finds its audience, and I made sure that producer saw the video of me performing it in Trafalgar Square to 15,000 backed by *The London Gay Big Band*. We've worked together since and I keep bringing new work to him and asking if it's "too niche".

I didn't intend to write that type of piece. I was just playing and being creative, it's good work so it found an audience.

In the world of drag everyone is a critic. Learn to ignore the noise and focus on yourself, your own journey and keep creating work you want to create!

Outside the Box Ideas

In the decade of drag showcases at the RVT, for *The Art of Drag* course, performers have created talking trees, sheep, a personified cucumber, belly dancers, one aerialist, puppets, a man-eating vagina, priests, nuns, tarts and vicars. Audiences have had tampons thrown at them, performers sat on them, have got very wet, have laughed, cried, been seduced and ridiculed. Most frequently they have asked: *"what the fuck was that?"* Performers are making brave work, redefining what a live performance can be, redefining what drag can be and breaking expectation.

Usually when creating work you decide on the style of what you want to create (a new song, a new comedy set, a new poem, etc). You can of course return to the specific chapter, looking for an idea, or exercise to get it going. However, sometimes the most exciting work defies categorisation. Drag acts are chameleons of the arts, keep changing, try to create something different, be unique.

Combining a few different performance styles into one piece, fusing together different styles, can create exciting work that is memorable and doesn't want to be labelled. It's time for one final exercise, one last creative exploration. This is an exercise I used a lot when creating solo theatre shows but many of the results, such as my *Stonewall* piece, have grown out of this and become standards in my drag repertoire. The exercise is my own development (and slightly mis-remembering) of a *Split Britches* exercise documented with Dr Sue-Ellen Case when they were discussing how they created their work. It was 20 years ago when I studied *Queer Theatre 101* under Dr Sue-Ellen Case at UCLA but what I discovered about myself, performance and my community at that time has completely shaped who I am as a person as a performer. This exercise was probably my biggest creative take away, and I am certain I have adapted it, forgotten bits and created something that looks nothing like their original exercise! I hope it opens as many creative doors for you as it has for me and you adapt it to work its magic for you!

EXERCISE 1: DO/SAY

You will need: Your notebook, your pen and your wildest dreams.

As an artist I hope you all have big aspirations of things you would love to *do* in drag and a long list of things you would love to *say* or explore on-stage. It's time to note them down. Draw up a quick table like Table 23.1 and fill in some *do* and some *say* options.

Don't worry about logistics such as how or why at this point – let this be your dream list. (For inspiration return to the table you created in *Chapter 1 – A New Beginning – Exercise 2*.) The *do* column is a place you could put any of those things you have always wanted to do on-stage. Some may just be fun things, visually exciting moments, or tricks you've seen on-stage and think you want to do! Or something you have always wanted to see on-stage but no-one else has been brave enough! The *say* could be political, irreverent, personal or rousing. It might be which political party to vote for, it might be your feelings about soup! Whatever it is that suits your brand, alter-ego and want to explore. But make it something you feel passionately about!

Do	Say
Aerial act	Never vote Republican
Juggle	Abolish the monarchy
Spoken word	I wish Starburst were still called Opel Fruits
Dress like a sheep	*High By The Beach* is Lana Del Rey's best song
Be soaking wet on-stage	Kate Bush is a national treasure

Table 23.1 An Example of a Table Assigning Things a Performer May Wish to "*Do*" and "*Say*".

The columns can go on forever. Do not limit yourself, keep adding more. The fun part is to now try and connect an idea on the left to an idea on the right. It's a case of trial and error, playing it though and seeing if there are any possible links between the two columns.

Brainstorm, theorise, daydream and have fun trying to find the strongest and weakest of links between the two. The point of this exercise is to find a creative *in* that excites you and an idea that will work on-stage. No-one is checking that you followed the rules (only one *do* meeting one *say*). Ideas will merge.

Once the idea is being developed it may lose one of the two initial elements – this is fine. This is a creative starting block – don't screw yourself to it – leap from it onto a new creative journey and see what you come up with. And then return and take another leap.

> I populated the columns above with some quick examples. How might I link them?
>
> An aerial act is a camp dream for many, but visibly involves spinning, or a pendulum. This might be swinging between two sides of an argument, or a political party. Also an aerial act is often up high so I could link to *High by the Beach*[1] in a punny way.
>
> Juggling, will I be good at this? No. Do I need to be good at it? It depends on the concept. Could each throw be representing the different reasons the UK have a monarchy? And my failure shows that if all elements are not in equilibrium then it loses momentum and falls apart...A stretch but who knows until we explore it! I'm noting it down and will let it brew!

> I don't know why I would want to dress like a sheep, but let's imagine I have a high fashion concept for it, or perhaps a high camp sheep concept, I could use Kate Bush's *Dream of Sheep*. Or sing *High by the Beach* and do a bleating sound on the word '*beeeeeeaach*' or perhaps it should be a mash up of the two. Are there any other bleatingly obvious links?

All of my ideas are clearly ridiculous and far-fetched; that's a wonderful ground to play in! Not everything needs to be obvious, straight-forward or expected. Hopefully from this exercise you have created a few unique idea embryos that you can let brew for a while, keep thinking about, find a way to get them on their feet and see if you can term them into a piece for you which is a bit of a departure from other pieces. It may be that during rehearsal the piece becomes a little tamer and doesn't feel as far-fetched. Great! Again, don't endgame. This exercise is just a simple go-to for generating new ideas to be creative without limiting yourself in style or form. Get on stage and do it!

You Will Never Be Ready, So Just Do It

Actually, you are ready. *Book the gig.* There is no time where a performer feels *fully* prepared or finished. Your craft is always improving, the alter-ego evolving, your point-of-view always refining. You will always have ideas for new bits, new pieces and new ways to create a live experience for an audience. But because you never feel ready, it's easy to hold yourself back. You need to throw yourself on-stage, possibly unsuccessfully, pick yourself up, review what happened and do it again. Repeatedly. That is the pattern I've been following for nearly 20 years, it's become a career but it hasn't got easier, because I refuse to play safe and just repeat the same process. Improving your craft is a lifetime commitment. And if you are anything like me the better you get the more critical of yourself you will become.

This handbook can help you prepare but it will be even more useful once you have started to get on-stage. One of the things I love most about the art of live performance is that it is constantly shifting. After every gig, even during the gig, I can make tiny micro-adjustments to improve the performance, my skills and the audience experience. Nothing is finite. But that means it take courage to share it, because you always want that extra bit of rehearsal, or time. Writing this handbook has been a process for me, and I'm reminded of a plaque I saw in a friends recording studio:

> **You can have my album when you prise it out of my cold, dead hand.**

Because I know this will be in print I feel it has to be perfect. I always want one day more, one more chance, there's always a little something I'd like to tweak. That's a good habit to nurture, always strive to be better than the last time. But sometimes you need to hand it over to the audience and let them respond to it. So, I'm putting the final words in this handbook, handing it over to the publishers and already thinking about how I would update it for a second edition.

I want to send you out into the world armed with ideas and inspiration but always with the underlying theme that you are a work in progress. Keep working, keep researching, keep evolving.

One of the concerns I had in writing a book was that it is seen as one person telling everyone what to do. One of the joys of *The Art of Drag Course* is that each week I pull different working drag acts into the room to give a different take on what drag can be, their process and how they do it! I am inspired by my peers, my community and people who are out there making it happen. I asked seven colleagues to talk to me, and you, about their creative process: why and how they do drag, their goals, aspirations and more. It was an eye opening experience for me and much of their wisdom has already been peppered through the book as quotes supporting various thoughts. Within their interviews was an awful lot of advice which has evolved into a top tips section.

It's now your turn to give it the audience, see what they make of it. Book a gig, find an open mic night. Give it to them, and then take it, review it, rework it, before giving it to them again. If you've been working through the handbook academically, keeping notes, researching and rehearsing – well done! But now go to the club, the reality of performance will hit you. I know a lot of the handbook's advice will make more sense after some on-stage experience. Remember: it will not be perfect. That's fine! Come back, review, refine it and then represent it. But at some point you have to take the leap of faith. If you haven't already – now is the time. Book that gig! Take what you have read and developed here into the world. The handbook will be here when you come back.

Have fun!

Snap a lash!

Note

1   I believe *Kintsugi* is actually Lana's best song but I chose a single so more people would be familiar with it and I thought *High By The Beach* gave easier *ins*. (Now, of course, I have ideas about smashing/deconstruction myself and reforming myself as something more beautiful that tells that story…)

Part IV

Praxis in Practice

Adam All/ @adamall_drag Photo: Emma Bailey

24
My Man: Interview with *Adam All*

Adam All is one of the world's most recognisable Drag Kings. A dapper, cheeky chappy with a geek-chic-streak, the embodiment of cartoon flavoured drag. He is a marvellous metrosexual mix of pop and politics. Married, both on and off stage, to his partner and collaborator the delicious drag queen *Apple Derrieres*, they are big fixtures of the UK drag circuit.

I've known *Adam* for over 15 years: a friend, colleague and collaborator. He's been a regular lecturer on *The Art of Drag Course* for the Parody week and we have shared many Pride stages together. He was the first Cabaret Winner of *Pride's Got Talent* in 2014 and was also the first ever drag king to reach the final of *Drag Idol* – the UK's nationwide drag contest. As co-creator and producer of *BoiBox*, one of the country's most successful drag king showcases, Adam champions kings, queers and emerging artists. We spoke about performance, process, persona and parody!

Why Did You Create *Adam All*?

The short answer is because I had to.

The long answer is because I felt I needed to say something. Having been accused of masculinity my whole life, yet denied maleness at every turn: *"you're too butch to be a woman"*, but *"you're not allowed to be strong, achieve masculine things because you're a girl"*. *"Good for a girl, but you'll never really be actually good"*.

I started paying attention to how people behaved, trying to understand *"What is this 'masculinity' that you're accusing me of. Why can't I just be me? Why not? Why is that not good enough? Or acceptable?"*

I studied men, and women. But a lot of the time with men I found an irregularity to what people said men were supposed to be like and what they were actually like.

Adam came about because I felt I had to show my findings and also to redeem myself from all of the accusations, misconceptions and misunderstandings of who I am. Adam came about as a healing method, I suppose. I think that's connected to the trauma of not fitting in. That's really common for queer people, really common for gender nonconforming people.

When Did He First Appear?

I dressed in drag a lot. From 16 right up until I actually started on the stage at 24. My transition from *saying* I was going to do it to *actually* doing it was the push of someone else. It was a drag queen who said *"shut up you, I've given you some backing tracks. You've got six weeks. I've booked you. You are doing it"*.

I was absolutely terrified! I knew I had to do it. I knew it was in me somewhere. Overcoming the massive stage fright; this real fear that you're literally flying in the face of the one thing that people have made you feel shit about your whole life. That was terrifying.

I went into panic mode; I had learned my set, so religiously that, I went into autopilot, tunnel vision. It was all black around my vision, I couldn't see very well, was shaking. I couldn't breathe properly! Full on stage fright for the entire half hour!

I know, after, I was really pleased with myself, because the next day my face hurt from grinning. Because I was *so* pleased – I finally owned it!

Is *Adam* Your Persona? A Character? You?

That's tough. I don't actually know anymore!

It's changed a great deal. To begin with, he was definitely character: *"it's not me I'm playing a character"*. I put the costume on, I go out there and even though it's my script, my voice, my face, it is a character. And so I'm telling you things through the medium of this idiot.

And Adam was an idiot to begin with! The point was, he was *trying* to be masculine and macho in that very toxic, masculine, macho way. And, occasionally he would let it slip down and you would see that underneath he wasn't really like that. That was my point. This is a game. This is a game that men play, and it doesn't make sense. And it's not good for anyone.

I was very rigid, I knew everything about the character. I wrote him like you would a character for a book. I listed his likes and dislikes, wrote about his past jobs and talked about his Mum, how many GCSEs he's got…Adam's a real human being. He's got a whole background. And I did that because that's how I was told to flesh out my characters.

But as he, as *I*, got more comfortable on the stage, I allowed more and more of myself through. To an extent, I think it's more me than character now.

Does He Know He's a Drag King?

You know, I think. Yeah.

Frustratingly, I have to tell my audiences that I am a drag king. Still, after 16 years: *"Hi, I'm Adam All. I'm a drag king"*. I still have to say that at the top of most of my sets, I'd rather I didn't have to, because I don't think he sees himself like that. He sees himself as a guy and his wife enjoying songs and facilitating a party.

For my first five or six years. I was very much against saying I am a drag king. I would just go into character and it would be Adam. I did lose a lot of audiences that way because they were like *"who is this weird guy?"* Because drag kings weren't a known thing.

Now, I make a real big point, I'll say to a host *"make sure you say I'm a drag king"*. I pass quite hard in drag and I think that a lot of people are very, very confused by that.

An *Adam All* Show – What Am I Getting?

Live vocals. You're going to get songs played out in very different contexts, which is going to make you laugh. It's a lot of comedy, and we're going to go on a journey of gender discovery.

It will be full of elation, happiness and joy. At the end of the show, you should come out of there going "*yeah, I feel really happy about who I am because it's okay to be me*".

And that's Adam at his best. You'll probably have quite a sore voice because you probably will sing along. Lots of bangers! Oh, and some stupid costumes as well, for a laugh.

Do You Have a Trademark Piece?

A strip! Probably my *Pants Off* [a parody of *We Don't Have To Take Our Clothes Off* by Jermain Stewart] routine is my calling card. It's probably my most viral video and it places the character most succinctly because it's a *nervous* strip. With a song that's nice and comfortably in my range.

Similar to saying that I'm a drag king, I'm still in a position where I need to show the strings [of how drag is created]. Showing drag is about gender, queerness, that's the point. It's not "*breaking the illusion*", it's a way of getting a point across. Drag queens have done so for millennia by taking their wigs off at the end of a show!

Do You Rehearse? How?

I rehearse rigorously. I certainly rehearse all of my songs to death! I want to know it upside down and inside out.

All of the ad-libs – exactly how the original singer does it. I'm quite fastidious about not adding my own riffs. Doing it the original way. I'm often taking the song out of context: *Somebody to Love*, for example, I'm making it a song about wanking. If I'm true to the original it doesn't distract from the point. The audience just go "*oh, I know this song, I'm focused on you doing your joke*".

I think my mannerisms are one of the things I worked the hardest on. Making sure that I exaggerate his gait, his arm movements, hand movements, all of the mannerisms and facial expressions. I have stood in the bloody mirror and worked on it, because I need this to look right. He's got to feel right to the audience.

How About Rehearsing the Banter?

I don't have to rehearse that as much as I used to! Originally, I wrote the script word for word. I'd write exactly what I wanted to say, and then I would reduce it to bullet points and rehearse it until I was off book. I don't need to do that as much because a lot of those off book pieces are in here [my head].

Also, growing as a performer, I do a lot of hosting of things like karaoke, that can't be rehearsed. That has to be ad-libbed. It just has to be free. You need to learn to be comfortable being completely free in your hosting style. And that's taken a while. But, yeah, I rehearse pretty hard.

Do You Have a Strict Approach to Your Drag, an Ethos?

I've worked really hard on the branding for Adam. Not just because it's easier to sell a product if people recognise it, but, because I'm trying to say what I'm trying to say!

There's a particular flavour, that 'cartoon flavour', an acceptable naughtiness, that has to be right. There are loads of great songs I'd really love to sing, but they just don't fit Adam – it's irritating! I'll spend ages learning a song, thinking, "*this is a really, really great*" but it's not Adam. So, you let go because it doesn't fit.

Do You Have a Pre-Show Routine?

Working with Apple, I really need to, like, connect with her properly. We need to talk through some of the set, maybe even do a little video moment, in character before we go out.

I will want to warm up. I'm a real pacer. When I'm backstage, I get ready really early – I'm worried I won't have enough time or a prop will fail and I will have to fix it. I don't like to be rushed! I like to stretch, there'll be some sort of physical warm up, some sort of vocal warm up, some sort of lubrication and pacing.

Any stage fright, nerves or anticipation I have learned to recognise as the same chemicals as excitement. They are the same. If you tell yourself before you go and "oh I'm really nervous", then you'll be nervous but if you go, "oh I'm really excited" then…

Do You Critique Your Own Work

I'm my own worst enemy. I really am, but I'm not as bad as my wife! She critiques the living daylights out of me, all of the time and very, very rarely will pay me a compliment.

I know when I'm good. I know when I'm on fire. I know when I'm doing well, but I also know when I fuck up. And I do heavily critique myself when I fuck up – it can take me days to get over.

How do You Find Inspiration for New Work?

If I don't know what to do, but need to make something new, the best thing is to stick the radio on. 80s and 90s music is pretty good because there's a lot of innuendo hidden in the songs. It isn't too blatant. Today's music, is a little bit too obvious, it's not funny. But in the 90s, there's a lot of stuff that you could misread as being about something else – which is where I like to find my little treasure trove.

I often will listen until something makes me laugh. If that song is in my range, and it makes me laugh – what could I do with this?

Recently a lot of my acts have been centred around costume, specifically revisiting costumes I wanted to have when I was a little person. The big gold knight that I made very recently was very specifically something I wanted to own as a kid. So it was living my seven-year-old dream!

Performers or Pieces that Influence Your Work?

The youngsters these days are a massive inspiration. There's so many drag kings coming up with fantastic ideas. I watched Dairy King for the first time the other day and I'm now slightly, stalky obsessed! Genius. I feel the same way about Oedipussi Rex. And Len Blanco.

There's loads of them with these really fucking great ideas that make me laugh. Very rarely am I ever on a line up with another drag king, so I don't get to watch other people's work. It's really nice to see them shine – it makes me very happy.

Anything You Wished You Learnt Sooner? Or a Top Tip to Finish On?

For the most part, it's to do with confidence. It grows with experience, I *now* know I can trust myself. There are moments where as long as I know who I'm introducing, or what I'm doing next, as long as I know what song is coming up, I can just trust that something relevant will come out of my mouth! And in the moment, I can feel the energy in the room and I should be able to say something relevant and, at least partially, funny. I can just relax and let that just be. But when I started, there's no way I could have done that. I would have just gone blank, which is why I wrote all my scripts!

Final thoughts…

Don't be underprepared.

Don't be an idiot.

Safety pins! You will need safety pins!

Simply Barbra /www.simplybarbra.com Photo: Devon Cass at devoncass.com

25
My Name Is Barbra: Interview with *Simply Barbra*

Simply Barbra is the worlds premiere Barbra Streisand impressionist. Performed by Steven Brinberg who brings her to life with warmth, humour and uncanny vocals *Simply Barbra* balances the fine line of pastiche, parody and pathos. Barbra fans come for the music and come back for the laughs.

As life-long Streisand fan (had you noticed?) I have had the pleasure of seeing Steven perform numerous times over the past 20 years. We spoke after a recent London performance about perfectionism, parody and finding fame in Streisand's inner circle.

Who Is *Simply Barbra*?

My *Barbra* is basically Barbra if she were in an alternative universe! And maybe had a bigger sense of humour about the world…and herself.

How did *Simply Barbra* Come about as an Act for You?

I was singing as myself, doing my own act, and I always knew I could do voices. I made a little segment where I did a bunch of other voices: it was Barbra, Julie Andrews and Cher. And Barbra was my favourite, and she got the best response.

One club owner in New York said, "*Why don't you do a whole act as Barbra?*" And I'm like "*I don't know if I could do that? I wouldn't know how to get made up or do anything and how would that work?*" And he said "*just try it, you know*". I put together an act pretty quickly. And I've been doing it ever since. It's crazy. It took off, you know. It's kind of amazing to me!

So Drag Was Never a Plan?

No. Not really, I did get dressed up as Mary Poppins when I was a little kid, just for fun. But no, it didn't occur to me.

An Evening with *Simply Barbra* – What Am I Getting?

It's like you're going to see Barbra: if she were in a little slightly altered state. To some people, they'll just get all the songs they know out of it. Others will be like "*but you're so funny. It's much funnier than she is*".

It's funny, when I started, I think I was more out there, imagining how she'd behave and everything. And as I've gone through time, we've sort of blended. I've worked a lot with the director of her concerts, and I've literally seen her do little *bits* in her shows that are her doing me, doing her, you know?

We've evolved. She's sort of morphed into me and I've morphed into her. I don't know if I've gotten more serious, but now I'll do a lot of 100% serious songs like *Send In The Clowns*. In the beginning, I think I was afraid: "*we've got to have a joke in there somewhere*". I didn't want to take myself too seriously. And now it's sort of like we're almost one.

Is There a Specific Calling Card or Trademark Piece?

When I started, we created this thing called the *Pioneer Album*, and it was Barbra talking all about the Pilgrims in America, and the pie, and I describe churning butter and being dressed like a farm wife and all this stuff…that became a medley of other songs. And that was what people were talking about when I started to get 'buzz' during my, you know, 15 minutes of notoriety in New York!

Stephen Sondheim, when he came to the show (he would send people to the show, it was unbelievable like "*oh, I'm sending Harold Prince and Arthur Laurents*") *Pioneer Album* is what I think he liked most, you know, because it was a parody.

I think that was what I was known for, and also the fact that I would throw in all these *other* voices when people were expecting just 100% Barbra.

It's Amazing When an Impersonator is Breaking Character to Do Impersonations

Yes! I'm trying to not break the spell. People say "*I closed my eyes, I thought it was her*". I'm like "*that's wonderful*". But then all of a sudden, you have to buy me as her, as Anthony Newley or somebody else that I'm doing. Somehow people accept it and really enjoy it. I guess because it's funny.

It Is Funny; I Laugh Just Thinking of Your Version of *Niagra*

Haha! I sent my CD to Marvin Hamlisch, which is how I started working with him, and (you know, he wrote *Niagra*), he loved it. He thought it was so great. And then I sort of stopped doing it once Viagra wasn't front page news anymore. That was sort of old, you know? But I suppose that could still fit.

How Do You Prepare and Rehearse for a Show?

I like to rehearse with the pianist, quite a lot. I mean, even when it's songs that I know, it's just good to go over them, to just make sure you have it. It's very handy, having somebody that you've worked with for a long time because there's just a shorthand that's, you know, if you screw up, if they screw up – it's pretty easy. That's pretty great.

What's not rehearsed sometimes is the dialogue. I have a general idea of what I'm going to say between the songs, but then something will just strike me as funny. And, you know, somebody sneezed, "*Gesundheit*" and then I went back to the song. That's more unrehearsed than the singing.

Rehearsing is important though, especially when we have a guest performer. They want to make sure they know all the stuff that's necessary: playing with the hands and the hair for example. I had one guy who I was singing with, and when I did the hair bit, afterwards he said "*oh, is my hair messy?*" I'm like "*No, that's supposed to be The Way We Were*". I guess he had no point of reference…so yeah. Rehearsal is good.

Do You Have a Specific Approach to *Barbra*?

Until I walk on the stage, I'm still me. Once the light hits, that's where I'm very careful to never break character. No matter what happens, I will still respond as Barbra. It's still theatre because I'm not myself. I'm playing somebody else. So it's very different rules than when I used to do me as myself, talking about myself. And it's it's totally theatre…of a different kind.

Do You Have a Pre-Show Routine?

Well, just being quiet. I want to look after my voice. And I like to make sure I have enough time to get ready. I find that whole aspect such a challenge. And when we were on tour recently in the UK, one venue wouldn't let us in quite early enough to do the soundcheck and get ready. And I was like "*that's not good*".

Do You Critique Your Own Work

I am like Barbra! I want everything to be the absolute best, and not for any other reason than I want it to be the best, that somebody should have the best, you know? Why not the best? Yeah, that's a good thing that she always got criticized for. But I think it's a good thing. Perfection.

I like to have the show videoed if it's possible, but it's not always possible. Then I always really tend to look at them. Well, I have this this kid who sort of works on a TikTok page for me. She grabs all these videos that come out and puts them on, and I usually say "*just show them to me first*". Because that's being very Barbra. If I didn't like the sound on that one, or if I didn't like my hair on that one, then I might veto it!

It is interesting looking at it and older videos. They just uncovered, after 24 years, Stephen Sondheim's 70th birthday concert at the Library of Congress, where I performed. And I'd never seen the video before: I was introduced by Nathan Lane! It's really quite great. Except I do remember that night, there was not enough reverb – that's where I become like her! 24 years later, that clip is still pretty great and everyone's responded well to it. Except I'm still like her: "*well, that was good…but, you know, the sound really wasn't very good*". I can't let that go, because it could have been better! I'm very much like her in that sense, perfectionism.

How Often Do You Update or Develop the Show?

Well, in recent years, it's been helpful, having all these milestones: we've already done a 50th anniversary of *Funny Girl*, of *Dolly*, of *Clear Day*…and then the year after that 50th anniversary of *A Star Is Born*. And then I can start doing, you know, 60th anniversaries…that makes it really easy to structure everything around that. Still having material beyond what's being celebrated, but that becomes the focus, if you will, for the show.

Then when I perform in a place that I've never performed before, like next week in Rhode Island, I don't really need a specific theme. And it's just billed as *Simply Barbra*. Most of that will still be included in there, but I might, you know, bring back something that I haven't done in years because they've never seen it before, never seen me before.

There's endless inspiration in what I can do. And it never gets old to me. You know, it's the classic case of, when you're on stage, like in legit theater in eight shows a week, that audience hasn't seen it before. That's how you keep it fresh. I've sung *People* a billion times at this point, and it's always new to me. I don't think I've ever been accused of walking through the show, I wouldn't know how to. And I wouldn't know how to cancel a show. I mean, I've powered through a couple of times but I have to do it!

Performers or Pieces That Influence Your Work?

I grew up without the internet, and I went to the library, I taught myself. I went to every theatre that showed old movies, and I was like *"I'm going to see every single Bette Davis movie"*. And I did, and was fascinated by people who were long gone when I was a kid. You know, the real Fanny Brice, and Carole Lombard.

Obviously the other icons, like Barbra, were always a strong influence from Judy and Liza, and Carol Burnett was a big influence to me. Then people like Julie Wilson, who became my good friend, such a wonderful singer/actress. And, gosh, I mean, I went to see Eydie Gormé, I loved her so much. Great voices have always fascinated me. Mostly female voices, except I really did like Anthony Newley, which is why I think I can 'do' him.

Anything You Wished You Learnt Sooner?

You know, it's funny. I mean, again, when I started, I didn't really *know* that there was no end date to this! I think I just thought, let's just try this out now and see what goes on.

I think I might have been more calm, even though I am sort of a calm well, I'm a contradiction. I'm calm, but I'm neurotic. But I'm outwardly calm, I never lose my temper. I think there were some times when I started where there were some various dramas along the way with managers and craziness and you just learn to say *"who cares?"* You just sort of let things go. I would have let a few more things go!

I know that people are always like, what would you tell your young self? I would tell my young self – I should have started sooner because I could *always* sounded like her! And maybe if I had started earlier when she was still, even more, popular…who knows what might have happened?

Ada Campe / @adacampe by Alexis Dubus Photography

26
Keepin' Out of Mischief Now: Interview with *Ada Campe*

An award-winning variety artiste *Ada Campe* is the alter-ego of Naomi Paxton. *Ada* is a fully realised character – a comedian, a host and a magician with a mischievous grin and a hunger to get in amongst the audience.

I've worked with *Ada* over the past few years on the London cabaret circuit, seen her in pantomime and shared a dressing room mirror more than a few times. She has also been the guest lecturer for Character Comedy on the course *The Art of Drag*. Currently *Ada* is working on her fifth full-length show – *Big Duck Energy* – we caught up to talk character, craft and cabaret.

Who Is *Ada Campe*?

Ada is a larger than life, quite old school, variety artiste. I imagine she's in her mid-60s. She's quite sprightly, has lived an interesting life, loves all things theatrical, and can't wait to be an overnight success! She does cabaret, comedy, magic and is very interactive. She predominantly does shows for adults but also performs for a family audience and almost always does a clean show.

I've got quite a specific backstory for her, but that's mainly from developing her solo shows. I'm developing her fifth solo show now for Edinburgh. There is a core storyline, a core history to her that I keep exploring and delving into. Her backstory is in a coherent and plausible timeline – she's not transplanted in time. I want her to be absolutely of the now. I wanted to put her at an older age than me by a couple of decades to open up more possibilities for story-telling and have her as a confident older woman on stage.

I never mention her direct family. She doesn't have kids, and I've never mentioned her parents. Everything is always once removed, so it's the found family or great aunts, you know, influential adults that were and are around her that aren't necessarily blood relations.

She is a moveable feast in many ways, because I need to be able to write more for her. I don't think she has the pressure like a more traditional standup comic does to know what's going on in the world and comment on it. I think it's slightly different for Ada, because there isn't an expectation that she's going to talk about the news. However if there are key national or world events happening that are extraordinary, I feel it's a disconnect to completely ignore them on stage. You can say to the audience, "*I'm not going to talk about this*", but they know that I know it's happening. So she is still absolutely in the present.

Is She Far Removed from You?

Ada can push boundaries that Naomi is not prepared to. I often find in the moment that Ada is quicker than me, bolder than me, in terms of comic responses and improvisation because that mask is on. She cannot help but be broadly a leftie lesbian, because that's what's going here on the inside. She is fantastical in look and in sound already, so she's already sort of once removed from me and the real world.

It all has to be me, because I'm doing it I suppose! But it's me without my specific insecurities or inhibitions. Really free – free to express myself in a way that I obviously don't feel I can do in real life. She does surprise me sometimes, but I think it's really just my own inhibitions. I'd love to be that energetic and that daft and that loud!

What Brought You to Cabaret?

I have early memories of being on stage, of very much enjoying not having to be myself. Memories of going to see a pantomime at a local theatre and being called up on stage – and I remember seeing that the Dame or the Ugly Sisters all had enormous amounts of makeup on! And I hadn't seen that from the audience. The audience saw one thing, one angle, but I became part of that world because I could see it from on stage. And I felt thrilled at the prospect of that, that one could transform oneself, one could be so boldly playful. I loved that energy. I loved comedy and variety as a teenager – I used to come to London to see the Comedy Store Players and the Players Music Hall shows. They were structured shows but the audience was a key part of both – the audience was included and necessary.

Comedy and theatre allowed me to escape my own physical persona, including what I looked like. I was really insecure about my physical self as a kid so that was hugely exciting for me. At drama school I ended up getting involved in physical theatre a lot, because I had dance training and knew how to use my body and voice. But it wasn't very joyful, physical but not joyful. I had theatre jobs in plays and shows for years, but when I began to work in comedy a little bit more, through doing character stuff in some radio and sketch work, and eventually through doing some cabaret, I found that there was a beast in me that had been waiting to come out! My first experience of performing in cabaret was in a late-night magic show and it felt like a space where anything was possible, where the audience and the performers created something special and unique that had an immediacy, an energy that I was and am drawn to.

I've a Ticket to See *Ada Campe*, What Can I Expect?

If possible I'd like to work with a live pianist or live band and do a welcoming song. I want to come out looking fantastic, I want to greet the audience and I want to get a couple of early laughs in. I want to make something specific about where we are or what's happening. I've got stories where you can 'insert name of town here', that kind of thing. At the top of Ada's longer form solo shows I love to tell a shaggy-dog story. Ada has a series of theatrical shaggy-dog stories that introduce her schtick and set the mood for the themes of the show. You spend seven minutes listening to a story that ends in a terrible pun, which helps puncture any sense of superiority!

And then I probably want to do something interactive. Something with the audience, I suppose that has ended up mostly being a magic trick, but, I'd want to do something with them. The sets are very different depending on the genre of the show, and the time constraints. If I'm MCing a comedy gig then I probably won't sing and just do gags and audience interaction instead. If it's a variety or cabaret gig then I'll sing and do magic.

How Do You Rehearse?

I don't rehearse enough. I'd love to rehearse more.

I feel like there aren't many opportunities for us to rehearse full out. Until you put it in front of an audience, you just don't know what the beats are, what people find funny, what works on stage, the logistics of what you're going to do, the sight-lines – any of that stuff! You have to do it with an audience, it has to grow as it happens.

I'd love to rehearse more, but I think often and especially for comedy you just have to do it in space with humans and work it up through trying bits live. My stuff isn't as set or visual as a circus act, or a burlesque act, something where it's a set piece to a musical track. I always want to be interactive and I always want to refer to the audience, even if it's quite scripted. I'm listening to them, I'm not listening to me.

Do You Have a Specific Approach to Becoming *Ada*?

I will growl before I go on stage, a little Ada growl because it makes me feel mischievous. I want to come in with a naughty grin on my face and be looking at the audience with curiosity.

Because I have put a lot of makeup on and also because I do vocal warm up, that sort of is my preparation. If I can listen to or see the audience before going on stage that's ideal to get a feel of the mood of the gig.

As time has gone on I've tried as much as possible not to be tricky and not to need things. When I first started I would wear gloves, black gloves, because I'd developed this whole thing "*she'd never have my hands! She'd have big, long nails*". I could see what kind of hands she'd have, and they wouldn't be my hands. The gloves stopped me doing some magic tricks but I couldn't perform without them. But one day at my first Edinburgh Fringe as Ada I ended up having to go on stage and do the show without them for some reason. And since then, I've not looked back!

I'd love a lovely dressing room and of course, I'd love a coffee and a fan! I'd like things that make me feel calm, that make me feel happy, feel focused. But I don't need them, because I never want to have to blame a bad performance on an inanimate object.

Do You Critique Your Own Work?

I record new stuff, mostly on audio for myself, on my phone. If I can get people to do it on video for me, when setting new things, great! I'm massively critical, hugely critical of myself, of timing. Hugely critical of sentence structure, always looking to improve and edit, nothing is ever completely set in stone. I'm always finding new rhythms. And I feel when stuff is set in stone, then you lose the energy of it because you find yourself in a rhythm. The audience can tell that it's a 'bit'.

Every time I'm in Edinburgh I try and audio record almost every solo show. So I can listen back to it on the walk in or the walk out, or I can come back to a moment and go, "*why isn't that working? Why did that work?*" I'm constantly trying to improve it.

How Does *Ada* Relate to an Audience?

If it's just me alone on stage, it's investigation. I always want to be in charge. I don't want to be mean to them or judgmental about their appearance. Broadly speaking, I want an audience to feel welcome so that they're going to do what Ada says! And I think that's just a sheer force of personality thing. Her expectation is that the audience are going to do exactly what she says. I am asking, but the expectation is that the response is going to be positive.

That's evolved over time. I used to come on in a much more sort of mysterious and creepy way and allow the silence to hang. But when it's a shorter set, you can't afford that time. Now I just want to come on and grab them.

How Do You Go About Creating a New Set or Show?

I have a permanent list of notes on my phone for when I think of funny little bits, ideas or names. Then if I'm looking for inspiration I'll go back and look through that. Some show ideas come from specific props or objects, or bits of research into theatre histories.

Are There Specific Performers or Pieces That Influence Your Work?

I didn't have a telly when I was young so mostly was influenced by films, books, music, radio and live shows. I loved the emotions and word play of the *Side by Side by Sondheim* record – an eight-year-old clinging to the radiator, going "*good times and bum times*" – and I loved Carol Burnett's physicality and comedy in the film *Annie*, that level of freedom and relaxation, confidence and experience!

I always was drawn to larger-than-life characters, to a kind of broad physical looseness that is just incredibly communicative. I was lucky, actually, to grow up in a time where women were doing comedy on TV. I missed the era of Joyce Grenfell but Maureen Lipman's books made me laugh lots. Loved the film *Stepping Out* with Liza Minelli – again lots of broad character comedy in that. Loved Terri Garr in *Tootsie*. Victoria Wood, *Acorn Antiques*, *French and Saunders*, of course. Patricia Routledge in *Keeping Up Appearances* and as Kitty. Josie Lawrence was a huge influence. I saw her in the *Comedy Store Players Live* but also on TV in *Whose Line Is It Anyway*.

I worked box office when Lily Savage was playing Miss Hannigan in *Annie* at the Victoria Palace Theatre and loved watching how playful Paul could be as Lily. The audience had a relationship with Lily and so while the story of the show was happening there was also a story going on between Lily and the audience, and I thought that was really interesting.

When Ada first did panto, I was so curious to see what it was like for the character to be playing a character. I loved it – it had a different energy. It was wonderful. This year will be my third panto as Ada!

Anything You Wish You Knew When You Started That You Know Now?

I wish I had sung earlier. I'd been so scared to do it and I'm an idiot! It's opened up so many more opportunities. It's fun for storytelling, and now I can't believe I waited so long.

I definitely should have been queerer sooner too. More openly out as Ada years ago! I don't know why I wasn't…well, I do. It's about confidence really. She's out and proud now!

And just to chill out…you know. Enjoy the moments. The only way to get better is having stage time, and being prepared to fail and carry on.

Le Fil / @iamlefil Photo: Scallywag Fox

27
The Way You Make Me Feel: Interview with *Le Fil*

Le Fil is UK drag artist, creative and pop-culture connoisseur. A cultural mixing pot, your favourite Chinese Yorkshireman, whose influences range from the Spice Girls to Terence Koh. His work transcends simple classification: fusing art forms, fashions and cultures to create unique live, artistic experiences. Drag is just one step on a conceptual journey through gender, politics and art.

Le Fil is known for his long-standing relationship with *Sink The Pink,* touring with Mel C and appearing on *Drag Race UK* and *Canada Vs The World*. I sat down with *Le Fil* shortly before the later aired to discuss pop-culture, pop-sculpture and a unique *Filosophy* of life!

Who Is *Le Fil*?

A pop artist and performer who uses drag as part of my work. My pronouns are he/him/they, in and out of drag, because I think a lot of my work, from now and right back when I was at art school, was about how to *re-vision* gender and how to *reinterpret* it, in a more political way. Essentially, smash gender stereotypes like how long a man's hair should be.

I am trying to assert that however feminine I may look, I am still a guy. It's a political thing. Which is why my name, Le Fil, is the masculine appropriation of la fille (the girl) in French. It's my artistic play on it, but it's also a shortened version of my name, Philip. It also means *The Thread*, which I think is weaving through all my disciplines I've ever done: ceramics, musical theatre, fashion, editorial and then drag…so that's my artistic entity.

And When Did You Decide on Drag?

Drag encompasses a lot of genres that I'm interested in. I always wanted to be a pop-star, but I also loved to design clothes, make performance art or perform other people's music. And I enjoy working in cabaret or theatre, as well as adverts or TV – and so, my career has evolved in a way that allowed for all that to happen. That's the beauty of drag, that it's still rooted in the underground so the potential of it is limitless. Your work is whatever you carve it to be. The freedom of drag is that it's not a genre, it's a creative expression that can fuel all the wider genres you want to be a part of.

Prior to drag, I was playing with my gender, but also thinking: "*I can expand the idea of what drag is*". It doesn't necessarily have to be about female impersonation. For me, it never was. Drag was about the amplification of authenticity and being able to be me, on a more heightened level. That's what pulled me into the world of drag, being the over-the-top version of myself.

DOI: 10.4324/9781003498797-31

Is That Who *Le Fil* Is, a Heightened Version of You?

The only thing that is different between Philip and Le Fil is, when I'm cooking in my house naked or something like that! That's the bits that you don't see. Whereas as soon as I switch on: the look in my mirror, I'm already feeling *Le Fil*…and for me it was always, an extension of me rather than a character.

It's the heightened version that you put out in public, but it's still very much me. It's just the me that I present, or I choose to present. I just wanted to be myself.

I've a Ticket to a *Le Fil* Show, What Am I Getting?

I have often called my shows *Pop Gigs With Extras!* Performance art: part concert, part installation. A mix of doing numbers and my music but told through twisted poetry or spoken word, loads of different things. I imagine it almost being Madonna meets Marina Abramović! In an ideal world, I would have all those elements of play.

Is There a Le Fil Trademark Piece?

I've written and released my own songs, but I think my actual trademark piece is just wafting my hair back and forth. I'm now known for using my own hair, which is so rare in drag – so people will expect that I'll be whipping my hair back and forth. When I was doing *Sink The Pink* nights, everyone expected me to lip-sync to Loreen's *Euphoria* as I performed that all the time, with lots of red organza. I call it organza-nography. I love dancing and wafting a piece of organza around myself. To make myself feel really beautiful.

Do You Rehearse? How?

It really depends on the show, so if I was just doing the lip-sync, like *Euphoria*, because I've done it so often, then it's ingrained in my body and I'm not having to think too much about it.

However, when I'm doing live stuff and I'm singing live, doing hosting or everything like that, I definitely rehearse. I want to sing my song a few times earlier in the day just to get my vocals up, because I notice personally, if I haven't warmed up. I will literally sing something to the ground if I'm learning something new. I want to get to the point where it's second nature, so I can always dip in and out of a song: be able to say something live and come back into it again.

Anything that I can control, I will rehearse in advance. I always rehearse my speech, I want to try and know which bits they might heckle or interact with. And then try to anticipate retorts, so that I can get a few answers ready to go if needed. As much as everything seems really organic, I try as much as I can to plan it.

And How Did You Rehearse for Drag Race, All Those Lip Syncs for Example?

Oh my God! I absolutely could not wing it! It's like 20 songs plus! I know you're familiar with the songs; we all know *Dancing Queen*. But do we actually know every lyric and every word? That was the difference. It was having to go back to songs that I was familiar with and learn it academically. Look at the lyrics, figure out, line by line. And then when I was doing that in my head at the same time, I could think of movement or think of how I want to deliver it. Does that song have a concept that I could turn visually into something? Can I make that my lip-sync about something, have a message?

Do You Have an Approach to Your Drag, an Ethos or Mantra?

It was always about new ways of seeing myself: My gender or identity, or how can I push myself to the pop-culturist-max. That's what I think about every time I go on, even on *Drag Race*.

My lyrics are all about my *Le Filosophical* book – a book of my personal philosophy I try to live by. It was always pushing that, and I think about that, but also think about the fact that I want to be an *Androgynous Asian Sensation*, "*your AAS*", and all that, fun stuff. It's really going out and being my most androgynous, philosophical, self. That's what I love.

Do You Have a Pre-Show Routine?

Everyone always takes the piss out of me because I like drinking hot water before I go on stage.

I want to properly warm up, I want to do my stretches. I'm going to do some of my tongue twists around my mouth, to make sure that I'm warm. My rider is really easy, so I'm surprised I'm not booked more!

Do You Critique Your Own Work?

I think the critique for me comes in rehearsal period more. By the time I present it, it's already been worked out: It's living, it's organic, so I'm not as harsh with myself. It's the rehearsal period where I'm the harshest. I will video everything, watch it back, and rework. But when I'm live and say something sounded kind of flat, "*whatever*", it was part of the whole show, no one's going to really know. "*Move on. Be in the moment*".

How Do You Get Creative and Find Inspiration?

My work is mainly within music, I'd say that's where I feel most creative. Usually it's about songwriting, mostly that really comes when I'm in the shower. In the most mundane parts of the day, where I'm just doing repetitive things. Most of my ideas come then without mood boards, and it's usually something in the background of my brain that's gone in by osmosis that comes to the front.

Things like *Drag Race*, where they are saying "*we need this outfit*". I need to be able to absorb that and send it into my brain's process. I need to research as much as I can. That stuff becomes the background work again, and then I go back to the shower. But I do mood boards, I read stuff, I read text, I read as much as I can, but also I *have* to give myself a deadline to get things moving and then that kickstarts the process. Then I'll reflect, re-do and keep on that cycle until it's done!

Performers or Pieces That Influence Your Work?

From an early age, *The Spice Girls*! Any performance that they did – "*Wow! There's a northern girl from Leeds there!*" I'm from Brighouse and that's the town near me, that was relatable.

But then I think as soon as I moved to art college and started doing stuff, my points of reference were Andy Warhol, Matthew Barney and Terrence Koh, a Chinese-Canadian artist who does black and white sculpture about life, death, sex – all the big things! But his work also exists in pop culture and fashion: he did a performance with Gaga, and I was like, "*wow, this is part of my mind!*" This cross –art, performance, pop culture, everything mishmash that's where I want to sit; creating art from the worlds of live performance art, pop culture and time mixing into that, into a *Le Fil* paste.

And I think of pop music and pop culture as a Trojan horse for all those types of activities. I think of even the work that I'm doing now, it's only a window for the work that I want to be doing in the future. A little foot in the door of all the different, weird ideas I want to try out!.

Any Final Piece of Wisdom?

Save money! For 15, 20 years of making I always felt I should invest it all back into my art! But you should save yourself a percentage. You need to be able to pay your rent so you can make art. You need to be able to eat food so that you can make art. And for a long time, I was always borrowing money. Save 10% or more for yourself, 20% for tax, 10% for union fees, memberships, 10% for work costs – and then the rest is bills and having a good time!

Hugo Grrrl / @hugogrrrl Photo: Lane Worrall /@laneworrallart

28
Simple Man: Interview with *Hugo Grrrl*

Hugo Grrrl is an award-winning drag king, host, producer and self-proclaimed doofus from Aotearoa New Zealand. *Hugo* gained notoriety as the winner of Season 1 of *House Of Drag*, a show which has since seen both judges and contestants appearing in *RuPaul's Drag Race Down Under*. This victory crowned him the first drag king and transgender man to win a drag reality TV show.

Drag really is a global phenomenon, so I needed voices from the opposite side of the world to me and had always wanted an excuse to talk shop with this dandy lad. *Hugo* now works as a comedy and cabaret producer, he is known for his many shows including *Naked Girls Reading* and *The Pun Battle* both of which he hosts. We spoke crisis, craft, consumerism and costumes.

Why Did You Create *Hugo*?

Well, I had a gender identity crisis. I started compulsively dressing in men's clothing, without much conscious thought behind it. Before this I was super femme: lipstick, dresses, heels every single day so it was quite a dramatic shift for me. I was surrounded by people working in cabaret, who just presumed I was working on a character, and I was like "…*sure*". A very excitable silly alter-ego of a man quickly fell out of me. I literally humped my bedroom mirror for months before finally getting on stage. There wasn't a lot of drag around, I was in Wellington, New Zealand at the time. Bugger all drag! But there was a lot of burlesque, so I started stripping, as a man. And that's how Hugo started.

So, You Needed Drag Personally?

Definitely. I owe everything to drag. It was a safe space to play while secretly, quietly testing out how masculinity felt on me. I think queer healing should be fun, or rather can be fun. So often we see representations of trans-ness that centre on suffering and discrimination, and those stories are important, but our identities deserve to be portrayed as something wonderful too. Drag shows gender queerness as something gorgeous and enviable and sexy and glamorous. That is magic. That's crucial.

I can't imagine not doing drag in some way, shape or form. One day I'll be an eccentric little old man hobbling around a dive bar stage somewhere. Drag gave me the tools to figure out I was trans. It gave me something to give a shit about. It gave me a reason to get sober. It totally saved me.

And Now, Is *Hugo* You? A Persona? A Character…?

It's a really good question. When I'm out of drag in a social setting people will often ask "*are you George or Hugo?*" And I say "*Shhh, don't tell but I'm actually the same person*". So, I'm not fussy about the

DOI: 10.4324/9781003498797-32

distinction, but George is who I am all the time, Hugo's the costume. But the two sides are inextricable. For example, the idea of changing my drag name is just nuts to me. Like I just am Hugo. He's just the louder, floppier, flashier, more feathery side of me.

What Should I Expect at a *Hugo* Show?

I run a lot of stuff! Drag cabarets, a comedy show called *The Pun Battle*, a raunchy literature show called *Naked Girls Reading*. At the moment my passion project is running the *Drag King Megashow* – a regular open-access night with up to 22 kings in each lineup. You'll never see a faster-moving drag show! We also run workshops and hangouts in the lead up to each gig, and get all the boys informed and excited. It's a joy to be part of.

The crowd at my drag show is very much dykes and sapphics, as well as queers and drag fans in general. If it's not a king-exclusive line up you'll also get your straight girly-pop drag fans but honestly they're the minority, it's rare that the TV drag fans demographic ever actually make it out to an IRL show.

And I usually host all my own shows. You'd probably describe my hosting as excitable and loud and complimentary, very enthusiastic. It's not an act, I am stoked to be up there.

And Is There a Trademark *Hugo Grrrl* Piece or Set?

I'm almost always on the mic when I'm performing! But when I do a cheeky lip sync, my go-to act is my peacock. The costume is a jumpsuit with peacock embroidery all over it. It's got a deep-v, giant shoulders and a codpiece to fake the big masculine shape. Then I pair it with a showgirl peacock feather collar and fans and do *Livin' La Vida Loca* in it.

I love it because peacocks are an emblem of flamboyant masculinity. And that's me! I am a show boy, my inclination is I want to feel gorgeous in drag. I feel I have a lot in common with drag queens in that way! I want to be dripping in jewels, I want giant hair. This is how I feel beautiful.

Is That Your Drag Brand?

Yeah, 'showboy' is definitely what I always strive for. It's a delicate balance though. Masculinity and good stagecraft have a very paradoxical relationship, right? Makeup's a good example – stage makeup is about opening up your face, but masc contouring requires you to lower your brow bone and add extra lines for facial hair and deep shadow – all things which close in and furrow your face. King makeup is so hard, honestly.

And masc performance is such a tricky line too. To be expressive on stage is to be large. Drag is an exaggeration of gendered traits and yet modern masculinity is basically defined by restriction and repression, what one *can't* do. Maybe that's why I love the iconography of a peacock – a reminder that masculinity in nature is fabulous, that human men can be fabulous too.

Do You Rehearse? How?

I do! But it depends on what kind of gig. Solo – I'll casually map some stuff out in front of my bedroom mirror, and leave room for improv on the day. But I'm way more diligent about group choreography. I reckon there's nothing cringier to watch than an under-rehearsed group act. It doesn't matter how good you are, there's no hiding if you don't know the dance moves.

And What about When Hosting? How Do You Rehearse?

I've been hosting for nearly ten years, which is wild. I've got a standard formula I generally fall into. It goes: big energetic entrance, call and response to get them loud off the bat, I'll explain what the show is and subtly set expectations, sing my praises for the cast. Then I introduce myself, give a bit of context for this strange man before them. Then housekeeping – with as many jokes in this section as I can muster 'cause logistics are boring. Then I'll do a giant audience warm up and when they're as loud as I think I'll get them, I'll call on the first act.

I rehearse this section before every gig, even though it's muscle memory now. I have a theory that if you get your audience onside in the first five minutes, you have got them for the whole thing. In fact, it might even be the first ten seconds of a show that are crucial! That entrance is everything. I run it at least twice with a tech pre-show, no matter how many times we've worked together. First impressions matter, I guess.

Do You Critique Your Own Work?

Yes but I'm not the most secure person, I doubt many drag performers are, that's why we overcompensate with sparkle! I tend to get overly critical when watching my live performance footage, and that'll stop me from being fully in the moment next time I'm on stage. So I try to limit myself from reviewing videos.

I will definitely review it from an experiential point of view though! Backstage I'll be like, "*that crowd was too straight for that joke*", "*doing that dance move there felt fun*" or "*I should delay that reveal to the next chorus*". It feels more constructive to review it in the moment.

And as a Career…? Do You Have a Plan? A Trajectory?

Yes and no! I know I don't want fame and fortune, it just doesn't seem fun! I've had the pleasure of knowing creative people who've gotten 'their big break' – and absolutely deserved it – and it slowly dawned on me that I don't think many of them are truly happier now. High stakes, high cost of living, highly critical eyes on you? Surely the cons outweigh the pros.

I think success is a calm nervous system. And I don't think anyone is being paid enough in drag to live a life of high stress. So I always choose the path of least chaos. For that reason I'm probably destined to be a local drag performer, and I'm honestly delighted by that idea. Making my local city a bit gayer, making people's bachelorettes, birthdays and Friday nights a bit brighter. Community is everything. I'll work for bugger all money as long as it's with and for great people.

Do You Have a Fixed Approach to Drag?

Not usually, however: This year I've had a no new costumes rule. I became really jaded with the superficiality of drag, the commercialism of it. Constantly spending money on gear for new Instagram content. I've just decided that I'm going to eject myself out of that rat race.

So I've been using what I have, fixing and repurposing old costumes, painting Op Shop suits, and making my own wigs. I've learnt so much and I've saved so much money. But it's very time-consuming, it's added a lot of stress this year. But it's been so worth it.

Also I just shamelessly rewear outfits – I'm a proud outfit repeater. It's so unsustainable not to be. In other art forms, a performer will have one costume that is their 'character's' and they're sorted for life. That look becomes iconic for them. It's so weird that drag basically has the opposite philosophy.

Do You Have a Specific Route in for New Work?

It is almost always a costume-first process for me. It's very rare that I find, for example, the song first. Generally, I'll be like "*I wanna be a sailor*" and then I'll figure out the act and track from there. For example, I made a kids' show called *Hugo's Rainbow Show* and that came from me thinking "*how cute would a drag cloud be?*", "*how would you make a rainbow foam wig?*", and then it developed from there.

Any Final Piece of Wisdom? Or Something You Wished You Learnt Sooner about Drag?

Probably that we need to work extra hard to actually create community in drag. In other art forms, there's opportunity to work on your art together. You'll spend hundreds of hours rehearsing a play together, or you'll all go to comedy scratch nights and watch each other bomb, or you compare bruises in dance class. In drag, there's no school or rehearsal or celebration of failure. We do all the work in isolation – sewing and teasing and stoning in our bedroom alone. And then we spit the product of all that work out in a high stakes, public environment and go home and obsess over what people say about it on the internet. No wonder we're all so neurotic. The irony is that most people get into drag because they're lonely, lost, vulnerable gender queer people – the people who need the most kindness and community out of just about anyone. So yeah, I'm really trying to get my drag friends in the room together as much as possible these days. I try to communicate really clearly and kindly. And I try not to gossip – now, that's a hard one to unlearn! But yeah, good relationships are everything – that's my biggest takeaway.

Me /@methedragqueen Photo: Corinne Cumming/Captured by Corinne

29
Let's Hear It for Me: Interview with *Me*

This is *Me*: notorious narcissist, glamour clown and professional idiot. *Me* is a lip-sync legend, host, producer and mentor. Mother to many, Mum to no one. During her career styles have changed: from gender-bending burlesque, through goth-slut-drag, to a modern interpretation of classic glam. *Me* is the third alter-ego previously performing as queerlesque artist *Mr. Mistress*, moving into drag and lip-sync with *Meth*. And now – just *Me*!

An international performer, producer of *The Meth Lab*, *Not Another Drag Contest* and themed nights as *Me & Herr* with longterm collaborator *Herr*. *Me* is also the guest lecturer on *The Art of Drag Course* for lip-sync.

With her husband, co-producer and drag academic Dr Joe Parslow she was part owner and founder of the hugely influential *Her Upstairs* in Camden, London (2016-2018). One can't discuss the current UK drag scene without talking about *Me*!

How Did You Start Performing?

I was performing my whole life, being on stage was a given from a very early age. My Mum was a choreographer of all the local am-dram, so, even before I was on stage, I was going to rehearsals with her and watching her choreograph the local Pantomime or show. My parents moved house so that I could go to a secondary school that had a theatre on site. In my head, I was going to be a musical theatre performer but as my teenage years developed, and my queerness started emerging, I was also weird, it was in the boom of the emo phase. It was actually through *The Dresden Dolls* and *Amanda Palmer* that I started being drawn into cabaret. They branded their style of music as Brechtian punk cabaret and I was like "*oh, what does all that mean?*" The shows that they put on would have walkabouts and incorporate performances too.

I was lucky enough at college to have a module on variety performance, where we got little tasters of circus, of stand up…looking at those self-contained cabaret style acts. I went to my tutors: "*I'd like to do a burlesque number for a variety show*". The module culminated in a performance and I made a burlesque routine to *Mandy Goes To Med School*, by The Dresden Dolls.

I think that was the first point that I realised all these amazing things about my identity, as a queer person. At that point I realised: "*I don't think musical theatre will be for me*". I didn't really like being told how I should look or what I should do.

When I moved to London for my degree, I threw myself out at promoters and slowly started getting gigs on the burlesque scene. In terms of falling into a career, that was one of those things where I threw as much out there as I could to see what stuck. It was through the grace of other people in the industry who worked with

DOI: 10.4324/9781003498797-33

me, they saw what I did, loved it, and they recommended me to people. It did that thing that careers often do…you know, that little first rock of the avalanche and before you know it: it's your entire life.

And Now? Who Is *Me*? A Persona, a Character, You?

How do you just define those things, I guess? She's not a character. But, I wouldn't say that nothing changes between Ben and Me. She is parts of me, but also parts of the characters and women that I've known in my life.

I don't see my drag as female impersonation. Even though I adopt a lot of those things, I wear breasts, I pad. But my intention is never to impersonate a woman. Why can't a man paint with all these colors and use these things?

I love musical theatre. I interject that into her both stylistically and performatively. Old school, trad throwbacks: I'd much rather do a Judy Garland than I would Billie Eilish. Not that I shy away from contemporary songs! But the sort of musical theatre icons I'm drawn to are often those rough, bawdy women: Mama Roses or Miss Hannigan as opposed to the leading lady.

There's definitely that trick that she can get away with saying things that I never could. She isn't afraid to be a bit catty, to have a little dig. Those faux compliments that are actually shade, but obviously, done with love.

Does She Know She's a Drag Act?

Yeah. I think that the further down my career I'm getting, the more I realise she is just for stage. Earlier in my career, I was doing club hosting things or those sort of like corporate gigs where you just sort of like milling around, and now I cannot stand it.

It's rare that I will spend more than five, ten minutes after a show before I just have to go and take her off and put her back in the suitcase. Now I'm turning down those sort of gigs, I need to be on that stage with a mic or with my acts. She just lives there. She's my performance outlet.

I Book for a *Me* Show – What Am I Getting?

First port of call, and to go completely against the narcissist brand, I don't actually like being the only one in the show! I've tried it. I thrive the best when I'm in a mixed variety bill. So there will also be some amazing people from across cabaret and drag. I can also have a break!

In terms of what I will be doing, I would ideally be hosting. I like to hold those sort of shows in the palm of my hands. I like to open, I like to close. The vast majority of my catalog are openers and closers. I'm drawn to those styles of performances, the sort of things that draw you in, give you a feel, a taste of what's to come, and then the big finish that puts a pin on the end of the night.

Content wise: a vast majority of my stuff is musical theatre standards. If we're getting some greatest hits out there, I still love to throw back to my spoken word mash ups because that's a joy. Knowing how technically proficient I am and how impressive a well-constructed mix is when done technically proficiently; I get off quite a bit by finishing with a really impressive bit of spoken word lip-sync.

Can You Talk Us Through One of Those?

My *Roar* mix is one that's been going for nearly ten years now. That's Katy Perry, interspersed with battle speeches from various films, across the ages. That one has become known as my signature. It was a Meth piece but it maintained a place in my repertoire, as Me.

Then the mirror, is *You Haven't Seen the Last Of Me* with my repeated endings. My eight-minute long torture device where she just won't leave the fucking stage! And that was the real quintessential thing that redefined my rebrand. It's one idea done through to its natural progression.

It's one of those ones that if I want to take it seriously, I can. If I want to be an absolute twat about it, I can. And, you know, *Roar* kind of looks the same almost every time now, I think, because I've been doing it so long. Which Is nice because you can see people doing certain movements along, in the crowd, the ones who really know it. Whereas *You Haven't Seen the Last Of Me*. I feel I've got a lot more freedom to play.

Do You Rehearse? And If So, How?

Not in a traditional sense of getting up on my feet and actually marking it through with my entire body. Most of my rehearsal, in terms of learning a song, getting it into my body is done when I'm traveling. I find something about the headspace of traveling really allows my brain to absorb lyrics.

I think I've just gotten to that cocky stage now where I know my capabilities. I put so much work into my technique, and my editing skills, I trust that I know what to do in front of a live audience. Often, the first time I perform a new song, in its entirety, will be when I step on stage in front of a crowd.

The amount of time I spend in GarageBand, in many ways, is a big part of the rehearsal. That's all about the structure, about timing of things. And again, that's a stage at which things start seeping into my brain.

When I branch into double acts and group work then we will have rehearsals so everyone knows where they're standing but I'm not a "*5,6,7,8, move 2,3,4*" performer. I like to leave room so that people can be in the moment, improv and then come together for certain key points.

Do You Have a Drag Ethos?

Something that's been stuck with me a lot recently, is the last line of Joe's book, which is:

> Plant your feet, take a deep breath, and remember, it's supposed to be fun.
>
> Joe Parslow[1]

Take the space, find your foundation, find your grounding. Take that breath, that moment for yourself. It's about how it's then shared with everyone else.

Other than that, it's just being authentic to myself. I don't actively strive for originality. I might accidentally stumble on it from time to time, but I'm also under no illusions that I am the most groundbreaking drag act in the world. I am authentic to what it is I want to do, and I think that shines through more than people desperately trying to do the next big thing.

Do You Have a Pre-Show Routine?

I'm a pacer. I can't help but sort of walk around a bit. I have to get into drag at least half an hour before stage time.

I do like a drink; I will have a maximum, usually, of 2 or 3 in a night. Just a little buzz.

Do You Critique Your Own Work?

Yeah. I use my husband, Joe, a lot! I'm always bouncing the ideas off him. I'm always wanting to get his feedback.

I also think I am naturally doing it in real time. This sounds awfully cocky, but I think my brain is capable of functioning in multiple ways: I can be in my body and be performing, whilst also a bit of my brain is also removed and critiquing what I'm doing. And that is informing the bit of my brain that's making the performance choices.

Is There a Way You Measure Success?

The longer you do it, I think the more you realise that term, success, is constantly shifting both from an industry standard and from a personal standard. I think it's useful for any new performer to learn pretty quickly that money is not a sign of success because that shifts and changes.

How much of your work are you actually enjoying? How much of it is fun? How much of it is artistically fulfilling? That's one of the reasons why I stopped doing brunches, because I wasn't having fun at them. Were they fulfilling me as an artist? Absolutely not.

Also, how much of an impact is your work making on the industry and on the community? And I'm also thinking about those things as very separate entities these days. I think the last ten years has been a really nice focus on who is our community, who has these spaces, who has the access to all of this stuff.

Now, we also need to think about this industry. How do we want this to survive? How are we maintaining artistic rigour, professional practice, those sort of things? If I can feel I've made some difference: both in how our community develops, and the strength of the industry that I'm a part of…I would consider that more of a success than everyone across the world knowing exactly who I am.

Where Do You Find Inspiration?

One of the reasons why I still do so much work with new performers is they are always coming up with some of the most incredible and inventive and exciting new work. Also, the energy of them. I'm under no illusions that the longer you're in the industry, the more jaded you can get about things and the more exhausted you are. Seeing the enthusiasm, and the love, and the drive, that younger and newer performers have for it is something that keeps me going.

Also, I'm a real fucking sucker for technique these days. If I know that you've really worked at your craft. That's enough for me. And I'm fully aware that means I've turned into my mother. But yeah, people who are fucking good at their jobs and good at their craft!

Any Final Pearls of Wisdom?

Walk away from the things that aren't right for you. It's totally cool. That might mean walking away from people, or spaces, or practices…you do not need to be in places and spaces or around people that are not doing, not giving you, what you need from them.

Walk away when it's not right. Trust your gut in those sort of things, because nine times out of ten, your gut will be correct.

Note

1 *Their Majesties – Drag Performance and Queer Communities in London* Joe Parslow (August 27, 2024 by Routledge).

Son Of A Tutu /@sonofatutu Photo: Cam Harle/@camharlephoto.

30
Mother: Interview with *Son Of A Tutu*

Son Of A Tutu is an award-winning drag queen, actor and activist. Raised in Nigeria *Tutu* turned to drag later in life, in her mid-forties, after a career in finance and on Wall Street. She found success on the UK drag scene after winning *Drag Idol UK* in 2011.

Now the host of *Drag Idol UK,* a resident at G-A-Y and an outspoken voice within the drag community *Tutu* has a prolific career working across the UK. She is also an accomplished actress who starred in the movie-musical *Everybody's Talking About Jamie* and won the Iris Prize for Best Performance in short film for *Lemon*.

Who Is *Son Of A Tutu*?

Son Of A Tutu is the drag persona of me, the queer person, and she has evolved over time. I believe there's a gender-bend element at the core of the gene and genius of queerness and at its most ripened, you find drag in all its glories. Beyond that point you find transness and I believe there's an element of transness in me personally. I hate using my civilian name: I go by Tutu both in and out of drag and use any and all pronouns but insist on "She" when in it. When I first started to find my way in drag, Tutu was a character but then I got lost between my art and my identity and had to figure that out. Now if Tutu wants to play a character in the pursuit of her art, she can but is not confined by it. As a community, our fears, desires, strengths, weaknesses, challenges, dreams and all facets of our experience are expressed through the art of drag. It is the most prevalent embodiment of queer culture. Son Of A Tutu is that person.

Has the Initial Character Gone?

If a performance piece requires it, she shows up. She is the forthright, gele-wearing, 'anti anti-immigration', Nigerian immigrant fighting intersectional injustice from the perspective of someone thriving, against the odds and threat of deportation and/or discrimination. She walks and talks (full Nigerian accent) differently and has a different smile. There were some development problems at the start but they have since been straightened out.

But day to day Tutu is an expression of self: an expression of my queerness. I was held back from being myself for so many decades due to my cultural background: my ethnic background, cultural disincentives, dis-encouragement…I was held back for so long. When I eventually overcame that, and found the courage to become the drag persona that I was born to be, I found my peace. I am one of those kids who was 'dragging' through their mother's closet before I lost my milk teeth, dressing up and putting on shows for my siblings and the neighbourhood kids; it is an intrinsic part of me. That's not to be confused with my nascent trans identity. They live side by side: gender is gender and art is art. I always say that had I not grown up in queer-hostile Nigeria in the 70s and 80s, I probably would have transitioned, but that's an enduring conversation I continuously have with myself. Through the first three decades of my life, I was emphatically discouraged from doing things of my nature – my black African queer self. Tutu has been my redemption arc, my happily ever after moment. The cliché but universal truth *"sometimes the biggest form of protest is just to show up as your authentic self"* is the story of my life.

How Did You Start Performing?

Right from a kid, before I knew what drag was, before I knew what queerness was, I was dragging it out and performing to people. It was always there.

I have not got any formal 'trained' skills whether it be singing, acting, hosting, any of the above. I just naturally had this interest, whether you call it aptitude or instinct for drag and most importantly, a burning desire that just wouldn't let go despite the tantalising distractions I accrued on the path my parent forced me on. I eventually rose to become a Wall Street finance director and I didn't start my drag journey until I was in my mid-forties. My father tried to beat drag out of me when I was ten years old but here I am. I entered *Drag Idol*, won it and drag has been my profession ever since.

I Come to a *Tutu* Show – What Am I Getting?

I love putting smiles on people's faces and thoughts in their heads. Tutu is here to give you a good time, make you forget your own woes, worries and cares, but also to make you leave with hope and, at least a curious thought. Nina Simone always said that *"it's an artist's responsibility to reflect the times that they live in"*. I like to do that, but I don't like to do it with a sledgehammer. A message has a better chance of reaching its intended if said recipient does not feel under attack. Joy and humour are great vehicles for conveying and sharing information, perspectives and experiences without bumping into impenetrable defences and/or resistance. This is the art of drag. I am not a lip-syncing dance diva but an engaging song and patter queen.

Is There a Specific Song or Set Piece I Should Expect?

I have come to love leading an audience through a 'take it to church' a cappella rendition of *"Take Me Home, Country Roads"*. I have all these forces: blackness, queerness, Britishness and fusing them together to produce something new but familiar, is my kink. I choose a white song and then get everybody involved, hands clapping, tambourines clacking, feet stomping and, riff riffing their way through a country and western song. Another staple is my *"And I Am Telling You"* parody which is a lament against the insane, hostility white nationalists seem to have to immigration. Railing against this absolute craziness that there is for the stigmatisation of others, including immigrants is my stock in trade.

Do You Rehearse? And If So, How?

As a soloist, it's more informal. All day long, subconsciously or consciously, I am thinking, learning a song or exploring the humour potentials of a subject.

What I'm not very good at doing is rehearsing the presentation. I let that happen through performance, trial it as I do it. Then slowly the presentation gets fine-tuned. But I do rehearse lines! A lot of my work is quick reactions, I like having an arsenal of witty remarks which are the bedrock of structured spontaneity; you build a treasure trove of one liners, or responses, that you deploy depending on the situation and what the interaction with an individual or room gives you. Through the day, I could be cooking, cleaning or sewing and something will come to me; I get my phone out, record it, develop it, memorise it, and fine-tune it. I'm always singing into the phone too, and then playing it back predominantly because I am my own singing teacher. Rehearsal is integrated into my everyday life. There's no real separation – it could pop up anywhere any time!

Do You Have a Pre-Show Routine?

I do a few vocal exercises, work on my articulation.

I like an alcoholic drink (or two hundred) but I refuse to drink before I go on stage, I have too much respect for drag as a profession. However, if I go on stage and somebody *offers* me a drink…that's part of my show! The most important pre-show ritual is: I don't like talking or giggling. I go inwards to centre myself before the show so that I can go outward when I'm on stage.

People don't realise, that in order to be that person on stage, it takes every ounce of social engagement energy inside you, to hold an audience for an hour or two. I have to go to that zone!

Do You Critique Your Own Work?

I am my own worst, most fervent critic, I am obsessed with watching videos of myself. I forensically review every note, every step, every intonation as I'm self-taught and the only way I can actually get to review what I've learnt (or not learned), is to watch it back.

I also have a natural distrust of people that pay me compliments especially if I feel I haven't earned it. Gratuitous kindness helps no one in the long run even when well-intentioned. What I value is constructive feedback, a golden nugget that will foster development.

Is There a Way You Measure Success?

As I didn't come into the profession in my teens or early twenties (as is the norm), I have no burning desire to become "*Britain's next Drag Superstar*". The practitioning of drag itself is what gives me joy and so I turn away half as much work as I accept, as I want to maintain the joy of the art itself and not the very real heights it can take you to (nowadays). I did all that in my previous life. That is not to say I am against the very tangible social mobility that drag affords; in-fact I am all for it. It, in and of itself does not motivate me. If I get there, fine; if not, fine. Success for me is leaving a stage with happy smiling faces and warm hearts in the audience. That's what I love. When I'm on stage, it's not for me. I give everything in the service of the audience, drag is a service that we're providing. I don't want to sound like I'm rudderless. I've been very lucky in that I've done things that I never set out to do, and have a relatively high profile within the industry. I have a generous degree of brand equity that had accrued from the passion and not the ambition. It stems from the fact that I was deprived of being 'me' for more than two-thirds of the life so far lived that finally being 'me' is the pleasure. I'm lucky that I can pay my bills and live a comfortable life with that. I am having the time of my life. When I worked in finance, I lived a good life but now, I am 100 times happier. For me, success is totally different because success is, "*oh my God, I am finally doing what my DNA said I should have been doing forty years ago*". I'm doing it, and I'm having a great time doing it, and I'm making other people have a great time doing it! That is success for me.

Inspiration

Whitney! Of course. Nina was always Mother! We have a slight physical resemblance, especially from the side and, we are similarly wired from an activism point of view. I just call her Mother.

Danny La Rue was my first drag, I remember as a young kid sitting on the living room floor, totally enraptured by him on television: I was transfixed. Later on in life, Boy George and the other was Leee John – *Imagination*. When Leee John's *Imagination* broke through this was so different: here are three queer presenting people, from hundreds of miles away (we had moved to Nigeria) speaking to my burgeoning queer self by and powerful decision makers put them on *Top of the Pops*.

Another important person was Flip Wilson who had a weekly sketch show – *The Flip Wilson Show* – on American prime time (the first black frontend show also loved by white America) TV in the 70s. His character "Geraldine" was the first black drag queen of my life!

Any Final Pearls of Wisdom?

Don't copy others. Be inspired by them.

Don't let people push you off who you are. Even if they mean well, find yourself!

Michael Twaits Photo: Simon J Webb for Jack The Lad Magazine

31
As If We Never Said Goodbye: Finale

Is that it…?

Are you a drag act now…?

I hope so. Or at least on your way there. This is the final chapter but it isn't "*goodbye*". I hope this handbook can remain with you throughout your career. When things get tricky dig in and try to find a solution. As a performer your craft and creativity is in constant evolution: there is always room for growth, find more inspiration or have a rebrand! As you pack your bag and totter towards the stage I wanted to leave you with a few final thoughts. Some from me that I haven't shoe-horned into other chapters, some that I did but it is worth repeating, but some advice I've been given, and others advice from my fabulous interviewees.

HAVE FUN

Because if you aren't, the audience aren't.

> **Nobody who fails to get fun out of his activities can expect them to be fun for anybody else.**
>
> Bertolt Brecht[1]

> They're not there to see complex, post-traumatic theatre. They're there to watch a cabaret show. Keep it simple, keep it effective.
>
> Me The Drag Queen

Find the Joy: If you aren't enjoying performing. It's not the career for you. If you aren't buzzing every time you come off stage then you have chosen the wrong career. It's too stressful to not enjoy every show!

That's your job. Keep them in the venue and keep them drinking.

Adam All

PACK THE DRAG BAG ESSENTIALS

A few things to make sure you have and make sure you use!

> A little handheld electric fan, these clubs and pubs don't have aircon.
>
> Le Fil

DOI: 10.4324/9781003498797-35

Deodorant: Wear deodorant. Have deodorant. You are running around under the lights, the adrenalin is pumping and are usually in close contact with an audience. Always have deodorant on hand.

An extension cable, multiplug.

Le Fil

A Drag Spritz: On top of the deodorant I'd also recommend finding an affordable drag fragrance to spritz on yourself and your costume so you smell fresh and pleasant. No one likes a stinky drag act.

Bring extra wet wipes.

Ada Campe

A Breath Mint: Have a pack of mints in your make up kit. Have one when getting ready. You are in close contact with many, many people!

I travel with a first aid kit, a drag first aid kit, to be able to fix anything! Nail clippers. Safety pins. Bobby pins.

Hugo Grrrl

A Towel: Lay it on the counter as you get ready, firstly to mark your area, but also to keep your areas clean. Then at the end of the night when you take make up off, you have a towel already!

I always have Sellotape on me.

Son of A Tutu

Black nail polish because you'd be amazed at what you can fix with black nail polish. Scuffs on shoes, for example.

Hugo Grrrrl

Look After Your Costumes

Drag is expensive! Treat your costumes with respect.

Clean Your Costumes: Lots of costumes are hard to wash but they do need it! Spray cleaners, spot cleaners and airing is essential at the very minimum. And if all else fails – *Febreze*!

Linen Fresh: I put tumble drying/fragrance sheets in my drag bags, and stuffed inside of shoes, to try and encourage the freshness back!

Undergarments: Don't forget to wash undergarments as they will just make a clean costume smell if not! Binding, padding, tights, packing, bras and corsets – all need washing!

Give It Some Air: After a gig if you have space and time let your Wig and Costume air for a moment in the dressing room before putting them back in a box/bag/suitcase. The wig especially will thank you. A wig gets all the heat of your head. If you take it straight off your head and then close it up in a box the moisture is all trapped in there and the style will droop. The style will not last as long, and it will begin to smell. Let it all air out as you are removing make up and doing the rest of the change back.

Unpack: After a gig – unpack your bag the next morning. When you packed it away you probably said to yourself *"I'll wash those brushes"* or *"I'll remember I need more lace glue"*. If you don't unpack it you won't.

Tucking/Binding: You only have one body – please be careful with it. You do not need to tuck or bind! I love seeing a drag king with big breasts, a queer with a large bulge! If you wish to do it – fine – but be safe, follow some of the safety advice on tutorials. These are VERY delicate parts of your body that shouldn't be strapped down for hours on end.

Work on Your Make-Up

Your make-up and aesthetic will keep improving.

Practice: You don't need to be a world-class make-up artist, but find time to practice. Every time you get into your drag – review your make-up and remember what worked, and what didn't!

Save Money: Cheap make-up can work just as well as expensive. When experimenting with new colours, finishes or textures try a cheap one first before spending too much money. When the colour/finish is right and you know you'll use it, then invest if you wish to.

Clean Brushes Are a Key to Beauty: Few drag acts seem to frequently clean their brushes! If you mix brushes in different colours, that's all mixing and being wiped on your face. Have a pot of clean brushes and a pencil case to put them in once used. After the gig you know exactly which ones need a quick wash.

Invest in a Skincare Regime: You are putting on and taking off so much make-up. Find products that help your skin recover – cleansers, toners, moisturisers, night creams. If you let your skin get dry, claggy and rough it will be harder to paint well with make up! Develop a post-drag skincare ritual. (And if you are canny with money you can declare them as tax deductible see *Chapter 3: The Economics of Drag*.)

It Won't Be Perfect, That's Not What Drag Is About

You are brilliant! Get out of your own way.

> If you have a hard gig, quiet, a death, a struggle, whatever, you can only be mad and frustrated and gutted until 11am the next day. Then you must draw a line under it and forget about it. As going into the next gig thinking you are shit will mean you will die.
>
> Equally, if you nail it, slam it, destroy it, whatever, you can only be smug about it until 11am the next day (in the past, I have set an alarm so I could get up and gloat for an extra half hour) as if you go into the next gig thinking you are God's gift to comedy, you will die. That is Millican's Law and it totally works. It means you move on quickly.
>
> Sarah Millican [2]

Managing Expectation: I trick myself into not overselling my skills. It manages my nerves. I say I'm a *"host"*, *"I'm an actor"* or a *"drag act who sings"*. Rather than *"a singer"*. Or that *"I'm funny"* rather than *"a comedian"*. I encourage you to do whatever little tricks you can to help you feel you are presenting yourself in a way you are comfortable with.

Keep Creating, Reviewing and Rehearsing

It's a never-ending process. Keep at it.

Keep Notes: I prefer real notes, but phones can do the job. When inspiration strikes write it down because you won't remember that song you randomly heard three hours later. Log everything!

> **Proper preparation prevents poor performance.**
>
> Adam All

Keep Creating: You never have enough repertoire – always be on the look out! Learn new songs, start the edit of a new track, plan a new costume.

Keep Rehearsing: Don't just wait until you are booked and 'need' a new act because rehearsing, and learning, is always stressful when rushed. Always have a few new numbers you are finessing and learning.

> I keep phone notes, I mean some of them I come back to and I've got no idea. But if something comes to mind I note it down. I've also got tons of playlists on Spotify!
>
> Me The Drag Queen

Record Rehearsals: When rehearsing alone use a phone/device to record as an outside eye and watch back!

Get in a Venue: Some venues are closed during the day and *might* be happy to have performers come in and rehearse in the venue.

Find Your Family: Performers and colleagues who you respect can be a great outside eye. They can watch the show, see you working with an audience and at a suitable time give you some feedback! But only if you ask!

> **Don't copy others. Be inspired by them.**
>
> Son Of A Tutu

Record Everything: Nearly everyone has a phone now that can record video and audio. When debuting work get that footage, not to share on socials, but so you can review your work later.

Document Your Work

To evaluate your work and, selectively, share!

Invest in a Mini Tripod: It doesn't need to be fancy but having something you can subtly film your act with, and possibly to get a little bit of content, is well worth it. (Otherwise you will break your phone by ambitiously balancing it somewhere you shouldn't!)

Go Quirky: There are many different types of mini camera where you can subtly place in an interesting position to get a different angle of shot for socials. Familiar content can become more eye-catching and dynamic when shot on an interesting lens or from a different perspective.

It's Not Live: Recorded footage does not do a live show justice. Don't overanalyse, or overshare it. The energy of the room disappears, the laughs feel off. Check what is useful to you, did you remember the choreography/script? Did you stay in the light?

Don't Over Share on Socials: Why am I coming to see the show if you've already shown me your set, costume and look online? I'll save my money thanks.

Tease Me: When you have a new costume it's always tempting to show it off straight away on socials. I would recommend not doing so! Once a costume has been seen, it has been seen. Save that "*wow*" moment for the audience in the space with you.

Drip Feed Details: I have a pattern of debuting a new outfit at a big event and then wearing it a lot in close succession before it is all over my socials. And then when it lands on my socials. I put it away for a little while.

Don't Be a Dick

Nobody wants to work with people who are hard work!

Be on Time: On time is fifteen minutes early! Turn that into a way of life.

> Backstage etiquette is actually really important. Being really nice to everybody is really important. In terms of me booking people, and re-booking, people for things. It's the people who were lovely that we want back.
>
> Adam All

Make Someone Happy: First time in the venue? Learn the technician's name and the producer's, promoter's. Second time in the venue: learn the bar staffs' names, security and the door staff. Thank them all on the way out using their name. People remember that stuff.

> I have communication tips for cast management: Ban group chats! Instead, you want to communicate all the information in one block whether that's one big email or a link to a Google doc which has all your instructions for the event in one place, it's just mandatory.
>
> Hugo Grrrrl

> Always take all of your music on a USB aswell. In about three different formats, just in case, and have it on your phone!
>
> Adam All

Say Thank You: Tag venues and publicly thank them for having you. "*Can't wait to be back*". Especially if you have a good follower range and can show some social media clout!

Look After Your Body

Getting into your drag isn't your pre-show warm up. Get your body ready!

Warmup!

Adam All

Do vocal exercises.

Son Of A tutu

Warm up.

Ada Campe

Have enough time to get ready.

Simply Barbra

Warm up.

Le Fil

Get Out of Your Way, Get On-Stage

You will never be 'ready' – you just need to do it!

Find A Moment For Yourself: Breathe. Remember what you are doing at the show. Remember why you are doing it. Go out and have fun.

> When I'm on-stage. It's not for me. I give everything in the service of the audience, it's a service that we're providing.
>
> Son Of A Tutu

> Plant your feet, take a deep breath, and remember, it's supposed to be fun. [3]
>
> Joe Parslow (shared by their husband *Me The Drag Queen*)

Basic Stage Craft

Slow Down: Get on stage and let the audience drink in how spectacular you look. You've got into drag. Let them see it before you start doing all the crazy stuff you have concocted. Breathe. You've got this.

Experience Helps: Get on stage – just do it! Learn from each experience, keep improving! Small steps are fine! Just keep working!

Know Your Exits: If you can't see anything other than a spotlight and the front row. Look for the Fire Exit signs. (They legally have to be on!) Staring into the abyss makes you look a little vacant so fix your eyes on those points at different points in your set, act like it's someone loving your set!

Confidence: Smile, make eye contact with someone you can see who is smiling. Remember that connection. How special this evening or show is to them. Connect to them, then spread that connection to the next audience member. They aren't one clump, they are room full of individuals.

Always Be You

People want an original, not a replica.

> A long time ago, I came to the realisation that sometimes the biggest form of protest is just to showcase your authentic self.
>
> Son Of A Tutu

> I wish I'd been cannier quicker. Probably more ambitious, more pragmatic, more set, more confident. But I guess it is what it is. And even though I'd rather not have had the journey, the journey is happening. So all I can do is try and do my best within it.
>
> Ada Campe

Be Yourself: People are coming to see you perform. So do *you*. Be yourself, unapologetically! Don't try to be someone else, or what you think someone else wants you be. Always be you!

Notes

1 Brecht, B., & Willett, J. (1964). *Brecht on Theatre: The Development of an Aesthetic.* [1st ed.] New York, Hill and Wang.
2 Sarah Millican is a British comedian (not a drag act) her 11am rule is one of the most useful things I ever read, so I had to share it here: quoting from her blog, 5th August 2012. http://sarahmillican.blogspot.com/
3 *Their Majesties* Routledge 2024.

Glossary

Act	1) An individual performer.
	2) The performance a performer does.
	3) The different Acts of a show, usually separated by an interval.
Ad-Lib	When a performer goes off script, usually with a quick, comic retort.
All Stars	Abbreviation of reality TV show *RuPaul's Drag Race All Stars*.
Alter-Ego	The person a performer choses to present as on stage. Usually a Character a Persona or somewhere in between. See *Chapter 9: Alter-Ego*.
An Edit/ Edited Track	A track that edits together from various sources to create one new, unique track. See *Chapter 16: Creating and Editing a Track*.
Anchors	Points for eye line/focus in a room. See *Chapter 8: Basic Drag*.
Aside	Speaking directed only at a specific person either in the audience, or off stage. Pretending other members of the cast/audience can't hear.
Backstage	The areas off stage and away from the audience. Dressing rooms, side of stage. Private areas for cast and crew only.
Beat	1) A pause, or break in the rhythm to add comedy or dramatic effect. The make-up on your face.
	2) The make-up on your face is *"your beat"*.
Bit	A small section of a a comedy set, usually on one subject or specific part of a story. Ie *"I might cut the duck bit tonight to keep it quick"*.
Blackout	When the lights go out on stage. I.e. Enter in a blackout.
Blocking	The physical movement, spacing and timings on stage.
Booker	The person who schedules a performer at an event. May be a producer, promoter or fellow performer.
Booking	Being programmed or scheduled to perform at a gig.
Breakdown	In castings a list of who, or what skills, are required by performers.
Breaking Character	When the performer stops presenting the character or persona and reveals themselves.
Camp	Eccentric, flamboyant, striking, out-of-the-ordinary and usually seen through a queer gaze.

Casting Director	The person in charge and making decisions for a casting in Film, TV and Theatre..
Centre Stage	The centre point on a stage. Usually the best place for site-line and focus.
Character	A persona outside of the performer's self with their own name, history and identity. Bought to life on stage by a performer but seen as a separate entity to the performer.
Close-Up	On camera shot which is just head and shoulders, or closer.
Cue	A signal for a performer or technician to do something.
Downstage	The area of the stage closest to the audience.
Drag Act	Any performer who uses Drag - queen, king, queer or other.
Drag Family	Drag acts who work and support each other. The closest of colleagues.
Drag Race	The general term to cover all franchises and variants of *RuPaul's Drag Race*. Covers *All Stars* and *Vs. The World* formats.
Fans	The people who like and support a performers work.
Fourth Wall	The imaginary divide between an audience and the cast on stage. In theatre the fourth wall usually remains in tact. In drag, cabaret it is often broken as acts interact directly with, or in, the audience.
Gig	A general term for a booking; it may be hosting a brunch, bingo, doing a show or a corporate but Gig covers all bases.
Happened Audience	An audience arrived at a venue, and the performance was secondary to their night out. Perhaps they didn't know a show was on. Or which performers might be on. A happened audience is generally more lively, a club/bar atmosphere. Audience members will come and go.
Haus/House	The drag family may identify as a collective who perform together but also work, support and develop together. Most Haus's have a set style and work towards a collective legacy.
Host (aka *M.C/Compere*)	The person who introduces performers to the stage. Usually they will welcome the audience with an opening set and often close a show as well.
Improvisation	When a performer speaks, or performs, spontaneously without a plan or script.
Line-Up	The cast on the show are *"tonight's line-up"*. One act following another.
Lip-Sync	A physical performance usually to music and spoken word where the performers lips match the words and appear to be in sync.
Look	The look is a term for the over aesthetic created by a drag act.
M.C.	*Master Of Ceremonies*. Another term for a *Host*.
Mid-Shot	On camera a shot that allows a little space for movement. Usually around the waste up so the face is still heavily featured.
Mime	1) The theatrical technique of suggesting action and character without words. 2) Another term for the act of Lip-syncing.

Glossary

Monologue	A solo speech or piece of text.
Motivation	The reason for doing something. Often the why behind a choice on stage. *"What's my motivation here?"*
Off-Book	Meaning the performer knows their lines, or lyrics, without a script or prompt.
Off-Stage	Any area in the venue which isn't the stage - backstage, the wings, the audience but not the designed stage space for performance.
On-Stage	Being in the designed stage/space where performances are intended to happen.
PA System	A *public address* system. It is the speakers, microphone, mixers, amplifier and all related equipment that is needed for stage performance to be amplified.
Padding	The pads and stuffing used to alter the physical shape of a drag performer.
Parody	The re-working, re-imaging or re-styling of an existing piece of work which is comic. See *Chapter 19: Parody*.
Peaks And Troughs	The variety found in performance: Variation of pace, tone, tempo, volume and more - to create interest for the audience. See *Chapter 8: Basic Drag*.
Performance Zones	Varying zones of a room to performer to, designed to create dynamic audience experience. See See *Chapter 8: Basic Drag*.
Persona	A heightened, altered and stage worthy version of your personality. See *Chapter 9: Alter-Ego*.
Piece	A section of a set - a song, a lip-sync, comic run, are all pieces that will make up a set of show.
Producer	The person who produces a show or event. Usually the one who will pay performers.
Promoter	Someone that works for the venue, programming, producing and booking nights. A promoter may engage an external producer to come in and produce shows or events at their venue.
Props	The objects used by performers on-stage.
Punters	Slang for audience members, usually punters are in a happened event, having a drink.
Queer	In this handbook is used as an umbrella term for anyone who identifies outside of the norm. Any member of the LGBT+ community and beyond.
Read/Reading	Verbally insulting another person. A vicious one liner about someone specific. See *Chapter 18: Comedy, Reading and Roasting*.
Realness	In terms of aesthetic, it is a drag performer who would 'pass' as the gender they are performing as.
Regulars	Those who come to see the same performers on a regular basis.
Repertoire/Rep	The pieces a performer builds up to perform time and again. See *Chapter 6: Building a Set, Range and Repertoire*.
Residency	A regular gig where the same performer is there at the same time each week, or sometimes each month.

Roast/Roasting	A longer version of reading. It may be a string of reads together to give someone a good roasting. See *Chapter 18: Comedy, Reading and Roasting*.
Run/Roll	A quick section of jokes.
Self Tape	A performer records an audience of themselves to camera and sends it to a casting director.
Set	1) the structure of the material that an act performs on stage
	2) the location with which something is filmed in TV and Film.
	3) In theatre the scenery and props on stage used to create a location or atmosphere.
Shade	A subtle, sneering expression of contempt for or disgust with someone. Usually dangerously close to the truth. See *Chapter 18: Comedy, Reading and Roasting*.
Show	The overall performance, not just your specific set.
Sight-Lines	The areas on stage, and in the space, where an audience can see you.
Stage Directions	Any details written in a script telling a performer where to move or how to act.
Stage Left	The left hand side of the stage when stood on it looking towards the audience.
Stage Right	The right hand side of the stage when stood on it looking towards the audience.
Straight Track	A track which is in essence the original song and plays from beginning to end.
Tech	1) Short for Technician.
	2) Short for Technical Rehearsal.
Technical Rehearsal	Rehearsing the technical elements of a set on stage - lighting, sound, costume changes, etc.
Technician	The person who is controlling the technical aspects of the show.
The Audience	1) The people watching a show or event.
	2) The space where the people watching the show or event are expected to be.
Track	The music/audio backing track for a live piece.
Ticketed Audience	Usually a sit down show where the audience have all paid for a ticket for a specific show which starts at a specific time.
Upstage	The area of the stage furthest away from the audience.
Wide-Shot	On camera a shot which is wide enough for the full body - head to toe, to be in and allow space for movement.
Your Drag	1) The clothing, mark-up, wigs, etc. you use to create your drag aesthetic.
	2) Your style or aesthetic of drag.

Acknowledgements

I need to thank the people who have helped me throughout my performance career, but also those who have put up with my performance career: my husband, son, family and friends who have spent decades with me missing events because of shows, turning up to events with remnants of eyeliner on and of course sequins and glitter being everywhere.

Huge thanks and love to the *Royal Vauxhall Tavern* for the ongoing support for *The Art of Drag Course* over the past decade. Specifically John and James who have made *The Art of Drag* at home there. The team there Dave Cross, Jason Reid and all the bar and security who make our graduates feel at home. Thanks always to Catia Ciarico for initially championing the course, finding it a permanent home and seeing in a drag course that was open to everyone. And of course Alexander Parsonage and Flavia Cannon at *Finger in the Pie* who first created and produced the initial two rounds of the course.

There are many collaborators on the course *The Art of Drag* who have made it a success and given me the motivation to build it into what it's become.

Those who have guest lectured and have enriched it along the way: Lolo Brow, Myra Dubois, Cookie Monstar, Rhys's Pieces, The Virgin X, Pie The Mime, Ada Campe, Joe Black, Stuart Saint and more. A special mention to two interviewees who have been with me on the course for nearing a decade – Me The Drag Queen and Adam All.

Adam All and Ada Campe are also, both in their own very different ways, responsible for me putting pen to paper. Their dressing room chats, post-show pints and constant mission to learn, improve and grow as artists. I am so pleased I could get some of your wisdom in interview form into the book. And am eternally grateful to Hugo Grrrl, Son Of A Tutu, Simply Barbra, Le Fil and Me The Drag Queen for giving up their time and insight to the book. The interviews were an integral part of the process that enriched the work and made me need to do a lot of re-writes!

My very old, very dear friend Cosmic who comes in to the course and imparts wisdom just days before the acts take to the stage. She stepped in for me when I rushed away on paternity leave and hosted a grad showcase. She gave me my first dress – and I took scissors to it! A constant source of support and entertainment and if I hadn't have met her in *The Edge*, Southampton (suitably she was lying on the flooring singing *Rescue Me* to a tiny crowd) would my drag journey have ever begun? Very naughty dear. By the time this book is published I expect she will, of course, have been cancelled.

A big part of the course is that the acts get their work documented and have a starting platform to move off from after the showcase is done: studio shots, live shots and a video. I've greatly enjoyed revisiting the archive of images and footage during this process. Who knows, maybe a coffee table book of drag debuts

Acknowledgements

could be in the future. Thanks to all the photographers – Joel Ryder (Joel Ryder Media), Richard McKenzie (The Burley Photographer), Claire Ford, Fox Al Rajim, Flavia Cannon, Carol J Moir and Simon J Webb (Jack The Lad Magazine). Videographers Sadie Sinner, Archie Onobu, and The Burley Photographer. And there is also a family of people supporting the acts at their showcases over the years: Emily Jane Flynn (Little Lady Luscious) and the legendary Andy Louder (much loved, much missed) who were with me at Madame Jojo's before. And now Allegra and Bella making our showcase so smoothly with a brilliant RVT tech team. The photography which features in the book and its cover are a mere snippet of the hundreds of fabulous performers who have stepped onto the stage in drag for the first time because of the course. (And I hope for those reading the book, they'll share their first time to @theartofdraguk.)

Richard Dobbs-Grove, at We Are Enriched, for all the graphics work over the years, finding a brand and agreeing to do a book cover too! (Also, who else would have agreed to go and see Barbra twice in one weekend – fabulous!)

Life is a long journey and people who inspire for a year or two have impact that lasts a lifetime. Thanks and love to Bette Bourne. Ben Evans and the team at OvalHouse Theatre where things really got moving for me. To the teachers and lecturers who helped me (slowly) find the beat of my own drum especially; Debbie Smith, Sax Jarrot, Alan Beck, Sue Ellen Case, Andrew Jarvis, Paul Clements and Sally-Anne Gritton.

My home from home: *The Phoenix Arts Club* for their ongoing support of me, and the book. Colin Savage, Ken Wright and Peter Dunbar. It's rare to find a residency that lasts a year: we've been together for eight plus years now!

And of course my partner in crime, the busiest fingers in the West End: Sarah Rose. If you ever see me singing on-stage and she isn't beside me, please understand I will be terrible! My whole career hangs on her ability to play the right key and follow me when I mess up.

Pride In London undoubtedly shaped my career, and politics, throughout the decade I was there. Thanks to Ian Massa-Harris-Mcfeely from bringing me in and being part my chosen family. Over ten years I worked with many incredible people (some of whom have become friends for life), also the *Pride's Got Talent* family and the many wonderful volunteers.

Finally, this book is love letter to the crazy people who decided that ten weeks in a room above a pub was better than joining any book club. Their insane ideas, love and enthusiasm have been constantly invigorating for me. My bonkers and beautiful draguates who are scattered across the country, and the world. You came to learn and have fun: and I ended up doing both with you all. Thank you: Frankie Sinatra, IntaStellar, Lady Thea, Maria Hurtz, Nell Points, Sue Burbia, Lady Glamour Nouveau, Walter Ego, Benjamin Butch, Chlamydia Jones, Dolly Trolley, Frankly Desire, La Verónica, The Black Flamingo, Rhys's Pieces, Ember, Fruit, Trevor Von Drivel, Bae Sharam, Holly Something, Connie Orff, The Emperor Of The Universe, Ivanka Manoff, Laura Nadia Hunt, Manny Splaine, The Countess Of Corsetshire, Morgue Anna, Geraldine Dorine Cockburn, TK Maxx, Kiikii, L'Amour Le Monde, Lorelai Spera, Orla Nothin', Ozzy Mandeus, Penny Comequick, Sally Slowcook, Scarlett Love, Vulgaire, Carrot, Flick, Aubrey Jean – The Vegan Queen, TvTv, Bunny Darko, Conkers, Debbie Del Rey, Gem The Clown, Henrietta The Eighth, Kallum Kiraly, Katastrofa Chernobyl, Ms Larissa Thorne, Steph Arendum, Miss Strawberry Moon, Lucy Fur, Allegra, Lola Del Fuego, Prinxx, Professor Q. Cucumber, Prospero Acronym, Will Actually, Perrie Alore, Phil Mashitter, Veneer, LX Motley, Hayley Bailey-Barnum, Hella Good, Valentine Smyth, Sindy Le Moist, Ai Wen Wong, Velvet Webb, Mx Anthropie, Maverick, Amanda Fox-Taylor, Abnorma Faye, Belladonna Bitters, Brucifix, Pussykat Bangkok, Mavis Blewitt, Dear Spora, Dee Dee Doo Doo, Sissy Lea, Miss Marikina, Letta Meatcake, Lady Fanny, Avaline A'love, Phyliss, Shandy Lear, An Nemia, Princess Eva After, Tabitha Manson, Sibyl Grimm, Cuntessa Queef, Lady Bush, Ruby Siren, Hot Rod, Samuel, Phil Me Up, Chelsea Delaney, Lady HD, Barb Barrick, CloClo Pops, Glimour, Ivan If A Boy, Kim Moan Ho, Red Velvet, Tim Tation, Nanao, Chiffon, Tilly, Laura Rose, Liz Dexamfetamine, Nigella Sins, The Lady T Glitters, Diva Dopamine, 404 Not Found, Axel Pose, Eevee Heartless, Glitzy Von Jagger, Kendal Mince, Rhoda Kill, YeeWhore, Shroomie, Mystic Mandy, Oliver Twinks, CJ Hopkins, Chase Bush, Michaela

George, Twerkish Delight, Bobby Dazzler, Bartholomew, Bryan Ayre, Eddie East, Filthy Habit, Jennifer Kool-Aid, Marco Mozzarelli, Miss Samantha, Seraphos, Bernie M, Danni Delicious, Adele Monte, Tipsy Hedren, Fergus, Bona Daddy and so many more! Thank you for letting me share *some* of your naked baby drag photos in the book and on the cover.

I can't wait to meet the next lot…

Further Credits

Lyrics Used: CABARET by Fred Ebb and John Kander – © 1966 Alley Music Corp (BMI)/Trio Music Company (BMI)/Carlin Music Delaware LLC. All Rights Reserved. Courtesy of Carlin Music Delaware LLC, 53-64 Chancery Lane, London, WC2A 1QS.

Front Cover:

Image (from left to right, top to bottom): Pussy Kat Bangkok, The Black Flamingo, La Veronica, Kallum Kiraly, Dolly Trolley, Twerkish Delight, Bae Sharam, Michael Twaits, Debbie Del Rey, Gem The Clown, Katastrofa Chernobyl, Vulgair, Seraphos, Chase Bush and Laura Nadia Hunt. **Photography:** Joel Ryder and Simon J Webb from across the years at The RVT and Underbelly, Southbank. **Design:** Richard Dobbs-Grove/We Are Enriched.

Rear Cover:

Image: Michael Twaits at *Her Majesty's Theatre*. **Photography:** Carol J Moir. **Design:** Richard Dobbs-Grove/We Are Enriched.

Index

acting 6, 155–166, 227, 231–237
aesthetics 4–11, 218, 302–303
agreed fee 20–23, 30–32, 36–37
Aja 182
Alaska 198
All, Adam 40, 53, 59, 72–73, 96, 151, 174, 205, 206–207, 241, 258–263, 301–307
All Stars see Drag Race
alter-ego 91–104, 137, 232–233
anchors 87–88, 121, 129, 184
approaching venues 13, 17–18, 45,
Art Simone 193
audience 81–88, 118–125, 240–242
auditions 234–236
autobiography 92, 246–247

Beau, Dickie 72, 169, 174, 182
being live/present 107–116, 119
BenDelaCreme 182, 198
box office split 30
Branding 8–10, 11–14, 261
Burnett, Carol 268, 274
business (acting 'business') 232
business (of drag) 5, 14–26, 45, 128, 130, 144
Butch, Kate 189

Camp, Ada 50, 59, 73, 83, 94, 118, 120, 130, 233, 270–274, 301–307
Carr, Alan 191
casting 17, 48, 234–236
catchphrase 15, 198, 220–224 *see also* language and lexicon
Channing, Carol 74, 218, 220
character 58, 91–104 *see also* alter ego; persona; impersonation
choices 107–114
choreography 67, 160–165,
Cider, Landon 72
Cleopantha 72, 173
collaborators 25
Collins, Tracey 72, 95, 217
comedy 189–201
commissioned track 172
confidence 87, 184

contracts 19–24
contradiction 93
corporate and private functions 22
Couleé, Shea 182
Cummings, Marti Gould 72

Del Rio, Bianca 119, 189
Derrieres, Apple 72, 206, 259, 262
Dick, Mo B. 72
drag contests 155–157, 234, 259, 283
drag family 25, 56, 304
drag mother *see* drag family
Drag Race 3, 39, 45, 71, 74, 76, 179–187, 193–201, 208–211, 221, 277–279
Dubois, Myra 119, 133, 189, 233

editing a track 169–177
Edwards, Alyssa 181
Elvis Lesley see Collins, Tracey
Etcetra Etcerta 193
Evans, Norman 72
expenses 29–41

fill/filling 139, 241, 243–244
finance/money 5, 22–23, 26, 29–41, 44–45, 53, 98, 280, 285, 292, 303
Fong, Regina 72, 169
framing 109–110, 136–138, 165, 246
fun 36–38, 44–45, 87–88, 149, 184

Garland, Judy 179, 182, 268, 290
Gaw-jus, Cheddar 72

haus/house *see* drag family
hecklers 122–125, 278
Hill, Murray 72
hosting 21, 119, 239–245
Hoyle, David 72
Hugo Grrrl 44, 73, 92, 141, 282–286, 301–307

impersonation 72, 111, 217–229
inspiration 71–77, 190, 247
invoices/invoicing 30–35, 40, 47

Index

Jimbo 198
jokes (structures, forms) 191–194
Jujubee 182

Katya 197
Kiki & Herb 72, 144

La Rue, Danny 72, 144
La Voix 73, 229
language and lexicon 60, 111, 140–145, 194, 218, 222, 229
Le Fil 35, 73, 276–280, 301–307
Le Gateau Chocolat 72
line learning 58–59
lip-sync: battles 181–182; rehearsal 54–58, 179–187; tracks/edits 72–73, 169–177

M.C./host 21 *see also* hosting
making an entrance 82, 129, 165,
marketing 14, 248 *see also* promotion and social media
Me The Drag Queen 48, 68, 73–74, 92, 95, 118, 125, 136, 139, 173, 179–184, 190, 241, 242, 288–293, 301–307
measuring success 43–51, 292, 297
mic technique 128
mindfulness 49
Minge, Ginger 197
Miss Fame 191
Miss Toto 72
Monet X Change 180–182, 198
money 29–41
monkey bars 64, 138–139, 144, 240
Monsoon, Jinkx 119, 198, 200
Montrese, Coco 181, 218

Naomi Small 179–182
nerves/anxiety 44, 148–149, 184, 262, 285, 303
networking 11–14, 19–21, 25–26, 39–40, 130
non-verbal acts 110, 143, 172–177

opinions *see choices*

pacing 83–85
parody 72, 85, 204–214 *see also* impersonation
payment in-kind 39
peaks and troughs 85–86, 161–163,183, 243
performance zones 85–88, 183
persona 92–100, 259, 295
photographers 15–16, 25
physicality 90–94, 100–103
Pleasure, Maxx 72
poetry 231–234, 252
poses 101–102, 161
Pride in London 38, 87, 244
progression 48
promotion 11, 14–15

promotional drive 15–16
puns 98–9, 174, 191, 198, 225

Raven 182
reading/shade 118,190, 195–201
rehearsal 53–60, 124–125, 165, 213; environment 54–55; for lip-sync 179–187; for singers 57–58; techniques 54–60
repertoire 64–69, 108, 155–156, 190
research: inspiration 71–77; repertoire 63–69, 157; stages/spaces 129–131; the audience 83–84; venues 13–24
riders 20, 279
roast 195–201
RuPaul 72, 76, 191, 196,

Savage, Lily 144, 233, 274
self-tapes 234–236
set 63–69
Shell Suit Cher see Collins, Tracey
Sight Lines 81, 129
Simply Barbra 73, 128, 203, 217, 264–268, 301–307
Sin Wai Kin 73
singing 57, 107, 147–153, 155–166
Snatch Game 220–228
social media 14, 17–19, 44–45, 111–113
solo show 239–249
Son Of A Tutu 44, 50, 54, 64, 73, 98, 294–298, 301–307
Split Britches 72, 75, 252
stages 127–131
stand-up 138, 189–201
Streisand, Barbra 3, 123, 217, 220, 223, 245, 264–268

talking 135–145
tax 29–41
technical rehearsals 20–25, 127–131
technicians 127–131
text (script, lyrics, etc.) 157–63, 231–234
the self 91–2
The Vivienne 221
tips (money) 30
tribute acts *see* Impersonation
Twaits, Michael 9, 73, 103, 141, 252

unions 21, 35, 280

Valentina 181
Velour, Sasha 72
Venues 13–24, 38–39, 45, 53, 127–131, 144, 304–305
Virgin X 72
Visage, Michelle 198, 200
vocal/vocal technique 1 103, 47–153

warm ups 56–57, 147–153, 262, 273, 279, 306
Wood, Victoria 190–192, 206
working for free 39
writing 55